Disclosing a Value System in a Living Will Could be in Your Best Interests

Disclosing a Value System in a Living Will Could be in Your Best Interests

By

Susan Farrall

CAMBRIDGE
SCHOLARS
PUBLISHING

Disclosing a Value System in a Living Will Could be in Your Best Interests,
by Susan Farrall

This book first published 2011

Cambridge Scholars Publishing

12 Back Chapman Street, Newcastle upon Tyne, NE6 2XX, UK

British Library Cataloguing in Publication Data
A catalogue record for this book is available from the British Library

ISBN (10): 1-4438-3210-3, ISBN (13): 978-1-4438-3210-6

THIS BOOK IS DEDICATED TO MY MOTHER AND LATE FATHER
WITH MUCH LOVE

TABLE OF CONTENTS

TABLE OF CASES

Airedale NHS Trust v Bland [1993] 1 All ER 821
B v An NHS Trust Hospital [2002] 152 NLJ 470
Banks v Goodfellow (1870) L.R. 5 Q.B. 549
Bolam v Friern Hospital Management Committee [1957] 1 WLR 582
Bolitho v City and Hackney HA [1997] 4 All ER 771
Breen v Williams (1996) 186 CLR 71
Canterbury v Spence (1972) 464 F. 2d 558
Chatterton v Gerson [1981] QB 432
Chester v Afshar 2004 WL 2289136
Cruzan vs Director, Missouri Dept. of Health 110 S.Ct. 2841
Earl of Oxford's Case (1615)
Estate of Park [1953] 2 All ER 408
Gillick v West Norfolk and Wisbech AHA [1986] A.C. 112
HE v A Hospital NHS Trust 2003 WL 21729346
In the Matter of Claire Conroy 486 A 2d 1209 [1985]
KC and NNC v City of Westminster Social and Community Services Dept. and IC (a protected party, by his litigation friend the Official Solicitor) [2008] EWCA Civ 198
Lindsay v Wood [2006] EWHC 2895 QB
Masterman Lister v Jewell; Masterman Lister v Brutton and Co [2002] EWCA Civ 1889
Maynard v West Midlands RHA [1984] 1 WLR 634
R v Bodkin Adams [1957] Crim LR 365
R v Brown [1993] 2 All ER 75
R v Cambridge Health Authority, ex parte B [1995] 2 All ER 129
R v Cox (1992) 12 BMLR 38
R v Howe [1987] AC 417
R (On the Application of Oliver Leslie Burke) v The General Medical Council [2005] EWCA Civ 1003
Re A (Medical Treatment: Male Sterilisation) [2000] 1 FLR 549
Re B (Consent to Treatment: Capacity) [2002] EWHC 429 (Fam)
Re C (Adult: Refusal of Treatment) [1994] 1 WLR 290
Re D (A Minor) (Wardship: Sterilisation) 1 All ER 326
Re Eve [1986] 2 S.C.R. 388
Re F (Mental Patient: Sterilisation) [1990] 2 AC 1

Re Guardianship of Estelle M. Browning, 568 So.2d 4
Re J (A Minor) (Wardship: Medical Treatment) [1990] 3 All ER 930
Re MB (Adult: Medical Treatment) [1997] 2 FLR 426
Re Quinlan 70 N.J. 10
Re SL (Adult Patient) (Medical Treatment) [2000] 2 FCR 452
Re T (Adult: Refusal of Treatment) [1992] 4 All ER 649
Re W (A Minor) (Medical Treatment) [1992] 4 All ER 627
Re Y (An Adult Patient) (Transplant: Bone Marrow) [1996] BMLR 111
Schloendorff v Society of New York Hospital (1914) 211 N.Y. 125
Sheffield City Council v E [2004] EWHC 2808
Sidaway v Board of the Bethlem Royal Hospital and the Maudsley Hospital and Others [1985] AC 871
Simms v Simms [2003] 1 All ER 669
W Healthcare NHS Trust v KH 2004 WL 2458658

TABLE OF LEGISLATION

De Prerogativa Regis 1324

Family Law Reform Act 1969

Judicature Acts 1873-75

Mental Capacity Act 2005

Table of Website

www.allaboutgod.com/god-is-love.htm
http://ww2.allina.com/anwim/GrandRounds/medicalfutility06/pages/slide38.html
www.ascensionhealth.org
www.braguelaw.com/5.html
www.ca/ef/topical-the-duty-of-benevolence.htm
www.ethox.org.uk/education/undergraduate-course/no-consent/4-the-assessment
www.fpnotebook.com/Neuro/Cognitive/MdclDcsnMkngCpcty.htm
www.godandscience.org/love/biblicallove.html
www.historylearningsite.co.uk/ancient-egyptian-medicine.htm
www.historylearningsite.co.uk/hippocrates.htm
www.historylearningsite.co.uk/medicine-and-ancient-greece.htm
www.medword.com/hippocrates.html
http://news.bbc.co.uk/1/hi/England/Norfolk/8284728.stm
www.scu.edu/ethics/practicing/decision/calculating.html
www.yourdictionary.com/good-faith

ACKNOWLEDGEMENTS

I wish to thank my supervisors, Ms Kay Wheat and Professor Michael Gunn, for their unswerving dedication, attentiveness, support, guidance and patience during the preparation of this book.

SUMMARY

Whilst doctors are recognised for being expert in medical matters they are nevertheless generally required by law to obtain the consent of a competent adult patient prior to administering a medical treatment.[1] The need for consent underpins the right of a competent adult patient to refuse treatment, even life preserving treatment. Accordingly, bodily inviolability is a fundamental principle of law and violation of it, even for benevolent reasons, is prima facie punishable. Instead of which a competent patient has a right to self-determine what shall happen to their own body. In this way the subjective decision-making standards and methods of a competent patient inform, and are made determinative, of any decision to accept or reject a medical treatment.

It is against this general background that the comments of Lord Goff in the case of *Bland* should be considered. There he suggested that the best interests test should comprise of something more than purely professional appraisal of a person's medical welfare.[2] To confine the test in this way, he said, would be inconsistent with the primacy given to the principle of self-determination and would '*downgrade the status of the incompetent person by placing a lesser value on [their] intrinsic worth and vitality*'.[3]

So as the title to this study suggests I am primarily concerned with legal provisions governing medical treatment decision-making processes in respect of formerly competent adult patients. More specifically it questions whether the values, beliefs and preferences of members of this

---

[1] The term generally has been used to denote the fact that the inviolability of persons is a fundamental principle of law and in a medical context this means that the administration of a medical treatment is dependent on some form of legal authority. As the primacy of the moral principle of autonomy is established in law doctors must obtain legal consent prior to administering a medical treatment. However, there are circumstances where the law remains paternalistic and medical treatment can be administered on the basis of an alternative legal authority, for example, the Mental Health Act 2007.

[2] Airedale NHS Trust v Bland [1993] 1 All ER 821 HL

[3] Airedale NHS Trust v Bland [1993] 1 All ER 821 HL

patient group should be more favourably promoted, i.e. used and made determinative, in medical treatment decision-making processes concerning them based on contemporary understanding and application of the moral principle of autonomy. Naturally this depends on whether a person's value system can be accurately ascertained, recorded and protected to ensure that it is most fully promoted and respected in the future should a loss of decision-making capacity leave them unable to determine matters contemporaneously.

Accordingly, the premise underlying this study is that the autonomous values, beliefs and preferences of a formerly competent person should be ascertained and recorded so that they can be understood and used by others to determine whether, and if so what, medical treatment is in the actual best interests of the patient. Essentially bodily integrity would be safeguarded if a surrogate decision-maker was able to determine what the patient would decide if they were competent to make that choice. A situation that is most desirable if we are not to downgrade the moral status of this particular group of incompetent patients.

INTRODUCTION

This study seeks to answer the question of whether the values or value system of a competent person, that have been disclosed in a living will, could play a role in medical treatment decision-making processes concerning them under the Mental Capacity Act 2005.[1]

Aims of the Investigation[2]

- To explore the goals of medicine as well as the key ethical principles of the medical profession to draw attention to the obligations that are significant to treatment decision-making processes
- To examine the moral principle of autonomy to establish the context in which a person is respected as an autonomous moral agent with the right to self-determination and to its significance in relation to the question of what a good life is or should entail
- To investigate the general legal framework for the provision of a medical treatment in respect of a capable patient to determine whether autonomy is the primary principle of medical law and if it is to consider whether patient values are also respected in law
- To inquire into the law in respect of the incapable patient to see what approach is taken to safeguarding the autonomy and welfare interests of formerly competent patients
- To research the nature and scope of an advance decision to refuse a medical treatment since these are an exception to the principle that a doctor must act in the best interests of a mentally incapacitated patient
- To analyse the concept of values and of a value system to see how these can be articulated so as to inform the assessment of

---

[1] In this regard I wish to thank Professor Michael Gunn, who acted as director of studies during the first year of my study, for inspiring me to undertake this project.

[2] In this regard I wish to thank Ms Kay Wheat for assisting me to develop a structure that helped me to focus more precisely on the theme of this work.

best interests and how they might be incorporated into advance decisions

- To inquire into the usefulness and effectiveness of the Mental Capacity Act 2005 in promoting autonomy when someone has disclosed a value system in a living will with a view to suggesting ways in which the law might be made to work better if the MCA is found wanting in this regard

Research Context

My research question seeks to address a social issue that directly or indirectly affects many members of society. It arises out of the fact that persons wish to survive and to lead a good or flourishing life and trust that medical science will, when necessary and appropriate, help them in that endeavour. We are fortunate to live in an era where death results far less frequently from serious injury or illness due to advances in medical science and this is obviously beneficial for those whose health is subsequently fully restored. However, contemporary medicine cannot always be relied upon to produce such a positive outcome and in cases where mental health has been unduly compromised doctors may continue to care for a patient in their best interests. Another consequence of our era is that people are living for longer. This has precipitated a proportionate rise in the incidence of diseases such as dementia and once a victim's decision-making capacity has been irretrievably compromised by mental deterioration, their future health and welfare needs will also be determined by reference to the best interests test. Accordingly, an increasing number of people are, or at risk of being, prevented from exercising their right to self-determine what shall happen to them in a medical context.

The irony is that this is taking place at a time when the primacy of autonomy and the right to self-determination have become more firmly established in medical law.[3] Certain significant influences contribute to this being so. Our law is intimately concerned with human welfare and morality and as statutory and common law provisions tend to support the view that we are all equal before the law it is important that the law should not be structured in such a way as to deny moral equality. Unfortunately,

[3] See, for example, *Chester v Afshar 2004 WL 2289136*

there is no definitive way to settle questions about human welfare.[4] Each person is a unique individual and as society is inherently pluralistic no consensus of opinion has formed around which goods and social practices we should adopt and why. If the law is to remain neutral in the face of competing and conflicting ideas about what a good life for humans should entail then one of its primary functions in regulating human conduct should be to recognise and protect certain basic liberties and freedoms of all persons.[5]

In this regard the fundamental principle of bodily inviolability is adopted in law to reflect the special significance[6] and importance members of society attribute to the human body and life.[7] Primacy is however accorded to the principle of autonomy.[8] Philosophical reflections as to the value of autonomy relate particular facts about humans and their nature to the view that human life has special significance. The dominant view is that humans have an intellect that gives them the capacity to think, to reason and to be rational and because they can be trusted to make decisions and act on their own behalf in accordance with a reasoned set of principles or laws they should have freedom to pursue a life of their own choosing.[9] Nevertheless, they like other creatures also receive information from their senses. Human beings are therefore confronted by a mixture of rational and non-rational impulses. However, the will, which is essentially autonomous, links these two aspects of them and it can be mobilised to

[4] For example, Mill and Bentham both considered that the principle of utility was the primary principle of morality but differed in their views about how the principle should be used to maximise human happiness

[5] Dworkin Ronald, Justice in Robes, 2006, The Belknap Press of Harvard University Press, Rawls and the Law, p.253

[6] There is general agreement that human life can be distinguished from all other life forms on the basis of the intellect. It therefore follows that this is the source of many of the concepts and ideas we use to uphold the notion that human life has special significance and importance, for example, dignity and morality and as each human life deserves to be respected as something special each of us should always be treated as an end and should never be treated merely as the means to the end of any other.

[7] *Re F (Mental Patient: Sterilisation) [1990] 2 AC 1 HL*

[8] *Re F (Mental Patient: Sterilisation) [1990] 2 AC 1 HL*

[9] See Immanuel Kant

override their more basic instincts.[10] Persons should therefore be treated as autonomous creatures of moral worth and dignity.

Therefore, the principle of autonomy is an important principle of law because it establishes the idea that person's value being in control of their own person and life.[11] A good life is in other words one where persons have freedom to pursue whatever is of value to them, i.e. a good life is one that is self-constructed. Accordingly, philosophical reflections on the value of autonomy support the view that mankind is better off when individuals are respected as sovereign masters[12] who willingly accept personal responsibility for their decisions and actions.[13]

Consequently, one of the ways that we show our respect for persons, in relation to medical treatment decision-making processes, is to allow them to self-determine, in accordance with their own values, beliefs and preferences, the matter of whether to accept or reject an offer of medical treatment, including cases where treatment may preserve life. In this way respect for autonomy is allowed to triumph over the sanctity principle; the desire to survive is a potent force within most rational persons but when good physical and/or mental health has been irretrievably compromised, it may not, on every occasion, be entirely irrational for some people to view an earlier death as being preferable to a continued life of intolerable mental or physical pain, indignity and restricted freedom.[14]

This is reflected in law as the general rule is that a doctor who administers a medical treatment without obtaining their patient's consent commits a battery.[15] This fact should be weighed against another. The underlying objective of medicine is to benefit the patient and physicians are people who possess skills and expertise in the practice of medicine. Moreover,

---

[10] When the will operates freely and independently persons are more inclined to act rationally on the basis of reasoned deliberation rather than on the basis of sense perception alone

[11] Bodily security is an essential pre-requisite to individual exercises of self-determination

[12] According to Kant persons should always be treated as an end and never solely as the means to the end of any other

[13] Most moral and legal philosophers support, or at least do not detract from this view, see Kant, Mill, Bentham, Dworkin and Raz

[14] *Airedale NHS Trust v Bland [1993] 1 All ER 821 HL; Re B (Consent to Treatment: Capacity) [2002] EWHC 429 (Fam)*

[15] *Re F (Mental Patient: Sterilisation) [1990] 2 AC 1 HL*

medical professionals are ethically and legally regulated to act in the best interests of their patients. They are in other words bound to practice medicine beneficently and yet in law this is an insufficient justification for divesting persons of their basic liberties and freedoms or right to autonomy. Consequently, the law preserves the right of a doctor to determine, as medical expert, the form of treatment the patient should receive in their medical best interests but it is quite clear that beneficence should not be allowed to override autonomy when it comes to accepting or rejecting an offer of medical treatment. This is to reflect the fact that persons confer value on a wide variety of goods and as such it is impossible to define well-being solely in terms related to medical well-being. And when welfare is considered more broadly doctors are in no better position than anyone else to know whether what is in someone's medical best interests will also be in their actual best interests all things considered.

To that end consent must be legally valid if it is to provide physicians with a defence to the crime or tort of battery. As autonomy is the primary value governing treatment decision-making processes doctors are required to ensure that patients have the requisite level of capacity to make the decision they purport to make and in this regard all adults are presumed competent to make decisions and act on their own behalf.[16] In cases of doubt a doctor will seek to determine whether someone is suffering from an impairment or disturbance of the mind or brain[17] that would prevent them from understanding[18] and retaining[19] relevant information so that it can be used[20] to make a decision which they can communicate.[21] The decision of the patient must also be the decision of the patient and here it is important that the patient reached their decision about what to do voluntarily in that it was their own will that had been expressed on the matter and not that of some other interested party.[22] Finally, all medical treatments carry with them potential benefits and harms that may or may not materialise in a particular instance. Consequently, in order for consent to be legally valid it should be informed also so that the purpose of the

[16] Mental Capacity Act 2005, s.1(2)
[17] Mental Capacity Act 2005, s.2(1)
[18] Mental Capacity Act 2005, s.3(1)(a)
[19] Mental Capacity Act 2005, s.3(1)(b)
[20] Mental Capacity Act 2005, s.3(1)(c)
[21] Mental Capacity Act 2005, s.3(1)(d)
[22] *Re T (Adult: Refusal of Treatment) [1992] 4 All ER 649 CA*

law, the inviolability of persons, is not frustrated but fulfilled.[23] In order to escape liability for the intentional tort of battery[24] doctors are required to inform their patients of the nature and purpose of medical treatment(s) and to inform them of the consequences of exercising their right of choice one way rather than another.[25] Doctors are also required to inform their patients of the risks inherent in treatment and to answer any questions they may field honestly and candidly.[26] Thus part of the reason why the patient's right to self-determination is legally protected is to enable them to arrive at a treatment decision having considered which harms they would wish to avoid and which risks they may be willing to assume in order to restore their personal sense of well-being. The question of whether the patient received sufficient information for their needs, i.e. to protect their own welfare and other interests, including that pertaining to risks which may or may not materialise, is thought to be a matter that should properly be considered in accordance with the standards proposed by the unintentional tort of negligence.[27] This is despite the fact that the way in which someone exercises judgment may be heavily influenced by information pertaining to the nature and severity of harms that may ensue from their decision when these entail a possible threat to their basic liberties and freedom of action in the future.

Self-evidently, the law's requirement for consent chiefly resides in the right of a competent patient to be maintained inviolate and free from bodily harm. Accordingly, the right to refuse necessary and appropriate medical treatment, even life-preserving treatment, is an essential element of autonomy. Moreover, the law determines that personal welfare and interests are best safeguarded by the subjective decision-making standards and methods of patients and therefore not only are their values, beliefs and preferences of paramount importance to decision-making processes concerning them but so too is their subjective evaluation of the benefits and burdens of the medical treatment they have been offered. Autonomy is then an important concept in the context of medical treatment decision-making because it allows patients to protect their own body[28] and welfare interests. It also serves to counter medical paternalism.

---

[23] *Chester v Afshar 2004 WL 2289136*

[24] The standard of disclosure to escape liability for battery is restrictive in the sense that information about risks, which may or may not arise, do not have to be given

[25] *Chatterton v Gerson [1981] QB 432*

[26] *Chester v Afshar 2004 WL 2289136*

[27] Ibid

[28] Through the act of giving or withholding their consent

However, because the right to bodily inviolability is obtained through the right to self-determination it is open to question whether the right to autonomy is necessarily contemporary. The principle of inviolability is non-discriminatory and therefore every person has a right to be maintained inviolate and free from harm which means that every person should have the right to self-determine what happens to their body. However, the patient's right to self-determination flows from legal capacity. An issue in relation to mentally incapacitated patients is whether they too enjoy a similar right to medical treatment or to the withholding or withdrawal of necessary and appropriate medical treatment as do competent patients to consent to, or to refuse to consent to, medical treatment.

In *Re F*, for instance, Lord Bridge thought it axiomatic that in cases of medical necessity treatment which is necessary and appropriate to preserve the life, health or well-being of an incompetent patient may lawfully be administered without their consent provided that a doctor has acted in the patient's best interests.[29] The incompetency of the patient should not in other words be used as an excuse to deny vulnerable persons their basic right to medical care and treatment. Whilst, in the case of *Bland*, Lord Goff suggested that to subject an incompetent patient to a medical treatment based purely on professional opinion of what was in their medical best interests would not only be inconsistent with the importance we attach to autonomy and to the right of self-determination but it would also downgrade the status of the incompetent person by placing a lesser value on their intrinsic worth and vitality.[30]

What should happen then when a person suffers a loss of decision-making capacity? Is the patient's right to autonomy greater in these circumstances than their right to beneficence or to the state's interest in the preservation and sanctity of human life?[31] Should a person in a persistent vegetative state who will never regain cognition and whose vital processes are being maintained by a mechanical respirator and nasogastric tube be required to accept bodily invasions of this nature and frequency?[32] Or is the right to bodily integrity so fundamental that the right to autonomy should not be disregarded solely on the basis that their condition prevents them from

---

[29] *Re F (Mental Patient: Sterilisation) [1990] 2 AC 1 HL, p.52*
[30] *Airedale NHS Trust v Bland [1993] 1 All ER 821 HL*
[31] Mental Capacity Act 2005; *Airedale NHS Trust v Bland [1993] 1 All ER 821 HL; In the matter of Karen Quinlan, 70 N.J. 10 Supreme Court*
[32] Ibid

exercising their right of choice?[33] If so, how is moral equality to be achieved? Upon what principle can autonomy best be protected, advanced and vindicated?

Conversely, what scope should be given to autonomy within the context of treatment decision-making on behalf of incompetent patients? Is there a danger, in a political democracy, that in respecting autonomy certain other important principles might fall into decline through misuse or become redundant through unthinking adherence to particular ideas about goods and social practices? For example, should a competent person be able to decide what happens to their incompetent self at some future point in time? Also, given the importance we attach to the sanctity principle and to the preservation of life how should the withdrawal of life-sustaining procedures, which will hasten the death of the patient, be regarded?[34] Finally, if we are not to abandon people to their autonomy isn't there a need for society not only to be just but to show that it is just also?

These various thoughts and comments stimulated my interest in the situation of formerly competent patients. More specifically I wished to examine legal provisions governing the doctor-patient relationship in respect of this patient group to determine whether their rights are coterminous with those of a competent patient and if not whether there was scope to improve upon current law.

Research Design and Methodology

This study is ultimately concerned with protecting and promoting the autonomy of formerly competent patients. As I wished to make suggestions for how the law might be made to work better in this regard it was possible for me to conduct a comparative study by seeking counsel from legal systems in alternative jurisdictions. The USA being foremost amongst them based on its long standing history of recognising and protecting the basic rights and freedoms of citizens constitutionally. There the Patient Self-Determination Act 1990, which is a federal law, seeks to promote patient autonomy but also to reduce costs associated with unwanted medical care. This statute requires hospital staff to inform patients of treatment options including the right to refuse treatment and by extension of right to die information and their advance directive options.

---

[33] Ibid

[34] Ibid

Allied to which most States implement legislative provisions of their own - Natural Death Acts.[35] For example, Idaho and California have both implemented legislation that sets out the procedures to be followed for limitation of treatment, including life-sustaining treatment when a patient is terminally ill or suffers from an irreversible condition. Issues surround the definition given to 'terminally ill' etc. They also establish documentation to cover specific health situations. These can be equated to a traditional advance decision except that completion of one of these establishes clear and convincing evidence of the patient's wishes, i.e. the advance directive is valid and applicable. Beyond that these statutes generally seem to encourage the appointment of a surrogate decision-maker, who must not be the patient's doctor, to make decisions on their behalf in good faith and in accordance with their former wishes under the principle of substituted judgment. Use of the best interests principle is reserved for those cases where the wishes of the patient are unknown. Of course an issue with this is that an increasing number of people will not have anyone that they can or may wish to appoint into that role. In those cases it is at least arguable that the law has been structured in such a way as to deny moral equality.

I was, however, more interested in conducting a theoretical study because I wished to examine the philosophical foundations of medical law to see how this particular area of law was derived as a prelude to examining the relationship between moral philosophy and law in relation to competent patients. The next question that had to be addressed was whether, and if so how, considerations that should apply to a competent patient are applied in a situation where a patient has suffered a loss of decision-making capacity. Essentially, I examine the legal frameworks that apply to medical treatment decision-making processes in respect of competent and incompetent patients to see how the law works in practice so that I could form a view that was both valid and reliable about why it might fail to deliver what it promises in a particular instance or might not work as well as intended.

As with all things ethical questions concerning the application of moral standards and ideas about what is right and wrong human conduct become refined and modified over time to take account of contemporary conditions

---

[35] Parallels can be drawn with Europe, I think, where the European Parliament issue Directives which require member states to achieve a particular legislative result without stipulating the means for doing so. Essentially state legislators have discretion to decide how to implement Directives.

possibly not envisaged by the likes of Kant and Mill. The contribution of medical science and technology for example to human welfare is outstanding but we must also learn how best to live with the consequences of its successes and limitations when these give rise to new moral dilemmas that are a source of considerable debate amongst members of society. In this regard contemporary moral and legal philosophers build on the work of their predecessors, whilst retaining its basic structure, to shine a light on the various factors that should be considered by those who attempt to find solutions to current ethical issues and I wished to draw on a valid and reliable body of knowledge that offered relevant, related and contrasting ideas about the value of autonomy so that I could make suggestions for how the law might be made to work better.

Since persons are moral subjects[36] a close connection exists between moral and legal systems, both are essentially concerned with human welfare and therefore with right and wrong human conduct. It was therefore possible for me to engage in classic legal scholarship which typically involves the synthesis, evaluation and critical analysis of key publications that are relevant to my area of study. The fact that data has been collected from some of the most distinguished academics in the field should ensure that my findings are valid and reliable. As data has been collected from a variety of sources to reflect alternative perspectives on the value of autonomy it is also possible to claim that the selection process was conducted objectively and with a view to reducing the incidence of biased interpretations and research outcomes.

Results

Legislation suggests that it is not uncommon for persons to worry about what might happen to them if they are no longer capable of making their own decisions. And based on the fact that a surrogate must act in their best interests their primary concern must be that in so doing they may not be loyal to them or to their wishes when they are themselves helpless to act. However, legislators are equally aware that a doctor's self-proclaimed mission or purpose in life is to heal and/or care for the sick. They are also minded that medical professionals are required to make decisions and act in difficult situations when under pressure and that it is unreasonable to

[36] The way we treat one another is derivative of our ideas about the significance of the human body and life

expect them to carry out their obligations fearing that they may be litigated against whichever way they decide things.

Accordingly, the issue of who decides and of how they decide what should happen to patients who suffer a loss of decision-making capacity has been debated since 1990 and the case of *Re F*, culminating in the recent enactment of the MCA. This conversation, concerning the doctor-patient relationship, was taking place at a time when the collective will sought constitutional protection of individual rights as a way to promote the various fundamental freedoms and liberty interests of all persons.[37] It was therefore apparent that an increased emphasis on patient autonomy in personal decision-making and respect for individual wishes based on values was upon us. The Act is an attempt to acknowledge this and to incorporate this perspective into law.

Initiatives that aimed to make respect for autonomy overriding in this context required the legislature to encourage competent patients to take steps in advance of a time when they might suffer from a loss of decision-making capacity and when decisions concerning their welfare might have to be made. Hence we have legal recognition of living wills or advance decisions. And, as priority is accorded to the advance decision of a competent patient, over what others may consider is in their best interests, the concept of precedent autonomy has become established within the legislative framework.

This means that paternalist intervention is preceded by the need to respect someone by means of giving them what they previously wanted. Essentially the legislature is saying that past decisions are important indicators of what the patient would want now when they are incompetent and unable to form a view contemporaneously. Treating someone in this way is the best way we have of respecting their autonomy and right to self-determination in the present. The problem is that, the concept, as currently defined and used under the MCA is given a fairly narrow window of opportunity to fulfil its purpose of empowering patients and of requiring others to respect their right to self-determination with regard to their own body and life.

However, it would seem possible to breathe new life into the concept of precedent autonomy if the values, beliefs and preferences that underpinned

[37] For example, the enactment of the Human Rights Act 1998

the decisions of the patient could be identified, expressed and preserved, for future use, in a living will. The idea in disclosing ones values or value system in this way is that it would be regarded as a relevant written statement of the patient that could be used to inform a best interests treatment decision but it could just as well be used to inform a capacity assessment. Accordingly, an advantage in disclosing one's values over conventional advance decisions is that it might conceivably be incorporated into an advance decision or could be used by others to inform a wider range of treatment decision-making processes under the MCA based upon the contents of the patient's living will.

The problem is that although the MCA could support such an approach to decision-making I fear that a doctor as surrogate decision-maker might be inclined to prioritise the current wishes and feelings of a sentient but incompetent patient, which are by their very nature experientially valid, over the autonomously chosen critical interests of their former competent self. In doing so they would apply the test of best interests test in a way that suggests the right to autonomy is necessarily contemporary. As such I argue that the MCA is in need of reform if a values-based approach to decisions taken on behalf of formerly competent patients is to work well and be prioritised. In this respect I draw upon the work of Pellegrino and Thomasma, amongst others, to propose that if beneficence is not to triumph over autonomy that a fiduciary principle is needed to underpin the nature of a doctor's duty at both stage one and stage two of a treatment decision-making process to indicate where loyalty should lie in respect of formerly competent persons.

To state the case in support of a values-based approach to decision-making I draw on the work and theoretical perspectives of Kant, Mill, Raz, Dworkin and Beauchamp and Childress, amongst others. My purpose in doing so is to ensure that a competent person's legally protected right to choose or reject medical treatment is safeguarded, not lost or diminished by virtue of subsequent physical or mental incapacity or incompetence.[38]

[38] *Re Guardianship of Estelle M. Browning, 568 So.2d 4*, para. 7

Summary Overview and Structured Analysis of Chapters

The focus of this study is informed by the circumstances in which the law sanctions the medical treatment of adult patients who lack the capacity to consent to that treatment. The law respects patients' right to self-determination, but nevertheless will permit treatment of a patient who is incapable of consenting in broadly two sets of circumstances: first, when the patient has previously (when capable) articulated an advance decision specifying circumstances in which s/he would not wish to be treated, and, secondly, when there is no such advance decision but the proposed form of treatment is in the best interests of the patient.

The law's respect for self-determination is underpinned by the ethical principle of the right of capable adults to autonomous decision-making, and therefore in the case of patients without capacity, the law has to devise ways of according a similar sort of respect to those patients. Given that, normally, the key players in assessing the scope of the advance decision or in assessing best interests will be doctors, attention to doctors' ethical obligations may be a significant factor in this assessment. In consequence, it is necessary to examine the ethical underpinnings of both the doctors' obligations and the rights of patients. One of the ways in which patients' rights can be respected is to respect their values. These can be articulated through an advance decision, and in the absence of such a decision, by reference to those values in deciding what is in their best interests. How such values can be ascertained and expressed forms the main focus of the work, together with a consideration of the adequacy of the current legal framework in accommodating this.

Chapter One –
Key Ethical Principles of the Medical Profession

The medical objective is to preserve the life, health and well-being of patients and as most rational human beings wish to survive and to live a good or flourishing life no obvious conflict of ends exists. However, the goals of medicine are not always compatible with one another and this fact is established by examining the use of life sustaining technologies and treatment in cases where the patient has entered into a persistent vegetative state. These patients will be subjected to ongoing physically invasive treatment and care to sustain their life when medical evidence establishes that they are insentient because an injury to the brain has totally and irretrievably compromised their cognitive capacity.

It is against this general background that the traditional moral responsibilities of medical professionals are examined. In this regard Hippocrates determined that doctors, as medical experts, should use their skill and judgment for the benefit of patients. Hippocrates thereby recognised the fiduciary nature of the doctor-patient relationship but permitted doctors to adopt a paternalist approach to decision-making and in so doing denied patient autonomy. First they should determine the form of medical treatment that the patient should receive prior to determining, in accordance with the moral principles of non-maleficence (do no harm) and beneficence (do good), whether that treatment should be administered, withheld or withdrawn in the patient's best interests.

As the framework for decision, i.e. identifying and reflecting on moral problems, is insufficiently fleshed out for practical application the ethical underpinnings of these principles are explored to gain relevant insight into those factors considered by doctors and also into how they discharge their various moral obligations when making treatment decisions for and on behalf of their patients.[39] This leads me to question whether these obligations, which are not always compatible with each other, amount to a form of paternalism that conflicts with the principle of autonomy. Ultimately I conclude that the framework proposed by Hippocrates is inadequate for determining questions that have to do with human life, death and quality of life.

Chapter Two – The Ethical Principle of Autonomy

Based on the notion that persons have an intellect and therefore have the capacity to think, to reason and to be rational, Kant proposed that persons should be respected as autonomous creatures of moral worth and dignity. Essentially, he was saying that subject to certain constraints, persons should have freedom to be self-governing and should not be directed or governed externally. Therefore, persons should have freedom, of body and mind, to live their life in accordance with laws of their own making.

Accordingly this chapter seeks to examine the moral principle of autonomy to show (1) that autonomy is synonymous with the idea of self-rule and therefore the values, beliefs and preferences of individuals are relevant to questions about what a good life for them is or should entail (2)

[39] Beauchamp, Tom L., Childress, James F., Principles of Biomedical Ethics, 2001, Fifth Edition, Oxford University Press, p.15/6

how the right to self-determination is derived from a particular conception of persons and their capacities (3) how the doctor-patient relationship is now informed by the principle of autonomy and as persons normatively considered should be respected as bearers of rights doctors are required to be appropriately beneficent to ensure that values are referable to human nature and ultimately to the nature of a particular person.

Chapter Three – The Law and the Capable Patient

Since the law is equally concerned with morality and human welfare this chapter seeks to ascertain whether autonomy is the primary principle of medical law. To this end the general legal framework for the provision of a medical treatment in respect of a capable patient is examined.

This chapter will show (1) that all persons enjoy a right to bodily inviolability that is protected by the tort/crime of battery and to be maintained free from bodily harm which is protected by the tort of negligence also but makes consent a defence to either claim. The need for consent resides in the right of an adult patient who suffers from no mental incapacity to self-determine the matter of whether to consent or to refuse to consent to a medical treatment, including life preserving treatment, in accordance with their own values, beliefs and preferences, thereby establishing the primacy of the moral principle of autonomy in law (2) what must happen in order for consent to be legally valid, i.e. a patient must be competent to decide or have capacity that is commensurate with the decision they purport to make, be provided with information relevant to their decision and must give their consent voluntarily (3) that the requirement for consent primarily resides in the right of an adult patient who suffers from no mental incapacity to be maintained inviolate thus the right to refuse necessary and appropriate medical treatment is an important part of what it means to respect patient autonomy.

Chapter Four – The Law and the Incapable Patient

As every person enjoys a legally protected right to bodily inviolability all persons have a right to be maintained inviolate and free from bodily harm. Plus this fundamental right is derived from the right to self-determination which means that every person ought to have the right to self-determine, in accordance with their own values, beliefs and preferences, what should happen to their own body. However, when decision-making capacity is lost the MCA requires a third party, and in relation to a medical necessity this will usually be a member of the medical profession, to make treatment decisions and act on behalf of the patient in their best interests.

A difficulty for legislators is that the law seeks to protect patients who are not capable of making a decision about treatment from the consequences of not being given treatment. However, they must also find a way to balance the patient's right to beneficence against maintaining respect for autonomous decision making. In other words is necessity and best interests equivalent to consent or do formerly competent patients enjoy a similar right to medical treatment or to the withholding or withdrawal of necessary and appropriate medical treatment as do competent patients to consent to, or, to refuse to consent to, an offer of medical treatment?

The focus in this chapter is therefore on the MCA, its provisions and any relevant common law commentary on these in terms of who is empowered to make decisions, who else may be involved in that process and the structure, standards and criteria that apply to surrogate decision-making processes and finally with whether, and if so on what basis, decision-makers are made accountable to patients for their decisions. As a prelude to all of that there is also an examination of the parens patriae jurisdiction of the court, which is no longer part of the law. The jurisdiction, which permitted courts to intervene in the affairs of incompetents, has been traced to a medieval statute De Prerogativa Regis 1324. This statute is interesting in distinguishing between formerly and never competent persons adopting a fiduciary decision-making standard in respect of the former though not the latter out of respect for the fact that they previously had the capacity for self-determination. It is introduced at this stage as it is intended to make reference to this later in the dissertation in consideration of best interests.

Chapter Five – Advance Decisions

As persons value being in control of their body, life and life plan the law makes provision for a competent person to refuse a specified medical treatment for a time in the future when they may lack the capacity to decide whether to consent or to refuse to consent to it contemporaneously. Founded upon the right to bodily inviolability advance decisions seek to limit unnecessary or unwarranted intervention in the lives of others by maximising decision-making capacity. The implication is that an advance decision of a patient that is both legally valid and applicable will be treated in the same way as if they had refused the treatment contemporaneously and is an exception to the principle that doctors must act in the best interests of their incompetent patients.

However it has been suggested that in a civil society compassion for the plight of one's fellow man should be overriding not autonomy. Therefore, in this chapter I first set out to consider whether (1) the prior wishes and feelings of a competent person should be binding later on when they are incompetent by exploring Dworkin's ideas about, inter alia, the integrity view of autonomy and contrasting these with those of Dresser who uses personal identity theory to challenge the authority of precedent autonomy (2) it is possible for persons to predict their preferences accurately and to then articulate them with the requisite degree of specificity.

This leads in to a review of the MCA in relation to advance decisions. As one is treated as though the patient had made the decision on the spot the general requirements of capacity, information and voluntariness apply. Next emphasis is placed on the fact that advance refusals are recognised to illustrate that the MCA does not intend autonomy to override a doctor's professional obligation to determine the form of treatment that it is in their patient's best interests to receive. Thereafter the patient's right to decide cannot simply be ignored. Attention therefore turns to how someone can decide on the existence, validity and applicability of an advance decision. The point is that if a healthcare professional concludes that an advance decision does not exist they may act in the patient's best interests alternatively if they conclude that it is not valid and/or applicable but that it is an expression of the person's previous wishes they must then consider what is set out in the advance decision when working out the person's best interests.

Eventually I conclude that some consideration should be given to developing a central registry if advance decision-making is to have any utility at all. Nevertheless validity and applicability are difficult standards to meet in seeming to require a patient to be very competent and/or to record a decision in conjunction with a medical professional close to the time that it will come into effect.

Chapter Six – Patients' Values and Value Systems

Given the fact that all persons rely on their values, beliefs and preferences to guide them when deciding whether to consent or to refuse to consent to a medical treatment this chapter is concerned with how those values, that were the source of a decision, can be ascertained and expressed. The idea is that a third party should be able to understand the values that the patient would consider so that they can use them, or apply facts to values, to make a decision that is broadly consistent with the one the patient would have made if they were competent to decide.

Disclosing one's values or value system is obviously beneficial in situations where more than one treatment decision is needed or where someone is deemed incompetent to decide for an extended period of time, such as might happen to those with dementia. However, if beneficence is not to override autonomy it is also necessary to consider how a value system might be incorporated into an advance decision. In this regard statutory and common law provisions suggest that in order for priority to be accorded to a value system one would have to be clearly established and applicable in the circumstances arising for decision. Moreover, the integrity with which personal decisions have been made to accord with one's values, beliefs and preferences would seem to be an important factor in establishing its reliability and credibility, i.e. has the patient evinced a settled and continuing intention to honour their values, beliefs and preferences if these are to be regarded as being determinative of what should happen to them in the future when they are no longer competent to express a view. Consequently, there is a second element to this chapter that is concerned with suggesting ways in which someone can construct their value system to make it functional, coherent and an inherently clear, convincing and reliable source of information about the personal value of their own life.

Chapter six is rounded off with a discussion that focuses on whether some limit should be imposed on autonomy, and therefore by definition on respect for the values of individuals, on public policy grounds.

Chapter Seven – How useful is the MCA in Promoting Autonomy through Advance Decision-Making and Decisions made in Patients' Best Interests?

The self-confessed mission of the MCA is to empower patients to make their own decisions and if not to place mentally incapacitated patients at the centre of decision-making processes concerning them. In this regard the MCA determines that the values, beliefs and preferences of a competent person, which can be clearly and reliably ascertained and understood by others, can play a role in medical treatment decisions.

My focus in this chapter is to therefore establish whether the MCA will support the use of a statement of values that has been constructed by a competent patient to distinguish whatever is critically or intrinsically valuable, which is synonymous with their reason for being or their life's purpose, from what is merely experientially or instrumentally valid. This question is posed in relation to three discreet aspects of decision-making under the Act, namely, capacity assessments, advance decisions and best interests decision-making.

An underlying objective of this work is to appraise whether, despite protestations to the contrary, the right to autonomy is in fact contemporary because regulation of the doctor-patient relationship under the MCA suggests that at various points beneficence will be in conflict with autonomy. The second part of this chapter is concerned with what should happen if the right to autonomy is not to be contemporary and with whether reform of the MCA will be necessary to accommodate the changes that are proposed.

CHAPTER ONE

KEY ETHICAL PRINCIPLES OF THE MEDICAL PROFESSION

This study is concerned with the principles, values and standards that should inform medical treatment decision-making processes and decisions taken on behalf of mentally incapacitated patients. The particular issue being considered is whether the values of a competent person, when they are known and understood by others, can play a role in medical treatment decision-making processes under the Mental Capacity Act 2005. That inquiry proceeds, in this chapter and the next, in ethics. The purpose in both is to legitimate the proposition, implicit in the research question, that the values, beliefs and preferences of competent patients are morally relevant to decision-making processes about whether to administer, withhold or withdraw medical treatment, including life preserving treatment, at a time when that person is no longer capable of making decisions on their own behalf.

Emphasis in this chapter is placed on the two most traditional and fundamental ethical principles of medicine, non-maleficence and beneficence. Argument will proceed to show why, in modern medicine, these represent an inadequate framework for analysis and decision about what ought to be done in the best interests of the patient. The chapter will be rounded off by a discussion that considers whether these obligations give rise to a form of medical paternalism that would conflict with the requirements of the moral principle of autonomy.

The Goals of Medicine

The goals of medicine can be stated in a variety of ways. Lord Bridge has referred to the administration of curative or prophylactic treatment which is appropriate to the patient's existing condition of disease, injury or bodily malfunction or susceptibility to such condition in the future.[1] In accordance with Sir Thomas Bingham MR the objects of medical care were to prevent the occurrence of illness, injury or deformity, to cure illness when it does occur, where illness cannot be cured to prevent or retard deterioration of the patient's condition and to relieve pain and suffering in body and mind.[2] Lord Goff was most succinct in summarising the medical purpose as action that is taken to preserve the life, health or well-being of another.[3]

Howsoever stated, the important point is that these are the ends that doctors are required to pursue in the best interests of patients.

Conflicting Goals of Medicine

An obvious problem with the goals of medicine is that they are not always compatible with one another. Now Hippocrates advocated that medicine should be practiced in accordance with an overriding philosophy that placed mankind in harmony with nature as the following extract reveals:

> *"Healing up to Hippocrates' time involved talking, praying and blatant shamanism; and Hippocrates was vehemently against all that. Occasionally, doctors would be hired to end a life, with or without the patient's consent; but Hippocrates based his healing on a natural philosophy that placed humankind in harmony with nature rather than in control of it; he based his interventions on observation, practicality, proof, and the constant self-warning not to do harm to the patient. His science was dedicated firmly to the patient's welfare. The physician sought honour though doing right by the sick person. No longer could the physician be hired to poison someone or to become a purposeful agent of death. He eschewed words as therapeutic, calling medicine the silent art. His written descriptions of some of his cases are masterpieces in clinical observation and deduction. He was thus the father of scientific medicine".*[4]

Although medical objectives have remained largely unaltered since the time of Hippocrates in another important respect medicine has changed

---

[1] *Re F (Mental Patient: Sterilisation) [1990] 2 AC 1 HL*, Lord Bridge, p.52

[2] *Airedale NHS Trust v Bland [1993] 1 All ER 821*

[3] *Re F (Mental Patient: Sterilisation) [1990] 2 AC 1 HL*, Lord Goff, p.74

[4] Bulger, Roger J., On Hippocrates, Thomas Jefferson and Max Weber: The Bureaucratic, Technologic Imperatives and the Future of the Healing Tradition in a Voluntary Society, The Tanner Lectures on Human Values, March 87, p.75

quite radically. In more recent times, advances in medical science and technology have altered the face and capacity of contemporary medicine. For example, technological developments such as respirators and ventilators are relied upon to substitute for the work of the heart and lungs just as a kidney machine can act as an artificial kidney. Each of these innovations can be relied upon to preserve life. Prosthetic devices may not actually preserve life but improved functionality must surely contribute to patient health and well-being. Yet more recently brain-computer technologies[5] benefit patients who suffer with severe movement disorders or paralysis following a stroke or accident.[6] Recipients with a functioning central nervous system have an implant inserted in the brain to receive neural messages that it translates and relays to a computer to help the patient to communicate with others. It is anticipated that further developments, using this form of technology, will emerge in the not too distant future leading to an even greater sense of independence for this patient group.[7] These are thrilling prospects for those that await them whilst the rest of society might simply marvel at the sort of possibilities now contemplated by medical science.

In consequence medical science has moved us to a stage where contemporary medicine can offer an extensive and effective range of beneficial treatments to prevent,[8] sometimes cure[9] and even control the progress or ill-effects of disease and injury.[10] Indeed such is the success of medical science that more recent developments demonstrate an ability to improve upon that which nature had already determined and to maximise

---

[5] Otherwise referred to as 'Braingate' technologies

[6] Wolpe, Paul R, Ethical and Social Challenges of Brain-Computer Interfaces, American Medical Association, Journal of Ethics, Virtual Mentor, Feb 07, Volume 9, no.2, 128-131

[7] For example, being able to switch on a light or the t.v. or perhaps to open and close curtains or to switch the heating system on and off

[8] For example, immunisation programmes. Diagnostic methods such as blood or saliva tests and scanners can also be targeted to detect early signs of health abnormalities

[9] For example, modern surgical procedures and methods have improved the skill and efficiency of surgeons just as drugs such as antibiotics clear infections

[10] For example, treatment such as kidney dialysis also there are a wide range of drugs that are not curative but which nevertheless aim to control the progress or symptoms of disease, such as chemotherapy or statins, and to thereby improve health and personal well-being

human potential to live a full and active life.[11] These developments are consistent with the medical objective which is to preserve the life, health and well-being of the patient.

However, the news is not all in one direction for medical science has increasingly placed physicians in a position to alter and control human life and not simply to cure or palliate the symptoms of sickness and disease.[12] For example, medical scientific and technological innovations enable physicians to intervene and control events at the end of life. These are to be distinguished from the more conventional form of cardiopulmonary resuscitation that has been practiced for many years in hospitals, emergency response units and by those who have been trained in first-aid in the work environment, for example, which aims to re-start a non-beating heart following cardiac arrest. Although intervention in these circumstances might be life-saving it can be categorised as an advanced form of first-aid because it involves mouth to mouth ventilation and chest compressions which continue for a relatively short period to see whether the heart can be revived and if so whether it has the further capacity to provide life support. To that extent we can say that the capacity to control or to influence events at the end of life has been with us for some considerable time.

The difference is that in contemporary medicine more advanced life support technologies are relied upon to revive a non-beating heart, and more importantly in this context, to support and sustain life. A ventilator breathes air into the lungs which oxygenates the blood, sustains the heartbeat and keeps vital organs alive,[13] whilst a nasogastric tube can be inserted to administer drugs as well as to feed patients artificially and mechanically with nutrition and hydration.[14] Consequently, human life can be artificially preserved and sustained for many years. Still, the use of life saving and sustaining technologies such as respirators, ventilators and nasogastric tubes becomes contentious when life is artificially prolonged without any obvious benefit to the future health and well-being of a patient

---

[11] For example, organ transplantation, infertility treatment, genetic and anti-aging treatment

[12] Anderson, Emily E., What we Talk About when we Talk about Goals, American Medical Association, Journal of Ethics, Virtual Mentor, Jun 07, Volume 9, no.6, 407-409, p.408

[13] *Airedale NHS Trust v Bland [1993] 1 All ER 821*, Lord Browne-Wilkinson

[14] Ibid - Sir Stephen Brown P

in a persistent vegetative state, for example, which challenges the view that we should seek to preserve or prolong life in all circumstances.

Has medical science precipitated the elevation of the goal of preserving life?

Lord Keith has previously stated that:

> *"The object of medical treatment and care is to benefit the patient. It may do so by taking steps to prevent the occurrence of illness, or, if an illness does occur, by taking steps towards curing it. Where an illness or the effects of an injury cannot be cured, then efforts are directed towards preventing deterioration or relieving pain and suffering"*.[15]

In some circumstances therefore the first imperative may be to prevent a person from dying and we have seen that physicians have the means at their disposal to do so, and as persons generally value life and view death as the ultimate harm there is an incentive to seek the survival of the patient. However, a presumption in favour of life can lead to a situation where more aggressive forms of medical intervention will secure the survival of some patients with brain damage.[16] This illustrates the point that it will not always be possible for doctors to save the life, health and well-being of their patients. Instead a physician will be required to choose which goal should be pursued in their patient's best interests.

Identifying the Legitimate Medical Goal

When taken as a whole the goals of medicine appear to have been informed by mankind's natural fear of death, disease and suffering. However, they have not been accounted for in any great detail and therefore the goals lack clarity.[17] Furthermore, there is no unifying theory to render the goals a coherent whole or that can bring each specific element into a state of coherence.[18] In the absence of either a fully specified set of goals or an overriding or unifying theory the goals can be shown to be internally inconsistent raising dilemmas about which goal should be pursued in the best interests of the patient.

---

[15] Ibid - Lord Keith

[16] Ibid - Sir Stephen Brown P

[17] Beauchamp, Tom L., Childress, James F., Principles of Biomedical Ethics, 2001, Fifth Edition, Oxford University Press, p.339

[18] Ibid

This is not a trivial matter when we have observed that medical decisions have consequences for the individual patient that can only be known retrospectively. The difficulty for physicians is that they are trained to achieve professional competence in the diagnosis and treatment of illness and disease. Undue reliance on a scientific theory that places mankind in harmony with nature is unsatisfactory because it presents too narrow a view of what it means to live a worthwhile life and therefore of whether quantity or quality of life is more important? Who then should decide and on what basis should they decide what should happen, i.e. which goal to pursue and where a choice exists what form of treatment will be in the best interests of the patient?

Medical Ethics

The purpose of ethical discourse is to determine what one ought to do or aim at when confronted with a moral problem.[19] Typically reliance is placed on a set of ultimate ends, values or principles that are relevant to the evaluation of the problem and a method or rational procedure for determining from those values what should be done or what one has most reason to do.[20] Consequently a moral conclusion is derived from a process of specifying, weighting and balancing the various factors under consideration which is what anybody might do to resolve a personal issue; they list possible courses of action then consider the pluses and minuses of each option to see which course of action to pursue on balance.[21]

In relation to medical ethics we typically think of the Hippocratic Oath because it was the first code of its kind that established a core set of values, customs and practices to help physicians determine what the legitimate goal of medicine should be based on what it would be ethical for them to do in the prevailing circumstances.[22] Several transcripts of the Oath exist and when consulted each varies a little from another but all are to similar effect in requiring physicians to:

---

[19] Sidgwick Henry, The Methods of Ethics, 1981, Seventh Edition, Hackett Publishing Company, Chapter IV, p.2; Beauchamp, Tom L., Childress, James F., Principles of Biomedical Ethics, 2001, Fifth Edition, Oxford University Press

[20] Ibid

[21] Beauchamp, Tom L., Childress, James F., Principles of Biomedical Ethics, 2001, Fifth Edition, Oxford University Press, p.15/23

[22] Gillon, Raanan, Philosophical Medical Ethics, 1986, John Wiley and Sons, p.9

> *"Follow that system of regimen which, according to my ability and judgment to, I consider for the benefit of my patients and abstain from whatever is deleterious and mischievous. I will give no deadly medicine to any one if asked, nor suggest any such counsel; and in like manner I will not give to a woman a pessary to produce abortion. With purity and with holiness I will pass my life and practice my art. I will not cut persons labouring under the stone, but will leave this to be done by men who are practitioners of this work. Into whatever houses I enter, I will go into them for the benefit of the sick, and will abstain from every voluntary act of mischief and corruption; and, further, from the seduction of females or males, of freemen and slaves. Whatever, in connection with my professional service, or not in connection with it, I see or hear, in the life of men, which ought not to be spoken of abroad, I will not divulge, as reckoning that all such should be kept secret. While I continue to keep this Oath unviolated, may it be granted to me to enjoy life and the practice of the art, respected by all men, in all times. But should I trespass and violate this Oath, may the reverse be my lot".*[23]

Essentially Hippocrates sought to regulate the doctor-patient relationship to instil in the wider community the requisite level of trust in members of the medical profession and confidence in the art and practice of scientific medicine. This was achieved by establishing a unifying moral code for the practice of medicine that would bind all physicians. More specifically, the moral principles of non-maleficence and beneficence functioned as relevant guidelines for ethical medical practice whilst a series of requirements, imperatives or rules established the particular nature of the moral obligation that was owed to the patient. In particular, the Oath requires physicians to benefit the sick and to abstain from acts that were likely to cause harm or which may lead to the death of the patient. Moreover, doctors are instructed to use their ability and judgment for the benefit of patients. Therefore the view embedded in medical ethics, at that time, was that medicine should be practiced paternalistically. Accordingly, Hippocrates determined that decisions that have to do with life, death and quality of life should be taken by someone who is expert in medical matters but who is not directly affected by the decision.

The Ethical Principle of Non-Maleficence

The principle of non-maleficence places physicians under an obligation to abstain from acts that are likely to cause harm, and in particular those which might lead to the death of the patient. Therefore, Hippocrates

[23] www.medword.com/hippocrates.html

recognised the moral significance of human life but says relatively little about how that concept should be understood. Most obviously, the principle does not specify what constitutes harm or which acts are to be avoided. Consequently, the Oath promotes uncertainty about what is right and wrong conduct in relation to medical treatment decision-making processes. It is possible that the term is not fully defined since ideas about what is good and bad for persons tends to change over time through a combination of knowledge and experience. For that reason harm could be defined compatibly with the impersonal but universal rules and norms of the common moral system. This would at least ensure that the Oath retained relevance and that a wider range of harms could be considered alongside death including the prospect of a patient experiencing pain, disability, loss of pleasure, and loss of freedom.[24]

Still the harm that is to be avoided would be determined by an external assessor who must rely on the rather indeterminate nature and scope of the common morality for guidance on a matter that the principle of autonomy claims should be determined by the personal values, beliefs and preferences of the particular patient in the context arising for decision. This is potentially problematic when persons differ in their assessment of what constitutes harm. For example, it might cause me a great deal of anxiety to be thrust into the Australian outback with only a penknife and billycan to depend on for my survival but Ray Mears adapts very well to the austerity of the bush and with a similar set of resources positively thrives on the peace and challenges that await him there. Persons similarly differ in estimating the likelihood of particular harms arising. So whereas my mind might be overtaken by fears about encountering venomous snakes and spiders when contemplating a visit to the bush Ray Mears can put the likelihood of that particular risk arising into perspective and this allows him to make a rational, on balance, judgment about the benefits and burdens of spending time in the outback regions of Australia.

The Sanctity of Human Life

It is suggested in the Oath that the obligation not to actively cause a patient's death is categorical. The view that it is morally objectionable to kill can be traced to the sanctity of life principle which is synonymous with the idea that human life has special or moral value and should

[24] Gert, Bernard, Culver, Charles M., Clouser, K. Danner, Bioethics: A Systematic Approach, 2006, Second Edition, Oxford University Press, p.11

therefore be treated as sacred. In view of the advances that have been made in medical science a matter of particular concern is whether there is any basis for moral absolutism in respect of the sanctity principle that would require doctors to seek to preserve life in any and all circumstances. In other words does respect for the sanctity principle lead to situations where preserving life becomes an ultimate value? This matter will be considered through two opposing perspectives; one theological the other secular.

Sanctity Principle: Traditional Western Theological Perspective

Christian faiths take the view that human life is a gift from God which is to be preserved and cherished due to its having been created in the image and likeness of God.[25] In this tradition human life is given and taken away again according to God's sovereign will and it is inviolable because of its inherent moral worth or value and dignity.[26]

Human dignity, which is founded on the concept of '*Imago Dei*',[27] is fundamental to the religious perspective.[28] The idea that human beings have dignity is attributed to the intellect, i.e. human are created in the image of God and therefore inherit developed intellectual capacities, which distinguishes humans from all other living things. It is on this basis that humans have capacity for moral decision-making and the ability to rule over creation as 'created co-creators' and as stewards of the gifts of God.[29] Accordingly, dignity which is the source of human pride and self-respect is here tied to a particular ideal of what it means to live a good life and the concept of moral accountability is introduced to deal with those whose enthusiasm might wane for leading their life in conformity with God's moral laws.

In summary therefore the religious perspective could be taken to infer that mortals are prohibited from assuming control or intervening in matters that are subject to divine command and intervention; an incomprehensible position for humans to adopt given their nature and intellectual capacities.

---

[25] The Holy Bible, Cambridge University Press, Genesis, Chapter One, paras.26-8,

[26] Ibid

[27] Imago dei denotes the theological doctrine that human beings are made in the likeness and image of God

[28] Ibid

[29] Ibid

On the other hand human dignity resides in the intellect. Therefore, it could be argued that our mandate as created co-creators is merely to respect every human being as an equal and inherently valuable member of society with a right to a life of their own choosing that does not harm the equal rights of others, which the moral principle of autonomy encourages us to do.

Secular Perspective: Intrinsic Value

Although the sanctity principle has religious origins not all persons share the same religious outlook which inclines moral philosophers to use secular concepts to justify the special value we attach to human life. Value theorists use the term 'intrinsic value' to identify things that are intrinsically valuable either in themselves or for their own sake or as an end itself.[30] Things that have intrinsic value have an inherent quality that we think special and we recognise that by treating them differently.[31] Accordingly, things that have intrinsic value are distinguished from other things that we value in purely instrumental terms or as a means to an end. Something that is instrumentally valuable is valued merely in terms of its usefulness in helping us to get what we want.[32] Ronald Dworkin claims that money and medicine are examples of things that are instrumentally valuable. He states that '*no one thinks that money has value beyond its power to purchase things that people want or need, or that medicine has value beyond its ability to cure*'.[33]

Is human life instrumentally or intrinsically valuable?

Dworkin states that it is both. He says that most of us believe that human life has intrinsic value[34] but that we might also treat the value of someone's life as instrumental when we measure it in terms of how much there being alive serves the interests of others.[35] If Dworkin is right, when he says that human life has intrinsic value, what account of the concept

---

[30] Levinson, Jerrold, Intrinsic Value and the Notion of a Life, The Journal of Aesthetics and Art Criticism, 62:4, Fall 2004, p.319

[31] Dworkin, Ronald, Life's Dominion: An argument about Abortion and Euthanasia, Harper Collins, p.72

[32] Ibid, p.71

[33] Ibid, p.71

[34] Ibid, p.70

[35] Ibid, p.72

would support the view that human life should be distinguished from all other life forms as having unique moral importance?

To be in concert with the theological perspective a version is needed to sustain the view that human life is valuable just in itself.[36] Thus the intrinsic value of human life must be found in virtue of what it is and not in virtue of its connections or relations to other things.[37]

Dworkin states that something is intrinsically valuable if '*its value is independent of what people happen to enjoy or want or need or what is good for them*'. Dworkin's definition aims to persuade us that what is intrinsically valuable must also be objectively valuable. Jerrold Levinson similarly describes intrinsic value in objective terms when referring to self-contained value.[38] He states that something has self-contained value if it would be valuable even were there nothing in the world but it, or if it would be judged good, or something that ought to exist, entirely on its own.[39] Shelly Kagan is on the other hand a little more circumspect when it comes to the value that an object has in itself. He states that: *"[i]f the object's intrinsic value is had independently of all other objects, that value cannot depend at all upon any of the relational properties of the object; rather its intrinsic value must depend upon the intrinsic properties of the object alone.* However, he questions whether anything does have intrinsic value in this sense.[40] Darwin, on the other hand, might argue that human life has intrinsic value on the basis that mankind had evolved as the greatest achievement of the natural world.

Levinson posts an alternative viewpoint which he calls persistent value. Something has persistent value if it remains valuable, and to just the same degree, regardless of the situation in which it is embedded or the context in which it is viewed. Persistent value is thus roughly the same as unconditional value, or the value something possesses irrespective of, and unaffected by, situating, framing or contextualisation. George Moore is to similar effect stating that:

36 Levinson, Jerrold, Intrinsic Value and the Notion of a Life, The Journal of Aesthetics and Art Criticism, 62:4, Fall 2004, p.322
37 Ibid, p.321
38 Ibid, p.321/2
39 Kagan, Shelly, Rethinking Intrinsic Value, The Journal of Ethics, 1998, 2, 277-297, p.278/9
40 Ibid

> *"To say that a kind of value is intrinsic means merely that the question whether a thing possesses it, and in what degree it possesses it, depends solely on the intrinsic nature of the thing in question. ... The definition involves notions which I do not know how to define exactly ... I mean to say two different things at the same time. I mean to say (1) that it is impossible for what is strictly one and the same thing to possess that kind of value at one time, or in one set of circumstances, and not to possess it at another; and equally impossible for it to possess it in one degree at one time, or in one set of circumstances, and to possess it in a different degree at another or in a different set ... (2) The second part of what is meant is that if a given thing possesses any kind of intrinsic value in a certain degree, then not only must that same thing possess it, under all circumstances, in the same degree but also anything exactly like it, must, under all circumstances, possess it in exactly the same degree. Or to put it in the corresponding negative form: it is impossible that of two exactly similar things one should possess it and the other not, or that one should possess it in one degree, and the other in a different one".*[41]

His account of intrinsic value seeks to reinforce the view that all human life has an inherent intrinsic value which persists over time and space. This is similar to saying that humans have inherent moral worth and dignity and for that reason should be honoured.

What gives Human Life its Intrinsic, Innate, Value?

What notion of human life is presupposed by intrinsic value that it should be morally objectionable to kill, for example?[42] Perhaps the first point to make is that influencing circumstances such as sex, age, culture, education and so on are of secondary importance. Consequently, the value of experience is not a source of intrinsic value. Jerrold Levinson explains the matter this way:

> *"The value of an experience taken by itself, in other words, is subordinate to the value that it contributes to a broader whole, the life into which it enters and of which it is a part. The value attaching to a whole life is not the sum of the values of its parts assessed in isolation, for a life ... is an organic unity, a series of internally connected, mutually qualifying episodes, whose value depends not only on the value of the episodes that make it up, but on their order of occurrence and their relations to one*

[41] Moore, G.E., Principia Ethica, 1993, Revised Edition, Cambridge University Press, p.285/7

[42] Levinson, Jerrold, Intrinsic Value and the Notion of a Life, The Journal of Aesthetics and Art Criticism, 62:4, Fall 2004, p.325

another. It is thus a whole life being a certain complex way, and not its component experiences having certain characters that is the real bearer of intrinsic value.

...Although experiences widely construed, are a significant part of a life, they are not the whole of it. As underlined by Nagel, not all of a life is experiential. Certain aspects of a life, such as the faithfulness of one's spouse, the state of one's reputation, or one's degree of privacy in one's home, may lie outside what one has experience or knowledge of, and other aspects of one's life, such as one's intellectual legacy, the realisation of one's projects, or the flourishing of one's children, may outrun one's lifetime entirely. Yet these non experiential aspects of a life being a certain way, for instance, one's good name not being tarnished after one's death, one's not being spied on by hidden surveillance cameras during private acts, or one's daughter achieving success after one is gone, contribute importantly to the intrinsic value of that life. As Nagel puts it, 'a man's life includes much that does not take place within the boundaries of his body and mind, and what happens to him can include much that does not take place within the boundaries of his life. The notion of a human life, in other words, cannot be entirely recuperated as the notion of a series of experiences, even if such a series forms the core of such a life, because some ways a life is are not experiential in any sense".[43]

Consequently, it is lives being a certain way that is the proper subject of intrinsic value. Moreover, that something must be a non-arbitrary feature or characteristic of humans, or of human nature, that is not inconvenienced by the fact that as co-creators each one of us is, as it were, made to be just that little bit different.

In this regard Jeremy Bentham, the founder of the utilitarian movement, dismissed traditional ideas about morality and the importance of human life within it by appearing to displace the significance of the human intellect. He argued instead that an act should be judged morally right or wrong in accordance with its propensity to produce pleasure or pain[44] and therefore the ability to reason was secondary to the ability to suffer.[45] Consequently, he argued in favour of a moral system that would maximise happiness and on this basis mere sentience or conscious existence was the fundamental moral criterion for inclusion and consideration under his

[43] Ibid, p.325/6

[44] Bentham, Jeremy, An Introduction to the Principles of Morals and Legislation, 1823 (Re-Print), Clarendon Press, p.2

[45] Gillon, Raanan, Philosophical Medical Ethics, 1986, John Wiley and Sons, p.43/4

proposed utilitarian scheme. Accordingly, all creatures that could experience suffering and pleasure would be treated as moral equals and any moral decision would require the interests of all sentient beings affected by that decision to be taken equally into account.[46] Theoretically, the general utility of ongoing veterinary care for a lame yearling stallion with excellent bloodlines could be compared to that of giving an esteemed octogenarian scientist a hip operation. The morally correct choice is the one that would create the greatest happiness for the greatest number.

Another approach is to take the view that humans are more important morally speaking than other animals for reasons that are independent of considerations of pain and pleasure.[47] Natural rights theorists, for example, argue that human life should be distinguished from all other life forms as having unique moral importance and therefore all living and innocent human beings are moral equals in having equal natural rights including an equal right to life.[48] The term 'natural' is used to convey the idea that all humans enter life with certain basic moral rights that should not be denied.[49]

Who acquires the natural right to life and isn't the rather straightforward idea about being a member of the human species too simplistic? Indeed, incorporation of the term 'human being' has proved to be quite divisive.[50] One obstacle lies in determining the point at which human life acquires its unique moral importance.[51] If we adopt the view of the Roman Catholic Church, that humans have an integrated body, mind and spirit, then all innocent human beings acquire an equal right to life from the beginning to the end of their lives.[52] This is because humans start their lives with a soul, the morally crucial gift that places human life above all other life forms. However, there is some disagreement about when exactly ensoulment takes place, from fertilisation to the development of the primitive streak, in a developing embryo and as the soul is immaterial it is

---

[46] Ibid, p.47/8
[47] Ibid, p.44
[48] Ibid, p.43/4
[49] The Columbia Encyclopedia, Sixth Edition, 2001-07
[50] Gillon, Raanan, Philosophical Medical Ethics, 1986, John Wiley and Sons, p.8
[51] Ibid, p.44/5
[52] Ibid, p.44/5

a matter beyond proof.[53] Consequently the debate continues to rage on in relation to the morality of abortion.[54]

An alternative position is to hold that all viable innocent human beings acquire natural rights.[55] The question is whether viability is a justifiable criterion for differentiating between humans that can be killed and those that cannot.[56] At issue is the fact that medical technology has made it possible to preserve the life of many more infants that are born prematurely.[57] As medical science may yet move to a stage where a fetus may customarily be incubated outside of the womb viability[58] would appear to be an inadequate premise on which to differentiate between humans that acquire rights and those that do not.[59]

In the search for an innate characteristic or quality in humans, that grounds the scope of our moral obligations and that is relevant to ideas about moral equality, sentience would after all seem to confer some moral importance.[60] That said simple sentience or self-awareness is insufficient as a justification for differentiating between the moral status of humans and animals as Bentham argued. But within the class of sentient beings some argue that there is a morally more important subclass that possess the special attributes grounding the unique moral importance due to people, including their right to life.[61]

The identification of that subset is no less problematic but most philosophers tend to focus on some aspect of personhood as the morally relevant differentiating concept.[62] Kant determined that rational willing agency was the essential characteristic of persons and therefore the relevant moral criterion for distinguishing between entities that were owed moral obligations and those that were not.[63] Perhaps inspired by the

---

[53] Ibid, p.44/5
[54] Ibid, p.44/5
[55] Ibid, p.43
[56] Ibid, p.46
[57] Ibid, p.49/50
[58] Viability is a technical term and its meaning will change over time
[59] Gillon, Raanan, Philosophical Medical Ethics, 1986, John Wiley and Sons, p.47/8
[60] Ibid, p.43
[61] Ibid, p.43
[62] Ibid, p.46
[63] Ibid, p.50

biblical notion '*Imago Dei*' Kant suggests that as co-creators humans had an intellect and the capacity to think for themselves. However, he saw that this might incline persons to think only of themselves and to seek to prioritise their own interests. God, by contrast, loves all his children equally and thus has a good will towards all mankind. Kant arguably picks this up and determines that only a fully autonomous agent with a good will would contemplate moral imperatives[64] in categorical terms[65] thus leaving the will with no discretion but to obey the moral law. On this basis Kant argued that autonomous persons should have freedom to self-determine their own life path and to rule over the rest of creation as a moral legislator in a kingdom of ends.[66]

Nevertheless, there are situations in which persons cannot be considered autonomous agents when, for example, they are drunk or have taken hallucinogenic drugs. So must one's capacity to be a rational willing agent persist in order to be considered a moral agent and moral equal? Moreover, if human life is distinguished as something special on the basis of some functional feature of them then not all human beings will be treated as persons. About this Raanan Gillon explains that:

> *"One of the consequences of adopting ... the Kantian criteria for personhood is that not all living human beings are persons. Embryos, fetuses, very young infants, and humans with severely damaged or severely defective brains may be [un]able to think, and if the Kantian requirement of rational agency is to be met many older children and some adults will fail to fall into the net of personhood. Yet the idea that a single living human being starts its existence not being a person, develops into a person, and then at some stage may stop being a person while remaining a living human being seems to be intuitively plausible both as an account of what happens and also as a basis for at least some sorts of important moral distinction...*
>
> *Quite apart, however, from producing conflicting moral intuitions of this sort, the idea that living human beings can be persons at some stages of their lives and not at others produces many other sorts of philosophical difficulty, especially problems clustering around the concept of identity...*
>
> *Indeed there are undoubtedly grave problems associated with any of these theories about what properties ground a right to life, and the problems are*

---

[64] Rules or commands

[65] Rules that apply to all unconditionally or without exception

[66] A council of autonomous agents

> *manifested particularly clearly in consideration of the moral standing of very young human beings, of live but brain dead, and live but permanently unconscious, human beings, and of animals of varying attributes. Although such issues have received considerable philosophical attention fairly recently, the subject still represents a lacuna in ethics as a whole and medical ethics in particular".* [67]

In the absence of any real agreement about which biological features or characteristics of humans or their nature are morally relevant to the concept of intrinsic value secularists have some difficulty in asserting moral absolutism in respect of the sanctity principle. A presumptive interpretation is consistent with the idea that people generally seek their own survival and therefore value life but recognises also that there are circumstances under which that presumption can be rebutted.

Can the Principle of Non-Malefience be interpreted consistently with the Requirements of the Sanctity Principle?

The principle of non-maleficence insists that physicians must not do an act that will cause death just as they should not engage in activities that might be considered immoral or that cast a shadow over their moral purity. Essentially Hippocrates was mindful about doctors becoming the agents of death. He therefore sought to moderate their activities as a check against profligacy or perhaps to engender caution in relation to processes that are not readily reversible as future freedom of choice will have been forever restricted.[68] Accordingly, clinicians must not practice euthanasia and of course assisting a patient to commit suicide remains a crime.[69] Both acts are prohibited by the principle of non-maleficence. On the other hand, the principle of non-maleficence is contentious in differentiating between killing and letting die.

Acts and Omissions, Killing and Letting Die[70]

We are ultimately concerned with what is right and wrong conduct in relation to safeguarding or protecting the life of a moral subject. In this

---

[67] Gillon, Raanan, Philosophical Medical Ethics, 1986, John Wiley and Sons, p.51

[68] Glover, Jonathan, Causing Death and Saving Lives, 1990, Penguin Books, p.76

[69] *R (On the application of Purdy) vs DPP [2009] UKHL 45*; CPS, Policy for Prosecutors in respect of Cases of Encouraging or Assisting Suicide

[70] Gillon, Raanan, Philosophical Medical Ethics, 1986, John Wiley and Sons, p.126

regard the acts and omission doctrine says that, in certain contexts, failure to perform an act, with certain foreseen bad consequences of that failure, is morally less bad than to perform a different act which has the identical foreseen bad consequences.[71] Crucially, killing is rejected though it is sometimes morally permissible to allow a patient to die.[72] In particular the doctrine permits a doctor to withhold lifesaving treatment in the knowledge that the omission will probably lead to an earlier death.[73]

As both paths lead to the same destination, so to speak, it is open to question whether there is an ethical difference in how they got there, i.e. whether an agent, in this case a doctor, actively intervenes to bring about death as opposed to merely omitting to do an act that would preserve life and prevent death? Is there a moral difference between an act and an omission and if so what information explains the difference? Is it worse to kill someone than not to save their life or are there circumstances whereby the distinction is morally insignificant?[74] Clearly theological thought anticipates that some form of divine non-intervention will take place somewhere along the line otherwise the ultimate human destiny, of reunion with God, could not be fulfilled.

Is Culpability Key to Determining Acceptability of the Acts and Omissions Distinction?

Glover contends that the doctrine appeals to our intuitions about these things and that our intuitive response to killing differs from our response to not striving to keep alive.[75] He argues that we distinguish between duties and those good acts that go beyond the call of duty as such we must also recognise that if we were to abandon the doctrine, we might also have to abandon our present distinction between acts or moral duty and supererogation.[76] His argument is that a common moral system applies to all people in all places in prohibiting harmful activity but that we can have no similar obligation to benefit all people in all places because we could never fulfil such an obligation.

[71] Glover, Jonathan, Causing Death and Saving Lives, 1990, Penguin Books, p.92
[72] Gillon, Raanan, Philosophical Medical Ethics, 1986, John Wiley and Sons, p.126
[73] Ibid, p.126
[74] Glover, Jonathan, Causing Death and Saving Lives, 1990, Penguin Books, p.93
[75] Ibid, p.93
[76] Ibid, p.94

Nevertheless, Glover does contemplate situations where omissions can be blameworthy, such as when a doctor omits to provide medical treatment that will keep a person healthy for years to come because of the expense of the drug. Here, Glover suggests that many people would want to say that this is not a mere omission, but a positive act of withholding the medicine.[77] Consequently, he goes on to say that supporters of the act and omissions doctrine must explain which act and omissions are culpable and not simply insist that anything culpable must be counted as an act rather than an omission.[78]

Gillon's argument is preferred. He claims that the difference between killing and letting die is not itself morally relevant[79] and influenced by the special moral obligation doctors owe to their patients[80] he states that, '*although this [the acts and omission doctrine] may be a plausible defence for people who do not have particular obligations to help patients, that, indeed is the primary purpose of medicine. Thus it would be absurd for a doctor to try to justify an omission to provide lifesaving treatment for his patient on the grounds that he had no moral obligation to help his patient*'.[81]

The problem, he contends, is that the doctrine does not itself explain what makes the moral difference between actions that result in undesirable consequences and inactions that have the same consequences.[82] On the basis that an omission is by definition not simply any inaction but a morally culpable inaction Gillon states that there must be some additional

---

77 Ibid, p.95

78 Ibid, p.95

79 Rachel's offers the following example: Smith and Jones both stand to inherit fortunes if their 6 year old cousins predecease them. Smith drowns his cousin in the bath, making it seem like an accident. Jones intends to drown his cousin but on creeping into the bathroom sees the boy slip, bang his head, and slide unconscious beneath the water. Jones waits to make sure that the boy really does die and is ready to push his head back under the water if he should surface, but the boy drowns accidentally. The two cases are almost identical except that one is a case of an act and the other of an omission.

80 Gillon, Raanan, Philosophical Medical Ethics, 1986, John Wiley and Sons, p.156

81 Ibid, p.128

82 Ibid, p.127/8

moral information given before any particular inaction can be classified as an omission.[83]

What information is needed to decide whether a doctor's action or omission had led to a patient's death so that we could be more certain about whether a killing or letting die had occurred?[84] One proposal is to base the morally intuitive difference between killing and letting die on considerations of harm and benefit to the patient. A failure to provide life saving treatment would then have to be justified on the basis that it would not benefit the patient and would probably harm them.[85] However, Gillon states that whilst '*assessment of harm and benefit are essential to all medical interventions it is not equivalent to deciding whether it is the doctors action or omission that has led to the patient's death, that is deciding whether killing or letting die has occurred.*[86]

Another possible approach is to link ideas about what is good to omissions, an omission would on this account be defined by a failure, not just to do any good, but only the good that one ought to do.[87] The problem with this account, according to Gillon, is that no omission would be morally acceptable, because by definition all omissions would be morally unacceptable.[88] Indeed Gillon concludes that the widespread intuition that there is a morally important distinction between acts and omissions should be rejected.[89]

Should one's Motive in acting be Relevant to Moral Assessment?

Remember that doctors must not be motivated to bring about the death of their patients when considering how to treat them. Conventional application of the acts and omissions distinction seeks to pinpoint who or what was causally responsible for the patient's death prior to reaching judgment about whether, in the circumstances, an act or omission can be

[83] Ibid, p.129
[84] Ibid, p.129
[85] Ibid, p.129
[86] Ibid, p.129
[87] Ibid, p.129
[88] Ibid, p.129
[89] Ibid, p.133

said to have taken place.[90] Taking into consideration some of the practical difficulties that arise in medicine from trying to do one's best for the patient the doctrine, whilst morally incoherent, comes to the aid of medical professionals, though not lay persons, in circumstances where life-sustaining treatment is withdrawn from a patient in a persistent vegetative state.[91]

However, if the doctor-patient relationship was more appropriately defined to reflect the special commitments that arise under it then an individual's purpose would be key to determining the acceptability of an act or omission which is an idea that a contemporary application of Kantian philosophy would of course support.[92] Consequently, moral judgment would no longer be passed on the basis of conduct taken in isolation but would depend on preceding considerations, including pre-existing moral obligations and the understanding and intention with which the person acted.[93] Not only would the consequences of an action be relevant but, and on the basis that good and bad are, to an extent, illusory, the agent's motive or beliefs and intentions about what they did, at both stage one and stage two of a treatment decision, would also be relevant to moral assessment.[94] So in coming to a conclusion about whether an act or omission had occurred decision-makers would have to consider that at stage one a doctor would, for example, consider whether treatment might be futile or subject to constraints, whilst at the second stage the focus would be on whether the patient would find treatment intolerable or undignified perhaps because it was not critically beneficial to them.

A problem associated with moral evaluations that depend on finding out what the real facts of the matter may have been is that it can be difficult to be certain about what a person's intention in acting actually was.[95] Here again the way in which the doctor-patient relationship is defined may be crucial to moral assessment. For example, when a doctor acts in a fiduciary capacity additional duties are imposed to reflect a higher

[90] *Airedale NHS Trust v Bland [1993] 1 All ER 821*

[91] Ibid

[92] Kant, I, Groundwork of the Metaphysics of Morals, Edited by Mary Gregor, 2006, Cambridge University Press, p.27

[93] Ibid; Gillon, Raanan, Philosophical Medical Ethics, 1986, John Wiley and Sons, p.130

[94] Ibid

[95] Gillon, Raanan, Philosophical Medical Ethics, 1986, John Wiley and Sons, p.134

standard of moral accountability. Pertinent to the present discussion is the fact that decision-making processes should be transparent so that the grounds on which decisions are being made are disclosed and made explicit.

Preliminary Summary

To summarise the medical objective is to preserve the life, health and well-being of patients. However, the goals of medicine are not always compatible with one another and this point was illustrated by drawing attention to the situation of a patient in a persistent vegetative state. The illustration served double duty because it also helped to establish the point that decisions concerning medical treatment are often made for and on behalf of patients who are no longer competent to decide the matter for themselves. In these circumstances a third party must act in the best interests of mentally incompetent patients.

The Hippocratic Oath restricts ethical analysis of what action should be taken in a patient's best interests to the moral principles of non-maleficence and beneficence. In this regard the principle of non-maleficence places physicians under a moral obligation to not cause harm or to engage in activity that will lead to the death of the patient. This duty, which is pertinent to treatment decisions at the end of life, can be traced to the sanctity principle. Yet medical technological advancements that enable doctors to preserve life can prove contentious when they raise concerns about the ongoing benefits and burdens of continued medical intervention. And so the question was raised as to whether this foundational principle placed physicians under an absolute obligation of non-maleficence.

On this point it is apparent that the principle of non-maleficence prohibits doctors from causing death but distinguishes between killing and letting die or active and passive euthanasia. Whilst this intuitively appealing distinction might be important to end of life treatment decision-making processes concerning incompetent patients,[96] analysis shows that it can be difficult to justify what makes the moral difference between acts and omissions that have similar consequences.[97] Consequently, it has been suggested that the doctrine requires further explanation, including in respect of its limitations. For example, are there some actions and omissions

---

[96] *Airedale NHS Trust v Bland [1993] 1 All ER 821*

[97] Lord Browne-Wilkinson also makes this point in *Airedale NHS Trust v Bland [1993] 1 All ER 821*

for which doctors should be made morally culpable? In other words conceptual analysis and critical reflection of the doctrine is needed if we are not simply to say that anything culpable must be treated as an act rather than as an omission.

One suggestion is to say that culpability for morally offensive conduct cannot be ascertained from an assessment of the sequence of events in isolation. As such the agent's motive in acting is morally relevant information that should properly be considered. In this way conduct, ordinarily considered objectionable, would be subjected to thorough examination to ascertain how free will was exercised in a particular instance. Consequently, moral judgment would no longer be passed on the basis of a single act taken in isolation but would depend on preceding considerations, including pre-existing moral obligations and the understanding and intention with which the person acted.[98] Not only would the consequences of an action be relevant but, and on the basis that good and bad are, to an extent, illusory, the agent's motive or beliefs and intentions about what they did, at both stage one and stage two of a treatment decision, would also be relevant to moral assessment.[99]

Reconciling the Norms of the Common Moral System

If the existence of a common morality can be demonstrated by widespread agreement on most moral matters and the point of a common moral system is to lessen the amount of harm or evil that is suffered generally[100] how do we reconcile those thoughts with another equally relevant moral consideration; the idea that the range of harms that form the basis of the common moral system are not just different in kind they are ones that rational persons can and do rank differently.[101] For example, some people might be willing to endure post-operative pain, discomfort and immobility in exchange for the possibility that later on they will have greater freedom of movement in their hips. Just as all persons who endure surgical

[98] Ibid; Gillon, Raanan, Philosophical Medical Ethics, 1986, John Wiley and Sons , p.130

[99] Ibid

[100] Gert, Bernard, Culver, Charles M., Clouser, K. Danner, Bioethics: A Systematic Approach, 2006, Second Edition, Oxford University Press, p.11; Beauchamp, Tom L., Childress, James F., Principles of Biomedical Ethics, 2001, Fifth Edition, Oxford University Press, p.3 and p.401

[101] Ibid, p.12; Ibid

procedures forsake some temporary loss of freedom in order to avoid greater detriments to personal health and well-being.

Consequently, there is no objective way to rank the various harms that will resolve all controversies[102] and no one knows how others perceive quality of life issues. Nevertheless the Oath suggests that doctors should determine what is in a patient's best interests by weighing the objective values associated with the principle of non-maleficence against another set of subjective considerations which are introduced and upheld by the principle of beneficence to see whether, and if so how, what is objectively valuable would contribute to the good or welfare of the patient.

The Ethical Principle of Beneficence

The principle of beneficence asserts that persons have a moral obligation to do good for others and in medicine that obligation translates into a requirement to benefit or to contribute to the welfare of patients.[103] But in requiring positive action toward a beneficial end the primacy of the principle is disputed.[104] In accordance with the goals of medicine beneficence entails an obligation to promote the life, health and well-being of the patient. However, there is no specific moral rule that can tell a doctor what good is and therefore which actions will constitute doing good on behalf of the patient.[105] Of course most persons wish to survive and therefore value life but a majority of them will also wish to have a good life.[106] Yet each person is an individual with a unique character or personality and this means that all patients are likely to interpret their good in different ways, a point that tends to expose a fundamental difference between competent and mentally incompetent patients because those who fall within the latter patient group may no longer be capable of expressing a view that will be considered in any meaningful sense.[107] This is potentially problematic when doctors will have encountered patients, or else stories about patients, who have competently refused beneficial life-

---

[102] Gert, Bernard, Culver, Charles M., Clouser, K. Danner, Bioethics: A Systematic Approach, 2006, Second Edition, Oxford University Press, p.12

[103] Beauchamp, Tom L., Childress, James F., Principles of Biomedical Ethics, 2001, Fifth Edition, Oxford University Press, p.165

[104] www.ascensionhealth.org

[105] Ibid

[106] See, for example, Kant, I, Groundwork of the Metaphysics of Morals, Edited by Mary Gregor, 2006, Cambridge University Press, p.8 para.4.395

[107] See for example, Mental Capacity Act 2005

saving treatment that could restore health but would be detrimental to their personal sense of well-being.[108]

Similarly, we might ask what scope should be given to beneficence as some limit must be placed on the obligation to act for the benefit of others. In medicine that limitation is generally introduced as a matter governed by the availability of resources.[109] Consequently, we will now examine those concerns about the primacy and scope of the principle.

Ethical Justification

Beneficence refers to an action that is done to benefit another or that promotes the good of another or others.[110] It is to be distinguished from benevolence which refers to a character trait of being disposed to act for the benefit of another.[111] Accordingly the ethical justification for the principle of beneficence is related to human nature that persons wish not only to survive but also to lead a good life, the word 'good' is not here used to convey the notion of a life that is especially virtuous or moral but one that is satisfying to the individual whose life it is.

Hill explains why the principle of beneficence is significant:

> *"Virtually all people include engaging in enjoyable activities among their ends, and so it is a reasonable presumption, in most cases, that helping others to engage in enjoyable activities is a prime example of the sort of thing the moral principle of beneficence guides us to do. What beneficence directly requires that one promote (to some degree) is the realisation of the permissible ends of others, whatever these chosen ends may be. Enjoyable activities and other more particular ends become morally important (when not excluded by other principles) because these are what people choose to go for, not because the activities, or the pleasant experiences they bring, have an objective 'intrinsic value'.*

---

[108] For instance, a practicing Jehovah's Witness will refuse a blood transfusion

[109] Beauchamp, Tom L., Childress, James F., Principles of Biomedical Ethics, 2001, Fifth Edition, Oxford University Press, p.166

[110] Ibid

[111] Ibid

Beneficence merely illustrates how personal ends can have indirect moral significance as one attempts to work out specific applications of general moral principles".[112]

Rosamund Rhodes is to similar effect in claiming that:

"The 'do no harm' principle ... is [in part], an expression of medicine's fiduciary responsibility ... Some consequences of a medical intervention are beneficial, others, however, are harmful. It is always important for physicians to assess and compare both sorts of consequences and their likelihood in determining a course of treatment. Nevertheless, because what we call 'good' is highly subjective, for the most part, the ethics of medicine also requires incorporating the perspective of the patient and accepting the patient's view of the good or the patient's rankings of goods".[113]

Examining the Relationship between Non-Maleficence and Beneficence

The moral principle of non-maleficence is grounded in a particular fact of human nature; that humans have a natural desire to survive and thrive. In accordance with that principle doctors have an obligation to prevent or to not cause harm to their patients. These rules of conduct or moral prescriptions are though sometimes referred to as the moral minimum, i.e. what is essential for the preservation of human life. Moreover, a series of negative prohibitions, i.e. thou shalt nots, are relatively speaking, morally undemanding.

Persons, however, wish not only to survive but desire also to lead a good life. In concert with this objective the Oath commits medical practitioners to an obligation of beneficence.

Does the Obligation of Non-Maleficence assume Priority?

The principle of non-maleficence instructs physicians to abstain from acts that are likely to cause harm, and in particular those which might lead to

---

[112] Hill, Thomas E. Jr., Respect, Pluralism and Justice: Kantian Perspectives, 2003, Oxford University Press, p.28

[113] Rhodes, Rosamond, The Blackwell Guide to Medical Ethics, edited by Rhodes, Rosamond, Francis, Leslie P., Silvers, Anita, 2007, Blackwell Publishing, Chapter 4, p.86, f.7

the death of the patient. As doctors also owe their patients an obligation to do good a question frequently raised in connection with the principle of non-maleficence is whether it is synonymous with the maxim *primum non nocere* – above all, or first, do no harm.[114] This is because a rigorous interpretation of the maxim would make the avoidance of harm the most important medical consideration of all.[115] The consequences for patients, of such an interpretation, would indeed be extreme because the principle appears to suggest that if it is not possible to do good without also doing harm then it is better to take no action at all.[116] Accordingly we begin by examining whether the obligation of non-maleficence assumes priority.[117]

Difficulties Posed by the Maxim Primum non Nocere

What is entailed in achieving the ends of medicine when a doctor must weigh in the balance the possibility of taking beneficent action, and thereby doing some good, against the principle of non-maleficence when it is interpreted in accordance with the maxim *Primum non Nocere*? The important point to bear in mind is that the doctor must, according to this maxim, ensure that in doing good no harm would be caused.

In essence even where treatment offers potential benefits to longevity, health and well-being there could be little, and in some instances no, prospect of it being administered. If only because administering treatment would require a doctor to interfere with the physical integrity of the patient and the simple act of touching is deemed harm enough to constitute a battery.[118] Future harms may be contemplated as a reasonably foreseeable outcome of the administration of a medical treatment when, for example, a sample of blood is taken for testing or where a broken leg is set inside a plaster cast. Just as more serious physical harms or violations can be foreseen to arise from the vast majority of surgical procedures.

Patients are often exposed to other more latent forms of harm in medicine. These are the inherent risks associated with particular procedures and

---

114 Beauchamp, Tom L., Childress, James F., Principles of Biomedical Ethics, 2001, Fifth Edition, Oxford University Press, p.113; Gillon, Raanan, Philosophical Medical Ethics, 1986, John Wiley and Sons, p.80

115 www.ascensionhealth.org

116 Ibid

117 Gillon, Raanan, Philosophical Medical Ethics, 1986, John Wiley and Sons, p.80

118 *Re F (Mental Patient: Sterilisation) [1990] 2 AC 1 HL*

treatments. Most of us are by now familiar with the concept as even over the counter preparations, such as tablets for pain relief, are provided with information about possible risks and side-effects, including contra indications for use as well as guidance about when to seek medical advice should any of the risks on the list materialise.

However, a problem related to information about medical risks is that details pertaining to them are impersonal and often presented as a statistical probability, or of the chance, or odds, of the risk materialising at all.[119] Essentially information about a population risk[120] is silent about whether or not the risk, that one is being cautioned about, will occur in any particular individual at this particular time. Just as it does not allude to whether some feature of the patient or characteristic of the doctor or institution in which the procedure is practiced increases the chances of the risk occurring.

Of course drugs are licensed for use by the Medicines and Healthcare Regulatory Products Agency following clinical trials. Consequently, serious adverse advents resulting from the use of pharmacological preparations has, for the most part been eliminated, provided the drug is prescribed in accordance with its licence for use. Although a drug that is prescribed on the basis of an incorrect diagnosis could be adverse to the life, health and well-being of the patient.

Nevertheless risk is inherent in almost all activities not simply those attributable to medicine and medical practice. Accordingly, a strict interpretation of the maxim *primum non nocere* would prevent clinicians from doing any good at all because even the best actions would carry with them the prospect of some harmful results materialising.[121] Therefore to construe the principle of non-maleficence consistently with the maxim *Primum non Nocere* would not only render the medical profession inert it would also stunt medical progress which is contrary to the interests of patients now and in the future.

---

[119] See for example the cases of *Sidaway v Board of the Bethlem Royal Hospital and the Maudsley Hospital and Others [1985] AC 871and Chester v Afshar 2004 WL 2289136*

[120] The proportion of people in the population that may be affected

[121] www.ascensionhealth.org

Is Beneficence Equivalent to Non-Maleficence?

The symbolic value of the Oath when put into an historical context is that it does in a sense represent the baptism of medical science in setting out the conditions that should govern the application of human knowledge about disease and its causes and effects in the interests of all humanity. When viewed from this perspective it could be argued that the obligation to do good or to confer benefits served to restrict unethical and experimental medical practices and similarly cautions those who might be inclined to treat the disease and not the patient particularly at the end of life. On that assumption beneficence is not equivalent to non-maleficence. It demands something more positive to be weighed in the balance against actual and potential harms of treatment or non-treatment. Moreover, it appears that the obligation of beneficence is an overriding requirement because in the absence of a prophylactic justification for administering a treatment one is equally committed by the principle of non-maleficence to refrain from doing any harm for sometimes it is better to take no action at all when the risk is that further harm will be caused in the absence of any positive compensatory justification.[122] This restriction, Hippocrates must have thought, would at the very least differentiate practitioners of medical science from priests, shamans and magicians who at that time were similarly concerned with healing and human welfare but whose practices could not be objectively validated in terms of their therapeutic or beneficial effects.[123] In any event, Hippocrates enjoined others like him to instil trust and confidence in the moral integrity of medical professionals and therefore in the practice of scientific medicine. But above all else, Hippocrates determined that medicine should have a moral base and that beneficence, or the obligation to do some actual 'good', should be the master value.[124]

So in relation to the question whether beneficence is equivalent to non-maleficence Beauchamp and Childress have explained that whilst no sharp break exists on the continuum from not inflicting harm to providing

---

122 Though please take note of Butler-Sloss in *Simms v Simms [2002] EWHC] 2734 (Fam)*

123 Bulger, Roger J., On Hippocrates, Thomas Jefferson and Max Weber: The Bureaucratic, Technologic Imperatives and the Future of the Healing Tradition in a Voluntary Society, The Tanner Lectures on Human Values, March 87, p.75; www.historylearningsite.co.uk/hippocrates.htm

124 See for instance Beauchamp, Tom L., Childress, James F., Principles of Biomedical Ethics, 2001, Fifth Edition, Oxford University Press, p.168

benefit, principles of beneficence potentially demand more than the principle of non-maleficence does because agents must take positive steps to help others, not merely refrain from harmful acts.[125]

Accordingly, it is through the process of weighting and then balancing the benefits and burdens of a medical treatment or treatments that a physician is able to determine which form of treatment is most likely to benefit their patient. This is because physicians are not only morally bound to avoid causing harm to their patients but are equally committed to pursuing that course of action that is most likely to contribute to their welfare.[126]

Beneficence: Distinguishing Moral Duty from Supererogatory Acts

When we talk about the moral obligation to do good, or to make a positive contribution to the welfare of others, we distinguish between moral duties and those good acts that go beyond the call of duty.[127] An obvious example of an act of general beneficence is to donate a sum of money to charity. Many more might choose instead to donate their time, knowledge and skill for the benefit of others as lifeboat crews of the Royal National Lifeboat Institution do; volunteers do in addition put their own life and well-being at risk in attempting to help another. Yet others commit considerable emotional resources to personal acts of beneficence. Consider foster parents or a chaplain who works at the local hospice or for that matter a person who donates a kidney to help a loved one. It is also apparent that those who donate their money, time or resources in this way are often esteemed members of society. Indeed those who have during their lifetime selflessly committed themselves to promoting the good of others are more likely to be distinguished from their peers on the basis of such altruism through the honours system, for example. For members of society have determined that those who are motivated to be genuinely beneficent, i.e. to abandon self-interest for the sake of doing good for others, deserve to be publicly recognised for achieving a standard of moral excellence.

---

[125] Beauchamp, Tom L., Childress, James F., Principles of Biomedical Ethics, 2001, Fifth Edition, Oxford University Press, p.165

[126] Ibid

[127] Glover, Jonathan, Causing Death and Saving Lives, 1990, Penguin Books, p.94

Nevertheless, general beneficence, or the contribution that ordinary members of society should make to the good of others, would appear to be a personal rather than a moral issue, i.e. nice to do but not wrong to omit.[128] You may remember Jonathan Glover argued that a common moral system applies to all people in all places in prohibiting harmful activity but that we can have no similar obligation to benefit all people in all places because we could never fulfil such an obligation.

Therefore, we are obligated to follow some rules of beneficence impartially such as requiring efforts to rescue strangers in circumstances that pose minimal risk to ourselves many acts of beneficence are not obligatory.[129] Otherwise only exceptionally, as indicated above, may circumstances eliminate the discretion allowed by general beneficence.[130] Obligations of specific beneficence can arise from special moral relations, such as exist in families between parent and child for example, or from special commitments or promises of the type made by husband and wife, and roles with attendant responsibilities, e.g. trustee and beneficiary or solicitor and client.[131] The essential point here is that persons can be placed under a specific obligation to act for the benefit of another as a consequence of the nature of the relationship that exists between the parties.[132]

So whereas we are morally required to exhibit impartial adherence to rules of non-maleficence we are morally permitted to be partial in helping or benefiting those with whom we have special relationships and we are commonly not required to help or benefit those with whom we have no such special relationship.[133] Accordingly failing to act non-maleficently

---

[128] Hill, Thomas E. Jr., Human Welfare and Moral Worth: Kantian Perspectives, 2002, Oxford University Press, p.99; Gillon, Raanan, Philosophical Medical Ethics, 1986, John Wiley and Sons, p.73; Beauchamp, Tom L., Childress, James F., Principles of Biomedical Ethics, 2001, Fifth Edition, Oxford University Press, p.167-70

[129] Beauchamp, Tom L., Childress, James F., Principles of Biomedical Ethics, 2001, Fifth Edition, Oxford University Press, p.166

[130] Ibid, p.170

[131] Ibid, p.170/3

[132] Ibid, p.171; Dworkin, Ronald, Life's Dominion: An argument about Abortion and Euthanasia, Harper Collins, p.229; Rhodes, Rosamond, Medical Ethics, 2007, Blackwell Publishing, Chapter 4, p.75

[133] Beauchamp, Tom L., Childress, James F., Principles of Biomedical Ethics, 2001, Fifth Edition, Oxford University Press, p.168

toward a party is prima facie immoral as well as illegal whereas failing to act beneficently is very often not immoral or illegal.[134] Although Beauchamp and Childress argue that the principle of beneficence establishes an obligation to help others further their important and legitimate interests which perhaps explains why we are required to rescue strangers.[135]

In summary then, and with some exceptions, persons have only a limited obligation of beneficence toward others[136] although a personal commitment to be or to cultivate benevolence is undoubtedly a virtue in that it is an aspect of an individual's character that is morally commendable.[137]

The Oath: Doctors have Special Self-Imposed Supererogatory Moral Obligations to their Patients

Although the extent to which beneficence is morally obligatory is debated doctors have special, self imposed, supererogatory moral obligations to their patients, that is moral obligations that are over and above the ordinary moral obligations we all have to each other.[138] In accordance with the Hippocratic Oath, physicians pledge that they will come for the benefit of the sick according to their ability and judgment and will keep patients from harm and injustice.[139]

Does this mean that doctors are required to place the interests of their patients before their own?

About this Gillon states that:

---

[134] Ibid

[135] Ibid, p.166

[136] This situation can be contrasted with the one that pertains in some continental jurisdictions. The French impose a duty to rescue, for example.

[137] Hill, Thomas E. Jr., Human Welfare and Moral Worth: Kantian Perspectives, 2002, Oxford University Press, p.99-103; Sidgwick Henry, The Methods of Ethics, 1981, Seventh Edition, Hackett Publishing Company, Chapter IV, p.239; Gillon, Raanan, Philosophical Medical Ethics, 1986, John Wiley and Sons, p.73

[138] Beauchamp, Tom L., Childress, James F., Principles of Biomedical Ethics, 2001, Fifth Edition, Oxford University Press, p.165

[139] Ibid; Gillon, Raanan, Philosophical Medical Ethics, 1986, John Wiley and Sons, p.74

> *"Whatever the case in general ethics, it is undoubtedly true that members of the medical profession undertake to place the interests of their patients before their own in many circumstances. This undertaking differentiates them from, for instance, merchants, who, while they may also on occasion put their clients' interests first, will do so (qua merchants) only to further their own longer term interests, for example, when it is good for business to put themselves out for their clients. Although an element of self-interest undoubtedly exists in the practice of medicine ... the medical profession none the less conceives itself, and is conceived by society, as having a duty of beneficence to the sick in general and to its patients in particular".*[140]

One example of an occasion whereby a doctor undertakes to place the interests of their patient before their own lies in treating people with infectious diseases. Another notable example is that doctors may, even when out and about in their social time, be called upon to administer medical aid to a person in distress. Gillon presumes that the source of this additional moral obligation of beneficence taken on by doctors is a certain feeling of benevolence, good will or sympathy towards the sick.[141] At least he considers that there cannot be many who do not at least start off their medical careers with a desire to commit their working lives to helping the sick.[142]

Gillon's uncertainty on the subject prompts me to consider what is the source of the moral obligation to be beneficent? Morality is an institution that aspires to raise the bar, as it were, of human conduct. Clearly, not so far that its demands place unreasonable burdens on the majority of persons, but as informal rules of conduct are prescriptive and are not merely descriptive of what people actually do the intention must surely be to exalt persons, having due regard for their capacities and frailties, through maxims that give human life dignity.

In accordance with this view the principle of beneficence gives life to the biblical principle 'thou shalt love thy neighbour as thyself'. This means that human life should be conducted in a spirit of love and generosity towards others on the basis that love is one of the primary characteristics of God.[143] And in accordance with the concept 'Imago Dei' God has

---

[140] Gillon, Raanan, Philosophical Medical Ethics, 1986, John Wiley and Sons, p.73/4

[141] Ibid, p.74

[142] Ibid

[143] www.godandscience.org/love/biblicallove.html

similarly endowed us with the capacity to love.[144] However, in contrast to human love which is usually based on feelings and emotions God's love for us is spirit led and unconditional.[145] This means that we do not have to be especially lovable and neither do we have to make him feel good to be recipients of it.[146] Furthermore, God demonstrated his love for all mankind by sacrificing his only son to us and Jesus in turn sacrificed his life for our sin and so one of the ways that love is defined in biblical texts is through benevolent acts of giving.[147] Consequently, Christians who believe that love for all has supreme value will presumably desire to become as one with God's divine nature and to this end should strive to be patient, kind, truthful, unselfish, trusting, believing, hopeful and enduring and not simply jealous, boastful, arrogant, rude, selfish or angry.[148]

Nevertheless, some secular moral philosophers are less optimistic that humans can act altruistically as Hill explains:[149]

> *"Beliefs vary about what we can do for others, and these beliefs tend to influence in various ways views about what we should do for others.*
>
> *Some believe that altruistic conduct is impossible, and thus conclude that there is no moral obligation to be altruistic. Moral arguments for accepting other-regarding principles, on this view, must appeal at some point to self-interest. Hobbes is often thought to be a prime example. By nature, he held, we always act for the sake of some good for ourselves. What is called 'compassion', he tells us, is really one's 'grief for the calamity of another that ariseth from the imagination that a like calamity may befall oneself', and the laws of nature that prescribe accommodation and forbid hatred are derivative from the primary law directing one to further one's own interests.*
>
> *Others hold, less radically, that though concern for others for their own sake is occasionally possible, due to human nature such other regarding concerns can only be rare, unstable, and restricted in scope (e.g. to family, friends and associates). If one assumes that altruistic acts must be*

---

[144] Ibid

[145] Ibid

[146] www.allaboutgod.com/god-is-love.htm

[147] Ibid

[148] Hill, Thomas E. Jr., Human Welfare and Moral Worth: Kantian Perspectives, 2002, Oxford University Press, p.105; www.godandscience.org/love/biblicallove.html

[149] Hill, Thomas E. Jr., Human Welfare and Moral Worth: Kantian Perspectives, 2002, Oxford University Press, p.103

motivated by altruistic feelings, then the belief that altruistic feelings are severely limited tends to undermine belief in a general obligation to act for the sake of others. It seems pointless, and even dangerous, to expect people to act for selfless regard for others if, because of human nature, such motives are uncommon, unreliable, and narrowly focused... 'Ought' in this context implies 'can', and ... if most people are similarly lacking, then it seems doubtful that having and acting on the motive can be a basic moral obligation even for the few who have the capacity for it.

Many who agree that altruistic feelings are in fact rare in our world may nevertheless believe that this is an ideal motive, within human capacities, and that we are obligated to cultivate it. What our observations show, they may argue, is that people do not (often) act from altruistic feelings, but not that they cannot. Various explanations may be given for the fact that most do not develop and act from their capacity for this ideal motive. The failure may be attributed, for example, to pervasive problems that, according to some theological and social theories, can eventually be overcome or transcended.

If pressed with the objection that it is foolish and dangerous to expect people to act on motives that are in fact quite uncommon, idealists may reply in different ways. Some Christians may say that love for all, even though rare, has a supreme value and that one should have faith that God will prevent or compensate for the disasters that seem predictable when one trusts that people can be more loving than evidence shows them capable of being. Some revolutionary idealists, confronted with the same objection, may reply that indeed we should not count on most people, as currently conditioned, to act from anything less than selfish motives, but after the revolution, they may argue, radically altered social conditions will mould new personalities in which other-regarding motives dominate.

Another common view is that compassion and general benevolence are not only possible in rare circumstances but are powerful and pervasive features of human nature. This belief about human psychology can also influence moral views. For example, the belief makes it easier to affirm utilitarianism as a theory of moral obligation, for it sets aside the alleged problem that human beings cannot consciously strive for the greatest happiness for all without ulterior motives. Believing that general benevolence is a powerful natural motive would also make it more reasonable for utilitarians (and others) to believe that we need not and so (given costs) should not resort to state coercion, manipulation, and indoctrination to maintain a decent social order.

The Kantian position, by contrast, is that, once we see the reasons for doing so, we can guide our conduct by a limited principle of beneficence, no matter how warm or cold our feeling towards others may run. That we can do so, at least in normal circumstances, is not refuted by empirical evidence and is presupposed in our conception of ourselves as moral agents".[150]

It is against this general philosophical outlook that we return to consider the Hippocratic Oath. Hippocrates was presumably mindful that doctors had, through their education and training, acquired special knowledge, of medical science, and skills in the practice of medicine. In the knowledge also that health has no substitute in the battle to survive and thrive or to live a good life he recognised that doctors were uniquely placed to benefit others. Consequently, Hippocrates determined that medical professionals should not use their knowledge and skills merely to further self-interest just as they should not be used partially to benefit or to further the interests of a particular person or group. Rather, it is at least arguable, that he enjoined doctors to an obligation of beneficence in the belief that professional knowledge and skills ought to be used for the good of all patients regardless of their personal feelings toward them.[151]

Maximising Human Welfare – The Primary Obligation is to Maximise Human Health?

Is a doctor's obligation to benefit their patient overriding? The simple answer is no. Medical science has now progressed from its more humble origins of seeking to preserve life with what we may now regard as relatively ineffective treatments. This was a time when health and ill-health were each defined in relation to the presence or absence of disease and when the doctor's bedside manner was all important to patient wellbeing.

Scientific progress has therefore transformed medical practice for the benefit of patients however transformation does not take place in a vacuum for the success of modern medicine has altered medical practice in other noteworthy ways that are also relevant to patient care and well-being. The National Health Service operates under conditions in which it is funded out of public money where resources are finite and demand for services always outstrips supply. Consequently, a major issue for doctors in the delivery of healthcare is now how they should allocate those scarce resources to preserve the life, health and well-being of patients.

---

150 Ibid, p.104

151 www.ca/ef/topical-the-duty-of-benevolence.htm

The principle of utility[152] places value in achieving the greatest good for the greatest number and dictates that resources are maximised when doctors use their expert knowledge to form a diagnosis and give treatment advice. This is entirely consistent with the role doctors have been trained to perform and ensures that decisions governing the way in which medical problems are understood are taken by the person best equipped to appreciate the consequences of their decision-making and action on the available resources. Consequently, the obligation to confer benefits is constrained by other ethical considerations such as the need to weigh the cost of a medical treatment against its beneficial effects.[153] Similarly in a system where resources are finite doctors are also required to ensure a just distribution of available resources and in this way also the needs of 'my patients' compete with the needs of others in society.[154]

So in contemporary medicine doctors have a moral obligation to benefit their patient's health and to some extent the health of others.[155] In other words there will be times when moral obligations to others will supersede a doctor's duty to his or her patient. Essentially a doctor must act to maximise human welfare generally which is consistent with medicine's goal, rationale and justification.[156] Nevertheless, modern ethical considerations must be upheld alongside professional ethical values which can be traced back to Hippocratic times.

Maximising the Welfare of an Individual Patient

As the Oath instructs doctors to use their ability and judgment for the benefit of patients the view embedded in medical ethics, more traditionally construed, was that matters concerning the life, health and welfare interests of patients should be determined by a doctor, someone other than the person directly affected by the decision. The question is on what basis can a doctor make a reasoned judgment about what action to take in the best interests of a patient when the principle of beneficence is dependent for its content on how 'good' is defined?[157]

---

[152] Utilitiarian ethic – 'The greatest good for the greatest number'
[153] Gillon, Raanan, Philosophical Medical Ethics, 1986, John Wiley and Sons, p.97
[154] Ibid, p.77
[155] Ibid, p.164
[156] Beauchamp, Tom L., Childress, James F., Principles of Biomedical Ethics, 2001, Fifth Edition, Oxford University Press, p.173
[157] www.ascensionhealth.org

There is a gap that has to be filled and as good health is a feature of well-being it is possible that a doctor can do no better than to defer to a general moral theory of what the source of human welfare or good is and to interpret the principle of beneficence in conformity with it.

Utilitarian Good

Utilitarian theorists rely on a single principle and a single dimension of value as foundational to all moral decision-making.[158] They take the principle of utility to promote the greatest happiness or good.[159] Accordingly utilitarians focus on the consequences of actions and in particular their contribution to human welfare.[160] Therefore, the method for arriving at a decision about which action to take appears similarly uncomplicated.

Furthermore, the absence of an omniscient God who can foresee the total consequences of all actions[161] is compensated for in the utilitarian standard of right conduct by requiring decision-makers to be strictly impartial in the way that a disinterested or benevolent spectator would be.[162] Utilitarians, like Hippocrates, therefore consider that a third party should be able to determine what course of action will benefit or contribute to the welfare of others. This is because the principle of utility is intended to engender selfless decision-making based on biblical principles or common moral rules such as 'do as you would be done by' and 'love your neighbour as thyself'.[163]

What Contributes to Human Happiness?

Mill claimed that the principle of utility was in unison with facts of human nature in recognising that pleasure and freedom from pain are the only things desirable as ends and that whatever is desired is valued either for

---

[158] Bentham, Jeremy, An Introduction to the Principles of Morals and Legislation, Reprinted 1823, Clarendon Press, p.2: Mill, John Stuart, Utilitarianism, Second Edition, Edited by George Sher, Hackett Publishing Company, p.7

[159] Ibid

[160] Ibid

[161] Gert, Bernard, Culver, Charles M., Clouser, K. Danner, Bioethics: A Systematic Approach, 2006, Second Edition, Oxford University Press, p.11

[162] Mill, John Stuart, Utilitarianism, Second Edition, Edited by George Sher, Hackett Publishing Company, p.17

[163] Ibid

the inherent pleasure it brings or as a means to promoting pleasure and prevention of pain.[164] A problem for doctors is that the words pleasure and pain have to be interpreted and then given meaning in a medical setting. For example, a person who likes to play football might choose not to have their shoulder pinned, following dislocation, mid-season. An equally common phenomenon in medicine is that many patients are willing to delay gratification and may even be prepared to endure certain hardships on the way to recovery such as happens with cancer patients who receive chemotherapy. These examples, illustrate how the particular ends of an individual can influence medical treatment decision-making processes.

Consequently, doctors must first reflect on all possible options for action.[165] Second, determine all of the foreseeable benefits and harms that would result from each course of action.[166] Third, seek to identify the patient's wishes, preferences and concerns, then try to determine which are relevant and what weight these should assume prior to reaching a decision that should on balance produce more pleasure than pain for the patient after the costs have been taken into account.[167]

Such assessments are difficult to make for any person. How many of us when faced with a choice do not later reflect on what we elected to do and think that we would choose to do something different if we had our time again? What reason supports the view that doctors find the task any easier than the rest of us?[168] A doctor might be undecided about which body of medical opinion to follow.[169] Although one would hope that medical technical knowledge should in the end be helpful in alleviating that particular problem. Medical competence cannot however be relied upon to provide guidance about what is a good life for the patient.

---

[164] Ibid, p.7

[165] www.scu.edu/ethics/practicing/decision/calculating.html; Santa Clara University, Calculating Consequences: The Utilitarian Approach to Ethics; Gillon, Raanan, Philosophical Medical Ethics, 1986, John Wiley and Sons, p.70

[166] www.scu.edu/ethics/practicing/decision/calculating.html, Santa Clara University, Calculating Consequences: The Utilitarian Approach to Ethics; Gillon, Raanan, Philosophical Medical Ethics, 1986, John Wiley and Sons, p.70

[167] Ibid

[168] Gillon, Raanan, Philosophical Medical Ethics, 1986, John Wiley and Sons, p.71

[169] *Bolam v Friern Hospital Management Committee [1957] 1 WLR 582*

Consequently, there is reason to question the notion that a doctor, as technical expert, is in any better position to make such assessments than a patient who is, or may be, ignorant about medical matters.[170]

Well-Being

Thomas Scanlon provides insight into the uses and limitations of any general theory of well-being:[171]

> *"Any plausible theory of well-being would have to recognise at least the following fixed points. First, certain experiential states (such as various forms of satisfaction and enjoyment) contribute to well-being, but well-being is not determined solely by the quality of experience. Second, well-being depends to a large extent on a person's degree of success in achieving his or her main ends in life, provided that these are worth pursuing. This component of well-being reflects the fact that the life of a rational creature is something that is to be lived in an active sense – that is to say, shaped by his or her choices and reactions – and that well-being is therefore in large part a matter of how well this is done – of how well the ends are selected and how successfully they are pursued. Third, many goods that contribute to a person's well-being depend on the person's aims but go beyond the good of success in achieving those aims. These include such things as friendship, other valuable personal relations, and the achievement of various forms of excellence, such as in art or science...*
>
> *But this list of fixed points does not amount to a theory of well-being. Such a theory would go beyond this list by doing such things as the following. It might provide a more unified account of what well-being is, on the basis of which one could see why diverse things I have listed as contributing to well-being in fact do so. It might also provide a clearer account of the boundary of the concept – the line between contributions to one's well-being and things one has reason to pursue for other reasons. Finally, such a theory might provide a standard for making more exact comparisons of well-being – for deciding when, on balance, a person's well-being has been increased and by how much.*
>
> *I doubt that we are likely to find a theory of well-being of this kind. It does not seem likely, for example, that we will find a general theory telling us how much weight to assign to the different elements of well-being I have listed: how much to enjoyment, how much to success in one's aims, and so*

[170] Gillon, Raanan, Philosophical Medical Ethics, 1986, John Wiley and Sons, p.71
[171] Scanlon, Thomas M. Jr., The Status of Well-Being, 1996, The Tanner Lectures on Human Values, p.96

on... Plausible answers would depend on the particular goals that a person has and on the circumstances in which he or she was placed... It does seem that there are answers to such questions, but I do not think that they are likely to be delivered by anything that could be called a general theory. Even if there were such a theory, moreover, it would need to be not just a theory of well-being, but a more general account of what is valuable and worthwhile".[172]

How should Well-being be Assessed?

A narrowly defined concept of well-being might focus on a single good such as health.[173] What is in one's best interests would in these circumstances be equated with what is in a person's medical best interests and would tend to prioritise medical scientific data as well as medical expertise and experience over the personal wishes and experiences of the patient.

Welfare, so construed, would however tend to displace the idea that persons know best what is good for them and a conflict with autonomy would exist. Kant cautioned us against treating persons merely as the means to an end, including that of good health.[174] Persons are instead to be treated as rational beings with autonomy.[175] An autonomous person is someone who is bound to no higher authority, with a power to govern themselves in accordance with their own constitution, without needing the approval of any higher authority.[176] Therefore an autonomous agent identifies with the idea that moral, and non-moral, requirements are not externally imposed[177] but internally determined.[178] To act in a way that is

[172] Ibid, p.117-9

[173] In *Re F (Mental Patient: Sterilisation) [1990] 2 AC 1 HL* a persons best interests were synonymous with their medical best interests

[174] Kant, I, Groundwork of the Metaphysics of Morals, Edited by Mary Gregor, 2006, Cambridge University Press, p.37/38, para.4.429; Hill Jr, Thomas E., Human Welfare and Moral Worth: Kantian Perspectives, 2002, Oxford University Press, p.69, f.13 – Formulas of the Categorical Imperative, Formula of Humanity; Persons should never be treated merely as a means to an end

[175] Kant, I, Groundwork of the Metaphysics of Morals, Edited by Mary Gregor, 2006, Cambridge University Press, p.40/41, para.4.433; Hill Jr, Thomas E., Human Welfare and Moral Worth: Kantian Perspectives, 2002, Oxford University Press, p.33

[176] Ibid

[177] Culturally or by Divine Command

contrary to their beliefs, values and preferences causes them to experience inner conflict which is detrimental to their personal sense of well-being.[179]

Human welfare, according to Kant, should not therefore be assessed solely in terms of whether or not a person is in good health. As if to confirm Kant's viewpoint Julian Savulescu has also written that:

> *"Our well-being includes much more than our health. Indeed, arguably, health is an instrumental good which facilitates our engagement in worthwhile activity that we desire and which gives us pleasure. Cancer is bad because it stops us from completing our projects, seeing our children grow, doing what we planned with our partner, and so on. A symptom less disease, which does not affect length or quality of life, is of no practical importance. Whereas doctors may be concerned to promote health, patients may be concerned to promote their well-being more globally conceived'.*[180]

When welfare is assessed in accordance with a wider range of goods there is no disputing that a patient is in the best position to know what is good for them.

Which Factors are Morally Relevant?

If our notions of personhood are informed by the Kantian concept of autonomy what can safely be assumed about any particular individual? Do persons similarly share a commitment to particular human values that is mirrored by the goals of medicine? People often remark that the only certainty in life is death. A statement of fact that is hardly attention grabbing. The sentiment that lies beneath the statement is though quite interesting. For, in depicting death as an inescapable event that is a feature of every life, death is, somewhat ironically, cast as one of life's great levellers. It's going to happen to all of us. Yet little is known about it except that it marks the permanent ending of material existence. Only this much can we be sure of. Nevertheless this common thread in human experience is significant in fixing knowledge about a phenomenon that is

---

[178] Kant, I, Groundwork of the Metaphysics of Morals, Edited by Mary Gregor, 2006, Cambridge University Press, p.40/1, para.4.433

[179] Hill Jr, Thomas E., Human Welfare and Moral Worth: Kantian Perspectives, 2002, Oxford University Press, p.33

[180] Rhodes, Rosamond, Francis, Leslie P., Silvers, Anita, 2007, Medical Ethics, Blackwell Publishing, Chapter 1, p.23

familiar to all mankind. So we believe that death is the natural enemy of man and that understanding forms a necessary platform for persons to unite in valuing life and in seeking to prevent death.[181] Death is as it were the only universal experience we have in life.

To determine what is beneficial medical treatment requires us to go further. We must have knowledge about what people truly value in life. This is problematic when life presents itself in an unsystematic and incomplete package. The life that we have provides us with an opportunity to participate in a greater whole which offers no consistent foothold in human experience. Instead we are born onto the same planet but enter different worlds which are beset with irregularities and inconsistencies that have the power within them to divide humans. Whether as a consequence of the geographical space we occupy which might speak to religious beliefs, culture and ethnicity or to the circumstances we are born into and reflected in education, socialisation and experience. The timing of our birth is no less relevant in pointing to a person of a particular era and age. Just as the anatomy we are born with determines gender and polarises the sexes. This view of life is compounded by mankind's limited lifespan which serves to re-enforce our fragmented knowledge and experience of the world and its people. Consequently, the conditions necessary for a unified view of what is beneficial in life appear to be absent.

Essentially, all nation states and persons are similar in nature and will to that extent have values in common. They are also inherently autonomous and this means that the societies we live in and the people we live amongst are to that extent unique. Each is, as it were, built to be just that little bit different from another and therefore we should anticipate some diversity in the values that will inform a particular life based on a range of factors.[182]

---

[181] Life is objectively valuable and death is the ultimate harm

[182] Autonomy supports the view that persons should have control of their lives and bodies and that life should be lived in accordance with the subjectively held values, beliefs and preferences of the individual (and nation states)

How the Ethical Decision-Making Standards associated with the Principle of Autonomy are relevant to a Morally Desirable Outcome

When well-being is broadly construed it becomes tied to the issue of what a good life is. This is because a sense of well-being is what we will have when we are contented or, better still, happy with our lot in life. More generally the concept is associated with pleasure and the absence of pain;[183] pleasure generally induces that feeling of contentment whereas pain threatens to override or overwhelm most psychological states. This much we know. The problem is that controversy surrounds the issue of what will lead to the greatest amount of pleasure and conversely what will produce pain. The route to happiness is, as it were, not always entirely clear because there is no general agreement about what good is in this context or about how it should be pursued and evaluated.

For example, Utilitarians typically believe that good resides in states of affairs that are known to benefit mankind and take the principle of utility, which is considered the fundamental principle of all morality, to promote the greatest amount of human happiness for the greatest number.[184] Good is here evaluated as an objective property that is fixed by human nature.[185] Likeminded people do though differ about how to produce the desired consequences.[186]

Mill, for example, put forward an ideal or qualitative view of happiness and insisted that in estimating all things some pleasures are more desirable and more valuable than others irrespective of the quantity of pleasure yielded.[187] He recognised that people saw value in different things but nevertheless thought that the intrinsic goodness of various things could be

---

183 Sidgwick, Henry, The Methods of Ethics, 1981, Seventh Edition, Hackett Publishing Company, p.3

184 Mill, John Stuart, Utilitarianism, Second Edition, 2001, Hackett Publishing Company; Bentham, Jeremy, An Introduction to the Principles of Morals and Legislation, Reprinted Edition, Clarendon Press

185 Hill, Jnr. Thomas E., Human Welfare and Moral Worth: Kantian Perspectives, 2002, Oxford University Press, p.254; good could reside in a particular state of affairs that is known to benefit mankind, i.e. happiness. In that case good is evaluated as an objective property that is fixed by human nature

186 For example Mill and Bentham

187 Mill, John Stuart, Utilitarianism, Second Edition, 2001, Hackett Publishing Company, p.8/9

objectively measured so that comparisons could be drawn in the march toward pleasures being ranked in hierarchical terms. This enabled him to think that whatever would be capable of generating the greatest quality of pleasure for the greatest number could be determined externally by someone unaffected by the consequences of the decision.

By contrast, Jeremy Bentham, who was Mill's mentor in his formative years, thought that the principle of utility should be pursued quantitatively. A quantitative approach demanded that in estimating intrinsic goodness the consequences of a course of action should be calculated not just qualitatively but also in terms of the quantity of pleasure it produced.[188] Bentham claimed that by multiplying intensity by duration, it would be possible to calculate the quantity of pleasure a given pleasant experience contains.[189]

So whereas Mill appears to consider that one sort of pleasure, let's say buying a new item of clothing, could be compared to another form of pleasure such as attending a football match or reading a book, the intrinsic value of each being measured and compared in hierarchical terms for the quality of pleasure generated, Bentham thought that the longer a pleasure lasts and the more intense the experience, the better it was[190] and in construing the greatest good decision-makers would be required to think about and understand the force and true value of any pleasure and pain.[191]

Whilst we see that Mill and Bentham were each committed to the value of maximising human welfare or happiness they each held different views about how to pursue it and clearly differed in their methods of calculating or estimating human pleasure (and equally pain). Many others have speculated about what is the true source of human happiness by asking what a good life for humans is but many different visions of reality exist and one may be no less valid than another in this regard.

---

[188] For example, QALY's appear to have been modelled on this theory in relation to medical treatment decision-making

[189] Bentham, Jeremy, An Introduction to the Principles of Morals and Legislation, Reprinted Edition, Clarendon Press, p.29; Kagan, Shelly, 1998, Normative Ethics, Westview Press, p.31

[190] Ibid

[191] Bentham, Jeremy, An Introduction to the Principles of Morals and Legislation, 1823 (Re-Print), Clarendon Press, p.29

So perhaps the best we can say is that the pursuit of a good life is the guiding force in the lives of all rational persons who have an interest in personal well-being. However, happiness, if that is the ultimate end of human life, is a somewhat elusive creature that so often fails to respond to any form of command or expectation that is placed upon it.

The Kantian principle of autonomy is important in this respect in upholding the notion that the good life is best self-constructed because it allows each of us the freedom to determine, within certain confines, what our good is and if we feel bound by that understanding to therefore shape our life around those personally held beliefs, values and preferences. Indeed John Stuart Mill agrees because he has said that:

> *"The only freedom which deserves the name is that of pursuing our own good in our own way, so long as we do not attempt to deprive others of theirs or impede their efforts to obtain it. Each is the proper guardian of his own health, whether bodily or mental and spiritual. Mankind are greater gainers by suffering each other to live as seems good to themselves than by compelling each to live as seems good to the rest".*[192]

This statement suggests that individuals should have freedom from external constraints to pursue a life of their own choosing.[193] In other words persons and the autonomous choices they make should, in general and whenever possible, be respected. This indicates that diversity in the decision-making preferences of patients is to be expected and should not be suppressed by, for example, medical paternalism. Hence the obligations associated with the doctrine of informed consent have developed over time to emphasise a legal requirement that patients should be placed in position to make an informed choice about whether to accept or reject medical treatment.[194] As a consequence the doctor's duty to disclose information has increasingly been tailored towards what the patient must know in order that they may safeguard their welfare and other interests, including that of maintaining bodily integrity.

---

[192] Berg, Jessica W., Appelbaum, Paul S., Lidz Charles W., Parker, Lisa S., Informed Consent, 2001, Second Edition, Oxford University Press, p.23
[193] Ibid, p.24
[194] *Chester v Afshar 2004 WL 2289136*

Should a more paternalistic approach be taken towards the mental incapacitated?

The first point to make is that a patient may be considered incapable for any one of a number of reasons. Minors naturally fall into this category as time and experience have not combined sufficiently to induce maturity and wisdom. Alternatively, a knock on the head may render someone temporarily unconscious, or it could be that an elderly formerly competent person is suffering from dementia in which case capacity may fluctuate or be lost forever. And in some instances persons are incompetent but sentient whilst in exceptional circumstances the patient will be permanently insentient such as happens with those who enter a persistent vegetative state.

It is only natural that persons should want to protect those who are incapable of making treatment decisions themselves. In some situations there may be no option other than to adopt a paternalistic approach toward the incapable patient. This may be because the patient was never competent to register a choice or the wishes of the patient are unknown and are not reasonably ascertainable. Either way, necessary and appropriate treatment should, in these circumstances, be administered in their best interests for any alternative would be unthinkably immoral and therefore inhuman.

What is the role of the principle of autonomy in respect of formerly competent adult patients? Does the principle of autonomy continue to protect the right to choose what shall happen to one's body in a medical context?

In the Court of Appeal, Hoffmann LJ stated that to adopt a paternalist view, and deny that autonomy can be allowed to prevail, in such situations whilst appearing attractive can also have disturbing implications.[195] Do we insist upon patients accepting life-saving treatment which is contrary to their strongly held religious beliefs, for example?[196] He added that the principle of self-determination says that a person should be allowed to choose for themselves and that, if they are unable to express a choice we should try our honest best to do what we think they would have chosen.[197]

[195] *Airedale NHS Trust v Bland [1993] 1 All ER 821 HL*, Hoffmann LJ
[196] Ibid
[197] Ibid

A similar view was expressed in the House of Lords by Lord Goff. He stated that:

> *'To presume that the incompetent person must always be subjected to what many rational and intelligent persons may decline is to downgrade the status of the incompetent person by placing a lesser value on his intrinsic human worth and vitality'.*[198]

Therefore, if we are not to downgrade the moral status of mentally incapacitated patients then it is important that we should remain consistent between competent and incompetent patients. This means that decisions taken on behalf of a formerly competent patient should be made to accord with their former wishes even where a doctor or others do not consider it to be in their best interests to do so, such as when treatment and care that may restore health and prolong life would, if competence were notionally restored, be refused. To this extent, the principle of the sanctity of life yields to the principle of self-determination and the doctor's duty to act in the best interests of his patient must likewise be qualified.[199]

Dworkin writes compellingly on the subject that persons do not want to live or end their lives out of character.[200] He states that:

> *"Whether it is in someone's best interests that his life end in one way rather than another depends on so much else that is special about him, about the shape and character of his life and his own sense of his integrity and critical interests, that no uniform collective decision can possibly hope to serve everyone even decently. So we have that reason of beneficence as well as reasons of autonomy why the state should not impose some uniform general view by way of sovereign law but should encourage people to make provision for their future care themselves, as best they can, and why if they have made no provision the law should so far as possible leave decisions in the hands of their relatives or other people close to them whose sense of their best interests, shaped by intimate knowledge or everything that makes up where their best interests lie, is likely to be much sounder than some universal, theoretical, abstract judgment born in the*

---

[198] Ibid, Lord Goff

[199] Ibid

[200] Dworkin, Ronald, Life's Dominion: An argument about Abortion and Euthanasia, Harper Collins, p.213

> *stony halls where interest groups manoeuvre and political deals are done".*[201]

When welfare is assessed in accordance with a wider range of goods there is no disputing that a patient is in the best position to know what is good for them.

Conclusion: What is the moral standing of the Oath in contemporary medicine?

Although the principles of non-maleficence and beneficence continue to play a central role in medical ethics today it is a matter of personal choice whether a doctor swears allegiance to the Oath. For this ancient Code now suffers from the obvious criticism that it is outdated. Medical science has progressed from its humble origins to a position where contemporary medicine can, by contrast, offer a more extensive and effective range of preventative[202] and curative treatments[203] as well as metering out a collection of fairly comprehensive treatments that are capable of staving off the ill effects of poor health.[204] Indeed such is the success of medical science that it has properly entered into an era where treatment can be specifically tailored towards maximising human potential.[205] However, the National Health Service is publicly funded and operates on the basis of finite resources. And as demand for services always outstrips supply a basic function of medical ethics is to consider what the just allocation of a scare resource is. Another question of some moral importance in modern medicine is who should decide on the merits or otherwise of medical treatment, should it be the doctor who possesses expert knowledge in the field of medicine or should it be the patient who is for the most part relatively ignorant on the matter they seek expert advice about but who must bear the consequences of any decision. Respect for the principle of autonomy would accord primacy to the views of the patient. The Oath, by contrast, instructs doctors to use their ability and judgment for the benefit of patients. Therefore the view embedded in medical ethics, at that time,

---

[201] Ibid

[202] For example, immunisation programmes

[203] For example, modern surgical procedures and methods have improved the skills and efficiency of surgeons just as drugs such as antibiotics clear infections

[204] For example, treatment such as kidney dialysis also there are a wide range of drugs that are not curative but which nevertheless aim to control symptoms of disease and to thereby improve a person's quality of life

[205] For example, transplantation, fertility, genetic and anti-aging treatment

was that decisions that have to do with life, death and quality of life could be decided externally by someone other than the person affected by the decision. Paternalism was accepted in medical practice at that time. Consequently, the Oath is now best regarded as a symbolic source of moral authority regarding what it is appropriate and inappropriate for medicine to do in the name of preserving the life, health and well-being of patients in the 21st century.[206]

[206] Beauchamp, Tom L., Childress, James F., Principles of Biomedical Ethics, 2001, Fifth Edition, Oxford University Press, Chapters four and five; Gillon, Raanan, Philosophical Medical Ethics, 1986, John Wiley and Sons, Chapters 12 and 13

CHAPTER TWO

THE ETHICAL PRINCIPLE OF AUTONOMY

Immanuel Kant contended that persons should be respected as autonomous creatures of moral worth and dignity based on their capacity to reason and to be rational.[1] These, he argued, are the essential characteristics of persons which enable them to think, decide and act autonomously and in accordance with rational principles or laws which distinguishes them from all other creatures.[2] Therefore, persons should have freedom, of mind and body, to live their life in accordance with laws of their own making.[3]

Accordingly, Kant emphasises the supremacy of the principle of autonomy in the moral life which he grounds in a particular conception of persons and their capacities to explain why they should have freedom to be self-governing and should not be directed or governed externally as the utilitarian theorists Bentham and Mill had proposed.[4] Indeed Kant sought to constrain the scope and effect of utilitarian theory, perhaps fearing that there would be circumstances whereupon it would continue to have some bite, by claiming that in the moral life it is imperative that persons should always be treated at the same time as an end and never solely as the means to the end of any other.[5] Neither though did Kant advocate autonomy unconstrained.[6] He put forward a fairly demanding theory of right conduct based on the Categorical Imperative which required persons to consider whether the principle on which they acted could be univeralised, i.e. am I acting solely out of self-interest.[7] Consequently, it is inherent in Kant's theory that persons have duties to themselves and others when making

[1] Kant, I, Groundwork of the Metaphysics of Morals, Edited by Mary Gregor, 2006, Cambridge University Press, p.43, para.4.436
[2] Ibid, p.44, para.4.437; p.57, para.4.452
[3] Ibid, p.45, para.4.438
[4] Ibid, p.28, para.4.418
[5] Ibid, p.45, para.4.437
[6] Ibid, p.44, para.4.437
[7] Ibid, p.45, para.4.438

decisions and acting autonomously.[8] Of necessity therefore persons should not think and act on the basis of mere calculation alone rather the motive in choosing is an important element of such processes and in this respect Kant determines that only a good will has moral worth.[9] This is because only a person with a good will intends to think and act in accordance with the moral law and with what duty commands of them. Thus decisions and actions should be taken or done in a spirit of good will to all mankind.[10]

Hill, a contemporary Kantian philosopher, stresses why respect for persons is fundamental to Kant's idea of human dignity. He states that:

> *"Although Kant himself is often criticised for lapses into dogmatic rigourism, his principle of respect for persons is the product of his deep dissatisfaction with dogmatic, uncritical and pseudo-scientific moral theories that would impose their parochial norms on a world of richly diverse people who are capable of critical reflection and making their own choices. Respect for persons, Kant realised presupposes a practical conception of persons that must be normatively grounded, systematically developed, and responsive to a realistic (but not cynical) view of the human predicament. It must not merely reflect the substantive norms of particular communities or traditions, for it is needed as a framework for guiding moral reform within cultures and mediating conflicts among them".*[11]

To respect someone, in Kantian terms, is to respect them as an autonomous moral agent, indeed as an equal in moral matters, and therefore also as someone who has dominion over their own life and life plan insofar as this does not interfere with the equal rights and interests of others.[12] So to the degree that Maslow argued that humans were as predictable as all other creatures, in that they are motivated, or psychologically disposed, to satisfy their personal need of shelter, safety, care and only after these arrangements had been sorted out did they become concerned about personal development and eventually self-actualisation,[13] we can see in

---

[8] Ibid, p.31, para.4.421

[9] Ibid, p.7

[10] Ibid

[11] Hill, Thomas E. Jr., Respect, Pluralism and Justice, 2003, Oxford University Press, p.62

[12] Ibid, p.61

[13] Maslow's hierarchy of needs is a theory in psychology particularly that of human motivation

human life that within the hierarchy of needs there is considerable scope for diversity amongst and between individuals. As a result if someone thinks that a good life consists in living on a barge, for example, then we do not generally seek to persuade them that they have more reason to live on land in a traditionally constructed dwelling because it offers a greater measure of safety and security in the long term. Similarly, if a person with a degree in engineering is committed to the idea of spending their working life as a train driver we do not inquire over what factors they considered prior to arriving at their decision. Consequently, we respect their choice, even though it may not be ours, because we recognise each person is a unique individual as reflected in their beliefs, values and preferences and therefore in the way that they deliberate about things, including matters related to life, death and quality of life. What scope would have been given to personal freedom if it were otherwise? About this John Harris states that:

> *"Persons are capable of valuing their own lives. [There are] a vast variety of different reasons that people have for valuing their lives, and the different ways in which they think it important to organise their lives and the societies in which they live. Many of these differences stem from, or are expressive of, moral differences between people and are thus likely to remain important. It was the very intractability of these differences that made it seem unlikely that any agreement could be reached on a list of the things that made life valuable, and which made it seem more promising to concentrate on the fact that persons would be the sort of beings who had their own reasons or purposes for life, rather than on the content of those reasons or purposes.*
>
> *The recognition of the fact that we are likely to differ, and to go on differing, from one another as to what is important and valuable about life, and that this ability is itself part of the peculiar value that people's lives usually have, occupies a special place in moral theory. Those who accept that all the many differences between people, important as they are, do not of themselves make the life of one person more valuable, more worthy of preservation, than the life of any other, exhibit the basic attitude of their fellows which is often called 'respect for persons', and which is the starting point of morality.*
>
> *It is the starting point because it involves recognising that other people matter and so also that how they live their lives, and the quality of their lives, matters as well. It is precisely because they are so important that what they believe is so important, and it is because both they and their beliefs are so important that morality matters so much. There would be*

little reason even to get as far as disagreeing with others morally, unless it was accepted that they and their beliefs mattered".[14]

So manifestations in the moral life that have the potential to erode or eclipse personal freedom will to a similar degree undermine the principle of respect for persons as autonomous agents who are the primary source of moral and non-moral values, i.e. legitimate determinants of what is valuable in human life as well as what is personally valuable to them as valuers.

Accordingly, respect for persons entails the notion that each person should be respected as an autonomous moral agent and equal with a life of their own. Therefore, the subjectively held values and interests of individuals should be regarded by others as a legitimate source of authority about decisions and actions affecting them provided these do not cause others harm or interfere with their equal right to live a life of their own choosing. Consequently, we will be considering what respect is presumptively due to persons and the circumstances under which it can be forteited or lost.

What is Autonomy?

In brief autonomy refers to a right or state of self-government or self-rule.[15] The word 'autonomy' originally referred to the self-governance of independent city states.[16] Autonomy therefore defined those states that had a power to govern themselves in accordance with their own constitution.[17] They were not in other words bound to a higher authority and so did not need to seek direction from any further jurisdiction or power.[18] Thus the individual constitution of each unique state became the most relevant source of information about and authority of dominions.[19]

---

[14] Harris, John, The Value of Life, 1985, Routledge Publishing, p.192

[15] Tom L., Childress, James F., Principles of Biomedical Ethics, 2001, Fifth Edition, Oxford University Press, p.57/8; Gillon, Raanan, Philosophical Medical Ethics, 1986, John Wiley and Sons, p.60

[16] Tom L., Childress, James F., Principles of Biomedical Ethics, 2001, Fifth Edition, Oxford University Press, p.57/8

[17] Hill, Thomas E. Jr., Human Welfare and Moral Worth, 2002, Oxford University Press, p.33; Tom L., Childress, James F., Principles of Biomedical Ethics, 2001, Fifth Edition, Oxford University Press, p.57/8

[18] Ibid

[19] Ibid

The term later became extended and applied to persons.[20] Consequently, a person who has the capacity to think, decide and act freely and independently is autonomous.[21] By parity of reasoning autonomy of thought is related to the intellectual capacity to think for oneself which involves making decisions, believing things, having preferences and making moral assessments.[22] In order to act on the basis of personal deliberations persons must also have autonomy of the will.[23] Essentially this means that persons must have freedom to decide to do things on the basis of their own deliberations.[24] Perhaps we are all more familiar with the phrase 'willpower'. This term is used whenever a person exerts their will over their inclination. In so doing they are exercising their autonomous will or in religious terms we can say that personal willpower is the omnipotent force within each one of us.[25] Having thought and decided what to do autonomy of action is primarily concerned with the extent to which persons are willing to act on or back their own judgments. As a result autonomy of action requires that a distinction is drawn between having the freedom to do as one pleases such as happens when the inclination is dominant and acting autonomously which may also be doing as one pleases but on the basis of thought and reasoning.[26]

The Principle of Respect for Autonomy

Kantian philosophy is based on the premise that what exists in the world divides into two realms, the noumenal and the phenomenal worlds.[27] In the former what exists is intelligible to persons because things are represented as they are and therefore it can be governed by reason.[28] The phenomenal world, by contrast, is concerned with the way things appear

---

[20] Tom L., Childress, James F., Principles of Biomedical Ethics, 2001, Fifth Edition, Oxford University Press, p.58

[21] Gillon, Raanan, Philosophical Medical Ethics, 1986, John Wiley and Sons, p.60

[22] Ibid, p.61

[23] Ibid

[24] Ibid

[25] Ibid

[26] Ibid, p.60/1

[27] Ibid, p.63; Kant, I, Groundwork of the Metaphysics of Morals, Edited by Mary Gregor, 2006, Cambridge University Press, p.56, para.4.451

[28] Ibid; Kant, I, Groundwork of the Metaphysics of Morals, Edited by Mary Gregor, 2006, Cambridge University Press, p.57, para.4.452

and it is governed by sense perception.[29] Each of them, Kant judged, works according to universal laws but whereas a rational being can act autonomously according to their idea of laws a non-rational being is acted on, and their behaviour is heteronymous because it is determined by outside causes.[30] Think of a skittish horse that is concerned about a discarded crisp packet in the hedge row. Human beings are, by contrast, a mixture of the rational and non-rational but it is their will that links these two aspects of them and which enables persons to use their reason to produce effects on the non-rational world including the non-rational aspects of themselves.[31]

> *"Autonomy of the will is the property of the will by which it is a law to itself. The principle of autonomy is, therefore: to choose only in such a way that the maxims of your choice are also included as universal laws in the same volition".*[32]

Essentially Kant is saying that an autonomous will is the essential characteristic of persons who should therefore have freedom to self-determine their own life path.[33] They will recognise that in the real world persons must co-exist alongside other autonomous agents who like them are similarly interested in their own survival and in having an opportunity to lead a flourishing life. As a secure and stable community life is essential to individual exercises of autonomy reason will persuade them that their ability to survive and flourish will be seriously compromised in human communities that would adopt the rules of the jungle.[34] To this end reason will direct them to develop informal rules of conduct or a moral system that should apply to all persons, in all places at all times. So persons with an autonomous will choose to follow impartial moral principles of action, or in Kantian terms, Categorical Imperatives, '*act*

---

[29] Ibid; Kant, I, Groundwork of the Metaphysics of Morals, Edited by Mary Gregor, 2006, Cambridge University Press, p.56, para.4.451

[30] Ibid; Kant, I, Groundwork of the Metaphysics of Morals, Edited by Mary Gregor, 2006, Cambridge University Press, p.57, para.4.452

[31] Ibid

[32] Kant, I, Groundwork of the Metaphysics of Morals, Edited by Mary Gregor, 2006, Cambridge University Press, p.47

[33] Gillon, Raanan, Philosophical Medical Ethics, 1986, John Wiley and Sons, p.50; Harris, John, The Right to Die Lives! There is no Personhood Paradox, 2005, Medical Law Review, 13, pp.386-392, p.388

[34] A problem for evolutionary ideas about mankind is the notion of the 'Survival of the Fittest' which tends to encourage competition and undermines respect for moral laws

only on that maxim through which you can at the same time will that it should become a universal law', that engender equal respect for the life and welfare of all persons as a way to promote harmonious co-existence amongst a group of individuals who exhibit divergent moral beliefs, values and interests.[35]

As reason is being used to identify the need for objective moral laws persons are able to recognise the perspective from which moral judgments are made to a point where moral requirements are no longer deemed to be externally imposed, for example, by divine commands.[36] Instead persons with an autonomous will are both author of and subject to moral laws.[37] As such an autonomous person cannot act in any way contrary to their moral beliefs without inner conflict and self-disapproval.[38] And as the will is rational,[39] i.e. that persons can determine moral requirements through reasoning from a basic moral perspective, an autonomous individual can be relied upon to self-legislate in accord with moral laws just as if they were a legislator in a kingdom of ends.[40]

So in contrast to many other moral philosophers Immanuel Kant dared persons to think for themselves.[41] There was, according to him, no need of a God or any other external authority to inform us about the moral life since we have a mind and the ability to think, to reason and therefore to be rational, the distinguishing feature of persons, and as such it was within us all to think and act in accordance with Categorical Imperatives or universal laws of reason.[42] It was on this basis Kant deemed that persons should be both subject to moral laws and authors of them and as such morality should be self-constructed without the aid of a God or any other

---

[35] For example, Sanctity of life, Justice

[36] Hill, Thomas E. Jr., Human Welfare and Moral Worth, 2002, Oxford University Press, p.33; Gillon, Raanan, Philosophical Medical Ethics, 1986, John Wiley and Sons, p.64

[37] Ibid

[38] Hill, Thomas E. Jr., Human Welfare and Moral Worth, 2002, Oxford University Press, p.33

[39] It is independent or has not been acted upon and is thus autonomous

[40] Hill, Thomas E. Jr., Human Welfare and Moral Worth, 2002, Oxford University Press, p.33; Gillon, Raanan, Philosophical Medical Ethics, 1986, John Wiley and Sons, p.64

[41] Bragg, Melvyn, In our Time, Radio 4, Philosophy Archive, Altruism, note in particular the thoughts of Miranda Fricker of Birkbeck University

[42] Ibid

external authority.[43] Indeed it has been suggested Kant recognised that it was possible for persons to escape moral obligation if they did not care or did not believe in God, i.e. because something subjective within a person would release them from their moral obligations thereby letting them off the hook.[44] Kant therefore constructed a moral system that no one can escape and so when we act we must act on reasons that everyone can accept, i.e. a universal reason that can be applied to all people at all times without contradiction.[45]

Kant's ethics must therefore be classed as a theory that places what is right prior to what is good.[46] This is because it does not start with assumptions about what the end of human life is, i.e. that happiness, preference satisfaction or any other substantive ends are intrinsically valuable, objectively good or agent-neutral reasons to act as utilitarian theory does.[47] Instead, principles of right and duty or Categorical Imperatives are determined by rational reflection from a point of view that counts each agent as equally authoritative regarding moral principles and equally free to set and pursue individual ends within the limits set by these moral principles of action.[48]

In a sense Kantian moral theory encompasses many of the ideas and precepts found in traditional religious texts so it is a sort of divine theory without the aid of the divine. The important point, however, is that it permits of no external authority that is independent of our own reason.[49] The authority of moral principles is, as it were, the authority of our own reason, our best judgments, all things considered, as to what we ought to do.[50] Therefore, we respect the principle of autonomy when we respect persons, as moral agents with freedom to make decisions or to register

---

[43] Ibid
[44] Ibid
[45] Ibid
[46] Hill, Thomas E. Jr., Respect, Pluralism and Justice, 2003, Oxford University Press, p.27
[47] Ibid
[48] Hill, Thomas E. Jr., Respect, Pluralism and Justice, 2003, Oxford University Press, p.27; Gillon, Raanan, Philosophical Medical Ethics, 1986, John Wiley and Sons, p.64
[49] Hill, Thomas E. Jr., Human Welfare and Moral Worth, 2002, Oxford University Press, p.27; Gillon, Raanan, Philosophical Medical Ethics, 1986, John Wiley and Sons, p.64
[50] Ibid

choices that do not harm the interests of others or infringe upon their moral rights.[51]

Kantian ethics are then aspirational in the sense that he determined that human life has moral worth on the basis of some functional feature of persons, i.e. the intellect, which is why humans have freedom to develop a life as seems good to them and then said with freedom comes responsibility, to others, which imposes some limitation on self-interest.[52] Too much freedom, as with any hedonistic lifestyle, can at any rate be dangerous or at least counterproductive to human survival and flourishing in tending to ignite self-destructive tendencies in persons.[53] But Kant did not stop at the idea that human life has moral worth he also considered the idea of dignity and to that end viewed persons as free rational agents capable of abstracting from personal differences and therefore jointly legislating in a kingdom of ends the moral principles that constitute the basic moral framework within which they are free to set ends of their own.[54] To acknowledge the dignity of persons is then, according to Kant, to treat them as 'sovereigns' both in constituting general moral principles and in determining their own non-moral good.[55] Consequently, what is a good life for individuals is not determined by intrinsic values, such as happiness or pleasure and the absence of pain, but by the free choice of the individuals themselves.[56]

Mill on Autonomy

It is also true that Kant put forward a demanding concept of duty which might in all likelihood place too great a burden on the intellect. This is based on the argument that persons are expected to determine their moral duty from the Categorical Imperative and its various formulations. The pre-conditions of duty are widely held beliefs, most obviously the

---

[51] Gillon, Raanan, Philosophical Medical Ethics, 1986, John Wiley and Sons, p.64

[52] Bragg, Melvyn, In our Time, Radio 4, Philosophy Archive, Altruism, note in particular the thoughts of Miranda Fricker of Birkbeck University

[53] Idea taken from Rupert Everett who was speaking about Lord Byron

[54] Hill, Thomas E. Jr., Respect, Pluralism and Justice, 2003, Oxford University Press, p.25; Gillon, Raanan, Philosophical Medical Ethics, 1986, John Wiley and Sons, p.64

[55] Ibid; Kant, I, Groundwork of the Metaphysics of Morals, Edited by Mary Gregor, 2006, Cambridge University Press, p.47, para.4.440

[56] Hill, Thomas E. Jr., Respect, Pluralism and Justice, 2003, Oxford University Press, p.25

inviolability of persons, the sanctity of human life and justice or acting well toward others.[57] However, it is a feature of contemporary life that society is not morally homogenous. In a pluralistic society value diversity is the norm which presents obvious problems for those who would seek to do what is right. Remember that when Mill wrote his utilitarian theory he thought that only persons with an educated mind would have the capacity to determine what action would produce the greatest good.[58]

However, Mill, the great utilitarian thinker, also argued in favour of the moral obligation to respect people's autonomy on the utilitarian grounds that such respect would maximise human welfare.[59] On what basis could Mill have reconciled such apparently divergent ideas about moral philosophy? Gillon who quotes the philosopher John Gray offers the following explanation:

> *"In the first place, Mill's "absolutism" is only apparent, for he builds in the qualification that respect for an individual's autonomy governs absolutely provided that this does not harm others or deprive others of beneficial acts "which he may rightfully be compelled to perform". In the second place, Mill may be interpreted as arguing that the principle of utility (maximising overall welfare) entails this respect for autonomy, for the welfare to be maximised is "in the largest sense grounded on the permanent interests of man as a progressive being". Given that human happiness (in the broad Aristotelian sense of eudaemonia or flourishing) is constituted to a large extent in the exercise of people's autonomy and the people's autonomous requirements are so very different, indeed unique, it follows that respect for their autonomy will be at any rate a major obligation if the utilitarian objective of maximising welfare is to be achieved".*[60]

So it seems that both philosophers are agreed that we should respect autonomy in the interests of social harmony. However, Kant intended persons to legislate according to values inherent in their own constitution. This means that each person is entitled to a life in which the subjectively held values, beliefs and preferences, of a particular individual, which do not infringe the interests of others, should be respected in matters related to personal welfare and for sustaining respect for more objective or

---

[57] Bragg, Melvyn, In our Time, Philosophy Archive, Radio 4, Altruism

[58] Mill, John Stuart, Utilitarianism, Second Edition, Edited by Sher, George, Hackett Publishing Co., p.8/9

[59] Gillon, Raanan, Philosophical Medical Ethics, 1986, John Wiley and Sons, p.64

[60] Ibid, p.65

universal moral laws that are concerned with protecting human welfare more generally.[61] Consequently, Kant claimed that respect for the autonomy of others was a necessary feature of rational agency itself and thus of any rational agent whereas Mill (subsequently) argued that respect for the autonomy of others was required to maximise overall human welfare provided such respect did not harm others.[62]

The principle, both seem to be saying, enables us to order relationships between individuals and between those in a position of authority and the individuals they preside over.[63] Nevertheless, in relation to decisions concerning medical treatment it is only at stage two where the patient chooses whether to consent to an offer of treatment or to refuse to consent that respect for the principle of autonomy is made relevant to the decision-making process. Prior to that, at stage one, a physician will determine what treatment should be offered to the patient. Utilising the principles of utility and justice the aim is to consider what the likely consequences of their choice of treatment will be on the general human welfare. This is despite the fact that just as many contemporary philosophers have criticised Kant's ideas about duty[64] others have sought to challenge Mill's viewpoint that anyone can calculate with any degree of certainty what action will produce the greatest amount of good.[65]

The Doctor-Patient Relationship: Incorporating Respect for the Ethical Principle of Autonomy

Perhaps the first point to make is that respect for autonomy does not infer that doctors are released from their professional obligations of non-maleficence, which is a standard obligation all people share, and beneficence, which gives the doctor-patient relationship its special significance.[66] Rather, doctors, like the rest of us, must also have regard

---

[61] Societal change may force an alteration in the application of values

[62] Gillon, Raanan, Philosophical Medical Ethics, 1986, John Wiley and Sons, p.63

[63] Bragg, Melvyn, In our Time, Philosophy Archive, Radio 4, Altruism

[64] Pippin, Robert, in Raz, Joseph, The Practice of Value, 2003, Oxford University Press, p.103

[65] Smart, J.J.C. and Williams, Bernard, Utilitarianism For and Against, 2006, Cambridge University Press

[66] Gillon, Raanan, Philosophical Medical Ethics, 1986, John Wiley and Sons, p.164

for another standard moral obligation which is to respect the autonomy of others.[67]

Similarly, respect for patient autonomy does not mean that a patient can insist upon a particular form of treatment. The obligation of non-maleficence ensures that a terminally ill patient who suffers intolerable pain, for instance, cannot insist upon a doctor taking action that will release them from that burden but will also be the direct cause of their death, i.e. doctors are prohibited from killing their patients. Furthermore, doctors must be just as well as beneficent and so they must have regard for the medical welfare of all patients when deciding what treatment ought to be offered to an individual patient.

Essentially, the obligation to respect patient autonomy means that a doctor must be appropriately beneficent. Medical beneficence should therefore only be exercised to the extent that the patient wants or allows.[68] Primacy is, in other words, accorded to patient autonomy as opposed to medical paternalism and this means that a patient's wishes, rather than a doctor's, should be treated as paramount in relation to a decision to accept or reject an offer of medical treatment. As such doctors are morally required, in common with the rest of us, to respect the principle of bodily inviolability, which protects all persons against non-consensual physical interference, and have a general duty to obtain their patient's consent to a medical treatment as this most obviously demonstrates their willingness or agreement to proceed with what the doctor proposes to do.[69] Correspondingly, if the patient does not want to be helped or does not wish to consent to the form of treatment that is being offered to them then doctors must also respect their patient's decision to refuse treatment and to be instead maintained inviolate.[70]

The requirement that a doctor should obtain their patient's consent to a medical treatment therefore fulfils several functions. Most obviously the need for consent ensures that doctors respect their patients' bodily integrity which re-enforces the notion that the human body and life has special or symbolic value which explains why it is inviolable. As it is open to persons to exercise their autonomy by consenting to medical

[67] Ibid
[68] Ibid
[69] Ibid
[70] Ibid

intervention and to thereby relinquish their right to inviolability it is important that a person's autonomy is respected. In this regard Gillon claims that any consent to a medical intervention should bear the hallmarks of a voluntary, uncoerced decision, made by a sufficiently competent or autonomous person on the basis of adequate information and deliberation, to accept rather than reject some proposed course of action that will affect the patient.[71]

Decision-Making Capacity

As respect for the principle of autonomy is predicated on some functional feature of persons, i.e. the intellect, it is obvious that the right to self-determination, to make medical treatment decisions in accordance with one's own values, beliefs and preferences, depends on whether a person has capacity to think and act autonomously.

How much autonomy is sufficient for a person to be respected as an autonomous agent?

Mill, for instance, appears to have argued that respect for autonomy was required in so far as the people thus respected possessed a fairly basic level of maturity, or as he put it, a capability of being improved by free discussion.[72] Kant, contrastingly, placed emphasis on the fact that humans can reason and be rational and because rational agents necessarily have wills they are ends in themselves unlike entities that do not have wills and are at most mere means to an end.[73] In other words persons who have an autonomous will think and act on their own behalf and therefore in accordance with their own constitution, or values, beliefs and preferences, rather than merely following what others think and do.

Kantian philosophy therefore guides us to treat human life as both objectively and subjectively valuable. It is objectively valuable because it is part of our nature to reason and be rational. It is subjectively valuable because rational agents have freedom to develop a life plan. As such Kant argues that the particular nature of the individual concerned, as reflected in

[71] Ibid, p.113

[72] Ibid, p.63

[73] Gillon, Raanan, Philosophical Medical Ethics, 1986, John Wiley and Sons, p.64; Kant, I, Groundwork of the Metaphysics of Morals, Edited by Mary Gregor, 2006, Cambridge University Press, para.4.428

their values, beliefs and preferences, ought to be morally relevant to decision-making processes that concern them, i.e. it is incompatible with respect for autonomy to treat persons as the means to any end other than what is inherent in their own constitution.[74] Hence it is a categorical imperative that one must always act in such a way that you treat humanity, whether in your own person or in the person of any other, never simply as a means but always at the same time as an end.[75]

So whilst there is a presumption that all persons will have the requisite level of decision-making capacity, i.e. because the intellect is a functional feature of all persons, self-evidently not all persons will be considered autonomous in the sense that Mill or Kant prescribes. Infants and children certainly, and most teenagers, are likely to be insufficiently mature to be considered fully competent to be in control of their life in all situations, particularly when a fundamental interest such as life and health are at stake. Although on this point it is probably worth stating that it is a feature of contemporary society that adults are encouraged, if not required in some circumstances, to respect the growing maturity and autonomy of members of the younger generation.[76] This trend is generally positive in placing less emphasis on the notion that at some arbitrary point in time, customarily one's eighteenth birthday, some form of miraculous intervention takes place and overnight the person that existed yesterday is today rendered sufficiently competent to be considered autonomous to direct their own life. My point, then, is that whilst it is possible to justify a presumption in favour of decision-making capacity based on maturity alone emphasis should also be placed on the developing character and personality of the youngster, which is consistent with what Kant appears to be suggesting, i.e. emphasis should be placed on whether or not someone has capacity to be autonomous in that specific sense, i.e. to think and act in accordance with one's own constitution, rather than the more formal sense of being deemed competent on the basis of one's state of maturity which is what Mill appears to be hinting at.

---

[74] Ibid

[75] Kant, I, Groundwork of the Metaphysics of Morals, Edited by Mary Gregor, 2006, Cambridge University Press, para.4.429; Gillon, Raanan, Philosophical Medical Ethics, 1986, John Wiley and Sons, p.64

[76] It seems that children should no longer be seen but not heard. In relation to child abuse for example, persons in positions of authority might fall foul of the system if they did not take seriously the allegations of a child, even if these later prove to be unfounded. At another level consider how many children come home to an empty house because both parents are out at work.

Assessing Competence to Decide Autonomously

As previously mentioned all adults are presumed competent to make decisions on their own behalf. However, there is a danger that we might just be tempted to say that the person is competent to decide when a person's decision conforms to another's idea of what it would be reasonable for them to decide in the circumstances and to question that capacity whenever a decision stands out either because it does not conform with the reasonable expectations of others or because it is contrary to what most reasonable persons would decide in the circumstances, such as when a person refuses life-preserving medical treatment that would restore them to full health.

Of course doctors are placed in an unenviable position in this regard. The medical mission is to safeguard the life, health and well-being of patients, which are fundamental to human survival and flourishing. Respect for patient autonomy, on the other hand, determines that patients have the right to self-determination with regard to their own body, life and life plan. It is against this general background that Gert et al explain why the principle of autonomy has '*caught on so tenaciously*' stating that:

> *"One is that Kantian ethics was experiencing a renaissance and that his notion of autonomy was central to his account of morality. A second is that the society became increasingly aware that the medical profession was so markedly paternalistic that patient self-determination was almost nonexistent. A third was that the increase in medical technology resulted in several rational alternative treatments. A fourth was the aging of the population and the resulting increase in chronic diseases that could not be cured, only managed... A fifth, the increase in medical technology that could keep extremely sick people alive for a long time, together with an aging population that often had a rational desire not to be kept alive, even made it rational to refuse life prolonging treatment. So the emphasis on autonomy became the banner under which patients rallied to gain more control over their own health care. Allowing the patient to decide, what, if any, treatment he would receive became the main issue, and thus momentum and conviction, rather than conceptual clarity or theoretical soundness perpetuated the emphasis on autonomy".*[77]

Clearly there is a need for conceptual clarity concerning what should be assessed in order to determine that a person has, or does not have, capacity

[77] Gert, Bernard, Culver, Charles M., Clouser, K. Danner, Bioethics: A Systematic Approach, 2006, Second Edition, Oxford University Press, p.117

to think and act autonomously, i.e. has the capacity to make the decision they purport to make. Otherwise there is a risk that a doctor might override one's autonomous choice thereby depriving persons from exercising their right to decide. Furthermore, where capacity fluctuates, such as happens in the early stages of dementia, it is open to question on what basis a doctor can be expected to promote patient autonomy in the absence of any real notion of what contributes to a patient's sense of well-being.

What is it Relevant to Assess?

According to Kant a person with an autonomous will should think and act in accordance with a universal set of rational maxims or rules known as categorical imperatives.[78] At the same time the humanity formula counsels us to regard human life as objectively and subjectively valuable.[79] It is subjectively valuable because autonomy makes self creation possible.[80] Kant therefore encourages us to respect the personal rights and interests of each person including their views about how best to live where doing so presents no serious threat or harm to the equal rights and interests of others.[81] In this regard it is clear that people differ in terms of what they value. That is to say human nature determines that goals or ends, more commonly known as values, beliefs and preferences, will vary from person to person.[82]

Nevertheless Kant did not advocate autonomy unconstrained.[83] Accepting that nature imbued humans with the desire to survive and prosper,[84] Kant put forward a strong concept of duty that was intended to shape rather than constrain human inclination and self-interest. For example, he saw that

---

[78] Kant, I, Groundwork of the Metaphysics of Morals, Edited by Mary Gregor, 2006, Cambridge University Press, p.xv

[79] Ibid, p.xxii; Dworkin, Ronald, Life's Dominion: An argument about Abortion and Euthanasia, Harper Collins, p.72/3

[80] Ibid; Dworkin, Ronald, Life's Dominion: An argument about Abortion and Euthanasia, Harper Collins, p.224

[81] Ibid; Gert, Bernard, Culver, Charles M., Clouser, K. Danner, Bioethics: A Systematic Approach, 2006, Second Edition, Oxford University Press, p.117

[82] Ibid; Koehler, Derek J., and Harvey, Nigel, Judgment and Decision-Making, 2007, Blackwell Publishing, p.5

[83] Kant, I, Groundwork of the Metaphysics of Morals, Edited by Mary Gregor, 2006, Cambridge University Press, p.10, para.4.397

[84] Ibid, p.8, para 4.395

the way in which society is structured was of interest to all persons.[85] Consequently, he thought that persons should be committed to their own self-development because this would enable them to think more broadly about the true worth of their decisions and actions and of their consequences for society members generally, of which they are a part. He also thought that persons had a duty to preserve their life. Therefore, he was against suicide, perhaps considering acts opposed to the principle that persons generally desire to survive and flourish could only be explained on the basis that the will had been weakened by circumstances and rendered heteronymous.

Kagan picks up on this Kantian theme, i.e. the notion that persons have certain duties to themselves as well as to others, suggesting that it is necessary to reflect on the nature of autonomy, the central features of the model being pursued as well as its appropriateness and adequacy to our nature when assessing competence.[86] The point of such critical reflection is to not only aid understanding of what it means to be considered autonomous but to also indicate whether, and if so how, the imperative on which someone acts interferes with[87] or promotes[88] autonomy. For example, should persons always seek to maximise or prioritise self-interest to be considered autonomous? This is what he has to say:

> *"It might be, for example, that autonomy is only exercised if the person giving consent has at least minimal competence at evaluating the alternatives; or it might be that an autonomous choice must be at least minimally rational. Evaluating these claims would require a more careful investigation of the nature of autonomy ... But if anything like this is right, then not all consent will be morally relevant. And this issue may be important for settling the possibility of duties to oneself. Normally perhaps it is morally permissible for me to act toward myself in any way that I choose, including harming myself. For in the normal case, this will simply be living my life the way I want to, and will pose no threat to my own autonomy. But in certain cases, my consent may not suffice to make my act permissible. This might be especially so for actions that would destroy my autonomy, leaving me unable to control my life in the future. For example, it might be forbidden to sell myself into slavery or to take drugs that would leave me insane. In short, if morality is to adequately reflect our autonomy*

---

[85] Autonomy and the Kingdom of Ends

[86] Kagan, Shelly, Normative Ethics, 1998, Westview Press, p.280

[87] Actions that are contrary to what duty and the moral law demands

[88] Actions that are consistent with one's duty and moral law

this might actually require certain duties to oneself, and not merely duties to others".[89]

Kagan's final point might be relevant to the type of situation where a terminally ill cancer patient might be expected to forgo pain relief that might induce a state of unconsciousness, for example. Since whether or not the desire to be free of pain maximises self-interest in these circumstances could be debated. So too could it be argued that the desire is not autonomously willed because pain, particularly intense pain, overwhelms the volition and renders one heteronymous, i.e. an agent who is the means to an end of some other authority over the will.

John Harris has considered whether defects in reasoning or a particular bias might undermine autonomy. He states that:

"There are a number of ways in which an individual's processes of reasoning may be defective in ways that vitiate, or partially vitiate, the choices which they purport to justify or explain. First, some examples. Someone who smokes cigarettes because, there is no harm in it, or who believes that it is safe to drive home after an evenings drinking because I can take my drink, is if they genuinely believe what they say and act on the basis of that belief, operating under a substantial defect in reasoning. The same defects are characteristic of prejudices of all kinds. Where people allow received opinion or gut reaction to form the basis of their values, or when they form opinions based on manifestly implausible facts their autonomy is undermined...

Three main rules for avoiding the sorts of defects in reasoning that can undermine autonomy might be formulated as follows:

1. That there should be no mere parroting or blind acceptance of the views of others or of one's own society. This involves some active attempt to establish one's own views and to discover their truth or validity for oneself.
2. That where my choices are based on my reasons for them, that these reasons should not be vitiated by something like blind prejudice. And where the choices are based on some factual premise or claim, that there be a commensurate relationship between the strength of the evidence for those facts and the strength of the beliefs they support.
3. Where my choice is based on an inference from facts or propositions, that the inference should be valid...

[89] Kagan, Shelly, Normative Ethics, 1998, Westview Press, p.292

We should be clear that defects in reasoning will only damage autonomy where the defects undermine or tend to undermine the agent's capacity to make choices. Bad reasoning will always have this tendency, of course, but we must remember that some stated reasons are merely rationalisations and are known by the agent himself to be non-operative. Also, some genuine choices may be 'mere caprice' and none the less genuine for that". [90]

How then does a doctor determine whether their patient, who now expresses a desire to refuse treatment, is operating under some defect in their reasoning about treatment and its likely effects? Take for instance a person who is afraid of snakes, are they thinking more clearly when they decide not to go into the snake house at the zoo or when they summon the courage to take a peek inside or can whatever decision they make be attributed to a particular prejudice or bias that is operating on them at the time? About this Koehler and Harvey state that:

"Biases are often used to describe deviations from a norm but, in another more neutral sense, they can simply indicate a tendency to slant in one way rather than another. For instance, the term 'positivity bias' has been used to describe a preponderance of positive over negative evaluations in person perception and, more generally, in everyday language. This does not in itself indicate any errors of judgment, unless we believe that, in reality, positive and negative events should balance each other out. On the other hand the concept of a 'desirability bias' implies a tendency to assign exaggerated probability estimates to desired outcomes, not because of the amount of supporting evidence, but simply because we want them to come true. Such biases can be regarded as systematic, suboptimal judgments, sometimes labelled 'errors' or even 'fallacies'...

In studies of logical tasks, [it has been suggested] that many errors of deductive reasoning can be explained on the basis of a more general 'matching bias', namely the tendency to endorse conclusions that are linguistically compatible with the premises. Similarly, 'confirmation bias' in hypothesis testing can be conceived as a general strategy for testing hypotheses through verification rather than falsification procedures either by searching for positive instances rather than negative ones, or by finding observed confirmations more compelling than disconfirmations. It has alternatively been described as a general outcome of these and similar mechanisms (e.g. matching), reflecting the fact that hypotheses, for whatever reason, appear to be more easily retained than rejected.

---

[90] Harris, John, The Value of Life, 1985, Routledge Publishing, p.197

The concept of a bias in the latter sense, namely as a systematic deviation from a norm (or as an inclination towards one judgment rather than another), does not in itself imply one specific kind of explanation. Biases can be the result of cognitive limitations, processing strategies, perceptual organising principles, an egocentric perspective, specific motivations (e.g. 'self-serving biases' in social psychology), affects, and cognitive styles... The general approach has been to regard biases as a more or less regular by product of some more general principles of judgment"...[91]

Ronald Dworkin seems to suggest that decision-making capacity should be assessed in accordance with the degree to which a person's wishes or preferences are coterminous with or are expressive of the particular personality or constitution of an individual decision-maker for he states that:

"Competence is sometimes used in a task specific sense, to refer to the ability to grasp and manipulate information bearing on a given problem. Competence in that sense varies sometimes greatly even among ordinary competent people; I may be more competent than you at making some decisions and less competent at others. The medical literature points out, properly, that competence in this task specific sense is relative to the character and complexity of the decision in question. A patient who is not competent to administer his complex business affairs may nevertheless be able to grasp and appreciate information bearing on whether he should remain at home or enter an institution, for example... Competence in the sense in which it is presupposed by the right to autonomy means the general ability to act out of genuine preference or character of conviction or a sense of self".[92]

On this view it is the ability to think for oneself and in accordance with one's own values that should be assessed, i.e. can this person apply the facts of medical treatment to their values and arrive at a decision that is consistent with both. As persons are likely to differ in what they value as well as in how they value things by what standard should decision-making capacity be measured? Well if beneficence is not to triumph over autonomy then it is important that a doctor should not judge a book by its cover or seek to assess a patient's capacity to decide in accordance with their own values and standards. In this regard a functional, not outcome,

---

[91] Koehler, Derek J., and Harvey, Nigel, Judgment and Decision-Making, 2007, Blackwell Publishing, p.91/2

[92] Dworkin, Ronald, Life's Dominion: An argument about Abortion and Euthanasia, Harper Collins, p.225

based test for capacity should be most relevant to an assessment of whether or not someone has capacity to think and act autonomously in that sense.

Must Decisions be Rational?

The primacy of the principle of autonomy in the moral life is established on the basis of the human intellect, i.e. persons, normatively considered, are recognized for their capacity to think, reason and to be rational. However, Kant saw that it was impossible to account for persons solely in these terms. Persons are also social, sensory, emotional, spiritual beings with the capacity and drive to reproduce. Consequently, it is in their nature to form relationships of various kinds, to be sensitive, to feel and experience certain things, to be affectionate, emotional, empathetic, sentimental, and so on. As a result persons are subject to various stimuli which might affect their thinking and behaviour. Hence, it is relevant to ask what part reason should play in decision-making processes, i.e. must decisions be reasonable or rational.

Clearly, Kant intended that reason should remove sentiment in moral matters, such as whether it is just or in the public interest to provide a particular medical treatment, but it is less clear that sentiment, for example, should not have a role to play in matters related to the subjective value a life has for the person whose life it is. The problem with acknowledging this is that in some instances our sentiments may be acted upon or that we may be manipulated into a particular decision or course of action.[93]

A decision that is informed by human intuition poses an even greater challenge to rational decision-making particularly when the manner and timing of its calling foretells something that cannot be known by reason alone. Yet such feelings or instincts are not easily disregarded by those that have them when they have been validated over time to have foundation. So whereas personal willpower can be equated to religious ideas about God's omnipotence, the intuition can possibly be equated with religious ideas about omniscience, or that little bit of God within us all that heralds a form of foreknowledge or that allows us to perceive the imperceptible. Information gleaned from the subconscious, during sleep,

[93] *Re T (Adult: Refusal of Treatment) [1992] 4 All ER 649 CA*; *Re MB (Adult: Medical Treatment) [1997] 2 FLR 426 CA*

may be no less relevant to some individual decision-makers, which could account for why people sometimes choose to 'sleep on things'. Nonetheless, it is possible that we might just misinterpret what our instincts are telling us.[94]

It is also open to question by what standard rationality should be assessed. This is because decision-making is not an entirely neutral process when persons differ not only in terms of what they value but also in the way that they value things. For example, a person's worldview or attitude and approach will be reflected in the way that ones values, beliefs and preferences are weighed and therefore applied in practice. So there is scope for persons, similarly situated, to differ in deciding what should happen. Perhaps an example will help to make the point. Imagine that a group of co-workers in an office are organising a trip out to a local restaurant. Consider the conversation that ensues whilst they are all thinking about what to order from the menu:

> Skeptic – I doubt whether I will enjoy any of the dishes listed on this menu
>
> Objectivist – I'll have what everyone else is having
> Relativist – Can we split the bill according to what each person has ordered?
> Absolutist – This is the only restaurant in this city serving decent food at affordable prices and therefore it is the only restaurant that I will ever eat out at
> Subjectivist – The set menu is good, I agree, but please can I see the al la carte menu before I make my decision

Each is essentially pre-occupied with their own way of looking at things and this is what is being reflected in their attitudes and priorities when deciding what to eat. There is no indication that one is less rational than another if they are being true to themselves.

Is the subjectivist too fussy? The subjectivist does not intend to be difficult or awkward they merely want to decide in the light of all reasonably available information. They cannot be sure about what motivates others as it is possible to interpret human conduct in many different ways. Therefore, the subjectivist protects against falling victim to the values and interests of others by taking responsibility for making their own decisions

---

[94] Dworkin, Ronald, Life's Dominion: An argument about Abortion and Euthanasia, Harper Collins, p.73

in accordance with their own values. Thinking for oneself and taking personal responsibility for one's decisions and actions is what Kant advocates.

Now let us assume that the co-workers are reunited back at the office where the topic of conversation concerns the award of an annual bonus for sales performance:

> Skeptic – I've done alright – it's a jungle out there and only the fittest survive – he who dares wins, that's my motto
>
> Objectivist – Go out and grab it, I say, or someone else will
> Relativist – People sell to me, I sell to them. It's what makes the world go round, everyone does it and it's all the same. An eye for an eye and tooth for a tooth that is what tests or pushes the boundaries of what is acceptable sales practice
> Absolutist – I'm going to suggest a flat rate bonus scheme for all
> Subjectivist – I'm thinking of leaving because after I have explained the product/service, in detail, relatively few people tend to want it or can afford it

In this example we see that the subjectivist ensures that the interests of others are not compromised which is consistent and coherent with the notion of assuming personal responsibility for oneself since one is neither seeking to compromise or interfere with the interests of others. Instead of which they are supported, with appropriate information, to reach a decision in the light of relevant facts. In other words respect for personal autonomy is inconsistent with the idea of imposing, by one means or another, one's own values and beliefs onto any other. Consider religion and how we respond to Jehovah's Witnesses who knock on the door and seek to persuade us around to their world view. Creationists might, on the other hand, consider that the views of the evolutionist Richard Dawkin are equally offensive, because in pointing to the evidence that God did not create the earth and all of its creatures he asserts that it is preposterous that anyone should continue to believe in God and live a life that is informed by religious values and beliefs.

Consequently, some diversity in the approach of individuals to questions of value is to be expected. This is attributable to our nature and to the nature of individual decision-makers in terms of what they value and to the way in which they value those things. Therefore, it is important that reasonable differences between people in relation to question of value are mitigated by the test for decision-making capacity opening up the possibility that human emotion and intuition need not automatically be excluded from the decision-making process. The point it seems is that the ability to reason and to be rational should not be unduly compromised or overwhelmed by the human senses. To that extent we are allowed to love someone enough to donate one of our kidneys, or bone marrow[95], to them, even when to do so poses some risk to our own health and longevity. For example, a donor who subsequently suffered from cancer might not tolerate chemotherapy so well with only one kidney.

Clearly there is a need for conceptual clarity about what is most relevant to consider when determining that a person has, or does not have, capacity to make the decision they purport to make. A functional test for decision-making capacity is important in the various respects discussed in focusing on whether some form of cognitive impairment or disturbance prevents someone from being able to reason and to be rational, i.e. to think and act autonomously.[96] A two-stage test of this kind establishes a presumption in favour of decision-making capacity that should not be undermined simply because someone makes an unwise decision.[97]

Instead, persons must be able to comprehend or understand, retain and use information that is relevant to their decision. So it is the ability to think for oneself and in accordance with one's own values that should be assessed, i.e. can this person apply the facts of medical treatment to their values and arrive at a decision that is consistent with both. Accordingly, the outcome of a decision-making process or the choice or decision that is made should not have to conform to what a third party might expect you to decide in the light of the available information. Otherwise, the danger is that decision-making capacity would be objectively rather than subjectively appraised, which could have the effect of ushering us all into a state of conformity, and would bring forward the possibility that medical paternalism would again override patient autonomy. Although it has been said that the manner in which such a decision is made as well as possibly the timing of it might be significant to a finding of a lack of decision-making capacity.[98]

---

[95] *Re Y (An Adult Patient) (Transplant: Bone Marrow) [1996] BMLR 111*

[96] Mental Capacity Act 2005, s.2

[97] Mental Capacity Act 2005, s.1(4)

[98] *Re T (Adult: Refusal of Treatment) [1992] 4 All ER 649 CA*; *Re MB (Adult: Medical Treatment) [1997] 2 FLR 426 CA*

Information

Here again it is relevant to consider what is morally required of doctors if autonomy is to protect all persons against non-consensual physical interference since their consent must unequivocally demonstrate their willingness to proceed with what the doctor proposes to do. If, therefore, respect for autonomy is to supersede medical paternalism then it is important that doctors, as medical experts, should be required to provide their patients with information that is relevant or that is tailored to their needs, taking into consideration their values.[99] This is to enable patients with capacity to make an informed choice about whether to accept or reject an offer of medical treatment. Commenting on the role of information in relation to autonomous decision-making John Harris has stated that:

> *"Where beliefs or choices are based on false or incomplete information, or depend on such information at any crucial point, they will to that extent be less autonomous. So that where the agent is misinformed, or only told part of the truth, or where he is kept in total ignorance, his capacity to make the best choices he can will be undermined. This can happen of course by others deliberately deceiving him, for whatever motives, or knowingly giving only partial information, or it can happen by negligence or sheer mischance. It may of course also be the agent's own information gathering (or lack of it) that is at fault. And finally we should not rule out the possibility of the agent failing to understand, or understand the significance of, the information he obtains. Here too there is room for negligence, or deliberate obfuscation on the part of those supplying the information, and also for an unhappy and unwitting gulf between the medium of the message and the agent's ability to comprehend it".*[100]

Therefore, it is clear that the need for information is part of what it means to respect patient autonomy or more specifically the patient's right to self-determination, i.e. to make decisions, including medical ones, that accord with their wider interest in living a life that seems good to them. To this end it is important that information about medical treatment, in particular any risks of it, is tailored to meet the subjective needs of a particular patient rather than objectively assessed by a doctor to be material to what a reasonable person would want to know in the situation of the patient. A doctor's duty must, in other words, be tailored to meet the needs of their

---

[99] *Chester v Afshar 2004 WL 2289136*

[100] Harris, John, The Value of Life, 1985, Routledge Publishing, p.198

patient.[101] Clearly, patients should not be given so much information that it cannot reasonably be processed by them in the time available. Similarly, autonomy would be undermined if information were given in a form that could not be readily understood by the patient. This might happen if the doctor used overly technical terms since there would be an attempt to baffle the patient with science.

What other information might be relevant to a medical treatment decision? In particular should the patient be given any information about their doctor? I ask this question because it occurs to me that whilst a doctor will not labour over the benefit and burdens of a prescribed medication there is a reason for this. The manufacturer provides information about the risks and side effects of it. Furthermore, the doctor has access to one's medical notes which presumably act as a catalyst for why a certain medication ought not to be prescribed.

Where, however, the doctor is a surgeon who intends to perform an invasive surgical procedure is it reasonable, in these circumstances, for the physician to be required to provide patients with information about those risks and side effects that may be incurred as a consequence of it being them that is performing the said procedure. Certainly Gillon appears to think along these lines for he comments that a range of prima facie obligations derive from the principle of respect for patient autonomy including the provision of information about:

> *"[D]octors interests, qualifications, attitudes and moral stances to patients and potential patients as well as making it as easy as possible for patients to have a real choice of doctor".*[102]

With regard to his latter point it seems reasonable to argue that in order for a patient to exercise their right of choice meaningfully, they require information about the doctors experience and success rate, as well as perhaps about how success is being measured, in performing the procedure the patient is consulting them about, at the very least. Nevertheless, I do confess to feeling apprehensive about this idea not because there is anything wrong with it per se it is just that in practice it may well not be in the best interests of patients or the medical professions. The danger is that

---

[101] *Chester v Afshar 2004 WL 2289136*

[102] Gillon, Raanan, Philosophical Medical Ethics, 1986, John Wiley and Sons, p.166

exchanges of this kind could induce unhealthy competition between practitioners with information being presented or conveyed in measured terms. Patients might even be encouraged to engage in some form of cross-examination. Ultimately trust in the doctor-patient relationship would be forever undermined by undignified practices that it is in no one's interests to encounter or perpetuate.

The principle of making an informed choice is to safeguard patients against the consequences of making a non-autonomous decision. Accordingly, people need to gather or be given information that is appropriate to the choice confronting them. This is to facilitate an authentic reasoning process whereby patients determine what facts are most relevant to consider, how they should be weighted and so on, taking into consideration their values and attitude to risk.

So if autonomy not medical beneficence is to be overriding must patients always make an informed decision? We probably all know of someone who prefers not to hear unpleasant information particularly if it interferes unduly with their life plan or that affronts their identity or concept of themselves or possibly someone they care for. They would choose to sweep such information under the carpet rather than deal with it. In medicine it is possible to imagine that this might happen quite often in circumstances where people already burdened by illness, dependence and vulnerability might feel unable to cope with further disappointments. An otherwise healthy woman, disappointed at the results of IVF treatment, for example, might find it helpful to cling to the belief that she will become pregnant one day. So do clinicians have a special dispensation from telling the truth to their patients, and if so why and in what circumstances?[103] In this regard Roger Higgs argues that the importance that Kant attaches to reason has implications for medical practice in relation to the moral requirement for honest communication or truth telling and giving reasons. He states that:

> *"There can be no doubt that deceiving people will in some sense always diminish them. To treat people as an end in themselves, rather than as means to someone else's end, must mean that their own views of those ends – in the sense of aim and purpose – must be paramount when it comes to decisions about things that are theirs and that matter to them. If they are*

[103] Higgs, Roger, in The Blackwell Guide to Medical Ethics, Edited by Rhodes, Rosamond, Francis, Leslie P., Silvers Anita, 2007, Blackwell Publishing, Chapter 5, p.88

> *able to make choices for themselves in matters of their own welfare, if they are in other words autonomous people, they must be allowed to do so. Specifically, if there is a difficult decision to be made about treatment, the final arbiter must be that person to be treated, the patient. No one could make such a decision without being appropriately informed about the options, and their consequences, and the reasons for and against each, so the professional must give that person as accurate a picture as can be given, on which she can make her decision. Anything less means that the professional is set up as more powerful than the patient, and indeed more of a person than the patient: if the patient's choice is abrogated, she is reduced to a means to the physician's (perhaps perfectly laudable) ends. The choices might even include whether or not to continue as a patient at all. It is hard to see how an autonomous person's choice could possibly be respected in health care unless they were told the truth about their condition".*[104]

Kagan has also considered this matter but stresses what autonomy protects and therefore what is lost if a patient chooses not to take control of their own life. He states that:

> *"One basic idea of autonomy is to have the various aspects of one's life under one's control ... I can deliberate concerning how I want particular aspects of my life to go, choose amongst various alternatives and act so as to make my life the way I want it to be in that regard. But lies misinform me about how my life is going and what my options are; they distort my sense of what I can achieve and what needs attending to. The suggestion then is that being lied to interferes with my autonomy, by reducing my control over my own life. Accordingly lying to someone is wrong because it violates their autonomy".*[105]

It is fair to say that medical professionals have entered into an emotionally demanding profession. Consequently there is scope for arguing that there will be occasions where physicians might wish to spare their patients bad news for this very reason. None of us enjoy disappointing others the more so when it involves some fundamental interest of persons. This might lead to doctors justifying their approach to information sharing on the basis of what is proposed by their professional ethical code. Accordingly information that a doctor deemed was likely to do more harm than good

---

[104] Higgs, Roger, in The Blackwell Guide to Medical Ethics, Edited by Rhodes, Rosamond, Francis, Leslie P., Silvers Anita, 2007, Blackwell Publishing, Chapter 5, p.92

[105] Kagan, Shelly, Normative Ethics, 1998, Westview Press, p.111

would not be passed on to their patient based on some sort of professional privilege and as such medical paternalism not patient autonomy would be overriding. However, we also know that hard messages can be conveyed in an atmosphere of respect and compassion. Moreover, the evidence suggests that when people are denied access to significant information about themselves or their loved ones and only later find out about it they tend to feel somewhat aggrieved and disrespected.[106]

Of course there will be those who think that a doctor is in the best position to judge what should be done. They presumably do equate what is in their medical interests with what is in their overall best interests and perhaps in these circumstances there is no affront to autonomy if they have reason to want to defer to an expert, or at least to someone of greater experience, in medical matters. Others though might simply be deferential out of respect for their physician based on a traditional understanding of a profession whose mission in life is to care for the sick and disabled, a role that is today perhaps more appropriately assigned to practitioners in the hospice movement. Consequently, to think and act on the basis of such a belief is not consistent with exercising autonomy but with something else that is subjective within them, particularly if, for instance, the opinion of a nurse would not be regarded with an equal degree of reverential respect.

Treatment Refusals and the Duty to Respect Autonomy

Reason dictates that persons will be similarly motivated to seek their own survival, health and well-being. Good health has no substitute and besides poor health tends to compromise the freedom and independence we all enjoy. Nevertheless, there will be times when persons similarly situated might reasonably make different health choices. Crucially, medical treatment, that would preserve life and restore health, might be refused on the basis that it contravenes their beliefs thus causing them to suffer a loss of well-being.[107] So not everyone prioritises continued life or their own good health at all times and in all circumstances. As Gillon has written there are many competing interests in a person's life, including ones own and those of loved ones, the interests of those to whom we have special obligations and as persons are not entirely self-interested it is possible that

---

[106] The Bristol Inquiry and that at the Alder Hey Hospital would tend to support this statement

[107] See for example, *Re T (Adult: Refusal of Treatment) [1992] 4 All ER 649 CA*

anyone may choose to consider the wider interests of others in their community.[108]

Even amongst those who would prioritise health over other values persons might differ in their views about the benefits and burdens of a proposed medical treatment just as they might differ in estimating the likelihood of those various benefits and burdens materialising for subjective reasons. The question raised in situations where the medical purpose and reason align is whether a competent refusal of beneficial medical treatment must always be respected, including cases where treatment is life-preserving? On this matter Robert Veatch has written that:

> *"Some patients may decline certain benefits that have been offered them. Consider a terminally ill cancer patient who is told that a long and expensive course of chemotherapy has a modest chance of success. This treatment would involve considerable burdens on family members. Some people may conclude that it is indeed in their interests to receive the therapy, but nevertheless they do not choose to accept the offer because it conflicts with the interests of certain other family members (by consuming resources or imposing care-giving burdens)... Treating in the face of a refusal of treatment is not only a violation of patient autonomy; it is also a violation of the reasonable ethic of permitting people to make self-sacrifice in order to express their loyalty to the familial community of which they are members.*
>
> *... But what of cases in which the patient, perhaps through confusion or error, chooses to decline a beneficial treatment for other reasons beyond these? Many who defend patient autonomy to refuse consent to treatment do so because they believe that the patient may know his own interests better than the physician. We have seen ... how hard it is for the physician to claim that he or she knows the patients interests better than the patient does.*
>
> *But that is not always the case... The duty to respect autonomy has its real bite when there is good reason to believe that the patient really can be helped by violating his or her autonomy. Those committed to autonomy including anyone standing in the tradition of liberal philosophy will insist that the physician has a duty not to benefit the patient in these cases".*[109]

[108] Gillon, Raanan, Philosophical Medical Ethics, 1986, John Wiley and Sons, p.73
[109] Veatch, Robert M., Doctor Does Not Know Best: Why in the New Century Physicians Must Stop Trying to Benefit Patients; 2000, Journal of Medicine and Philosophy, Vol 25, No. 6, pp.701-721, p.712/3

Veatch appears to be saying that good communication is the key to an effective doctor-patient relationship which Gillon emphasises in his more integrated account of the doctor's duty to respect autonomy, and in particular an autonomous refusal of beneficial treatment, that is preferred simply because in respecting patient autonomy the moral integrity of the medical profession is also preserved, i.e. a doctor is not made a means to the ends of the patient but is respected as a medical expert and as someone who continues to honour their professional obligations of non-maleficence and beneficence. Anyway he put things in these terms:

> *"In most cases ... of a doctor's dealings with patients not only is there an independent moral presumption that he must respect their autonomy but, even if he is interested only in doing them good, he must generally respect their autonomy in order to do so.*
>
> *If one wants to do good for a patient one generally needs to find out what he or she actually wants one to do. Often this does not need much inquiry. Doctors, however, are often too ready to assume that they can tell what the patient wants, or even what is best for the patient, without asking. In even the simplest of interactions patients in similar circumstances want different things from their doctors The doctor who 'knows' what the patient wants without asking him is quite likely to get it wrong.*
>
> *Sometimes it is true that the patient's wants and needs may be in conflict... Conversely, he may want not to have what will benefit him...In each case the duty of beneficence requires at least discovery of what the patient does want and an explanation of why a different course of action would probably (for almost all such assessments are probabilistic) benefit him more. Such respect, even if an independent priority to respect for autonomy is rejected, is required by beneficence simply because the patient is more likely to do what the doctor considers to be medically optimal if the doctor explains why the patient's own preference is less likely to be beneficial. Conversely, the doctor is more likely to make a truly beneficial proposal if he knows and takes into account the patient's own preferences".*[110]

If a doctor's duty to disclose relevant treatment information is tailored to meet the needs of their patients there is less reason to be concerned that beneficial treatment will be refused erroneously or that misunderstandings will arise from the way in which information is framed.[111] For in these

[110] Gillon, Raanan, Philosophical Medical Ethics, 1986, John Wiley and Sons, p.75
[111] *Chester v Afshar 2004 WL 2289136*

circumstances the doctor will have knowledge of what the patient values and how they value those things and of their priorities in this regard. Whilst doctors must refrain from applying their own standards and methods for deciding as a basis for questioning the patient's capacity to decide the matter, such an approach does facilitate good communication and open discussion where any errors in reasoning can be accounted for and corrected.

Good, honest and open communication should ensure that treatment will be competently refused rather than resulting from the patient being misinformed or due to some misunderstanding or error. In other words respect for autonomy should not be used as an excuse to release doctors from their professional obligation to act in the best interests of patients when health is a fundamental concern of humans and when doctors are in a privileged position to assist patients to understand both the potential and limitations of a specialist subject, i.e. medical science.

Gillon summarises all that has been said in this section very well. He has commented that:

> *"In summary the principle of respect for autonomy asks the doctor to have at the back of his mind the question, would the patient, if he could consider it, wish me to do what I am doing or intend to do? If not, how can I justify it? Usually the best way to answer the first question is to ask the person concerned".*[112]

Voluntariness

Here we return once more to Kant's instruction '*so act that you use humanity, whether in your own person or in the person of any other, always at the same time as an end, never merely as a means*'.[113] We are by now familiar with the notion that we respect persons by treating them as ends in themselves rather than as simply the means to the end of any other. In relation to decision-making in general and to voluntariness more specifically we are concerned with whether the patient's will, which is essentially autonomous, remains under their control as in this context

[112]Gillon, Raanan, Philosophical Medical Ethics, 1986, John Wiley and Sons, p.166

[113] Kant, I, Groundwork of the Metaphysics of Morals, Edited by Mary Gregor Introduction by Christine Korsgaard, 2006, Cambridge University Press, para. 4.428

Kant's prescription amounts to a fairly strong moral injunction against coercion and deception involving as they do an attempt to take other people's decisions out of their own hands, by manipulating their wills perhaps for personal gain or ends.[114]

So, there will be cases in which it is appropriate for a doctor to consider whether the decision to consent, or to refuse to consent, to a medical treatment is really the decision of the patient. Crucially, the doctor must determine whether their will is operating freely and independently, i.e. without being under the control of another's influence, or whether it has been overborne or operated on in a way that violates or that eclipses autonomy in some significant way.[115]

Thus voluntariness in acting, as with information and capacity, can be considered under different lights.[116] At the far end of the scale we might think about the importance of being an effective legislator in a kingdom of ends, or in common parlance in exercising one's will in a democracy to influence ideas about what is just, good, bad, right and wrong about the current state of health care. Whilst Beauchamp and Childress have written that '*control of another person is necessarily an influence, but not all influences are controlling*'[117] doctors are required, amongst other things, to be just as well as beneficent and to ensure that the help that is given is not bought at too high a price.[118] Therefore, Kant, if not Mill, might see the potential for the personal convictions of medical professionals to remain hidden from view at the first stage of a treatment decision-making process but which might ultimately have a controlling influence over the decisions of patients. A state of affairs that is incompatible with Kantian ideas about respect in a Kingdom of Ends where persons come together as equals and joint legislators of moral laws. Consequently, it is essential that all material and relevant facts about treatment, various treatment options as well as how these are relevant to the patient and their health should be disclosed and not edited or obscured from view by doctors if we are to exercise our autonomy freely and independently because in

[114] Ibid

[115] Beauchamp, Tom L., Childress, James F., Principles of Biomedical Ethics, 2001, Fifth Edition, Oxford University Press, p.93; Harris, John, The Value of Life, 1985, Routledge Publishing, p.195

[116] Ibid

[117] Beauchamp, Tom L., Childress, James F., Principles of Biomedical Ethics, 2001, Fifth Edition, Oxford University Press, p.94

[118] Gillon, Raanan, Philosophical Medical Ethics, 1986, John Wiley and Sons, p.74

healthcare exercising one's autonomy should amount to so much more than freely and independently deciding whether to accept or reject an offer of medical treatment.

However, it is the case that doctors are more specifically concerned with the patient's response to an offer of treatment. In this regard defects in control might be attributable to conditions, rather than another's influence, such as debilitating disease, psychiatric disorders and drug addiction as these tend to undermine or diminish autonomy.[119] John Harris, for example, differentiates between genuine preferences which are expressive of the ability to control one's will and addictions or obsessions which he claims only 'sometimes' reflect the exercise of an impaired will.[120] It might be that someone purchases a specific perfume because they are addicted to the scent or obsessively inspect food labels to monitor their salt intake. Neither of which are examples of autonomy being undermined or diminished in any significant way. These terms are though more generally used in a negative sense to depict traits, habits or disorders that signal weakness of the will, that renders one the means to the end of some external authority which tends to undermine independence of thought and action.

Therefore, in the case of 'real addictions' or 'obsessions' it is at least open to question whether someone can be said to be in control of their life and themselves. In other instances the will may be impaired. This might be a particularly relevant consideration when the background condition is illness because suffering, which is again a personal matter, can certainly signify an impending destruction of the person as Cassell points out.[121] Consequently, paternalistic intervention could on occasion be legitimated by the need to restore or promote autonomy so that the will can once again operate freely and independently.[122]

---

[119] Beauchamp, Tom L., Childress, James F., Principles of Biomedical Ethics, 2001, Fifth Edition, Oxford University Press, p.93; Harris, John, The Value of Life, 1985, Routledge Publishing, p.196

[120] Harris, John, The Value of Life, 1985, Routledge Publishing, p.196/7

[121] Cassell, Eric, J., The Nature of Suffering and the Goals of Medicine, 2004, Second Edition, Oxford University Press, p.33

[122] Harris, John, The Value of Life, 1985, Routledge Publishing, p.200

What is entailed in overbearing the will of the patient?

More general forms of influence include coercion, persuasion and manipulation.[123] Coercion, according to Beauchamp and Childress, occurs when a person intentionally uses a credible and severe threat of harm or force to control others that displaces a person's self-directedness.[124] Gert et al, define coercion more objectively. They state that coercion involves a threat of sufficient evil or harm that it would be unreasonable to expect any rational man in that situation not to act on it.[125]

As terms such as 'credible' and 'sufficient' have not been defined these will have to be interpreted in a particular context. However, it does appear that Gert et al wished to draw a clear distinction between coercion and lesser forms of pressure, such as persuasion. In so doing they sought to eliminate the possibility of persons, who are inclined to surrender their will too easily, i.e. anything for a quiet life, from claiming to have been coerced into making the decision. By contrast, Beauchamp and Childress do, in referring to a person's self-directedness, appear to draw a link between the particular personality or character of the coerced agent and the threat that influenced them. The problem I fear is that in practice it might be quite difficult to recognise a coerced consent or refusal of a patient in the absence of any knowledge about their personality, character and values because of the many factors that are likely to be operating at any one time, i.e. how does anyone determine what was causally responsible for the decision in the absence of such information other than to simply challenge the decision of the patient on the ground that it does not correspond to that of a reasonable patient perhaps.

Persuasion can be contrasted with coercion because a person who is persuaded believes in something through the merit of the reasons advanced by another.[126] So whilst coercion violates autonomy, reasonable persuasion does not. However, it is interesting to note that Beauchamp and Childress distinguish appeals to reason from appeals to emotions whilst recognising

---

[123] Beauchamp, Tom L., Childress, James F., Principles of Biomedical Ethics, 2001, Fifth Edition, Oxford University Press, p.94

[124] Ibid

[125] Gert, Bernard, Culver, Charles M., Clouser, K. Danner, Bioethics: A Systematic Approach, 2006, Second Edition, Oxford University Press, p.232

[126] Beauchamp, Tom L., Childress, James F., Principles of Biomedical Ethics, 2001, Fifth Edition, Oxford University Press, p.94

that in healthcare it might be difficult to separate emotional responses from cognitive ones.[127]

Thinking back to our earlier discussion you may remember that Kant intended that reason should remove sentiment in moral matters but that it was less clear that sentiment should not have a role to play in matters related to the subjective value a life has for the person whose life it is. The difficulty this poses is that persons are exposed to the danger that their sentiments may be acted upon or that we may be manipulated into a particular decision or course of action.[128] Your reason or capacity to make a decision for yourself, would if this should occur, be treated as if it were merely an instrument for another's use which violates the respect persons are owed.[129] Therefore, it might be relevant to consider whether what someone says or perhaps does is determined by what they think will work to get the result they want.[130]

Yet again it would seem that personal knowledge of the patient and their values might provide relevant insight into whether it is their reason or their emotions that have been operated on. Think of a person who values peace and harmony and whose will is in a weakened state having been fatigued by illness and suffering. Consider also the possibility that an underlying conflict of interests or wills exists between them and their significant other. No words may actually be exchanged instead a current inability to tolerate the discomforts associated with discordant rhythms[131] might actually be all it takes to persuade them as to the merits of another's point of view.

Finally, let us consider manipulation. According to Beauchamp and Childress manipulation is a generic term that can be applied to forms of influence that are not persuasive or coercive.[132] So the essence of

[127] Ibid

[128] Dworkin, Ronald, Life's Dominion: An argument about Abortion and Euthanasia, Harper Collins, p.73

[129] Kant, I, Groundwork of the Metaphysics of Morals, Edited by Mary Gregor Introduction by Christine Korsgaard, 2006, Cambridge University Press, p.xxiii

[130] Ibid

[131] Think of being massaged and then of being with someone who is a fidget and or restless. If the atmosphere was water you would see ripples created by the energy that is being generated.

[132] Beauchamp, Tom L., Childress, James F., Principles of Biomedical Ethics, 2001, Fifth Edition, Oxford University Press, p.95

manipulation, they say, is swaying people to do what the manipulator wants by manipulating information, for instance, to alter a person's understanding of a situation, thing or person even and to thereby motivate them to do what the agent of influence intends.[133]

Of course doctors are in a particularly powerful position to influence the views of their patients because they possess special knowledge, skills and training in medical science and its wider application in medical practice. This is in essence what justified and indeed perpetuated paternalism as the dominant culture within medicine, i.e. the doctor knows best what is good for you. However, a move to respect patient autonomy in medicine signalled a proportionate rise in the obligation to embark on a process of demystification of a specialist subject. The object was to help patients to decide for themselves, in the light of all relevant and material information, what should happen in their actual best interests.

Nevertheless, the imbalance of power between a doctor and his patient places doctors in a position to influence the views of their patients and this is why the use of therapeutic privilege, for example, is so controversial. A doctor might, exceptionally, have very good reasons for withholding information from their patients but they might also use the privilege to manipulate patients into consenting to, what is in their view, a medically desirable procedure.[134] The problem is that information can be manipulated in various other ways that are virtually impossible to eliminate unless medical professionals are committed to honouring their moral obligations as Beauchamp and Childress have pointed out:

> *"The manner in which a health care professional presents information – by tone of voice, by forceful gesture, and by framing information positively (we succeed most of the time with this therapy) rather than negatively (we fail with this therapy in 35% of the cases) – can also manipulate a patient's perception and response, and thereby affect understanding and voluntariness.*
>
> *Nevertheless, one can easily inflate the threat of control by manipulation beyond its actual significance in health care. We typically make decisions in a context of competing influences, such as personal desires, familial constraints, legal obligations, and institutional pressures. These influences need not be controlling to a substantial degree. From the perspective of decision-making by patients and subjects, we need only establish general*

[133] Ibid
[134] Ibid

criteria for the point at which autonomous choice is imperilled, while recognising that in many cases no sharp boundary separates controlling and non-controlling influences".[135]

Perhaps Beauchamp and Childress are right about the threat of control by manipulation of information in medicine. Although in this context it is difficult to discount the viewpoint of Joseph Raz who has argued that human values can have some sort of historical and social justification as well as or in place of philosophical justification.[136] And on the basis that values depend on culture he argues that once a cultural value has come into existence it can be sustained, revived, and applied independently of particular social practices.[137] In response Korsgaard has pointed out that when values are derived from the social practices of some historical community that we are unable to establish what they value simply by appealing to the social fact that they are valued by members of the community.[138] Consequently, the concern is that unless we are able to trace values to their actual source there is no certain way of knowing whether we are entitled to rely on them in philosophical reflection and practical deliberation.[139] So in relation to paternalistic manipulation of treatment information, at both stage one and two of a treatment decision-making process, Korsgaard appears to be saying that there is no certain way of knowing which of the many factors the doctor considered was overriding and therefore we cannot know whether this was on reflection a good or bad instance of paternalistic practice.

Perhaps the final word should go to Gillon who states that:

"It is uncontroversial to assert that the principle of respect for autonomy has had little mileage for most of medicine's long history except, perhaps, when patients have been doctors' social equals or superiors (Plato alluded to this distinction when he differentiated between the doctor-slave patient relationship, in which the patient did what the doctor told him to do without discussion and that was the end of the matter, and the doctor-rich citizen relationship, in which explanation and discussion were the norm). The medical sociologist Dr Ann Cartwright is not alone when she says she

---

[135] Ibid

[136] Raz, Joseph, The Practice of Value, 2003, Oxford University Press, see Pippin, Robert p.103, see also Wallace R. Jay p.1/2

[137] Raz, Joseph, The Practice of Value, 2003, Oxford University Press, see Wallace R. Jay p.4

[138] Ibid, p.9

[139] Ibid, p.12

likes her doctor to treat her 'as an equal', but this is by no means a medical norm.

The implications for the doctor-patient relationship of taking the principle of respect for autonomy seriously are legion. Among the more important are the following prima facie duties: to give the patient at least what he or she considers to be adequate information, and often more if the doctor knows that more information will probably be appreciated and relevant to good decision-making; not to lie to or otherwise deceive the patient (unless he or she deliberately chooses such deception); and to allow the patient to have at least strategic control over which course of action to pursue – that is, the doctor may advise, but the patient is then given the opportunity to decide whether to accept that advice. If this principle is taken seriously, a patient's rejection of medical advice should not lead to a shrugging of the shoulders, a cooling of attitude, and 'if you can't trust my advice, perhaps you'd better find another doctor'. What should follow instead is a genuine attempt to understand the patient's reasons (or other motives) for rejecting the advice and search for the next best option.

One of the keys to respect for autonomy is good communication, and thus respect for patients' autonomy requires doctors to acquire and maintain skill in communicating with them – not just in telling but also in understanding".[140]

[140] Gillon, Raanan, Philosophical Medical Ethics, 1986, John Wiley and Sons, p.165

CHAPTER THREE

THE LAW AND THE CAPABLE PATIENT

In previous chapters we focused on ethical principles that are relevant to medical treatment decision-making processes where the primary concern is to safeguard and protect the life, health and welfare of persons. We also sought to gain a better understanding of the nature of the principles under consideration[1] and their purpose in decision-making processes so that we could better understand the moral obligations and conflicts that attend and define the doctor-patient relationship. The law, like ethics, is equally concerned with human welfare and morality or what is right and wrong human conduct and so in this chapter we will be examining whether, and if so how, those moral principles and obligations inform medical law and practice in respect of the capable patient.

The General Legal Framework for the Provision of a Medical Treatment

It is a fundamental principle of law that every person's body is inviolate. Consequently any touching of another person, however slight, can amount to a battery in the absence of a valid consent.[2] The principle of inviolability is interpreted broadly to ensure that every person has a right to be maintained inviolate and free from physical interference. Moreover, in prohibiting the first stages of physical violence every person is protected against any form of physical harm also.[3]

Hence the general legal framework for healthcare delivery and in particular the administration of a medical treatment is informed by the law of battery because it is a recurring feature of medical practice that doctors

---

[1] This was to draw attention to a deeper structure of values and standards that are the source of the moral obligations that attend and define it.

[2] *Re F (Mental Patient: Sterilisation) [1990] 2 AC 1 HL*, Lord Donaldson MR, p.11

[3] Ibid

will interfere with the bodily integrity of their patients. Moreover, the nature of medical practice suggests that in many instances some harm will be caused. Of course no actual bodily harm will be caused when a stethoscope is placed on the chest to hear a heart beat. On the other hand some physical harm can be anticipated to arise from the administration of a medical treatment or procedure, at least initially. Surgery is the most obvious example of a physically invasive procedure which results in actual bodily harm.

However, the law of battery makes consent a defence to the infliction of bodily harm in the course of some lawful activities.[4] Here we should bear in mind the fact that medicine is a lawful activity that one can consent to on account of the fact that although harm is an anticipated feature of medical endeavour the overall objective is to benefit patients, i.e. physicians are required to administer curative or prophylactic treatments which they believe are appropriate to the patient's existing condition of disease, injury or malfunction or susceptibility to such a condition in the future.[5] Medical treatment and procedures should then most often lead to beneficial outcomes such as when a surgeon removes a burst appendix or troublesome tonsils. The initial discomfort associated with the administration of a vaccination eventually subsides and provides medium to long term benefits. Similarly, some drugs can induce severe side effects that are initially problematic but which later return the patient to health.[6]

It is therefore plain that the need for consent is to ensure that a competent patient has freedom to choose whether to accept an offer of medical treatment or to reject it because they prefer instead to be maintained inviolate. So in law the question of who should decide about the benefits and burdens of a medical treatment or procedure, i.e. should it be the doctor, who is motivated by the principles of non-maleficence and beneficence to exercise judgment and act only in the best interests of a patient, or should it be the patient who is relatively ignorant about disease, its progress, about treatment(s) and of what the possible consequences of any choice might be for their future health and well-being, has been decided in favour of the patient.

---

[4] *Re F (Mental Patient: Sterilisation) [1990] 2 AC 1 HL*

[5] Ibid, Lord Bridge, p.52

[6] For example, Chemotherapy

Accordingly, we can say that the law bases its view on the invasion of physical integrity on the strong moral conviction that everyone[7] has the right of self-determination with regard to their body. [8] This is the point that Justice Cardozo makes when he states that:

> *"Every human being of adult years and sound mind has a right to determine what shall be done with his own body; and a surgeon who performs an operation without his patient's consent commits an assault".*[9]

Andrew Grubb adds a little gloss to this familiar statement of law:

> *"The law relating to consent is of central importance in medical law. Under the common law, the legality of a medical treatment or procedure will largely turn upon whether the patient has given a valid consent to it. Treatment without consent may amount to the tort of battery or the crime of assault. Consent, or more accurately the need for it, is the legal reflection of the ethical principle of respect for autonomy. In this particular context, this notion might be better expressed as respect for a person's bodily integrity stemming from a right of self-determination. It is a fundamental principle now long established, that every person's body is inviolable".*[10]

To summarise, the principle of inviolability is upheld by the law of battery to protect all persons against non-consensual physical contacts. Consequently, a doctor who administers a medical treatment to a capable patient in the absence of a legally valid consent will commit the tort of

---

[7] Absent any other relevant legal justification that would constrain or limit an individual's rights such as happens when autonomy is lacking perhaps in order to defend the interests of others, e.g. the Mental Health Act 2007 makes provision for persons with mental disorders to be treated without consent to prevent them from causing harm to themselves or others. Alternatively, in the case of mental incapacity where autonomy may be either temporarily or permanently diminished or not present non-consensual medical intervention must arise from the need to act beneficently to protect and promote the legitimate interests of the vulnerable person

[8] Mason J.K., McCall Smith, R.A., Laurie, G.T., Law and Medical Ethics, 2002, Sixth Edition, Butterworths, para 10.6

[9] *Schloendorff v Society of New York Hospital (1914) 211 N.Y. 125*, p.129

[10] Grubb, A., Principles of Medical Law, 2004, Second Edition, Oxford University Press, para. 3.01

battery or the crime of assault.[11] A legally valid consent is then a defence to an activity that would otherwise be unlawful. The need for consent reflects the primacy the law accords to the moral principle of autonomy through which patients exercise their right to self-determine what shall happen to their body in a medical context. Thus a competent patient has freedom to choose whether to accept or reject an offer of medical treatment and to exercise judgment in accordance with their own values, beliefs and preferences.

The Law of Battery

The law of battery charts the circumstances under which bodily interference with another person's person will be unlawful. Consequently, it is important in establishing the scope of the right to self-determine what shall happen to one's own body in a medical setting. For example, is a doctor required to obtain consent to conduct a physical examination of a patient or to perform a minor procedure such as to take a sample of blood? We might equally consider whether it might be detrimental to patient care if consent were required to justify an empathetic response.

The Scope of the Right to Freedom from Physical Interference and Harm

In *Re F* Lord Goff stated that the effect of the principle of inviolability is to protect everybody not only against physical injury but against any form of physical molestation.[12] Therefore, is it possible that any intentional touching of another person that does not cause harm will constitute a battery? Berg et al explain that:

> *"A battery occurs when one person engages in conduct that is intended to, and does, cause harmful physical contact with another person, as when, for example, a person throws a punch in a barroom brawl or hits someone with a rock. Less obviously, a battery is also committed by contact, or*

[11] The basis of a civil law suit for a battery is that a person's right to bodily security has been violated by a touching which may have caused them harm. In respect of civil actions for a battery the remedy sought is damages, however awards will be nominal in cases where there has been an invasion of a right in the absence of any actual bodily harm whereas in criminal cases the court has a wider range of penalties to choose from including imprisonment

[12] *Re F (Mental Patient: Sterilisation) [1990] 2 AC 1 HL*, Lord Donaldson MR, p.72

touching, that is offensive, but not necessarily harmful, at least not in the sense of causing bodily injury. Spitting can be a battery. Contact with another person is ordinarily considered offensive if it occurs without the consent of the person being touched. Thus, a physician who fails to obtain a patient's consent to a medical procedure that involves a touching of the patient commits the tort of battery even though the medical procedure may have helped rather than hurt the patient. This is because the right of bodily integrity is the legally protected interest, and thus the patient can be wronged even if not physically harmed".[13]

Is Hostility a Necessary Ingredient of a Battery?

As an intentional tort the original purpose of the law of battery was to curb or capture aggressive and unpleasant behaviour that was intended to cause injury or harm to others from fist or sword fights or bar room brawls.[14] The conduct of medical professionals stands in stark contrast to that of bar room brawlers in being informed by the principles of non-maleficence and beneficence. These create a moral obligation to act only in the best interests of patients. Consequently, the question arises whether hostility or any other adverse mental state is rightfully a necessary ingredient of a battery? However, in *Re F* Lord Goff confirmed that the motive of the aggressor is not a necessary ingredient of a battery because the offence is triggered by any intentional touching of another's body in the absence of a lawful excuse.[15] Does this rule out emotional responses that might be attributed to sympathy, for example?

Exceptions to the General Rule

Clearly not all cases of physical interference without consent are unlawful. For instance, paternalist intervention is permitted to allow parents to chastise their children and police officers, as well as citizens, may make a lawful arrest as well as take action to prevent crime and so on.[16] A further general exception is created to allow for the vicissitudes of everyday life, i.e. those types of physical contacts that are generally acceptable in the

---

[13] Berg, Jessica W., Appelbaum, Paul S., Lidz Charles W., Parker, Lisa S., Informed Consent, 2001, Second Edition, Oxford University Press, p.132

[14] Grubb, A., Principles of Medical Law, 2004, Second Edition, Oxford University Press, para. 3.05

[15] *Re F (Mental Patient: Sterilisation) [1990] 2 AC 1 HL,* Lord Donaldson MR, p.73

[16] Ibid, p.72

ordinary conduct of everyday life.[17] So a doctor who inadvertently bumps into a patient in the corridor does not commit a battery. Therefore, it is also assumed that the law does not intend to immunise medical professionals against the effects of the news they deliver. Accordingly, physical contacts that are derived from the human capacity to empathise with the situation of a fellow human being should not be prohibited by the law of battery. After all no one suggests to a business man that he should obtain consent prior to shaking the hand of a contemporary.

Criminal Liability for Assault

It is possible that a doctor who intentionally touches a patient without consent could be charged with the criminal offence of assault.[18] However, it is unlikely that charges would be pressed under the criminal law unless it could also be shown that the doctor acted maliciously or was grossly negligent in withholding information.[19] The law does not as it were intend to make criminals of medical professionals.

Consent

English courts have unreservedly accepted that a patient's body is inviolable such that any physically invasive medical treatment or procedure, however trivial, is unlawful unless authorised by consent or other lawful authority. The question then is whether consent is always necessary and if it is whether it is also a sufficient condition for a patient to be treated?

The Need for Physical Contact

A battery is only committed if there is a touching.[20] Consequently, a patient who agreed to take a drug orally, having been totally misled as to the nature of the drug, could not sue in battery because the claim would be

---

[17] Ibid, p.72/3

[18] Herring, Jonathan, Medical Law and Ethics, 2008, Second Edition, Oxford University Press, p.134; Stauch, Marc, Wheat, Kay, Tingle John, 2002, Second Edition, Sourcebook on Medical Law, Cavendish Publishing, p.105; Grubb, A., Principles of Medical Law, 2004, Second Edition, Oxford University Press, para. 3.31

[19] Herring, Jonathan, Medical Law and Ethics, 2008, Second Edition, Oxford University Press, p.134

[20] Ibid, p.136

based on the notion that the patient did not consent to the touching.[21] They might pursue an action in negligence whereupon the argument would be that although there was an apparent consent the doctor had acted negligently in failing to provide a sufficient amount of information or had made some sort of misrepresentation concerning the treatment. [22] So whereas the approach in battery is to protect the patient's right to bodily integrity when making a decision about medical treatment, attention in negligence is on ensuring that doctors follow a responsible body of medical opinion when disclosing treatment information. [23]

Limits to Consent

Here it is important to keep in mind that consent is a defence to an activity that would otherwise be regarded as a battery on the grounds of unlawful bodily interference. There is no absolute right to self-determination as we shall see and therefore consent works more as a shield than a sword.

Consent is a necessary though not sufficient condition for a patient to be treated

A patient cannot compel a doctor or NHS Trust to provide treatment of their own choosing. This is primarily because doctors cannot be forced to provide a treatment that is not clinically indicated to be in the best interests of the patient or which cannot be provided because of limited resources.[24] Neither can patients rely on the courts to force a doctor or NHS Trust to treat a patient in a manner contrary to their wishes.[25] Andrew Grubb establishes three reasons for this. As a matter of policy, the court will not make an order compelling a doctor to treat a patient in a manner contrary to his clinical judgment[26] and professional[27] duty.[28] Also it would be impracticable and uncertain for the court to enforce a mandatory order in

---

[21] Ibid

[22] Ibid, p.135

[23] Ibid

[24] Grubb, A., Principles of Medical Law, 2004, Second Edition, Oxford University Press, para. 3.08

[25] Ibid

[26] Bolam determines that a doctor must act in accordance with a respectable body of medical opinion

[27] In accordance with the principles of non-maleficence and beneficence

[28] Grubb, A., Principles of Medical Law, 2004, Second Edition, Oxford University Press, para. 3.08

this context.[29] Finally, the courts are most reluctant to enter into investigations about the proper allocation of resources within the health service.[30]

Requirements for Consent to be Legally Valid

Consent must be legally valid and in this respect the law requires, inter alia, that a patient must have capacity to make the particular treatment decision under consideration, must give their consent freely, that is their will should not be overborne, and the patient must have received information about the nature and purpose of medical treatment, at the very least.

Decision-Making Capacity

The legal requirement is that persons should have mental capacity or be competent to self-determine the matter of what shall happen to their body in a medical context.[31] Capacity is the term used to indicate that a patient has the ability to understand treatment information in order to arrive at a decision to consent or to reject an offer of treatment. Understanding is demonstrated when a patient is able to comprehend treatment information,[32] retain it[33] and then use or process that information[34] prior to arriving at a decision to consent or to reject an offer of treatment that they can communicate.[35]

The Ability to Understand

All adults are presumed to have the ability to understand treatment information.[36] No rebuttable presumption exists in relation to minors as here the law is more paternalistic, particularly toward those under the age of 16.[37] Consequently, the consent or refusal of a person in this age group

[29] Ibid
[30] Ibid
[31] Mental Capacity Act 2005, s.3 (a); *Re C (Adult: Refusal of Treatment) [1994] 1 WLR 290*
[32] Mental Capacity Act 2005, s.3(a)
[33] Ibid, s.3(b)
[34] Ibid, s.3(c)
[35] Ibid, s.3(d)
[36] Ibid, s.1(2)
[37] Family Law Reform Act 1969, s.8

will only exceptionally justify a doctor in administering or withholding appropriate and necessary medical treatment.[38] In relation to adults the question of whether or not a patient has decision-making capacity has been made a question of fact.[39] That is to say the law adopts a functional rather than an outcome[40] based test for decision-making capacity. Incapacity has therefore been linked to an impairment or disturbance in the functioning of the mind or brain, whether temporarily or more permanently, that prevents someone from understanding information that is relevant to the decision they are being asked to make.[41] That is the sole basis for determining that a person suffers from a lack of decision-making capacity and then only after a doctor has taken all reasonably practicable steps to help the patient to make sense of relevant treatment information.[42]

Outcome Test

An outcome approach would focus on the decision itself and in particular its consequences for the welfare of the patient; indeed the stalking ground of an outcome based test of capacity would be treatment refusals since it is unlikely that a doctor would seek to question a patient's judgment in consenting to their offer of treatment. Such an approach does however conflict with respect for the principle of autonomy, and in particular the right to make decisions, in accordance with one's own unique set of values, beliefs and preferences, that must be respected by others. Consequently, the law is very clear that a person must not to be treated as unable to make a decision merely because they make an unwise decision.[43] Accordingly, capacity should not be measured by whether the decision appears unwise to others as the patient's right of choice to consent, or to refuse to consent to, medical treatment exists notwithstanding that the reasons for making the choice are rational, irrational, unknown or even non-existent.[44] This is an example of legal neutrality or to put the matter another way in a pluralistic society a specific purpose of the principle of autonomy is to accommodate and mediate reasonable differences in the beliefs, values and preferences of citizens.

---

[38] *Gillick v West Norfolk and Wisbech AHA [1986] A.C. 112 HL, p.112/3*

[39] Grubb, A., Principles of Medical Law, 2004, Second Edition, Oxford University Press, para. 3.70

[40] Mental Capacity Act 2005, s.1(4)

[41] Ibid, s.2(1)

[42] Ibid, s.1(2)

[43] Ibid, s.1(4)

[44] *Re T (Adult: Refusal of Treatment) [1992] 4 All ER 649 CA*

Functional Test

Consistent with the right to self-determination a functional approach to capacity focuses on whether an impairment or disturbance in the functioning of a person's mind or brain[45] has rendered them unable to make a particular decision.[46] Therefore, a person has capacity to consent to or to refuse to consent to a medical intervention when they are able to understand,[47] retain,[48] and use or process,[49] information that is relevant to their decision in order to arrive at a choice that they can communicate.[50] The aim of a functional based approach to capacity is to safeguard persons against the consequences of making a non-autonomous decision by placing emphasis on the way in which the decision was made rather than on the decision itself. The problem is that it is difficult to refute the possibility that questions regarding decision-making capacity will tend to arise when a patient refuses to consent to a medical treatment that is intended to preserve the life, health and/or well-being of the patient.

Refusals

Whilst the law specifically outlaws an outcome test of decision-making capacity it has been said that a greater level of capacity may be required to refuse a medical treatment that is needed to preserve the life, health or well-being of the patient.[51] This does not mean that the patient is required to display greater reasoning powers rather they should be able to understand more information the more serious their decision and for that reason the decision-making process will be subject to greater scrutiny in such circumstances.[52] Whether this is consistent with what happens in others areas of one's personal life is open to debate. Take for example someone who wants to buy a property with a mortgage that will exceed the normal lending limit based on their income. There is little doubt that their mortgage application would be scrutinised more closely by the lender, particularly if they were self-employed, because of the increased level of

---

[45] Mental Capacity Act 2005, s.3.5(i)
[46] Ibid, s.3.5(ii)
[47] Ibid, s.3(1)(a)
[48] Ibid, s.3(1)(b)
[49] Ibid, s.3(1)(c)
[50] Ibid, s.3(1)(d)
[51] *Re T (Adult: Refusal of Treatment) [1992] 4 All ER 649 CA*
[52] Kennedy and Grubb, Medical Law, 2000, Third Edition, Butterworths, Chapter 5, p.627

risk assumed in the transaction. On the other hand persons seem to be able to obtain a permit to keep a licensed weapon on their premises without having to submit to any form of psychological test.

The Ability to Understand What

The law has the dilemma that its requirements should not be sufficiently onerous as to exclude a majority of persons from the right to choose whether to accept or reject an offer of medical treatment. So, in order that a doctor's touching does not constitute a battery the law merely requires a patient to understand the nature and purpose of the proposed treatment or procedure[53] and, as a competent patient must also use and weigh treatment information in the balance, to comprehend the likely consequences of deciding to exercise their right of choice one way rather than another.

Information

Obtaining patient consent prior to administering a medical treatment will protect medical professionals from liability for unlawful touching, i.e. a battery, if that consent is real.[54] Given the context making an informed choice about whether to accept or to refuse treatment, and to thereby maintain bodily integrity, would seem to be of the utmost importance. Consequently, we will now examine the issue of what information doctors are required to disclose to patients in order for their consent to be regarded in law as real.

The Historical Development of a Law of Informed Consent

If a patient is to exercise the right to self-determination meaningfully, that is in accordance with their own values, beliefs and preferences, it would seem essential that a doctor, as expert in matters of health, should be placed under a legal duty to provide information that is tailored to meet the needs of each individual patient.

Evidence suggests, however, that the contrary was once true, as the customs and practices of the medical profession initially informed the law:

---

[53] *Chatterton v Gerson [1981] QB 432*

[54] Jackson, Emily, First Do No Harm, edited by Sheila McLean, 2006, Ashgate Publishing, Chapter 17, p.274/5

"Early medical practice codes did not speak of consent - it was more likely that a physician would conceal his actions from the patient than seek his or her consent to treatment. However, patient consent is not completely a modern legal creation. Historically, the notion that physicians must inform patients about what will be done to them has its origins in English eighteenth-century law. In the 1767 case of Slater v Baker and Stapleton[55]*, the court held that because the professional custom among surgeons was to obtain consent from their patients before beginning treatment, it was only fair to impose liability on a physician who failed to meet this standard of care.*

> *"It appears from the evidence of the surgeons that it was improper to disunite the [partially healed fracture] without consent; this is the usage and law of surgeons: then it was ignorance and unskillfulness in that very particular, to do contrary to the rule of the profession, what no surgeon ought to have done".*

Not only was it customary for the surgeon to obtain the patient's consent, the court observed, but "indeed it is reasonable that a patient should be told what is about to be done to him that he may take courage and put himself in such a situation as to enable him to undergo the operation". Thus, one rationale for the custom was that physicians needed patients' cooperation if surgery were to be performed without the use of an anaesthetic, as was then necessary. The court's observation regarding the role of communication shows a pragmatic or consequentialist justification for informed consent, rather than one focused on information disclosure as a good in itself or on a patient's right to control what happens to his body. In line with this justification, there is a good deal of evidence to suggest that physicians historically saw the requirements for consent as minimal, requiring that little or no information be disclosed before permission to proceed was obtained".[56]

What emerges from this passage is that the sole purpose of disclosing information was to inform the patient of the nature and purpose of treatment in order to aid the medical objective. This is perhaps unsurprising when nowhere within the original formulation of the Oath does it refer to providing patients with information necessary to inform their choice about whether to consent to or to refuse to consent to medical intervention, rather it refers to the doctor using his 'ability and judgment' in the care of his patients.

---

[55] *95 Eng. Rep. 860 (K.B. 1767)*

[56] Berg, Jessica W., Appelbaum, Paul S., Lidz Charles W., Parker, Lisa S., Informed Consent, 2001, Second Edition, Oxford University Press, p.42

Accordingly, the medical profession was the legally recognised source of what the patient should be told.[57] Clearly one's perspective is to a very great extent responsible for governing personal conduct and it is here apparent that medical paternalism prevailed over respect for the principle of autonomy and all that it entails. On the other hand, this was a time when the restorative capacity of a patient's own constitution may have been the most important aid to recovery since medical practice would have been far less sophisticated with fewer options for treatment and more brutal techniques employed to restore patient health and well-being. Nevertheless, 'old habits die hard'. Practices once established prove difficult to change. Part of the reason why parents chastise children for disagreeable behaviour is to cultivate within them an understanding of the undesirable consequences that ensue from inconsiderate conduct. It also provides an opportunity to introduce the idea that virtue lies in the development of self-discipline because it has the ability to rule over inclination and the harmful tendencies that it can ignite. It is in developing this capacity that we acquire dignity as a human being which engenders notions of self-respect and respect for others.

How then has the judiciary, in fulfilling its role in the public supervision of the medical profession, exercised its authority to elevate the customs and practices of the medical profession in relation to patient autonomy? For any claim to uphold the principle of bodily inviolability will sound a little hollow unless the law is developed around and dominated by the principle of self-determination.[58]

---

[57] Wear, Stephen, Informed Consent: Patient Autonomy and Physician Beneficence within Clinical Medicine, 1993, Kluwer Academic Publishers, p.8

[58] Berg et al state at p.134 that courts have wrestled with the problem of whether an informed consent case ought to be treated as a battery or negligence. At stake is the fact that there are differences between them that can make a great deal of difference in terms of what a patient must prove and whether damages are available. More fundamentally, the difference between the two theories reflects different underlying values that a legal doctrine of informed consent might seek to protect.

Battery Theory of Law[59]

The basis of a claim in battery is that consent is not real because it was not informed and as a consequence a legally protected right to freedom from physical interference and harm has been violated.[60] This suggests that a battery is substantiated by any failure of a physician to obtain the informed consent of their patient in relation to the nature and purpose of a treatment or procedure, associated risks and possible consequences for health and well-being.[61] Accordingly, a physician who failed to give the patient adequate information would offend the legal principle because the patient's permission to proceed would not amount to consent. Thus the patient could recover damages for the offence and presumably for any harm that occurred as well.[62]

The problem is that although a battery theory of law goes more precisely to an infringement of patient autonomy whenever patients are deprived of material information Emily Jackson has stated that:

> *"Judges have tended to confine the use of battery to the extremely rare case in which the patient was not told about the nature of the treatment they received. Provided the patient was informed in broad terms about the proposed treatment and agreed to it, her consent will be effective and no action in battery will lie".* [63]

Crucially a complete lack of consent is actionable as a battery and it has been determined that a physician will escape liability whenever a patient is informed as to the nature and purpose of a medical treatment or procedure.[64] Disclosures in relation to risks inherent in medical treatment,

---

[59] Berg et al confirm at p.134 that when the legal theory (as opposed to the factual theory, i.e. the elements that must be ascertained to establish a case) in question involves the tort of battery a person is saying that they did not consent to bodily contact, i.e. a doctor has failed to obtain their patient's consent or has deprived them of the personal right to choose and in doing so intended to cause harmful or offensive contact

[60] Ibid

[61] Herring, Jonathan, Medical Law and Ethics, 2008, Second Edition, Oxford University Press, p.135

[62] Berg, Jessica W., Appelbaum, Paul S., Lidz Charles W., Parker, Lisa S., Informed Consent, 2001, Second Edition, Oxford University Press, p.132

[63] Jackson, Emily, in First Do No Harm, edited by Sheila McLean, 2006, Ashgate Publishing, Chapter 17, p.275

[64] *Chatterton v Gerson [1981] QB 432*

which may or may not materialise, are considered by way of the law of negligence, a non-intentional tort, in spite of the fact that the harms envisaged may be material to the way in which a patient exercises their right to self-determination. An issue of particular relevance in this context is that non-disclosure of such risks would effectively deny patients the opportunity to refuse medical treatment and to exercise their right to maintain bodily integrity.

To summarise, the duty to obtain a patient's consent is protected by the tort of battery, however the duty to ensure that a patient has been given enough information (whatever that might mean) is part of the doctor's ordinary duty of care to act in the best interests of their patients, meaning that a failure to offer sufficient information might ground an action in negligence.[65] So has a professional privilege to withhold treatment information been maintained in law?

Negligence Theory of Law[66]

The law of negligence is concerned with prudence and imposes a general requirement that persons act or refrain from acting in ways that one could reasonably foresee might cause harm to others.[67] Therefore, negligence, like battery, has a role to play in underpinning the legal right to freedom from bodily interference and harm. In law a physician has a professional and legal duty to exercise reasonable care and skill when treating patients whether that involves examination, assessment, diagnosis, advising on the need for treatment, providing information about alternative forms of treatment, carrying out treatment, post-operative care and, most importantly in this context, providing information about risks.[68]

The *Bolam* test is used to determine whether a doctor has acted in breach of his duty.[69] It asks whether a doctor has acted in accordance with a responsible and competent body of medical professional opinion or with a

---

[65] Jackson, Emily, in First Do No Harm, edited by Sheila McLean, 2006, Ashgate Publishing, Chapter 17, p.273

[66] According to Berg et al at p.134 under negligence theory the right vindicated is the right to be free from bodily injury caused by substandard medical practice. Unlike battery if the negligence causes no bodily injury to a patient, no remediable wrong is considered to have occurred.

[67] *Chester v Afshar 2004 WL 2289136*, para 22

[68] Ibid, para. 4

[69] *Bolam v Friern Hospital Management Committee [1957] 1 WLR 582*

practice that is accepted as proper within the profession with regard to the duty of care. The standard of care is thus determined by the medical profession; the reasonable doctor standard.

Informed Consent[70] - The Duty to Provide Information about Risks[71]

In *Sidaway* the majority in the House of Lords approved the *Bolam* standard and in condoning 'professional privilege'[72] the reasonable doctor standard became the standard of the prudent doctor. Lord Diplock said that:

> *"When it comes to warning about risks, the kind of training and experience that a judge will have undergone at the Bar makes it natural for him to say (correctly) it is my right to decide whether any particular thing is done to my body, and I want to be fully informed of any risks that may be involved of which I am not already aware from my general knowledge as a highly educated man of experience, so that I may form my own judgment as to whether to refuse the advised treatment or not.*
>
> *No doubt if the patient in fact manifested this attitude by means of questioning, the doctor would tell him whatever it was the patient wanted to know; but we are concerned here with volunteering unsought information about risks of the proposed treatment failing to achieve the result sought or making the patient's physical or mental condition worse rather than better. The only effect that mention of risks can have on the patient's mind, if it has any at all, can be in the direction of deterring the patient from undergoing the treatment which in the expert opinion of the doctor it is in the patient's interest to undergo. To decide what risks the existence of which a patient should be voluntarily warned and the terms in which such warning, if any, should be given, having regard to the effect*

---

[70] Please see Berg et al at p.22 where they refer to the ethical justification of informed consent. There they point to the philosophy of Kant as he argued that persons have the capacity to be moral and rational and on this basis they should also to be treated as an end or as someone that has self-ruling capacities. This is what makes persons valuable and so in order to act ethically persons must act with respect for other persons as intrinsically valuable, self-legislating beings. Accordingly, deception of whatever kind will deprive someone of the information necessary to make decisions for themselves, in accordance with their own constitution, and they are treated as the means to the end of another.

[71] Berg et al state at p.18 that the primary goals of informed consent are the protection of patient welfare and the promotion of autonomy

[72] Withholding treatment information in the interests of the patient

> *that the warning may have, is as much an exercise of professional skill and judgment as any other part of the doctor's comprehensive duty of care to the individual patient, and expert medical evidence on this matter should be treated in just the same way".*[73]

Lord Scarman, dissenting from majority opinion, was drawn to the reasoning in the judgment of the U.S. case of *Canterbury v Spence*[74] which favoured an alternative, prudent patient, approach which more closely equates the need for information and the right to decide upon its materiality, with the patient's right of self-determination. Reflecting on the views of the majority Lord Scarman said that:

> *"The implications of this view of the law are disturbing. It leaves the determination of a legal duty to the judgment of doctors. Responsible medical judgment may, indeed, provide the law with an acceptable standard in determining whether a doctor in diagnosis or treatment has complied with his duty. But is it right that medical judgment should determine whether there exists a duty to warn of risk and its scope? It would be a strange conclusion if the courts should be led to conclude that our law, which undoubtedly recognises a right in the patient to decide whether he will accept or reject the treatment proposed, should permit the doctors to determine whether and in what circumstances a duty arises requiring the doctor to warn his patient of the risks inherent in the treatment which he proposes.*
>
> *The right of self-determination – the description applied by some to what is no more and no less than the right of a patient to determine for himself whether he will or will not accept the doctor's advice – is vividly illustrated where the treatment recommended is surgery. A doctor who operates without the consent of his patient is, save in cases of emergency or mental disability, guilty of the civil wrong of trespass to the person: he is also guilty of the criminal offence of assault. The existence of the patient's right to make his own decision, which may be seen as a basic human right protected by the common law, is the reason why a doctrine embodying a right of the patient to be informed of risks of surgical treatment has been developed in some jurisdictions in the U.S.A. and has found favour with the Supreme Court of Canada. Known as the 'doctrine of informed consent', it amounts to this: where there is a 'real' or a 'material' risk inherent in the proposed operation (however competently and skilfully performed) the question whether and to what extent a patient*

---

[73] *Sidaway v Board of the Bethlem Royal Hospital and the Maudsley Hospital and Others [1985] AC 871 HL*, p.895

[74] *Canterbury v Spence (1972) 464 F. 2d 558*

> *should be warned before he gives his consent is to be answered not by reference to medical practice but by accepting as a matter of law that, subject to all proper exceptions (of which the court, not the profession, is the judge), a patient has a right to be informed of the risks inherent in the treatment which is proposed. The profession, it is said, should not be judge in its own cause: or, less emotively but more correctly, the courts should not allow medical opinion as to what is best for the patient to override the patient's right to decide for himself whether he will submit to the treatment offered him".*[75]

On this view doctors would be invited to consider firstly, what were the nature of the risks of the treatment they proposed to carry out and secondly, whether a patient would be likely to consider that the risk(s) identified were of any material consequence to them. Essentially Lord Scarman was arguing that patients should be the arbiter of what constitutes a material risk. However, as judgment about what would be material to a patient remained a question of medical opinion risk could only be assessed objectively from the standpoint of a reasonable patient. Nonetheless, a 'prudent patient' standard would have the effect of disempowering the medical profession as an objective test could be applied by the court independently of any medical opinion or practice.[76]

Some years later the *Bolam* test was modified by the decision of the House of Lords in the case of *Bolitho.*[77] There it was decided that even if the *Bolam* test were satisfied it was still open to the court to find that the requisite standard of care had not been met in cases where professional opinion did not prove to be capable of withstanding the logical analysis of the court. In those cases the judge would be entitled to hold that the body of opinion was not reasonable or responsible. Disclosure of risk did though appear to be specifically excluded from the judgment of Lord Browne-Wilkinson when he said that '*the assessment of medical risks and benefits is a matter of clinical judgment which a judge would not normally be able to make without expert [medical] evidence*'.[78]

---

[75] *Sidaway v Board of the Bethlem Royal Hospital and the Maudsley Hospital and Others [1985] AC 871 HL*, p.882

[76] *Chester v Afshar 2004 WL 2289136*, para. 53

[77] *Bolitho v City and Hackney HA [1997] 4 All ER 771 HL*

[78] Ibid, p.243

The scope of the doctor's duty, in relation to disclosure of information, was again discussed by the House of Lords in *Chester v Afshar.*[79] Essentially custom and practice, within the medical profession, continued to inform the law of what information, in relation to risks, was sufficiently material to a treatment decision that it should be disclosed to a patient. However, the court recognised the growing significance of patient autonomy in relation to medical treatment decision-making and on this occasion the majority[80] were minded to more closely equate the need for information, and the right to decide upon its materiality, with the patient's right to self-determination.

A novelty of this case which involved the non-disclosure of a small[81] but, in material terms, significant inherent[82] risk of surgery[83] was that it could not also be shown that the patient, upon receiving the appropriate warning, would never have undergone surgery and therefore even if the risk fell within the scope of the duty to disclose the all or nothing 'but for' test of causation would eliminate liability for damage that occurred out of a failure to disclose information about a small, though materially significant, inherent risk of surgery.[84] If a lack of informed consent was remediable as a battery rather than as negligence the patient would have a right to recover damages for the inadequate disclosure alone, even if not physically injured by the physician's treatment. This is because the patient is wronged by a failure to obtain consent or the deprivation of the right of personal choice which is sometimes called a dignity harm.[85] In contrast, the right vindicated under negligence theory is the right to be free from bodily injury caused by substandard medical practice. If the negligence causes no bodily injury to the patient, no remediable wrong is considered to have occurred.[86]

If the patient's right to self-determination was to be vindicated in this case the court would need to find some way around the standards that ordinarily

---

[79] *Chester v Afshar 2004 WL 2289136*

[80] Lords Steyn, Hope, Walker; Lords Bingham and Hoffmann dissented from the majority view

[81] Estimated to materialise in 1-2% of cases

[82] An unavoidable risk of surgery

[83] The risk is that of cauda equine syndrome or, in more familiar terms, paralysis

[84] *Chester v Afshar 2004 WL 2289136*, para.1

[85] Berg, Jessica W., Appelbaum, Paul S., Lidz Charles W., Parker, Lisa S., Informed Consent, 2001, Second Edition, Oxford University Press, p.134

[86] Ibid

apply in negligence particularly that established by the ordinary rule of causation. This demanded that a standard should be set by law for physicians rather than one which physicians may or may not impose on themselves.[87] In speaking of the scope of the duty to inform Lord Hope reasoned that the right to make the final decision and the duty of the doctor to inform the patient if the treatment may have special disadvantages or dangers go hand in hand. Thus the duty is owed to enable the patient to make their own decision about whether or not to undergo the course of surgery that had been proposed.[88] Lord Hope thought about what the patient might have done if adequately informed of the inherent risk.[89] One suggestion was that the patient would have delayed their decision in order to mull over the benefits and burdens of treatment and non-treatment and to seek a second opinion on the matter. This argument raised the possibility that the patient would not have consented to undergo surgery at the particular point in time in which it took place.[90] The point however was to illustrate the choices that remained open to the patient and to highlight the fact that the right to choose '*was for her to take, and for her alone*'.[91] On this Lord Hope said that, '*the function of the law is to protect the patient's right to choose. If it is to fulfil that function it must ensure that the duty to inform is respected by the doctor. It will fail to do this if an appropriate remedy cannot be given if the duty is breached and the very risk that the patient should have been told about occurs and she suffers injury*'.[92]

Consequently, if the court were to give full effect to the patient's right of self-determination it was then necessary to consider how causation could be established when the patient would not have refused absolutely to undergo surgery if told of the risks but would merely have postponed any decision until later.[93] The concern was that the patient had not made an informed choice about whether to undergo the treatment because the doctor had failed to act in accordance with his underlying moral responsibility to disclose information pertaining to risks.[94] Did justice

[87] *Chester v Afshar 2004 WL 2289136*, para.53
[88] Ibid, para.55
[89] Ibid, para.56
[90] Ibid, para.56
[91] Ibid, para.56
[92] Ibid, para.56
[93] Ibid, para.60
[94] Ibid, para.80

require the normal approach to causation to be modified on policy grounds? About this Lord Hope stated that:

> *"I start with the proposition that the law which imposed the duty to warn on the doctor has as its heart the right of the patient to make an informed choice as to whether, and if so when and by whom, to be operated on. Patients may have, and are entitled to have, different views about these matters. All sorts of factors may be at work here – the patient's hopes and fears and personal circumstances, the nature of the condition that has to be treated and, above all, the patient's own views about whether the risk is worth running for the benefits that may come if the operation is carried out. For some the choice may be easy – simply to agree or to decline the operation. But for many the choice will be a difficult one, requiring time to think, to take advice, and to weigh up the alternatives.*[95]
>
> *To leave the patient who would find the decision difficult without a remedy, as the normal approach to causation would indicate, would render the duty useless in the cases where it may be needed most. This would discriminate against those who cannot honestly say that they would have declined the operation once and for all if they had been warned. I would find that result unacceptable. The function of the law is to enable rights to be vindicated and to provide remedies when duties have been breached. Unless this is done the duty is a hollow one, stripped of all practical force and devoid of all content. It will have lost its ability to protect the patient and thus to fulfil the only purpose which brought it into existence. On policy grounds therefore I would hold that the test of causation is satisfied in this case".*[96]

Informed Consent: The (In) Significance of Chester v Afshar

To what extent does the judgment in *Chester v Afshar* safeguard patient autonomy? If the right to maintain bodily integrity is not to lose its significance as an essential pre-requisite to individual exercises of self-determination then it is crucial that there should be no room for conflict between the doctor's duty and the patient's right to be informed. Elaborating on this matter Lord Hope stated that, '*the imbalance between doctor and patient is due to the patient's lack of information. It is the function of the law to redress the imbalance by providing patients with the right to be given that information, or more accurately imposing a duty on doctors to provide it*'.[97] Consequently, the right to make the final decision

[95] Ibid, para.86
[96] Ibid, para.87
[97] Ibid, para.58

and the duty of the doctor to inform the patient of the benefits and burdens of treatment go hand in hand.[98]

Significantly, a legal standard of disclosure had been established that was unaffected in its scope by a professional privilege to withhold information that might alarm a patient.[99] This suggests that in the future courts will not be content to accept the explanation that patients tend to give disproportionate weight to such information and would as a consequence refuse to consent to, what would in all probability turn out to be, highly beneficial treatment. Appearances therefore suggest that, other than very exceptionally, professional privilege will no longer justify medical paternalism. Time has, it seems, been called on standards of disclosure that were once accepted as proper.

Summary: The Aim of Protecting and Enhancing Patient Self-Determination

Berg et al have stated that:

> *'The predominance of negligence theory appears to have been based largely on judicial reluctance to stigmatise physicians with the label of having committed a battery, thereby lumping them into the same category as barroom brawlers, rather than on any clear analysis of the different effects of one option or the other'.*[100]

Should the law be used to manage clinician behaviour? Stephen Wear thinks not. He believes that only those physicians who are committed to the enterprise of respecting patient self-determination will succeed in doing so. He states that:

> *"The law can neither accurately calibrate nor sufficiently motivate the necessary behaviours by itself. It can at most mandate minimal requirements. Such minimal requirements then need ethical supplementation and support, lacking which they tend to produce ineffective information disclosure rituals as many feel has been the actual result, when clinicians hyper-inform patients to the point of information overload to guard against a charge of inadequate disclosure.*

---

[98] Ibid, para.55

[99] Ibid, para.55

[100] Berg, Jessica W., Appelbaum, Paul S., Lidz Charles W., Parker, Lisa S., Informed Consent, 2001, Second Edition, Oxford University Press, p.135

Our focus should regard the ethical character and opportunities of informed consent, not how it was flawed in cases where negative outcomes also occurred. Part of the problem with the legal doctrine is that informed consent thus comes to be perceived by both patients and physicians as involving threats to which the physician must respond not as a vehicle for respecting and promoting patient self-determination and enhancing the patient-physician dialogue. Equally, the sort of guidance and standards that a court might offer in evaluating a suit for damages is not necessarily going to be the same as if it were asked to speak to how informed consent could best protect and enhance patient self-determination".[101]

Academic comment that informed the judgment of Lord Hope in *Chester v Afshar* is to similar effect:

"Part of the imbalance between doctor and patient is due to the patient's lack of information, and, on one view, it is the function of the law to redress the imbalance by providing patients with the 'right' to be given that information, or perhaps more accurately imposing a duty on doctors to provide it... the law cannot play a direct role in setting out detailed rules by way of guidance to doctors, but that it can have a powerful symbolic and galvanising role and that this is its major strength".[102]

Lord Hope considered that litigation on informed consent could provide a stimulus to the broader debate about the nature of the doctor-patient relationship.[103] But whether suits in negligence can be regarded as the most appropriate vehicle to stimulate such a debate is open to question when the financial implications of a course of action, unattractive as they are, combine so unappealingly with the human costs involved in the enterprise, in terms of the uncertainties that prevail and the delays that ensue. Consequently, there is reason to claim that litigation on informed consent is an inappropriate vehicle for micro managing the behaviour of clinicians.

A battery theory of law may fair no better in facilitating respect for informed consent amongst clinicians who would choose to drown patients in technical information that could not be adequately processed within the time allowed. Judicious use of language can also lead to misunderstanding and confusion as to its significance amongst the uninitiated a position that

---

101 Wear, Stephen, Informed Consent: Patient Autonomy and Physician Beneficence within Clinical Medicine, 1993, Kluwer Academic Publishers, p.9

102 *Chester v Afshar 2004 WL 2289136*, para.58

103 Ibid

is compounded by a general reluctance to challenge respected members of the medical profession. It's a little like the psychology engendered by road speed cameras, once one is aware of their presence it is possible to adapt behaviour to accommodate its demands whilst otherwise pleasing oneself, even within the speed restriction zone.

Concluding Comments

It is possible to conclude or to read into the case of *Chester* that we might now be in an era where use of 'but for' analysis is no longer required and hence we have as good a protection of informedness under negligence as we would get under battery.[104] However, I remain unconvinced. The point is that *Chester* does not propose to eliminate the distinction between these torts and as negligence is an unintentional tort it is apparent that liability for the unintended consequences of one's actions will continue to be subjected to some form of limiting principle in order to contain the cost of a mistake.

Perhaps then the 'happy ending' of a more substantive right to truly informed consent for patients does rely upon further ethical supplementation of the iterative process between law and professional guidance that is capable of manifesting and sustaining a change in approach, if not the basic attitude of medical professionals, to this particular moral issue. The problem is that moral principles, rules and ethical conventions are limited by the fact that these are not legally enforceable were they ever to be disregarded in an individual case. So we return to consider what is the function of the law and in this case it is to redress an imbalance in knowledge between doctors and their patients which can be resolved by re-defining the relationship to take account of its fiduciary nature. This should eliminate the potential for any conflict in the interests of the respective parties to arise in terms of determining what information the patient should be told as part of the process of obtaining their consent to a medical treatment.

---

[104] This was proposed by my internal and external examiners

Voluntariness

Consent must be given voluntarily and freely.[105] The issue here then is whether the decision, to consent, or to refuse to consent, is really the decision of the patient. Has the patient exercised their own will freely and independently in choosing or was their will overborne. So whereas the law of capacity is concerned with whether the will is subject to some form of internal limitation,[106] voluntariness is, contrastingly, concerned with external constraints that overbear the will, or to be more precise the effects of undue influence or coercion.[107] What circumstances have been found to give rise to undue influence?

Particular Relationships

When considering the effects of outside influence Lord Donaldson has remarked that the relationship of the persuader to the patient can be of crucial importance.[108]

Perhaps then it could be argued that a doctor, as expert in medical matters, stands in a position to unduly influence or coerce a patient because of the inherent inequality in their positions. As stated earlier the principles of non-maleficence and beneficence are a primary source of influence in medical training and would tend to foster paternalistic attitudes at both stage one and two of a treatment decision-making process on the basis of a doctor's superior knowledge and experience in medical matters. Paternalistic tendencies might also be strengthened by patients who generally regard doctors as professional people of status for whom they have great respect whereas mentally incapacitated patients are vulnerable simply because their own values, beliefs and preferences may not be fully respected in situations where these come into conflict with those of their carers, i.e. the potential to override the patient's values exists when a patient is no longer competent to speak on their own behalf and to have their views respected by others.

---

[105] Grubb, A., Principles of Medical Law, 2004, Second Edition, Oxford University Press, para. 3.166

[106] Impairment or disturbance in the functioning of the brain

[107] *Re T (Adult: Refusal of Treatment) [1992] 4 All ER 649 CA*

[108] *Re T (Adult: Refusal of Treatment) [1993] Fam 95*, Lord Donaldson, p.114

Undue influence

Here the concern is that a person may have succumbed to some form of external pressure that has overpowered the will without having also convinced their judgment.[109] Essentially what is said or done does not carry any personal conviction because what is expressed is the product of a will that may have been preyed upon.[110]

The problem lies in determining which pressures and their effects should be regarded as having invalidated consent. Threats that act on a person's fears or hopes clearly exert an undue influence.[111] Moral commands might be similarly regarded when asserted and then responded to for the sake of peace and quiet, or for peace of mind or to escape social discomfort.[112] And in this regard it has been said that of all influences religious influence is the most dangerous and the most powerful such that the courts will go to some length to protect persons against it.[113]

Enthusiasm is, on the other hand, not ordinarily to be treated as having an undue influence, unless it is the product of external influence.[114]

Coercion and Shared or Collaborative Decision-Making

Coercion most commonly arises when one person seeks to apply pressure by force, perhaps through violence or confinement or maybe even tone and framing of information, and if done successfully the coercion will be seen to have had an undue influence on the other.[115]

Consequently, coercion takes many forms and on some occasions very little pressure may be required for it to have an undue influence.[116] It is at least possible therefore that a doctor's recommendations regarding treatment could be regarded as coercive in some circumstances.

---

[109] Ibid, Butler-Sloss LJ, p.118
[110] Ibid
[111] Ibid
[112] Ibid
[113] Ibid, p.119
[114] Ibid
[115] Ibid
[116] Ibid

Persuasion Distinguished from Undue Influence

Not all influences are unlawful and in particular mere persuasion, which appeals to the affections, or which seeks to invoke a sense of gratitude or pity is permitted. [117]

Summary

In order for consent to be legally valid it must be given voluntarily and freely. Crucially a patient's decision to accept or reject medical treatment should not bare the hallmarks of undue influence.[118] This requires that a decision to consent to or to refuse to consent to, medical treatment is made in accordance with the values, beliefs and preferences of the actual patient and not those of a third party.

Certain relationships stand out for possible scrutiny because there is an awareness that one party may be in a dominant position in this regard to the other; parent and child, husband and wife, religious advisor and parishioner are amongst some of the most obvious examples. Whilst the law states that any external influence that overbears the will invalidates consent some influences are deemed to be stronger than others; '*influence may be subtle, insidious, pervasive and where religious beliefs are involved especially powerful*'. [119]

Can it be argued that the law of consent is equally subtle, insidious and pervasive in determining that a patient has capacity to make a decision notwithstanding that the reasons for making the choice are rational, irrational, unknown or even non-existent in the knowledge that a cause or motive for exercising judgment one way rather than another may later be questioned. Or to put the matter another way it is at least arguable that the subjectively held beliefs, values and preferences of patients that are seemingly accommodated by the law of capacity can, in certain circumstances, be exposed to the subjective scrutiny of others in relation to the issue of whether consent was in fact given voluntarily.

---

[117] Ibid, p.118

[118] *Re T (Adult: Refusal of Treatment) [1993] Fam 95*, Lord Donaldson, p.114

[119] Ibid, Butler-Sloss LJ, p.120

Refusals of Consent

Lord Donaldson has stated that:

> *"An adult patient who ... suffers from no mental incapacity has an absolute right to choose whether to consent to medical treatment, to refuse it or to choose one rather than another of the treatments being offered ... This right of choice is not limited to decisions which others might regard as sensible. It exists notwithstanding that the reasons for making the choice are rational, irrational, unknown or even non-existent".*[120]

Butler-Sloss LJ has also commented that:

> *"A man or woman of full age and sound understanding may choose to reject medical advice and medical or surgical treatment either partially or in its entirety. A decision to refuse medical treatment by a patient capable of making the decision does not have to be sensible, rational or well considered".* [121]

Whilst Staughton LJ confirms that:

> *"An adult whose mental capacity is unimpaired has the right to decide for herself whether she will or will not receive medical or surgical treatment, even in circumstances where she is likely or even certain to die in the absence of treatment".* [122]

It is therefore plain that in ordinary circumstances an adult patient who suffers from no mental incapacity may self-determine the matter of whether to accept or reject an offer of medical treatment.[123] In a situation where consent to treatment is necessary, a refusal by a competent adult patient acts as a veto to the prohibited treatment.[124] A decision to act in the face of such a refusal would be unlawful amounting to a battery. [125]
The refusal will be total when a person refuses any offer of treatment but it can also be partial such as when a Jehovah's Witness refuses a blood

---

[120] Ibid, Lord Donaldson, p.102
[121] Ibid, p.116
[122] Ibid, p.120
[123] Ibid, p.102
[124] Grubb, A., Principles of Medical Law, 2004, Second Edition, Oxford University Press, para. 3.10
[125] Ibid

transfusion. In either case the refusal is legally effective to prevent the prohibited treatment even though the doctor's intention will be to benefit the patient. In this way the principle of autonomy trumps the principle of beneficence as the patient's right to self-determination triumphs over or outweighs paternalistic medical intervention.

Sanctity Principle

Does respect for the sanctity principle lead to situations where preserving life becomes an ultimate value? In other words does respect for the sanctity principle lead to moral absolutism? This question is significant in respect of end of life decision-making because it tends to uphold the view that all human life is equally valuable and should not be intentionally destroyed.[126]

Nature of the Treatment - Preserving Life

However, a treatment refusal is legally effective to prevent the prohibited treatment even if the patient may or will certainly die. Consequently, a patient who is competent to decide may refuse any treatment including life-saving or preserving medical treatments, such as a blood transfusion,[127] artificial ventilation[128] and even artificial feeding.[129] In this way the principle of the sanctity of human life similarly yields to the right of self-determination which preserves an autonomous choice.

Countervailing State Interest in the Preservation of Life

However, Stauch et al ask whether it might be argued that there is a countervailing State interest, as opposed to private acts of paternalism which justify overriding a patient's refusal of certain forms of treatment?[130] In this regard it has been said that:

---

[126] Herring, Jonathan, Medical Law and Ethics, 2008, Second Edition, Oxford University Press, p.466

[127] *Re T (Adult: Refusal of Treatment) [1992] 4 All ER 649 CA*

[128] *B v An NHS Trust Hospital [2002] 152 NLJ 470*

[129] *Airedale NHS Trust v Bland [1993] AC 789 HL*

[130] Stauch, Marc, Wheat, Kay, Tingle John, 2002, Second Edition, Sourcebook on Medical Law, Cavendish Publishing, p.106

> *"The State's interest in preserving life may be seen as embracing two separate but related concerns: an interest in preserving the life of the particular patient, and an interest in preserving the sanctity of life.*
>
> *While both of these State interests in life are certainly strong, in themselves they will usually not foreclose a competent person from declining life-sustaining medical treatment for himself. This is because the life that the State is seeking to protect in such a situation is the life of the same person who has competently decided to forgo the medical intervention; it is not some other actual or potential life that cannot adequately protect itself".*[131]

Neither is a refusal of life-saving or preserving treatment viewed as an attempt to commit suicide.[132] This is because '*refusing medical treatment merely allows the disease to take its natural course; if death were eventually to occur it would be the result, primarily, of the underlying disease, and not the result of a self-inflicted injury*'.[133]

Thus the right to self-determination, which includes the right to refuse life-preserving treatment, will normally outweigh the interest of the State in promoting the sanctity of life.[134] And in relation to treatment decision-making at the end of life this can be significant: '*the choice the law makes is to reassure people that the courts do have full respect for human life, but that they do not pursue the principle to the point at which it has become almost empty of any real content and when it involves the sacrifice of other important values such as human dignity and freedom of choice*'.[135]

Conclusion

The fundamental principle of bodily inviolability is upheld by the law of battery to protect everybody against non-consensual physical contacts.[136] And as even the mere touching of another without consent is capable of

---

[131] *In the Matter of Claire Conroy 486 A 2d 1209 [1985]*, Schrieber J
[132] *B v An NHS Trust Hospital [2002] 152 NLJ 470*
[133] *In the Matter of Claire Conroy 486 A 2d 1209 [1985]*, Schrieber J
[134] Herring, Jonathan, Medical Law and Ethics, 2008, Second Edition, Oxford University Press, p.504
[135] *Airedale NHS Trust v Bland [1993] AC 789 HL*, Hoffmann LJ
[136] *Schloendorff v Society of New York Hospital (1914) 105 NE 92*

amounting to a battery it is clear that the law's requirement for consent resides in the right to be maintained inviolate.[137]

Crucially the right to maintain bodily inviolability is a common law right and there is a correlative duty not to interfere with that right.[138] Consent is though a defence to activity that would ordinarily constitute a battery. Doctors, who have no special immunity in law,[139] must therefore obtain their patient's consent prior to administering medical treatment if they wish to avoid liability from suit.[140]

However, consent must also be legally valid and as patients control what happens to their bodies through the act of giving or withholding consent it is clear that respect for a person's bodily integrity stems from the right of self-determination.[141] To this end a medical professional is required to validate, by way of an established set of criteria, that the decision to accept or reject treatment has been taken in accordance with the patient's own values, beliefs and preferences.

137 *Re F (Mental Patient: Sterilisation) [1990] 2 AC 1 HL*, page13
138 Ibid
139 *Chatterton v Gerson [1981] QB 432; Chester v Afshar 2004 WL 2289136*
140 *Schloendorff v Society of New York Hospital (1914) 105 NE 92*
141 Grubb, A., Principles of Medical Law, 2004, Second Edition, Oxford University Press, para. 3.01

CHAPTER FOUR

THE LAW AND THE INCOMPETENT PATIENT

The fundamental principle of bodily inviolability is upheld by the law of battery to protect all persons against non-consensual physical contacts. Thus all persons enjoy a legally protected right to bodily security and therefore to be maintained inviolate and free from bodily harm.

The non-discriminatory nature of the principle of bodily inviolability suggests that everybody should have the right to self-determination with regard to their own body.[1] An issue in relation to a mentally incapacitated patient is whether they too enjoy a similar right to medical treatment or to the withholding or withdrawal of necessary and appropriate medical treatment as do competent patients to consent to, or, to refuse to consent to, medical treatment. This is because these patients, unlike their competent counterparts, are deemed incapable of exercising their right to self-determine, in accordance with their own beliefs, values and preferences, what shall happen to their body in a medical context. A third party, usually a doctor, will instead seek to determine the matter for them. So if the right to maintain bodily integrity is not to lose its significance we must ask what approach is taken in law to safeguard the welfare and autonomous interests of formerly competent adult patients.

Ethical Considerations: Autonomy and the Significance of the Individual Ethical Voice vs Paternalism

There are two reasons why autonomy is an important concept in relation to healthcare and treatment; autonomy not only allows patients to protect their own sense of well-being or happiness but also serves as a counter to medical paternalism.[2]

---

[1] Mason, J.K., McCall Smith, R.A., Laurie, G.T., Law and Medical Ethics, 2002, Sixth Edition, Butterworths, para. 10.6

[2] Berg, Jessica W., Appelbaum, Paul S., Lidz Charles W., Parker, Lisa S., Informed Consent, 2001, Second Edition, Oxford University Press, p.19

Arguments against paternalism tend to focus on the dangers that can arise whenever a person or group is in a position to exercise power and authority over others. In relation to physicians that idea tends to lead to discussion of events during the twentieth century which called into question the trustworthiness of the medical profession when it was discovered that some individual members had engaged in eugenic practices[3] which they sought to justify by claiming that it would lead to an improvement in the human gene pool and ultimately therefore of the human race.[4] This example illustrates what can happen when doctors have too much discretion in the exercise of their professional powers and/or act as agents of the state rather than the patient. The danger in these circumstances is of beneficence being inappropriately construed to promote a hidden agenda based on a particular conception of the common good, i.e. an opportunity will exist for hidden values to be manifest in the decisions of doctors about what form of treatment is in the best interests of the patient.[5]

Advances in medical science have further emphasised the need for a patient centred medical decision-making model.[6] About this Berg et al state that:

> *"Technological advances in medicine created treatment options that allowed physicians to keep patients alive even when they had few chances of recovery and very poor quality of life. Patients who did not want to be dependent on ventilators or dialysis presented the possibility that medicine's capabilities could clash with patients' deeply held values. What individual patients asserted against medical paternalism was, in essence, that health was not the only value of importance to them. Patients whose vision of a good life included a death unencumbered by technology found that their vision of their own well-being clashed with the 'do everything' mandate of acute care medicine. Many physicians were themselves increasingly uncomfortable with the path charted by their perceived professional mandate to promote health and preserve life at all costs. It was growing less clear that doing 'what is best for the patient,"*

[3] Killing or the compulsory sterilisation of humans deemed less perfect

[4] Berg, Jessica W., Appelbaum, Paul S., Lidz Charles W., Parker, Lisa S., Informed Consent, 2001, Second Edition, Oxford University Press, p.20

[5] Pellegrino, Edmund D., and Thomasma, David C., The Conflict between Autonomy and Beneficence in Medical Ethics: Proposals for a Resolution, 1987, Journal of Contemporary Health Law and Policy, 3, 23/46, p.23

[6] Berg, Jessica W., Appelbaum, Paul S., Lidz Charles W., Parker, Lisa S., Informed Consent, 2001, Second Edition, Oxford University Press, p.20

the paternalistic mandate, entailed aggressive medical intervention. Asking what the patient wanted provided a way out of this dilemma".[7]

The Legal Framework for Making Decisions and Acting on behalf of Mentally Incompetent Adults

As a prelude to our discussion about the MCA we should start off by considering how things might be in the absence of any guidance or information of any kind. One obvious problem that springs to my mind is that any surrogate decision-maker would have a free hand to decide matters in accordance with their own values and preferences if they felt able to decide matters at all. What might that be like? It is possible that the unscrupulous would take advantage of a vulnerable person. The indecisive would be rendered inert, exhausted from all that conjecturing. Whereas the well-intentioned busy-body or the over zealous would happily seize the opportunity to take matters into their own hands and direct affairs according to their own values and perceptions. Aging punk rockers might seek wisdom in the words of Malcolm McLaren whilst other worldly folk might look for inspiration in a 'sign'. Defensive creatures would be too busy covering their own back to do any good. The easily offended would be too put out to focus on anything but themselves and the overly sensitive couldn't possibly cope with the responsibility. Those who are important would delegate responsibility to someone else unless of course it was an executive decision that had to be made. And no matter what goes on around self-centred types it's always all about them.

However, mayhem can be brought into order and in this regard the Mental Capacity Act 2005 (MCA) establishes the legal framework for acting and making decisions on behalf of someone who is no longer competent to make their own decisions.[8] Significantly, the 2005 Act brought together, improved upon and then formalised the preceding judge made or common law in respect of persons who lack capacity. As a consequence the common law remains relevant to the task of interpreting the provisions of the MCA.

So what we have is a framework[9] that maps out who is empowered to make decisions on behalf of a person that has lost decision-making

[7] Ibid, p.20/1
[8] Mental Capacity Act 2005 Code of Practice, Introduction
[9] Mental Capacity Act 2005

capacity and who else should[10] or may be involved in that process.[11] This is supported by further statutory provisions that provide guidance about how a surrogate decision-maker should approach their decision-making responsibilities.[12] These measures have the effect of instituting a formalised decision-making structure with decision-making criteria to regulate the decision-making process which together establish the nature of the legal obligation a surrogate decision-maker owes to the incompetent person. As the pre-conditions of duty have been constituted it is plain that in law mentally disabled persons, like their competent counterparts, are intended to have a claim over the decisions and actions of surrogate decision-makers.[13]

In this regard the Act embodies a set of principles that must be applied by surrogates to first establish that a patient lacks the requisite capacity to decide themselves. Crucially, the MCA maintains the presumption that a person must be assumed to have capacity to make their own decisions unless it is established that they lack capacity.[14] This means that a capacity assessment by a potential decision-maker should only be undertaken if there is evidence to suggest that the presumption might be rebutted.[15] In this respect a person is not to be treated as unable to make a decision merely because they make an unwise decision.[16] Moreover, a person must not be treated as unable to make a decision unless all practicable steps to help them to do so have been taken without success.[17]

Accordingly, the MCA invites those it empowers to tread a difficult path as they must balance the need to protect those in need of medical treatment and/or care but are incapable of giving or withholding their consent to it with maintaining respect for an individual's right to make their own decisions.[18]

---

[10] Ibid, s.4(7)
[11] Ibid, s.15
[12] Ibid, s.4
[13] Ibid, s.5
[14] Ibid, s.1(2)
[15] Jones, Richard, Mental Capacity Act Manual, 2008, Third Edition, Sweet and Maxwell, p.16, para.1-029
[16] Mental Capacity Act 2005, s.1(4)
[17] Ibid, s.1(3)
[18] Idea taken from my supervisor Kay Wheat; Mental Capacity Act 2005 Code of Practice, para.1.4

Incapacity

For the purposes of the MCA, a person lacks capacity in relation to the matter in question if at the material time they are unable to make a decision because of an impairment or disturbance in the functioning of the mind or brain[19] which may be of a temporary or more permanent nature.[20] Consequently, anyone assessing capacity must use the two-stage test. At the first stage it is necessary to consider whether a person has an impairment or disturbance that affects the way their mind or brain works, and if so at the second stage to consider whether that impairment or disturbance means that they are unable to make a specific decision at the time it needs to be made.[21]

The statutory test therefore focuses on a person's ability to understand information and apply it to their situation in order to make a decision.[22] For the purposes of the Act a person is unable to make a decision for themselves if they are unable;[23] to understand information that is relevant to the decision in hand;[24] to retain that information;[25] to use it or weigh it as part of the process of making the decision;[26] or to communicate their decision.[27]

The Law Adopts a Functional not Outcome Based Approach to Decision-Making Capacity

Consistent with the foregoing the Act adopts a functional, not outcome or status based, approach to decision-making capacity. As a consequence doctors and carers are cautioned that a lack of decision-making capacity cannot be established merely by reference to a person's age or appearance[28] or the simple fact that they suffer from a particular condition, for example some sort of mental illness, which would indicate that the law adopted a status-based approach to capacity. On its own therefore an

---

[19] Mental Capacity Act 2005, s.2(1)
[20] Ibid, s.2(2)
[21] Mental Capacity Act, Code of Practice, Chapter Four, para.4.3
[22] Mental Capacity Act 2005, s.3; Code of Practice, Chapter Four, para.4.1
[23] Mental Capacity Act 2005, s.3(1)
[24] Ibid, s.3(1)(a)
[25] Ibid, s.3(1)(b)
[26] Ibid, s.3(1)(c)
[27] Ibid, s.3(1)(d)
[28] Mental Capacity Act 2005, s.2(3)(a)

aspect of personal behaviour, such as might be exhibited by those who suffer from an obsessive compulsive disorder or who engage in self-harming practices,[29] should not lead to unjustified assumptions being made about someone's capacity to decide.[30]

It is also consistent with aims of a functional test for capacity that a fresh capacity assessment should be undertaken for each and every decision that a person might be required to make and at a time when the decision in question needs to be made.[31] You might recall the decision in *The Estate of Park*[32] which recognised that a person can be capable of deciding to marry but not to make a will.[33] Potential decision-makers should not therefore think that just because a person lacks the ability to make one decision that they lack the ability to make any decision particularly when what has to be decided is of a more minor nature as less information or perhaps more accurately less complex information has to be processed to arrive at a choice.[34] Although at least one commentator considers that assessments in the case of routine decisions, such as what clothes a person should wear or food they should eat, if they happen at all, are most likely to be fairly superficial.[35] Nevertheless, the approach is consistent with respect for the principle of autonomy and might be particularly relevant to those who require ongoing treatment and care and are confined within an institutionalised setting.

An outcome based approach to decision-making capacity does by contrast conflict with respect for the principle of autonomy in tending to focus on

---

[29] Jacob R., Clare I.C.H., Holland A., Watson P.C., Maimaris C., Gunn M., Self-harm, capacity, and refusal of treatment: Implications for emergency medical practice, 2005, Emergency Medical Journal, 22: 799-802

[30] Mental Capacity Act 2005, s.2(3)(b)

[31] Mental Capacity Act 2005, Code of Practice, Chapter Four, para.4.4; Gunn, M.J., Wong, J.G., Clare, I.C.H., and Holland, A.J., Decision-Making Capacity, 1999, Medical Law Review, 7(3) 269, p.270; Jones, Richard, Mental Capacity Act Manual, 2008, Third Edition, Sweet and Maxwell, p.16, para.1-029

[32] *Estate of Park [1953] 2 All ER 408*

[33] Gunn, M.J., Wong, J.G., Clare, I.C.H., and Holland, A.J., Decision-Making Capacity, 1999, Medical Law Review, 7(3) 269, p.270; Jones, Richard, Mental Capacity Act Manual, 2008, Third Edition, Sweet and Maxwell, p.16, para.1-028

[34] *Re T (Adult: Refusal of Treatment) [1992] 4 All ER 649 CA*: Gunn, M.J., Wong, J.G., Clare, I.C.H., and Holland, A.J., Decision-Making Capacity, 1999, Medical Law Review, 7(3) 269, p.270/1

[35] Jones, Richard, Mental Capacity Act Manual, 2008, Third Edition, Sweet and Maxwell, p.16, para.1-029

the consequences for someone of their decision. Accordingly, the freedom to make a decision in accordance with one's own constitution or value system could be undermined by the need to usher non-compliant individuals into a state of conformity with a consensus viewpoint or with the views of the potential decision-maker.[36] Instead the principle of autonomy permits each of us to develop our individuality or character and personality and to make decisions in conformity with it.[37] The potential for diversity in the decisions of persons similarly situated is to be expected and is precisely what a functional based test for capacity allows for. This is confirmed in the Mental Capacity Act Code of Practice which states that:

> *"Everybody has their own values, beliefs, preferences and attitudes. A person should not be assumed to lack capacity to make a decision just because other people think their decision is unwise. This applies even if family members, friends, or healthcare or social care staff are unhappy with a decision... There may be cause for concern if somebody repeatedly makes unwise decisions that put them at significant risk of harm or exploitation or makes a particular unwise decision that is obviously irrational or out of character. These things do not necessarily mean that somebody lacks capacity. But there might be need for further investigation, taking into account the person's past decisions and choices. For example, have they developed a medical condition or disorder that is affecting their capacity to make particular decisions? Are they easily influenced by undue pressure? Or do they need more information to help them understand the consequences of the decision they are making?"*[38]

A functional approach to decision-making capacity was also emphasised at common law as Lord Donaldson has previously stated that:

> *"The patient's right of choice exists whether the reasons for making that choice are rational, irrational, unknown or even non-existent. That his choice is contrary to what is to be expected of the vast majority of adults is only relevant if there are other reasons for doubting his capacity to decide".*[39]

---

[36] Gunn, M.J., Wong, J.G., Clare, I.C.H., and Holland, A.J., Decision-Making Capacity, 1999, Medical Law Review, 7(3) 269, p.281

[37] Mental Capacity Act 2005, Code of Practice, Chapter Two, para.2.10/1

[38] Ibid, para.2.11

[39] *Re T (Adult: Refusal of Treatment) [1993] Fam. 95 CA*, Lord Donaldson, para.113

The rejection of the outcome approach was emphasised in *Masterman-Lister v Jewell* where Wright J. said that:

> *"In principle, legal capacity depends on understanding rather than wisdom: the quality of the decision is irrelevant as long as the person understands what he is deciding".*[40]

Whilst in *Masterman-Lister v Brutton & Co* Chadwick L.J. said:

> *"English law requires that a person must have the necessary mental capacity if he is to do a legally effective act or to make a legally effective decision for himself. The authorities are unanimous in support of two broad propositions. First, that the mental capacity required by the law is capacity in relation to the transaction which is to be effected. Second, that what is required is the capacity to understand the nature of that transaction when it is explained".*[41]

Finally, in *Sheffield City Council v E* Munby J. said:

> *"The general rule of English law, whatever the context, is that the test of capacity is the ability (whether or not one chooses to exercise it) to understand the nature and quality of the transaction".*[42]

Assessing Patient Capacity to Decide

Contrary to what a functional approach to capacity prescribes a patient's decision, in particular its consequences for longevity, health and well-being, and the manner in which it is made, might in practice be the only reason one has to question a person's capacity to decide. In *Re T*, for example, Lord Donaldson said that '*doctors faced with a refusal of treatment have to give very careful thought and detailed consideration to*

---

[40] *Masterman-Lister v Jewell [2002] EWHC 417 QB*; Jones, Richard, Mental Capacity Act Manual, 2008, Third Edition, Sweet and Maxwell, p.15-16, para. 1-029

[41] *Masterman Lister v Jewell; Masterman Lister v Brutton and Co [2002] EWCA Civ 1889*; Jones, Richard, Mental Capacity Act Manual, 2008, Third Edition, Sweet and Maxwell, p.15-16, para. 1-029

[42] *Sheffield City Council v E [2004] EWHC 2808*; Jones, Richard, Mental Capacity Act Manual, 2008, Third Edition, Sweet and Maxwell, p.15-16, para. 1-029

the patients' capacity to decide'.[43] This gives rise to an obvious concern that a doctor will say a patient is competent to give their consent to treatment when the patient is compliant with medical expert opinion and conversely to claim that the patient is not competent to decide if they raise objections or refuse a necessary and appropriate treatment or procedure.[44]

Moreover, the person who is required to assess an individual's capacity to decide will be the person who has the power to make the decision in respect of, or to act on behalf of the patient in question.[45] So that will be either a doctor or a carer depending on whether the decision in hand is a day-to-day matter or one concerning the health and welfare of the patient.[46] Whilst the MCA institutes safeguards to protect the interests of all concerned a formal procedure for the assessment of capacity has not been established and no statutory form confirming incapacity needs to be completed.[47] Neither is there a requirement to involve or obtain a second opinion from a particular professional such as a psychologist or a psychiatrist, in the assessment[48] although there is nothing to prevent a doctor or carer from obtaining a second opinion from another professional, particularly for complex decisions.[49]

Nonetheless the decision of a doctor or carer may be challenged and in this situation the decision-maker would need to show that they had reasonable grounds for believing that the person lacked the capacity to make a particular decision at the time when it needed to be made.[50] Such consideration are reflected in the thoughts of Lord Donaldson in *Re T* who made references to the fact that doctors have to give very careful thought and detailed consideration to the patient's capacity because if a person is not capable of making a decision *Re F* determines that a doctor is required

---

43 *Re T (Adult: Refusal of Treatment) [1992] 4 All ER 649 CA*, p.661; Gunn, M.J., Wong, J.G., Clare, I.C.H., and Holland, A.J., Decision-Making Capacity, 1999, Medical Law Review, 7(3) 269, p.291

44 Gunn, M.J., Wong, J.G., Clare, I.C.H., and Holland, A.J., Decision-Making Capacity, 1999, Medical Law Review, 7(3) 269, p.275; Jones, Richard, Mental Capacity Act Manual, 2008, Third Edition, Sweet and Maxwell, p.20, para.1-033

45 Jones, Richard, Mental Capacity Act Manual, 2008, Third Edition, Sweet and Maxwell, p.16/7, para.1-029

46 Ibid

47 Ibid

48 Ibid

49 Mental Capacity Act 2005, Code of Practice, Chapter four, para.4.65

50 Mental Capacity Act 2005, s.5

to make decision in the patient's best interests.[51] If however, a doctor, as the potential decision-maker, is in any doubt about whether a patient lacks capacity to make the decision in question he or she is permitted to resolve any doubts in accordance with the civil standard, i.e. based on a balance of probabilities.[52] Whilst these two considerations appear somewhat incongruous this is an example of the balance that is struck between beneficence and autonomy, or protection and self-determination.

Although where the decision was finely balanced and the situation was non-urgent a doctor should, as a matter of principle, seek to delay treatment for as long as possible or at least until all practicable steps had been taken to assist the patient to make their own decision.[53] Practical guidance and information is contained within the Code of Practice about what can be done to improve a patient's ability to satisfy a capacity test and to therefore make their own decision.[54] Potential decision-makers are encouraged to connect with patients more effectively by using simple language or alternative communication techniques such as sign language or pictures and structuring information in a way that aids understanding.[55] Another suggestion is to engage the services of a relative or someone else who is more familiar with the patient, as they might be able to elicit a decision from them where others have failed to do so.[56] Of course it remains important that the decision is arrived at voluntarily and so anyone who seeks to support the patient to make a decision should take care not to unduly influence or pressurise them into making a decision they would not otherwise have made.[57]

However, the underlying significance of this provision is that physical interference in the absence of consent ordinarily constitutes a battery. Consent is the concept that gives rise to respect for the principle of autonomy and so developing a person's capacity is part of what it means

---

[51] *Re T (Adult: Refusal of Treatment) [1992] 4 All ER 649 CA*, p.661; Gunn, M.J., Wong, J.G., Clare, I.C.H., and Holland, A.J., Decision-Making Capacity, 1999, Medical Law Review, 7(3) 269, p.290

[52] Mental Capacity Act 2005, s.2(4)

[53] Ibid, s.1(3)

[54] Mental Capacity Act 2005 Code of Practice, Chapter two, para.2.7

[55] Ibid, Chapter Three

[56] Ibid, Chapter Four, para.4.36

[57] Ibid, Chapter Two, para.2.8

to show respect for that principle.[58] Consequently, this provision aims to prevent unnecessary intervention in the lives of patients.[59] Moreover, there is research to show that this type of action can yield positive results in some instances.[60] Gunn et al, for example, have demonstrated that the skills of some amongst a group of patients who appeared to be incapable of making a decision to have a blood test could be maximised to a point where they were competent to make the decision to have a blood test themselves.[61]

On the other hand this group of researchers could not exclude the possibility that potential decision-makers may be required to exercise their judgment, when making an assessment of capacity, based on an overall impression of the person.[62] Whilst the MCA rejects a status based approach to capacity assessment the reality is that it might be quite difficult to eliminate personal feelings from the judgments of potential decision-makers. This is potentially problematic because it places too much emphasis on something that is subjective within them. For example, it is a fact of life that people have quite different ideas about who they like and why and in the early stages of contact this also has to do with impressions that are created, since there is little else to base our opinions on. Yet we all know that it is true of many married couples that when they first met neither party may initially have made a spectacular impression on the other. Consequently, their decision to marry must have been formed on the basis of something more substantial following a period of getting to know one another rather better.

What Information must the Patient Understand?

The adoption of a functional rather than an outcome or status based test for capacity suggests that the law requires a competent process, i.e. informed decisions, rather than a competent outcome, i.e. a responsible decision. Consequently, a person can have capacity to make some decisions but not others and this will in part depend on the amount or complexity of the

58 Gunn, M.J., Wong, J.G., Clare, I.C.H., and Holland, A.J., Decision-Making Capacity, 1999, Medical Law Review, 7(3) 269, p.276

59 Mental Capacity Act 2005 Code of Practice, Chapter two, para.2.6

60 Gunn, M.J., Wong, J.G., Clare, I.C.H., and Holland, A.J., Decision-Making Capacity, 1999, Medical Law Review, 7(3) 269, p.276/7

61 Ibid, p.269

62 Ibid

information that is relevant to the transaction and that the patient must be able to understand.

In relation to a medical treatment or procedure, and in order for any resulting consent to be real, case law determines that a patient must understand information that is presented in broad terms pertaining to the nature and purpose of the particular form of treatment that is being proposed[63] and of each treatment where a choice of treatments are open to them and finally the likely consequences of treatment and non-treatment or of accepting or refusing treatment.[64]

A doctor must also inform the patient of the advantages and disadvantages of treatment and describe how different people experience different reactions or side effects to treatment. [65] In this regard disclosures as to risks was initially treated as a matter of clinical judgment that was directed by the *Bolam*[66] principle, i.e. a practice accepted as proper by a responsible body of medical opinion.[67] The case of *Sidaway* modified that situation somewhat by taking into consideration circumstances in which the disclosure of a particular risk might be so obviously necessary, or material, to an informed choice on the part of the patient that no reasonably prudent doctor would fail to mention it.[68] A doctor's privilege in deciding about the relevance or materiality of treatment information was however dealt a distinct blow in the case of *Chester v Afshar* when Lord Hope reasoned that the right to make the final decision and the duty of the doctor to inform the patient of special disadvantages or dangers of treatment go hand in hand. Consequently, a standard had been set by law for physicians rather than one which physicians may or may not impose on themselves.[69] Professional paternalism related to treatment disclosures was effectively laid to rest as the doctor's duty to inform had been tailored to meet the needs of individual patients.[70]

---

[63] *Chatterton v Gerson [1981] 1 QB 432*

[64] Mental Capacity Act 2005, Code of Practice, Chapter 3, para.3.7

[65] Ibid, Chapter 2, para 2.8

[66] *Bolam v Friern Hospital Management Committee [1957] 1 WLR 582*

[67] *Sidaway v Board of Governors of the Bethlem Royal Hospital [1985] 1 All ER 643*; Jones, Richard, Mental Capacity Act Manual, 2008, Third Edition, Sweet and Maxwell, p.21, para.1-034

[68] Ibid

[69] *Chester v Afshar 2004 WL 2289136*, para.53

[70] Jones, Richard, Mental Capacity Act Manual, 2008, Third Edition, Sweet and Maxwell, p.22, para.1-034

It is therefore clear that in law a functional approach to capacity demands that the patient must be able to understand relevant treatment information so that it can be applied to their own situation, in particular its significance and potential effects with regard to their existing values, beliefs and preferences.[71] Understanding is demonstrated in other words by someone who is able to apply facts to values as part of the decision-making process. The problem is that the Act cannot state what information will be relevant in each case and so it becomes a matter that is left to the discretion of the doctor. In this respect it is important to note that in accordance with the MCA information must be tailored to an individual's needs and abilities.[72] So whilst it is important that a person has access to all the information they need to make an informed decision that information can presumably be presented in broad terms to aid their understanding of it whereupon there is a danger that the true meaning and significance of it might get lost in translation.[73] This of course means that if the patient fails to understand the true significance of the information they are being given then they may also fail to apply it meaningfully to their own situation. Moreover, the standard with regard to disclosure appears once again to be determined by members of the medical profession. Although, the Code of Practice does emphasise the importance of providing information that is factual bearing in mind the decision must be that of the patient not the doctor.[74] There is also the ever present danger that a medical professional will manipulate the situation to gain patient consent or to determine where treatment is refused that the patient is incompetent to decide and must therefore be treated in their best interests. However, if respect for autonomy, not beneficence, is the primary value in healthcare ethics and law then no gap should exist between what the patient needs to understand taking into consideration their values, beliefs and preferences and the doctor's duty to provide that information and where necessary assistance to aid their actual understanding of it.

What Key Abilities are involved in a Functional Approach to Decision-Making?

Consistent with a functional approach to capacity the Code of Practice informs us that what matters is that a patient should have the ability to

---

[71] Gunn, M.J., Wong, J.G., Clare, I.C.H., and Holland, A.J., Decision-Making Capacity, 1999, Medical Law Review, 7(3) 269, p.280

[72] Mental Capacity Act 2005, Code of Practice, Chapter 3, para 3.8

[73] Ibid, para 3.9

[74] Ibid, Chapter 2, para 2.8

carry out the processes involved in making a decision.[75] As a person is unable to make a decision if they cannot, understand information about the decision to be made, retain that information in their mind, use or weigh that information as part of the decision-making process or communicate their decision four specific abilities should be assessed: the ability to understand information about treatment; the ability to appreciate how that information applies to their situation; the ability to reason with that information; and the ability to make a choice and express it.[76]

Understanding

As patients are not expected to demonstrate their ability to arrive at a choice that is actually wise, prudent or competent when assessed in the light of their actual values, beliefs and preferences, i.e. the outcome of the deliberative process is not what is being tested for or assessed, appearances suggest that there is no need for a patient to demonstrate actual understanding of the treatment information.[77]

However, according to the Code of practice there is a difference between unwise decisions, which a person has the right to make, and decisions based on a lack of understanding of risks or the inability to weigh up the information about a decision.[78]

In respect of the latter the Code confirms that a decision of the patient can form part of a capacity assessment, particularly if someone repeatedly makes decisions that put them at risk or result in harm to them or someone else.[79] This results in a situation where patients must actually understand the information that is relevant to their decision.[80]

So we arrive at the somewhat confusing situation whereby a general understanding of the information a patient must be told for a physician to

[75] Ibid, Chapter 4, para.4.2

[76] Mental Capacity Act 2005, Code of Practice, Chapter 4, para.4.14; Tunzi, Marc, Can the Patient Decide? Evaluating Patient Capacity in Practice, 2001, American Family Physician, Vol.64 No.2, p.299; Gunn, M.J., Wong, J.G., Clare, I.C.H., and Holland, A.J., Decision-Making Capacity, 1999, Medical Law Review, 7(3) 269, p.280/3

[77] Mental Capacity Act 2005, Code of Practice, Chapter 4, para.4.2

[78] Ibid, para.4.30

[79] Ibid

[80] Mental Capacity Act 2005, Code of Practice, Chapter 4, Quick summary

escape liability for the intentional tort of battery will suffice, i.e. the patient must be told in broad terms the nature and purpose of medical treatment and of the likely consequences of accepting or refusing treatment,[81] whereas patients must actually understand information pertaining to risks and side effects that form part of the doctors duty in negligence. The problem is that the relationship between information and how it relates to any individual patient and in particular their values is co-dependent and so it is somewhat disingenuous to maintain a distinction between what the patient must be told in battery and negligence, i.e. no real divide exists. For instance, a battery theory of law seeks to maintain a position whereby its requirements will be satisfied by medical knowledge, i.e. diagnosis and prognosis, whereas it has been determined that in negligence a doctor must also know something more about the patient and in particular their values, beliefs and preferences because patients must understand how information about risks relates to their own situation. Whilst the judgment in *Chester v Afshar* maintains the distinction between battery and negligence its strength lies in recognising that the same degree or level of knowledge and understanding that is relevant in negligence is pertinent in battery also because the patient must appreciate what the likely consequences will be for them of accepting or refusing treatment. Crucially, the patient must understand what the possible benefits and harms of treatment are in order to fully appreciate what the consequences for them may be if they should decide one way rather than another.

Retaining Information

According to the Code of Practice a patient must be able to hold information in their mind long enough to use it to make an effective decision.[82] The latter points suggests that a person's memory should work sufficiently well to enable them to make a decision in conformity with existing values or to at least appreciate that their current decision entails a departure from them.

Using or Weighing Information

Sometimes a condition, which may or may not be of a psychiatric nature, can interfere with a person's ability to understand information.[83] It is also

[81] *Chatterton v Gerson [1981] 1 QB 432*
[82] Mental Capacity Act 2005, Code of Practice, Chapter 4, para.4.20
[83] www.ethox.org.uk/education/undergraduate-course/no-consent/4-the-assessment

the case that sometimes people can understand treatment information but an impairment or disturbance, such as a compulsive disorder or phobia, prevents them from using or weighing it. For example a person with anorexia nervosa may understand treatment information about the consequences of not eating but their compulsion not to eat might be too strong for them to ignore.[84] In *Banks v Goodfellow*, for instance, Lord Cockburn C.J. remarked that, '*one object may be so forced upon the attention of the invalid as to shut out all others that might require consideration*'.[85]

So potential decision-makers are invited to consider whether the patient has the capacity to apply facts to values and through a process of reasoning and deliberation arrive at a decision that suits them best, i.e. does the patient have a general understanding of their condition and treatment; can they apply that information to their situation, i.e. how their life will be affected by their medical condition if untreated, and how their future life prospects may be improved by treatment, together with the possible risks to them of treatment, and is the patients' decision consistent with the facts and values of this case.[86] Dan Brock has written about this process and he states that:

> *"Besides the capacity to understand relevant information, decision-making competence requires the capacity to use that information in a process of reasoning and deliberation. That process largely consists of "if/then" reasoning – if I choose this, then these will be the consequences. Also required is the capacity to entertain at once or serially, and to compare the consequences of, alternative choices or courses of action. These are capacities that ordinary people regularly exercise in going about their everyday lives, and so they will be available for medical decision-making unless special circumstances impair them.*
>
> *Finally, patients require values, preferences, plans and purposes for their lives that they can use to evaluate the desirability of the consequences of*

---

[84] Mental Capacity Act 2005, Code of Practice, Chapter 4, para.4.21/2

[85] *Banks v Goodfellow (1870) L.R. 5 Q.B. 549*, p.569; Gunn, M.J., Wong, J.G., Clare, I.C.H., and Holland, A.J., Decision-Making Capacity, 1999, Medical Law Review, 7(3) 269, p.272

[86] *Chester v Afshar 2004 WL 2289136*; Brock, Dan W., Medical Ethics, 2007, Blackwell Publishing, Chapter 7, p.128; www.fpnotebook.com/Neuro/Cognitive/MdclDcsnMkngCpcty.htm; Tunzi, Marc, Can the Patient Decide? Evaluating Patient Capacity in Practice, 2001, American Family Physician, Vol.64 No.2, p.299

> *alternative treatments, including the alternative of no treatment, and to select the one that will be best for them. This is not to say that people must already possess articulated values with determinative relative weights that could then be applied in a straightforward and mechanical way to yield a decision about treatment. Serious medical choices often confront patients with new and difficult choices that go beyond their previous experiences. What is then necessary is the capacity to decide what value to place on various alternative consequences and outcomes so as to be able to reach a decision about a course of action. This too is a capacity that ordinary people also exercise in non-medical circumstances when they are faced with new and unfamiliar choices. It is important to distinguish this third capacity to have and apply values because some accounts of competence require only capacities for understanding and reasoning. These accounts are defective, however, because a patient's values can be impaired as well. Perhaps the most important example is when severe depression distorts patients' values so that they no longer care about the harm, even including death, that may come to them without treatment. There may be no failure in their understanding or reasoning about this outcome, but they 'no longer care' about the harm that will come to them. Here, mental illness that distorts what they value from what it would otherwise be can result in incompetence to decide about treatment".*[87]

Consequently, a seemingly irrational or incoherent choice may trigger a capacity assessment or might at least alert a physician to assess decision-making capacity more carefully. This is despite the fact that the outcome of the decision-making process is not part of what is being measured and therefore patients are permitted to make an unwise decision. Several factors might explain the decision, for example it may be due to a change in mental status although some changes in mental status might only be temporary in which case it is possible that treatment could be delayed until such time as the patient is able to make their own decision.[88] Alternatively necessary and appropriate treatment might be refused for unknown or irrational reasons and the patient may not be willing to discuss their decision. Although there will be cases where patients refuse treatment for unusual or idiosyncratic reasons which are not irrational when examined in more detail.[89] It might also be the case that a risky treatment or procedure is accepted too readily without apparent consideration of the associated

[87] Brock, Dan W., Medical Ethics, 2007, Blackwell Publishing, Chapter 7, p.129/30

[88] This change may be caused by hypoxia, infection, medication, metabolic disturbances, an acute neurologic process or other medical problem

[89] Tunzi, Marc, Can the Patient Decide? Evaluating Patient Capacity in Practice, 2001, American Family Physician, Vol.64 No.2, p.299/300

risks and benefits which would suggest that the patient had failed to adequately process treatment information as well as how it applied to their values and thus to their current situation in the time available.[90] Finally, a patient might be known to have a condition, such as a learning disability or an acknowledged fear or discomfort of institutional settings or perhaps even disproportionate respect for members of the medical profession, that places them at risk of impaired decision-making which might also lead some patients to consent to treatment without apparent consideration.[91]

In all such situations a doctor's task is to understand the patient's reasoning and how they arrived at their decision. They will therefore be interested in what the patient understands about their medical condition and of the proposed treatment and why it has been accepted or rejected in order that any misunderstandings can be corrected.[92] This form of approach may also throw light on the fact that the patient has made a choice that is consistent with their values and should be respected even though it may not be the choice that most other persons would make, for example a Jehovah's Witness who is critically ill and refuses a blood transfusion that would return them to full health.[93] In other cases serious impairments in the patient's decision-making may be uncovered that resist correction by way of further explanation and there could be many reasons for this, for example the patient may be gripped by fear about undergoing treatment or a procedure.[94] The question will then be whether the patient's decision-making is sufficiently impaired for them to be judged incompetent to decide.[95] This raises an analogous question about how much uncertainty in the patient's decision-making is compatible with affirming their competence to decide.[96] At issue is the fact that the patient either retains or loses the right to make decisions about treatment.[97]

---

[90] Ibid

[91] www.fpnotebook.com/Neuro/Cognitive/MdclDcsnMkngCpcty.htm;
Tunzi, Marc, Can the Patient Decide? Evaluating Patient Capacity in Practice, 2001, American Family Physician, Vol.64 No.2, p.299/300

[92] Brock, Dan W., Medical Ethics, 2007, Blackwell Publishing, Chapter 7, p.131

[93] Ibid

[94] Brock, Dan W., Medical Ethics, 2007, Blackwell Publishing, Chapter 7, p.131; *Re MB (Adult: Medical Treatment) [1997] 2 FLR 426 CA*

[95] Brock, Dan W., Medical Ethics, 2007, Blackwell Publishing, Chapter 7, p.132

[96] Ibid

[97] Ibid, p.133

Brock argues that we need a principled answer to this question so that competence determinations do not depend in an arbitrary way on the preferences, values and idiosyncrasies of different evaluators, i.e. in this situation I would do this or in these circumstances most of my patients choose to accept the treatment that I propose.[98] He therefore reflects on what principal values or interests are at stake for the patient in whether they retain or lose decisional authority and determines that patient's have an interest in autonomy and in their well-being.[99]

With regard to the patient's interests in self-determination Brock states that:

> *"This is the interest of people in making significant decisions about their lives for themselves according to their own values or conception of a good life. It is important to understand that this interests does not depend on an assumption that individuals will always make the decision that is best for them, according to either their own or anyone else's conception of what is best for them... We want to make our own decisions because that is the way we exercise some measure of control over and take responsibility for our lives, even recognising that we will not always make the best decision".*[100]

On the question of well-being Brock focuses on the harm principle and the fact that most people have a natural wish to avoid anything that is likely to have a harmful impact on well-being. He says that:

> *"In some cases patients' refusal of their physicians' treatment recommendations could have a great and harmful impact on their well-being, including in some cases leading to their preventable death. Sometimes not refusing all treatment but insisting on a far from optimal treatment can also have serious adverse effects on patients' well-being. Individuals' reasonable and near universal concern for their own well-being supports steps to protect it when their seriously impaired decision-making capacities result in a treatment choice that would be seriously harmful to them. This is not an imposition that most patients would not want, though they may be resisting it at the time. Most patients would want others to act to protect their well-being if their decision-making is*

[98] Ibid, p.132
[99] Ibid, p.133
[100] Ibid

seriously impaired and has resulted in a choice likely to be seriously harmful".[101]

Of course Brock acknowledges that in most instances no conflict will exist between expressing a treatment choice that is in accord with a patients' well-being and respecting their self-determination.[102] On those occasions, he argues, the patient's decisional authority and treatment choice should be respected.[103] But when the patient's decision-making capacities are seriously impaired resulting in a harmful choice these two values will be in conflict and must be balanced.[104] Although here Brock concedes that it is not possible to state precisely how they should be balanced or traded off because the matter remains ethically controversial due to the fact that different people attach different weight or importance to their own self-determination and well-being.[105] In essence therefore potential decision-makers or evaluators should seek to avoid two possible mistakes; on the one hand, failing to adequately respect the patient's self-determination when the patient has sufficient decision-making capacity and on the other hand failing to protect the patient's well-being when the patient's seriously impaired decision-making capacity has led to a seriously harmful choice.[106]

Fluctuating Capacity

Conditions like manic depression can mean that a person has capacity to make decisions on some occasions and not at others.[107] Temporary factors such as acute illness or severe pain may also affect some people's ability to make decisions. Other examples include the effects of distress or even medication.[108] The question is whether these are factors that might escape the attention of someone assessing another's ability to make a decision. In relation to the effects of medication Baroness Finlay of Llandaff has previously stated that:

---

[101] Ibid, p.134
[102] Ibid
[103] Ibid
[104] Ibid
[105] Ibid
[106] Ibid, p.134/5
[107] Mental Capacity Act 2005, Code of Practice, Chapter 4, para.4.26
[108] *Re T (Adult: Refusal of Treatment)) [1992] 4 All ER 649 CA*

"If I can give you two specific and very common instances, one where patients have been anxious, which is understandable because they are facing dying, and where the benzodiazepine group of drugs such as Midazolam are used to remove the churning drive of anxiety without sedating the patient so they can still function but they are relieved in part of this desperate feeling of anxiety, butterflies and churning inside. With some of these patients you can have a conversation and they appear to understand everything that is said and have recall. The following day they have no recall whatsoever of that conversation. It may have been a few hours later in some patients. Another situation which arises is where patients' calcium goes up and that occurs in about ten per cent of all cancer patients. They become confused. That is a gradual onset and the outset is difficult to diagnose. They may appear to be arguing rationally but when their calcium level has been brought down and is treated they then are behaving differently and they have no recall of that previous conversation to the direction that they were trying to give in expressing what they wanted. Also they may completely change their mind which is a terribly important situation for a clinician. The difficulty is in judging whether they have capacity or not because at any one point in time the conversation appears to be logical and consequential. There are lots of other situations which arise, particularly with patients on steroids, where the steroids may have created a very mild steroid psychosis which can be difficult to diagnose and just presents as emotional immobility. Again their thinking and perception is distorted".[109]

A Formal Capacity Assessment Tool:[110] Potential Decision-Makers should have regard to the Values of the Patient in Deciding[111]

The Code of Practice in support of the MCA confirms that anyone who believes that a person lacks capacity should be able to prove their case[112] by giving reasons and providing objective evidence in support of their belief.[113] A decision to restrict autonomy therefore requires a clear and convincing assessment that a patient's decision regarding care was non-autonomous necessitating beneficent intervention to prevent unintended,

[109] Jones, Richard, Mental Capacity Act Manual, 2008, Third Edition, Sweet and Maxwell, p.19/20, para.1-032

[110] Tunzi, Marc, Can the Patient Decide? Evaluating Patient Capacity in Practice, 2001, American Family Physician, Vol.64 No.2, p.299

[111] Jones, Richard, Mental Capacity Act Manual, 2008, Third Edition, Sweet and Maxwell, p.19, para.1-032

[112] Mental Capacity Act 2005, Code of Practice, Chapter 2, para 2.5

[113] Ibid, Chapter 4, para 4.63

irreparable harm to them.[114] However, harm is difficult to define in this context because what is deemed harmful varies from one person and set of circumstances to another.[115] Plus people differ in estimating the likely harm that will ensue from their decisions and actions and if autonomy not harm is the dominant consideration then it is important that potential decision-makers should have at the forefront of their mind the patient's right to refuse necessary and appropriate treatment, including life-preserving treatment.[116]

If harm were to become the dominant principal there is a danger that what is in one's medical best interests would become the overriding consideration when what we seek to establish is whether there is a lack of congruity with the patient's values not those of the doctor. Therefore, is there an argument for establishing some sort of link between decision-making capacity and competence in terms of arriving at a decision that is consistent with what has gone before and an expectation that a seemingly inconsistent response can be appreciated and explained, for example, my diet consists of a lot of fresh fruit but now that I am older I find that too much acid tends to create problems with digestion. If so one way of balancing respect for autonomy with the need to act beneficently is to emphasise how the subjective nature of the particular patient is likely to influence their decisions about personal welfare which is an idea that more recent case law tends to support.

For example, in *Re B*[117] there is a reference to the significance of distinguishing between capacity and best interests in the context of consent to treatment[118] and in this regard Butler-Sloss P. stated that:

> *"If there are difficulties in deciding whether the patient has sufficient mental capacity particularly if the refusal may have grave consequences for the patient, it is most important that those considering the issue should not confuse the question of mental capacity with the nature of the decision*

---

[114] Mental Capacity Act 2005, s.3(4); *Re T (Adult: Refusal of Treatment) [1992] 4 All ER 649 CA*; Tunzi, Marc, Can the Patient Decide? Evaluating Patient Capacity in Practice, 2001, American Family Physician, Vol.64 No.2, p.301

[115] Ibid

[116] *Re T (Adult: Refusal of Treatment) [1992] 4 All ER 649 CA; Re B (Consent to Treatment: Capacity) [2002] EWHC 429 (Fam)*

[117] *Re B (Consent to Treatment: Capacity) [2002] EWHC 429 (Fam)*

[118] Jones, Richard, Mental Capacity Act Manual, 2008, Third Edition, Sweet and Maxwell, p.18, para.1-031

made by the patient, however grave the consequences. The view of the patient may reflect a difference in values rather than an absence of competence and the assessment of capacity should be approached with this firmly in mind. The doctors must not allow their emotional reaction to or strong disagreement with the decision of the patient to cloud their judgment in answering the primary question whether the patient has the mental capacity to make the decision".[119]

In *Masterman-Lister v Jewell* Wright J. said:

"Although the opinions of skilled and experienced medical practitioners are a very important element in the evidence to be considered by the court, that element has to be considered in conjunction with any other evidence that there may be about the manner in which the subject of the enquiry actually has conducted his everyday life and affairs".[120]

Finally, in *Lindsay v Wood* Stanley Burnton J. said:

"When considering the question of capacity, psychiatrists and psychologists will normally wish to take into account all aspects of the personality and behaviour of the person in question, including vulnerability to exploitation. However, vulnerability to exploitation does not of itself lead to the conclusion that there is a lack of capacity. Many people who have full capacity are vulnerable to exploitation, or more so than most other people. Many people make rash and irresponsible decisions, but are of full capacity. The issue is whether the person concerned has the mental capacity to make a rational decision".[121]

These decisions are a reflection of the priority that is accorded to autonomy in law and more specifically to the right to make decisions in accordance with one's own value system even when the decision will have consequences for one's own life, health and well-being. Therefore, it seems reasonable to argue that a finding for or against decision-making capacity should be based on whether the patient is able to understand, use and weigh treatment information in the balance and can comprehend the

---

[119] Ibid

[120] *Masterman-Lister v Jewell [2002] EWHC 417 QB*, para 16; Jones, Richard, Mental Capacity Act Manual, 2008, Third Edition, Sweet and Maxwell, p.19, para.1-032

[121] *Lindsay v Wood [2006] EWHC 2895 QB*, para.18; Jones, Richard, Mental Capacity Act Manual, 2008, Third Edition, Sweet and Maxwell, p.19, para.1-032

likely consequences of deciding to exercise the right of choice one way rather than another in the light of their own values, beliefs and preferences.

However, whilst there will be clear cases of patient incompetence, such as when a person is unconscious or in a persistent vegetative state, on what basis should a doctor decide in other instances of borderline or fluctuating competence whether the patient is competent or incompetent to make their own decisions in the absence of any knowledge and understanding of the patient and their values, beliefs and preferences other than on the basis of medical knowledge and clinical experience? In other words knowledge of the patient and their values should mark the designated starting point for a discussion on capacity because an absence of such knowledge will potentially leave doctors unsure of what they are aiming for when assessing whether the patient is competent to decide. Moreover, different doctors might come to different conclusions about the patient's ability to decide. Therefore, the patient's own value system introduces coherence where currently there is none in deciding whether the patient is competent to decide.

The Power to Decide and Act on behalf of Persons who Lack Decision-Making Capacity

As a person who lacks decision-making capacity is not capable of making decisions and acting autonomously they are prevented from consenting to or refusing to consent to a medical treatment and instead someone else must make decisions and act on behalf of the patient.[122] The mentally incapacitated patient is deemed to be incapable of furthering their own welfare and other interests. On the other hand English courts have unreservedly accepted that a patient's body is inviolable such that any physically invasive medical treatment or procedure, however trivial, is unlawful unless authorised by consent or other lawful authority.[123] So on what authority is medical intervention justified and in particular is it possible to consent to treatment for and on behalf of a mentally incapacitated patient?

---

[122] Mental Capacity Act 2005; Brock, Dan W., Medical Ethics, 2007, Blackwell Publishing, Chapter 7, p.135

[123] Mental Capacity Act 2005, s.5; *Re F (Mental Patient: Sterilisation) [1990] 2 AC 1 HL*

Next of Kin: No Automatic Power to Consent

Contrary to popular belief family members have no legal right to consent to medical treatment on behalf of their mentally incapacitated relative.[124] Nevertheless, the courts have stated that medical practitioners should consult relatives and friends prior to administering treatment when the interests of the patient will not suffer from any ensuing delay.[125] This is desirable for two reasons. First, because it may reveal that the patient has made an anticipatory choice which would be binding on the practitioner if it was valid and applicable in the circumstances giving rise to decision.[126] Alternatively information may be revealed as to the personal wishes of the patient and the choice they would have made if in a position to decide and these are factors that a physician would be bound to take into account in deciding what is in the best interests of the patient.[127]

Indeed some academics have suggested that whilst the doctor's position in such a case is not easy, because of the many factors they must consider, the involvement of friends and family in the decision-making process could be of value in diminishing the likelihood of a patient feeling aggrieved at the invasion of their bodily integrity.[128]

LPA's: Conferring Power and Authority to Consent

Alternatively persons can create a lasting power of attorney (LPA) to formally appoint and confer authority on a specific other(s) to make welfare, including health, decisions on their behalf.[129] Whilst a strict set of formalities must be observed or complied with in creating an LPA[130] it does mean that the appointed person or donee may either consent or refuse to consent to medical treatment on behalf of the donor unless their rights in this respect are restricted because the donor has capacity to make the particular healthcare decision,[131] or has since made a legally valid and

---

[124] *Re T (Adult: Refusal of Treatment) [1992] 4 All ER 649 CA*
[125] *Re T (Adult: Refusal of Treatment) [1993] Fam. 95 CA*, Lord Donaldson, para.103
[126] Ibid
[127] Ibid
[128] Mason, J.K., McCall Smith, R.A., Laurie, G.T., Law and Medical Ethics, 2002, Sixth Edition, Butterworths, para. 10.16
[129] Mental Capacity Act 2005, s.9, Code of Practice, Chapter 7, para.7.21
[130] Mental Capacity Act 2005, s.9(2)&(3)
[131] Ibid, s.11(7)(a)

applicable advance decision to refuse the proposed medical treatment,[132] or the decision concerns life-preserving treatment which an attorney has no power to accept or reject on behalf of the donor unless the LPA specifically authorises this.[133] The donor can of course restrict the powers of the attorney either by specifying the powers that the donee is granted or by specifying the types of decisions that the donee is not empowered to make.[134]

Selecting a Surrogate Decision-Maker

Obviously people differ in their reasons for making certain arrangements and so it is often dangerous to make assumptions and generalisations about what prompted or motivated them to do so. However, that is precisely what I am now about to do. It seems to me that the factor influencing anyone that would go to the trouble and expense of creating a lasting power of attorney is a strong desire to appoint someone they trust to make decisions in accordance with their pre-existing values, beliefs and preferences. This must surely be the case when they were not content to leave matters in the hands of a stranger, albeit someone, such as a doctor, who is professionally and legally required to make decisions and act in their best interests.[135]

The primary concern could not therefore have been to choose someone who cares about their well-being per se as Brock has suggested. A preferable view is that the attorney, who will most likely be a close relative or friend of the patient and will therefore be both familiar with and to them, will, most importantly, also be someone who is familiar with their personal values and attitudes to life or more specifically to what constitutes a good life for them and death also and can to that extent be relied upon to care enough about their personal sense of well-being to make decisions in conformity with them.[136] Arguably therefore, the donor

---

[132] Mental Capacity Act 2005, s.11(7)(b) However, in accordance with Mental Capacity Act 2005, s.25(2)(b) if the advance decision pre-dates the LPA a donee has the right to consent to or refuse the treatment in question but they can also choose to uphold the advance decision of the donor

[133] Mental Capacity Act 2005, s.11(7)©

[134] Mental Capacity Act 2005, s.11(8)(b); Jones, Richard, Mental Capacity Act Manual, 2008, Third Edition, Sweet and Maxwell, p.49, para.1-096

[135] Mental Capacity Act 2005, s.4

[136] Brock, Dan W., Medical Ethics, 2007, Blackwell Publishing, Chapter 7, p.136

seeks to appoint someone they trust to uphold their former autonomous wishes in decisions concerning them.

What this suggests, is that when there are doubts about whether a patient's partially or questionably competent preferences should be respected, physicians should be guided by the patient's previous values and beliefs and not simply by the patient's best medical interests as those might be understood from a medical perspective and in creating an LPA an attorney has been cast into the role of providing the relevant insight.[137] So in this situation diminished competence does not eliminate obligations based on respect for a patient's autonomy as expressed in their history of values and beliefs.[138]

Predicting Preferences

Will the attorney be able to accurately predict what the patient would have wanted? The evidence is mixed. Fagerlin and Schneider, for example, have reported that although we might hope that intimates already know the patient's mind, so that only modest demands need be made on their interpreting skills, many studies show that when surrogates are asked to predict what treatment the patient would choose approximately 70 per cent of predictions was correct.[139] Considered in the context of life and death decision-making these authors do not find these results particularly inspiring.[140]

Brock provides an explanation for why surrogate decision-makers might find it difficult to predict the patient's preferences:

> *"Since surrogates will usually be a close family member or friend of the patient, their job will be to use their knowledge of the patient to attempt to decide what the patient would have wanted in the circumstances. Sometimes this will be relatively clear as a result of previous explicit discussions with the patient about the patient's treatment wishes, although these too will usually have been relatively general and so require some*

---

[137] McCullough, Laurence B., Medical Care for Elderly Patients with Diminished Competence: An Ethical Analysis, 1984, Journal of the American Geriatrics Society, vol.32 part 2 pp.150-153, p.152

[138] Ibid

[139] Fagerlin, Angela, Schneider, Carl E., 2004, Enough The Failure of the Living Will, Hastings Center Report, March-April, p.36

[140] Ibid

interpretation by the surrogate for the decision at hand. In other cases, in the absence of explicit prior discussions, surrogates will have to use their general knowledge of the patient's values and desires to make a judgment about what the patient would likely have wanted. In either case, surrogates will often have to make judgments in the face of some uncertainty about what the patient would have wanted".[141]

Mixed Values

Laurence McCullough focuses on the problem that all too often surrogate decision-makers mix their own values with those of the patient and this leads to uncertainty in the decision-making process. This is what he has to say:

"Recognition of the importance of the patient's value history helps to clarify the role of family members in the case of patients with diminished competence: they become an important source for helping the physician to construct the required value history. Because family members mix their own values and beliefs with the patient's values histories, the physician might be uncertain how to proceed in light of requests of family members for or against diagnostic and treatment interventions. In these circumstances, the physician should help family members to distinguish their own values and beliefs from those of the patient, by having them focus on what the patient would want.

Determining a patient's value history post hoc will frequently be a difficult matter. As a consequence, the best way to base diagnostic and treatment decisions on a patient's value history is to develop that history in advance of the patient's decline to a condition of diminished or partial competence".[142]

There is also the issue of whether the donee will at some stage begin to relate to their family member or friend as an incompetent person who has needs and desires that conflict with those of their previous competent self. In many respects this would be an entirely natural thing to happen if they cared about them and continued to have a relationship of sorts with the patient. On the other hand it is not unknown for persons to desert a sinking ship so to speak. Richard Jones, for example, has noted the

---

[141] Brock, Dan W., Medical Ethics, 2007, Blackwell Publishing, Chapter 7, p.138

[142] McCullough, Laurence B., Medical Care for Elderly Patients with Diminished Competence: An Ethical Analysis, 1984, Journal of the American Geriatrics Society, vol.32 part 2 pp.150-153, p.153

comment of the House of Lords Select Committee on Medical Ethics that personal relationships are not immutable.[143] So at either extreme there may be some difficulty in ensuring the continued objectivity of the proxy decision-maker (even when acting in good faith).[144]

Conflict of Interests

This, like most others, is potentially a difficult area. There is some evidence that in respect of LPA's for property and affairs that financial abuse will arise in a small proportion of cases.[145] Potential conflicts can also arise between the attorney and patient in respect of welfare matters.[146] For example, a decision to place the patient in a care home might have the effect of reducing the potential inheritance of the donee.[147] We have also observed in previous chapters that people are capable of behaving altruistically and will therefore consider or promote the interests of others, in particular family, friends and close associates, above their own self-interests when it comes to making decisions including those concerning their own health and welfare.[148] In this regard Brock has remarked that it should not always be assumed that surrogates should never give weight to their own interests, since in some cases there may be good reason to believe that the patient selected this surrogate in order for them to be able to do just that.[149]

Monitoring

Certain formalities must be complied with in order for an attorney to be permitted to make welfare decisions on behalf of another. In particular an LPA must be registered at the office of the Public Guardian.[150] Whereupon it becomes a function of that office to oversee the role of the donee and where necessary to investigate any complaints about the way in which they are discharging their powers and authority.[151] If a serious

---

[143] Jones, Richard, Mental Capacity Act Manual, 2008, Third Edition, Sweet and Maxwell, p.48, para.1-094
[144] Ibid
[145] Ibid
[146] Ibid
[147] Ibid
[148] *Re Y (An Adult Patient) (Transplant: Bone Marrow) [1996] BMLR 111*
[149] Brock, Dan W., Medical Ethics, 2007, Blackwell Publishing, Chapter 7, p.139
[150] Mental Capacity Act 2005, s.58(1)(a)
[151] Ibid, s.58(1)(h)

complaint was lodged or if the Public Guardian had misgivings about the conduct of the attorney they can report the matter to the court[152] and the court could give directions regarding how the LPA should be used. Alternatively they could decide, if sufficiently concerned about the welfare of the patient, to revoke the LPA.[153]

What Duties does an Attorney have?

The MCA imposes certain duties that apply to anybody who is required to make decisions and to take action on behalf of a mentally incapacitated person or patient. More specifically an attorney must follow the Act's statutory principles;[154] make decisions in the donor's best interests;[155] have regard to the guidance contained in the Code of Practice;[156] act within the scope of the authority the LPA provides for[157] and in certain circumstances to comply with any directions, or decisions, the Court of Protection might make,[158] such as producing records or specific information or documentation.[159] Finally, an attorney cannot usually delegate their authority to someone else unless specifically authorised by the donor.[160]

Fiduciary Duty

An attorney appointed under an LPA acts as the chosen agent of the donor.[161] Under the law of agency an act of an agent that is done within the scope of their authority is binding on the principal which in this case will be the donor.[162] As such an attorney's role carries with it a great deal of power.[163] However, a donee is also bound by a number of common law

---

[152] Ibid, s.58
[153] Ibid, s.22(4)(b)
[154] Mental Capacity Act 2005, s.9(4)(a); Jones, Richard, Mental Capacity Act Manual, 2008, Third Edition, Sweet and Maxwell, p.52, para.1-105
[155] Ibid
[156] Mental Capacity Act 2005, s.42(4)(a); Jones, Richard, Mental Capacity Act Manual, 2008, Third Edition, Sweet and Maxwell, p.52, para.1-105
[157] Ibid, s.9(4)(b); Ibid
[158] Ibid, s.23(2)(a); Ibid
[159] Mental Capacity Act 2005, s.23(3)(a)&(b); Code of Practice para.7.65
[160] Mental Capacity Act 2005, Code of Practice para.7.61
[161] Mental Capacity Act 2005, chapter 7, para.7.58; Jones, Richard, Mental Capacity Act Manual, 2008, Third Edition, Sweet and Maxwell, p.52, para.1-105
[162] Ibid
[163] Mental Capacity Act 2005, Code of Practice, chapter 7, para.7.58

duties towards the donor when they act as their agent.[164] Amongst other things a donee must act with due care and skill and in good faith when making decisions. Acting in good faith means that an attorney should act with honesty and integrity at all times.[165] This means that an attorney must try to ensure that their decisions do not go against a decision the donor made while they still had capacity.[166] One assumes therefore that an attorney should be required to respect the value system of a donor that was disclosed in a living will, for instance. In this way the pre-existing values, beliefs and preferences of the patient are made relevant to decisions concerning them.

Additionally, an attorney must not permit their own interests to conflict with those of the donor, i.e. they must not take advantage of their position and in particular must not benefit themselves but benefit the donor.[167] Neither must an attorney allow any other influences to affect their decisions or the way in which they act.[168] This could mean that an attorney should not be influenced by the values and preferences of the incompetent where these would conflict with their former autonomously held values. More importantly, these features spell out the special nature of the relationship that exists between the parties and also explains why it is treated as a fiduciary relationship in law.[169]

What Standard should the Surrogate Apply in Making Decisions?

Here the Act is somewhat anomalous in adopting the standard of best interests[170] in preference to that of substituted judgment which would require an attorney to make the decision the donor would make if competence was notionally restored.[171] Is the difference between these two standards more imagined than real? Well, to decide what is in

---

[164] Ibid; Jones, Richard, Mental Capacity Act Manual, 2008, Third Edition, Sweet and Maxwell, p.52, para.1-105

[165] Mental Capacity Act 2005, Code of Practice, chapter 7, para.7.63

[166] Ibid, para.7.63

[167] Mental Capacity Act 2005, Code of Practice, chapter 7, para.7.60; Jones, Richard, Mental Capacity Act Manual, 2008, Third Edition, Sweet and Maxwell, p.52, para.1-105

[168] Mental Capacity Act 2005, Code of Practice, chapter 7, para.7.60

[169] Ibid

[170] Mental Capacity Act 2005, s.1(5)

[171] *Re T (Adult: Refusal of Treatment) [1992] 4 All ER 649 CA*

someone's best interests decision-makers must have regard to the statutory principles and welfare checklist. In this regard they must consider, so far as is reasonably possible, the patient's past and present wishes and feelings, and in particular any relevant written statement they may have made at a time when they had decision-making capacity;[172] the beliefs and values that would be likely to influence their decision if they had capacity[173] and any other factors that they would be likely to consider if able to do so.[174] An attorney must also take into account, if it is practicable and appropriate to consult them, the views of anyone the person has named as someone to be consulted on the matter in question or on matters of that kind,[175] anyone engaged in caring for the person or who is interested in their welfare,[176] i.e. medical professionals, any other donee of an LPA[177] and finally any deputy appointed by the court.[178]

Taking these factors into account a best interests decision is likely to differ from one based on, or that was more closely approximated to the standards and practices upheld by substituted judgment. This is because best interests fails to incorporate a method for deciding. As a consequence the standard does not apportion any particular weight to the pre-existing autonomous wishes, values and beliefs of formerly competent patients. Moreover, the designated decision-maker, in this case the attorney, must consult significant others in order to obtain their views, including those of the doctor who recommended the treatment currently under consideration.

Regard must also be had for the principle of the least restrictive option, which could be construed as an organising principle.[179] Essentially decision-makers are encouraged to consider what other options for treatment exist that are as effective as the one proposed but in a way that is less restrictive of the patient's (future) rights and freedom of action.[180] So non-treatment is an option.[181] As I have previously commented this provision has a warm glow about it because it is both thoughtful and

---

[172] Mental Capacity Act 2005, s.4(6)(a)
[173] Ibid, s.4(6)(b)
[174] Ibid, s.4(6)(c)
[175] Ibid, s.4(7)(a)
[176] Ibid, s.4(7)(b)
[177] Ibid, s.4(7)(c)
[178] Ibid, s.4(7)(d)
[179] Ibid, s.1(6)
[180] Ibid, s.1(6)
[181] Ibid, s.1(6)

thought provoking as it reminds decision-makers, if a reminder were needed, to place the patient at the heart of the decision-making process.[182] Cynics might, of course, argue that this principle has been couched in terms that seek to persuade an ambivalent attorney around to a consensus viewpoint, i.e. well we could try this, regarding treatment or non-treatment on the grounds that the decision will least offend against the donor's rights and interests which is a pretty powerful argument when faced with indecision and one that might help soothe a troubled conscience. Yet aside from all of that the provision, though well-intentioned, fails to state exactly whose rights and interests are being promoted. Is it those of the incompetent or their former competent self? As these could be quite different things bearing in mind the former has a right to beneficence through which their current wishes and feelings deserve respect whilst the latter has a right to self-determine matters in accordance with their former values, beliefs and preferences. If, as seems likely, these are in conflict the standard does not enlighten us about how they should be balanced? So as the law stands a person who wanted to ensure that health and welfare decisions were taken in accordance with their former values has two options. They can either attempt to make an advance treatment decision or impose any conditions or restrictions onto the decision-making process and to make these known in the LPA as the attorney must comply with these.[183]

A Doctor's Right to Challenge

Both doctors and donees are required to work in the patient's best interests. The attorney should be given information about the nature of the treatment that is being proposed and its consequences for the patient. Essentially, the attorney is given the information that the patient would have received if competent to decide.[184] However, 'best interests' is open to interpretation simply because the test is not fully defined and does not incorporate a method for deciding. This might lead to differences in the factors that were considered by the parties.[185] Differences could also emerge from the way in which certain factors under consideration have been weighted or ranked during the decision-making process.

---

[182] Mental Capacity Act 2005, Code of Practice, see the Foreword by Lord Falconer

[183] Mental Capacity Act 2005, s.9(4)(b)

[184] Jones, Richard, Mental Capacity Act Manual, 2008, Third Edition, Sweet and Maxwell, p.55, para.1-114

[185] Ibid, p.56, para.1-119

An LPA, unless restricted, gives an attorney a right to refuse treatment that has been recommended in the patient's best interests by a medical professional. This is an important function of any attorney when the law's requirement for consent resides in the right to be maintained inviolate. Yet an attorney might not accurately reflect the patient's wishes for any number of reasons including those discussed earlier in this chapter under 'predicting preferences'. The possibility that a conflict of interests will arise should not be dismissed out of hand either. In this regard Richard Jones reports that the problem is not common but neither is it rare and illustrates how such a conflict can arise; the following example was given in evidence to the Joint Committee for the Mental Capacity Bill by Baroness Finlay:[186]

> *"A lady aged 59 was very ill. Her family appeared to be very concerned about her pain and constantly asked for her diamorphine to be increased. However, we remained unconvinced that her pain was really that severe. In fact, the patient declined increasing doses of diamorphine. Her 60th birthday arrived and was passed with minimal celebration, after which the family visited very little. She became depressed and spoke to one of the night nurses, explaining that the problem was that on her 60th birthday, her fixed-term life insurance policy expired. The family would not now inherit what they thought they would if she had died, and if her drugs had been duly increased".*[187]

The reality that one's attention is being drawn towards is that an attorney has the power to refuse a treatment or procedure on behalf of the patient, although an attorney has no right to refuse life-sustaining treatment unless specifically authorised in the LPA.[188] Therefore, a non-medical donee can override a doctor's clinical judgment as to what treatment the patient should receive.[189] And it might be perfectly possible for a donee to maintain, with some justification, that what has been decided is in the best interests of the patient. However, where a doctor, as medical expert, concludes that the donee has not arrived at a fair and reasonable view of best interests they may as a consequence challenge the decision of the donee in the Court of Protection.[190] This is done by making an application

---

[186] Ibid, p.53, para.1-105
[187] Ibid
[188] Ibid, p.55, para.1-114
[189] Ibid
[190] Ibid, p.56, para.1-119

for a ruling or decision to override that of the donee on the ground that they are not acting in the best interests of the patient.[191]

The question highlighted by some is whether doctors will have the time, energy and motivation to ask a court to override a donee whose determination of best interests appears to them to be defective or questionable.[192] You see it has been argued that a doctor who has no previous experience of the patient and who is confronted by a donee who articulates their views plausibly and forcefully might not have the strength of purpose and the degree of self-belief to refer the matter to the Court.[193]

Exceptions

Most obviously an attorney has no right to insist that a particular form of treatment be provided to the patient. The question of what treatment the patient should receive in their best medical interests remains a matter for the doctor to decide in accordance with what is acceptable medical[194] and professional ethical practice.[195] In addition an attorney has no automatic right to consent to non-therapeutic interventions or treatments such as an organ donation or to refuse basic care, including artificial nutrition and hydration and grooming because such treatment would always be in the best interests of the patient.[196]

One final point of some note is that medical professionals who administer treatment, in contravention of an LPA which provides for an attorney to make the decision in question, is protected from liability unless they are satisfied, at the time of making the decision, that an LPA exists.[197] A similar exception exists in relation to urgent treatment, i.e. treatment that is life-sustaining or that is intended to prevent serious deterioration in a patient's condition.[198] So if there is no time to contact the donee, the healthcare professional may treat the patient in their best interests and

---

[191] Ibid, p.55, para.1-114
[192] Ibid
[193] Ibid, p.56, para.1-119
[194] *Bolam v Friern Hospital Management Committee [1957] 1 WLR 582*
[195] In accordance with the principles of non-maleficence and beneficence
[196] Mental Capacity Act 2005, s.45; Code of Practice, chapter eight, para.8.1
[197] Mental Capacity Act 2005, s.5; Jones, Richard, Mental Capacity Act Manual, 2008, Third Edition, Sweet and Maxwell, p.55, para.1-114
[198] Mental Capacity Act 2005, 6(7)

report the matter to the donee later. [199] This could be an avenue of hope that a medical professional might use to their advantage in any dispute with an attorney about what is in the patient's best interests.

The Jurisdiction of the Courts

Does the court have power to consent on behalf of an adult incompetent patient? The new Court of Protection has no power to consent to treatment on behalf of a mentally incapacitated patient though the court has power, to decide whether a person has capacity to make a particular decision, i.e. questions must be real rather than merely hypothetical,[200] and to make declarations on financial or welfare matters affecting people who lack capacity to decide,[201] based on what is in the best interests of the patient.[202] The Court of Protection's jurisdiction to make declarations is founded on the inherent jurisdiction of the High Court which may be used in appropriate cases to meet circumstances unmet by the scope of legislation.[203] That jurisdiction was not displaced by the MCA.[204] This is consistent with the common law position that was established in *Re F*.[205] In that case the House of Lords determined that the court had no statutory power to consent to treatment because its common law power had been revoked but that it remained open to the court to use its inherent jurisdiction for the protection of vulnerable adults who lack decision-making capacity to make a declaration that a medical treatment or procedure was in a patient's best interests.[206]

---

199 Mental Capacity Act 2005, s.5; Jones, Richard, Mental Capacity Act Manual, 2008, Third Edition, Sweet and Maxwell, p.55, para.1-114
200 The court is not to be used as a legal advice centre
201 Mental Capacity Act 2005, s.15; Code of Practice, chapter 8, Quick summary
202 Herring, Jonathan, Medical Law and Ethics, 2008, Oxford University Press, p.161
203 *KC and NNC v City of Westminster Social and Community Services Dept. and IC (a protected party, by his litigation friend the Official Solicitor) [2008] EWCA Civ 198 CA*; Jones, Richard, Mental Capacity Act Manual, 2008, Third Edition, Sweet and Maxwell, p.61, para.1-137/8
204 Ibid
205 *Re F (Mental Patient: Sterilisation) [1990] 2 AC 1 HL*
206 Ibid

Prerogative Power: The Parens Patriae Jurisdiction

The parens patriae jurisdiction emanates from an ancient prerogative[207] power of the sovereign to care for the welfare and other affairs of persons of unsound mind.[208]

Power was conferred by Royal Warrant under the Sign Manual[209] and subsequent Warrants extended that jurisdiction to the Lord Chancellor and eventually to other judicial officers.[210] However, in *Re F* all members of the Court of Appeal and House of Lords agreed that their power to exercise the jurisdiction ended on the 1st November 1960. Section 1 of the Mental Health Act 1959 swept away previous legislative provisions dealing with incapable adults and at the same time revoked the Warrant under the Sign Manual thus removing the jurisdiction from the common law completely.[211] Rejecting the view of the majority Neill LJ was inclined to think that the power remained but had fallen into a state of abeyance so that it was incapable of being exercised adding that '*it would require clear statutory words to remove from the Crown a prerogative power which has vested in the Crown since at least 1325*'.[212]

The Significance of the Jurisdiction: To Benefit an Incompetent

The importance of the jurisdiction is that it permitted a court to consent or to refuse consent to medical treatment on behalf of an incapable patient.[213] Indeed case law dating back to 1603 confirms that the jurisdiction had never been limited by definition and therefore those who exercised power under it had an inherent right to do whatever was for the benefit of an incompetent.[214] In this regard the jurisdiction is interesting in distinguishing between formerly and never competent persons, adopting a

---

207 A privileged form of power that is limited to a person of a particular rank
208 Kennedy & Grubb, Medical Law, 2000, Third Edition, Butterworths, page 827
209 A royal sign manual is the name given to the autographed signature of the monarch which is placed on a document or warrant conferring the appointment of someone to a particular position of authority
210 Kennedy & Grubb, Medical Law, 2000, Third Edition, Butterworths, page 827
211 Mason, J.K., McCall Smith, R.A., Laurie, G.T., Law and Medical Ethics, 2002, Sixth Edition, Butterworths, para. 10.32
212 *Re F (Mental Patient: Sterilisation) [1990] 2 AC 1 HL*, page 26
213 Mason, J.K., McCall Smith, R.A., Laurie, G.T., Law and Medical Ethics, 2002, Sixth Edition, Butterworths, para. 10.31
214 *E v Eve [1986] 2 S.C.R. 388*, para 40

fiduciary decision-making standard in respect of the former though not the latter.[215] This reflected the need to maximise the interests of the beneficiaries and ensured that those charged with exercising the power could in the future be held to account for their decisions and actions.

The Jurisdiction Distinguished between Formerly and Never Competents

As previously indicated the prerogative was originally exercised by the monarch, as the parent of the country, to care for persons of unsound mind. The jurisdiction therefore came into effect when it was found that a person was in need of protection and it had been determined that they were no longer capable of acting on their own behalf.[216] However, in accordance with the statute De Prerogativa Regis 1324 an important distinction was made between lunatics and natural fools or idiots.

Consequently once the jurisdiction had been invoked different administrative arrangements were created for persons who were similarly situated. The King took jurisdiction over natural idiots as a guardian and lunatics as a trustee.[217] Lunatics were presumed to be temporarily incompetent adults who previously had the capacity for self-determination and therefore a life that would be characterised by the conventions of the day. This would include engaging in transactions, managing things and people, and making and enforcing promises.[218] As a response the statute provided an administrator who was responsible to him. Moreover, the lunatic was given a right to an accounting which he would be able to enforce upon his recovery. All of the legal obligations owed by the King and the administrators were duties owed to the lunatic and to his household as an extension of himself.[219] Whereas the section governing idiots states explicitly that its purpose is to prevent the disinheritance of the idiot's heirs.[220]

---

[215] Payton S., The Concept of the Person in the Parens Patriae Jurisdiction over Previously Competent Persons, Journal of Medicine and Philosophy, 1992, December, 17(6), p.626
[216] Ibid, p.621
[217] Ibid, p.626
[218] Ibid, p.628
[219] Ibid
[220] Ibid

Right to an Accounting regarding Property and Affairs: Fiduciary Decision-Making Standard Implied

A fiduciary standard is implied in the use of this prerogative power in relation to previously competent persons.[221] This is based on the fact that decision-makers must adopt an attitude of respectful friendship toward the incompetent person, just as though they were to be accountable to the person himself, were he to recover his faculties and become competent once more.[222] Consequently, decision-makers were required to maximise the interests of the beneficiaries and to exercise loyalty and good faith in the performance of their duties.[223] There is therefore an underlying concern with the agent's state of mind or more precisely with preventing them from taking advantage of their position and this is achieved by introducing the notion of an accounting which is intended to promote honesty, transparency, fairness and an absence of intent to do harm when acting on behalf of an otherwise vulnerable person.[224]

The State meanwhile must not impose policies or advance interests of its own in the supervision of the affairs of an incompetent, apart from interests arising legitimately out of the state's institutional interest in providing competent administration for the benefit of the incompetents themselves.[225] As a surrogate decision-maker could be required to give an account of decisions made and action taken on behalf of a complete stranger, State responsibility would appear to reside in the provision of a comprehensive decision-making framework that would assist surrogate decision-makers to carry out their more specific duties. The framework for decision would set out which criteria are relevant to consider and put forward a method for deciding the weight that should be given to the individual factors under consideration. This should narrow the scope for paternalistic tendencies to emerge, would prevent arbitrary and other misuses of executive powers and lead to certainty and confidence in surrogate decision-making processes.

---

[221] Ibid, 605-45

[222] Ibid

[223] Ibid

[224] www.yourdictionary.com/good-faith

[225] Payton S., The Concept of the Person in the Parens Patriae Jurisdiction over Previously Competent Persons, Journal of Medicine and Philosophy, 1992, December, 17(6), 605-45

State Administration

The obligations of the King were initially passed down to the Lord Chancellor. At that time this office was awarded to men of the cloth who were required to exercise judgment in accordance with what their conscience told them was the morally correct thing to do. This created the problem that decision-making was to an extent arbitrary reflecting the values and influences of the decision-maker. Eventually, as the work of the Lord Chancellor's office grew it became necessary to delegate responsibility to a senior member(s) of the judiciary in the Chancery Courts whereupon decision-making processes were governed by legal principles and rules.

However, as keeper of the King's conscience in the exercise of so widely drawn power, the Lord Chancellor required a flexible system of principles, rules and remedies that could be adapted to meet the needs and circumstances of a particular case. Accordingly, the power was exercised by giving effect to the court's equitable jurisdiction. Common law rules, principles and remedies were deemed to be too inflexible to be of any use to decision-makers in deciding how to benefit an assisted person.

Equitable remedies[226] proved popular and came to rival and conflict with those of the common law as people generally seemed interested in the court ordering someone to do something or prohibiting some act as opposed to claiming damages for detriments suffered. The effect of this was to bring the separate jurisdictions of equity and the common law into dispute. In the end it was settled that in the event of a conflict between equity and the common law, equity would prevail.[227]

Yet ultimately it was decided that certainty in the legal system was of greater value to the public and so the courts of the common law and equity were merged to produce one unified court system in which both systems of law could be applied by the same courts.[228] This led to a simplified administrative system of law and greater judicial accountability for judgments handed down due to the loss of the independent status previously enjoyed by Chancery Court judges. Thus producing a legal

---

[226] Injunctive relief

[227] *Earl of Oxford's Case (1615) 1 Ch Rep 1*

[228] Judicature Acts 1873-75

system based on precedents that were relied upon to introduce conformity where previously there was none.

Summary

The parens patriae jurisdiction enabled the court to consent or to refuse medical treatment on behalf of an incompetent patient. However, the effect of the revocation of the Sign Manual was to remove the jurisdiction from the common law.[229] Accordingly, the courts no longer have power to consent or to refuse to consent to medical treatment on behalf of a mentally incapacitated adult patient which falls outside of the scope of Mental Health legislation.[230]

Court Appointed Deputies

As previously indicated the Court of Protection can make declarations,[231] decisions, or orders on health and welfare matters affecting those who lack capacity to make their own decisions.[232] However, in circumstances where the need to make decisions is ongoing, such as might happen when a person suffers a brain injury or has dementia, the court can decide to appoint a deputy in a situation where there is no LPA.[233] In deciding whether it is in someone's best interests to appoint a deputy the court must apply the Acts principles, the best interests checklist[234] and have regard for two further principles that provide guidance about the practice of conferring discretionary decision-making powers.[235] The first counsels the court to make the decision itself[236] whilst the second guides the court to limit the scope and duration of deputy powers.[237]

A decision to appoint a deputy requires the court to decide who to appoint. The selection process will focus on the likelihood of someone being a reliable and trustworthy agent of the incompetent. In this regard they must

---

[229] Mason, J.K., McCall Smith, R.A., Laurie, G.T., Law and Medical Ethics, 2002, Sixth Edition, Butterworths, para. 10.32
[230] Ibid
[231] Mental Capacity Act 2005, s.15
[232] Ibid, s.16(2)(a)
[233] Mental Capacity Act 2005, s.16(2)(b); Code of Practice, chapter 8, para.8.25
[234] Mental Capacity Act 2005, s.16(3)
[235] Ibid, s.16(4)
[236] Ibid, s.16(4)(a)
[237] Ibid, s.16(4)(b)

consider whether the person has the requisite level of skill and competence to fulfil the responsibilities of that office and to carry out the task they have been given.[238] Often the person appointed will be a member of the incompetent's family or someone else who knows them well, accepting of course that the patient did not care to make them an LPA. However, this cannot be the solution in cases where the incompetent has no extended family, i.e. brothers and sisters or children of their own, their parents might be dead or quite elderly and they might also be divorced or separated - a lot of ifs, I know, but it is not so uncommon nowadays. Also, bear in mind that court involvement will often be precipitated by ongoing disputes between family members or family members and medical professionals about what is in the patient's best interests. Consequently, the court could decide that the patient's interests would be better served by someone who is independent of the family.[239] The issue then is whether the deputy is more likely to be influenced by medical opinion, i.e. whatever form of treatment the doctor recommends is in the patient's best medical interests, simply because they have no prior knowledge of the patient but at the same time may not feel able to rely on information, imparted by family and/or friends, about the patient's former autonomous values, beliefs and preferences to weigh in the balance. Accordingly, it is possible to see that a practical solution to a legal problem can yield undesirable consequences for the patient, whose rights and interests are at stake, bearing in mind that a deputy's powers to consent or to refuse a medical treatment or procedure are limited only so far as refusing life-sustaining treatment. These decisions are taken on behalf of the patient by the court.[240]

In all other important respects the discussion about LPA's will apply to a court appointed deputy. Consequently, a deputy has a general legal duty to make only those decisions that fall within the scope of their authority or as outlined by the Court.[241] They must also follow the statutory principles[242] and have regard to the guidance contained in the Code of Practice when making decisions in the patient's best interests.[243] Indeed the court can revoke the appointment of a deputy or vary the powers

---

[238] Code of Practice, Chapter 8, para.8.32
[239] Ibid, para.8.33, 8.38, 8.39
[240] Mental Capacity Act 2005 s.20(5); Code of Practice, Chapter 8, para.8.46
[241] Mental Capacity Act 2005, s.16(5)
[242] Ibid, s.1
[243] Ibid, s.4

conferred on them if they act,[244] or propose to act,[245] in a way that contravenes that authority or is not in the best interests of the patient. Additionally, the court may request that a deputy submit reports to the Public Guardian at various intervals.[246]

Lastly, and most importantly in the context of this thesis, the MCA confirms that a deputy is to be treated as 'the agent' of the incapacitated patient when they make decisions and act on their behalf.[247] This means that the deputy, like an LPA, has legal duties arising from the law of agency to the person they represent so that in addition to the ordinary duty to act with due care and skill in the performance of their duties a deputy is made a fiduciary to the patient and must not therefore take advantage of their position but should instead seek to maximise the interests of the patient whilst avoiding possible conflicts of interest.[248] Consequently, a deputy must act in good faith in carrying out their legal duties, which means that they must act with honesty and integrity at all times in determining what should happen in the patient's best interests.[249] In this regard the Code of Practice explains that a deputy must try to make sure that their decisions do not go against a decision the person made while they still had capacity unless it would be in their best interests to do so![250]

Medical Professionals

If the medical welfare of all other adult patients who suffer loss of decision-making capacity was not to suffer some other lawful authority was needed to justify a decision to administer treatment in the absence of patient consent.

The Defence of Necessity: An Exception to the Need for Consent

In this regard the MCA establishes that a doctor who administers a treatment or procedure in the absence of consent may still not be liable for

[244] Ibid, s.16(8)(a)
[245] Ibid, s.16(8)(b)
[246] Ibid, s.19(9)(b)
[247] Mental Capacity Act 2005, s.19(6); Code of Practice, chapter 8, para.8.55-68
[248] Ibid
[249] Mental Capacity Act 2005, s.19(6); Code of Practice, chapter 8, para.8.63
[250] Mental Capacity Act 2005, Code of Practice, chapter 8, para.8.63

a battery where they can raise the defence of necessity.[251] The defence could be raised where it would be unreasonable as opposed to inconvenient to delay medical intervention[252] and where it could be shown that the doctor acted in the best interests of the patient[253] and there is no known objection to treatment, for example, a prior decision of the patient to refuse the proposed treatment.[254]

What Aspects of a Person's Treatment and Care does the Doctrine of Necessity Govern?

The MCA determines, in cases where someone suffers a loss of decision-making capacity, that the principle of necessity should displace respect for the fundamental principle of bodily inviolability.[255] In a civilized society patients should not be denied medical care and treatment simply because they are unable to consent to it. Nevertheless, as the right to bodily inviolability is derived through the right to self-determination the general law seeks to prohibit doctors from administering a medical treatment without first obtaining the authority of their patients. Thus the law's requirement for consent resides in the fundamental right of all persons to be maintained inviolate so emphasising the importance of the right to refuse necessary and appropriate medical treatment. If, therefore, we are not to downgrade the status of mentally incompetents it is equally important that necessity should not be a defence that applies

---

[251] Mental Capacity Act 2005, s.5(1)(a); *Re F (Mental patient: Sterilisation) [1990] 2 AC 1 HL*, page 75; Mason, J.K., McCall Smith, R.A., Laurie, G.T., Law and Medical Ethics, 2002, Sixth Edition, Butterworths, para. 10.12.; Grubb, A., Principles of Medical Law, 2004, Second Edition, Oxford University Press, para. 3.55; Stauch, Marc, Wheat, Kay, Tingle John, 2002, Second Edition, Sourcebook on Medical Law, Cavendish Publishing, p.169

[252] Mental Capacity Act 2005, s.5(1)(b)(i); *Re F (Mental patient: Sterilisation) [1990] 2 AC 1 HL*, page 75

[253] Mental Capacity Act 2005, s.5(1)(b)(ii); *Re F (Mental patient: Sterilisation) [1990] 2 AC 1 HL*, page 75

[254] Mental Capacity Act 2005, s.5(4); *Re F (Mental patient: Sterilisation) [1990] 2 AC 1 HL*, page 75; *Re T (Adult: Refusal of Treatment) [1992] 4 All ER 649 CA*; Mason, J.K., McCall Smith, R.A., Laurie, G.T., Law and Medical Ethics, 2002, Sixth Edition, Butterworths, para. 10.12.; Grubb, A., Principles of Medical Law, 2004, Second Edition, Oxford University Press, para. 3.55; Stauch, Marc, Wheat, Kay, Tingle John, 2002, Second Edition, Sourcebook on Medical Law, Cavendish Publishing, p.169

[255] Mental Capacity Act 2005, s.1(3)&(5); s.2(1); s.3; s.4; s.5; *Re F (Mental Patient: Sterilisation) [1990] 2 AC 1 HL*

indiscriminately. In particular, it seems reasonable that medical professionals should be required to distinguish between those who are likely to regain competency and those who have been rendered permanently or semi-permanently incompetent.

Temporarily Incompetent Patient – Emergency Cases

In respect of patients rendered temporarily incompetent, perhaps as a result of an accident, Lord Goff determined, in the case of *Re F*, that physicians should do no more than is reasonably required, in the best interests of the patient. This would enable patients who are expected to both re-gain consciousness and the requisite decision-making capacity to be consulted about the prospect of further treatment.[256]

Permanently Incompetent Patients

In circumstances where incapacity is of a permanent or semi-permanent nature the defence can be raised to justify a wider range of treatment and care. About this Lord Goff has previously stated that:

> "*Where the state of affairs is permanent or semi-permanent, as may be so in the case of a mentally disordered person, there is no point in waiting to obtain the patient's consent. The need to care for him is obvious, and the doctor must then act in the best interests of the patient, just as if he had received his patient's consent to do so. Were this not so, much useful treatment and care could be denied to the unfortunate*".[257]

The (Ir)Relevance of an Emergency

As the principle can be used to meet the needs of permanently incompetent patients, who are likely to require ongoing care of a fairly basic nature, it is established that the principle is one of necessity and not emergency, i.e. the doctrine cannot be defined exclusively in relation to medical interventions.[258] This means that the defence could be relied on by carers, relatives and friends, who were also involved in looking after the patient.[259]

---

[256] *Re F (Mental Patient: Sterilisation) [1990] 2 AC 1 HL*, page 77
[257] Ibid
[258] Ibid, page 75
[259] Ibid, page 76

No Requirement for a Pre-Existing or Continuing Relationship

If the necessity itself provided the justification for intervention taken on behalf of the assisted person it was inevitable that there should be no requirement for a pre-existing or continuing relationship between the patient and carer.[260] This is to an extent a practical matter since physicians may move to another hospital, auxiliary staff may change jobs and relationships between the permanently incompetent person and their family and friends may change over time.

A further consequence of this inherent flexibility is that the interventions of both professional and non-professional persons can be justified by the principle. The actions of physicians are determined, inter alia, by their professional body, Hippocratic traditions, ethics committees and by professional Codes of Practice that may have been issued by a regulatory body such as the General Medical Council or the National Institute for Clinical Excellence. Medical professionals are also subjected to external supervision, most notably by way of laws that are intended to regulate the activities of physicians. Therefore, there is reason to suppose that the actions of a professional person should of necessity accord with the action that a reasonable person would take when acting in the best interests of the assisted person. Unfortunately, non-professionals are not similarly regulated and yet these people will play a significant role in the treatment and care of the permanently incompetent patient.

Possible Limitations on the Defence of Necessity – Unforeseen Treatment

What should happen in respect of treatment that is necessary to preserve the health and well-being of the patient but yet is unconnected to the source of the urgency that impels immediate action? The House of Lords confronted the problem in *Re F* but provided no answer to it preferring instead to leave the matter open until it became a real rather than a hypothetical issue.

The law of consent upholds the principle of bodily inviolability and establishes the patient's right of self-determination with regard to their own body, life and life plan. Therefore, a competent patient has the right to consent to, or to refuse to consent to, medical intervention in accordance

---

[260] Ibid, page 77/8

with their own values, beliefs and preferences. Since this places the patient in a position of being able to choose a course that others think unwise, one might have expected their Lordships to determine that in such circumstances the doctor must wait until it is possible to obtain the patient's consent. Accordingly, a physician who discovered a small, malignant growth that was unconnected to the immediate surgical goal and which presented no immediate threat to the health or well-being of the assisted person should postpone a decision to remove it until such time as the patient could be consulted and their consent obtained. If the patient was not immediately expected to regain consciousness and/or competency it is likely that a decision to treat need not be postponed as the patient would appear to fall within the scope of the term 'semi-permanently incompetent'. But how should the matter be decided in circumstances where the patient was expected to regain competency following surgery but suffered from a heart complaint that did not respond well to anaesthesia?

It is perhaps fair to conclude that their Lordships would have dealt a significant blow to the fundamental principle of bodily inviolability had they sanctioned such intervention in the absence of an actual set of facts which were capable of justifying an extension to the principle of necessity. On the other hand, judicial reticence upon the matter placed physicians in an unenviable position and patients an uncertain one.

Necessity: The General Principles

Necessity should not be treated as a blanket defence that can be raised in respect of any acts taken on behalf of a mentally incompetent person, particularly one who is expected to recover capacity to decide.[261] Physicians cannot therefore take advantage of unconsciousness to perform procedures which are not essential for the patient's immediate survival or well-being.[262] Indeed the treatment undertaken must not be more extensive than is required by the exigencies of the situation.[263] In such a case physicians must consider whether the person will be able to make the decision in the reasonably foreseeable future and if so whether the purpose

---

[261] *Re F (Mental Patient: Sterilisation) [1990] 2 AC 1 HL*

[262] *Re F (Mental Patient: Sterilisation) [1990] 2 AC 1 HL*; Mason, J.K., McCall Smith, R.A., Laurie, G.T., Law and Medical Ethics, 2002, Sixth Edition, Butterworths , para. 10.12

[263] Ibid

for which intervention is required can be achieved by some other less intrusive means.[264] On the other hand a doctor is justified by necessity in proceeding without the patient's consent if a condition is discovered in an unconscious patient for which treatment is necessary in the sense that it would be, in the circumstances, unreasonable to postpone the operation to a later date. Postponement of treatment is, however, to be preferred if it is possible to wait until the patient is in a position to give consent.[265] Moreover, necessity acts as a general legal authority for carers to intervene and act reasonably in a patient's best interests relating to general day to day matters of care, such as giving medication, providing help with feeding or other matters of personal management.[266] Consequently, the distinction between necessity and convenience is often delicately balanced.[267]

Best Interests

Those who raise the defence of necessity must also show that the action taken by them was the action that a reasonable person would take when acting in another's best interests.[268] Taking into consideration the legally protected interests of all patients on what basis does any surrogate decide what should happen in another's best interests? Remember that the primacy of the moral principle of autonomy has been established in relation to a competent patient to prioritise the patient's own viewpoint of what is in their medical and other welfare interests. So when welfare is construed broadly to encompass a wider range of goods rather than the solitary good of medical welfare a beneficent doctor cannot ordinarily be expected to know what will most benefit the patient, i.e. promote well-being.[269] This brings us to the crux of the matter. If a mentally incapacitated patient is to enjoy a similar right to medical treatment or to the withholding or withdrawing of necessary and appropriate medical treatment as do competent patients, to consent to, or, to refuse to consent to, medical treatment then it is essential that the best interests test should

---

[264] Ibid, para. 10.36; Mental Capacity Act 2005, s.1(6); s.4(3)&(4)

[265] Mason, J.K., McCall Smith, R.A., Laurie, G.T., Law and Medical Ethics, 2002, Sixth Edition, Butterworths, para. 10.14; Mental Capacity Act 2005, s.1(6); s.4(3)&(4)

[266] Ibid; *Re F (Mental Patient: Sterilisation) [1990] 2 AC 1 HL*

[267] Ibid, para. 10.15

[268] Mental Capacity Act 2005, s.1(5); s.4; s.5(1)(b)(ii); *Re F (Mental Patient: Sterilisation) [1990] 2 AC 1 HL*, page 75

[269] *Schloendorff v Society of New York Hospital (1914) 211 N.Y. 125*

comprise of something more than a purely professional appraisal of a person's medical welfare.[270] To confine the test in this way would, as Lord Goff suggested in the case of *Bland*, '*downgrade the status of the incompetent person by placing a lesser value on [their] intrinsic worth and vitality*'.[271]

Test Criteria: The Development of the Test of Best Interests

The aim here is to examine what the test of best interests focuses on and we start with its invocation at common law. In *Re F* the House of Lords determined that a person's best interests would be satisfied whenever a doctor administered curative or prophylactic treatment which they believed was appropriate to the patient's existing condition of disease, injury or bodily malfunction or susceptibility to such a condition in the future.[272] The effect of the court's decision was to leave the matter of what was in a patient's best interests to members of the medical profession who were required to decide what should be done, in accordance with the *Bolam* principle.[273] As *Bolam* merely requires a doctor to conform to a practice accepted as proper by a responsible body of doctors the *Re F* formulation of best interests was deemed unduly paternalistic in focusing entirely upon professional appraisal of what was in a person's medical welfare interests. In the absence of any other factors to weigh in the balance against the *Bolam* principle it is unsurprising that this formulation of best interests was susceptible to the criticism that what was in a person's best interests was equivalent to what was in their medical best interests. And as non-consensual bodily violations were justified on the basis of *Bolam* a 'prudent doctor' standard governed best interests treatment decision-making processes.

Best interests was subsequently revised to place greater weight on the autonomously held wishes and views of formerly competent patients. This had the effect of increasing unity in the situation pertaining to competent and incompetent patients, i.e. the doctor makes an offer of treatment and the patient has the right to choose whether to accept or reject the doctor's offer in accordance with their own values, beliefs and preferences.[274] A

[270] The obligation to act beneficently should be similarly qualified
[271] *Airedale NHS Trust v Bland [1993] 1 All ER 821 HL*
[272] *Re F (Mental Patient: Sterilisation) [1990] 2 AC 1 HL*, Lord Bridge page 52
[273] Ibid
[274] *Re A (Medical Treatment: Male Sterilisation) [2000] 1 FLR 549 CA; Re SL (Adult Patient) (Medical Treatment) [2000] 2 FCR 452 CA*

two-stage was introduced; at the first stage professional opinion was determinative of the treatment that the patient should receive, but at the second stage that decision should be considered in the light of a welfare appraisal that took into account a person's ethical, social, moral and emotional viewpoint.[275] Assessment of what was in another's best interests required a doctor to consider, inter alia, the uncoerced past and present wishes and feelings of the patient, even when these have not been expressed in an advance directive, as well as any beliefs and values that might influence their decision one way or another and any other factors that the patient might have considered if they were able to.[276]

This common law test now has statutory status. The MCA requires surrogate decision-makers to consider, when determining whether it is in someone's best interests[277] to administer, withhold or withdraw a particular medical treatment, the person's past and present wishes and feelings and in particular any relevant written statement made by them when they had capacity;[278] the beliefs and values that would be likely to influence their decision if they had capacity[279] and any other factors they would be likely to consider if able to do so,[280] in so far as such information can reasonably be ascertained.

The Personality of the Patient is Relevant to Best Interests[281]

Medical paternalism that was once such an evident feature of best interests was being constrained by the act of requiring doctors to consider a wider range of factors when deciding questions about the welfare of the patient. Thus the two-stage test helpfully distanced best interests from its former association with a 'prudent doctor' standard and focused attention instead on the personality of the particular patient.[282]

---

[275] *Re SL (Adult Patient) (Medical Treatment) [2000] 2 FCR 452 CA*

[276] *Re T (Adult: Refusal of Treatment) [1992] 4 All ER 649 CA; Airedale NHS Trust v Bland [1993] 1 All ER 821 HL*

[277] Mental Capacity Act 2005, s.4

[278] Mental Capacity Act 2005, s.4(6)(a)

[279] Mental Capacity Act 2005, s.4(6)(b)

[280] Mental Capacity Act 2005, s.4(6)(c)

[281] Mason, J.K., McCall Smith, R.A., Laurie, G.T., Law and Medical Ethics, 2002, Sixth Edition, Butterworths, para. 10.36

[282] Grubb, A., Principles of Medical Law, 2004, Second Edition, Oxford University Press, para. 3.55

Best Interests Ensures the Lawful and Ethical Treatment of an Incompetent Patient[283]

The test requires doctors to consider what is in the overall best interests of a particular patient. And in accordance with the welfare appraisal doctors are required to engage in an evaluative process that takes into account a wide range of factors to determine what is, all things considered, in the patient's best interests.[284]

A variety of concepts were introduced as a set of organizing principles for the initiation of inquiries. However, these gave rise to the problem that it was impossible to fully define the test. For instance, what other factors might the patient have considered? The absence of a comprehensive account of the welfare appraisal and method for deciding which particular features of the morally relevant factors under consideration were most relevant to the decision-making process, i.e. whether the patient's past or present wishes should be accorded greater weight, suggests that what is in a person's best interests is to an extent unknowable.[285] This has led to criticism; that the test of best interests is a vague concept that permits a wide ranging discretion even when the test is tempered by factors to be taken into account.[286]

Best Interests not Substituted Judgment[287]

The best interests of an incompetent patient are determined by asking what a reasonable person would decide in the position of the patient. Thus all factors of the test are to be comprehended objectively, i.e. the test embodies an objective decision-making standard. Any decisions that have been based upon it should therefore reflect the opinions and standards of ordinary people living in the community. It is subjective only to the extent that decision-makers are required to consider what is in the best interests of an individual who suffers from a particular condition or handicap after

---

[283] Mason, J.K., McCall Smith, R.A., Laurie, G.T., Law and Medical Ethics, 2002, Sixth Edition, Butterworths, para. 10.36

[284] The welfare appraisal took into account a person's ethical, social, moral and emotional viewpoint

[285] Establishes the primacy of the principle of Beneficence

[286] Mason, J.K., McCall Smith, R.A., Laurie, G.T., Law and Medical Ethics, 2002, Sixth Edition, Butterworths, para. 10.37

[287] Grubb, A., Principles of Medical Law, 2004, Second Edition, Oxford University Press, para. 4.147

taking into consideration the patient's own wishes and feelings on the matter.[288]

Best interests can therefore be distinguished from a substituted judgment decision-making standard which prioritises the subjective decision-making standards of the patient and does for that reason generally involve a more detailed inquiry into what the patient would actually want done.[289] Crucially, substituted judgment makes the patient's own wishes and feelings determinative of what should happen rather than a factor that is merely taken into consideration. Substituted judgment does however raise other important questions such as whether it is possible to look at the situation from the point of view of the patient and to make decisions on the basis of what they would have wanted regardless of what may be thought by others to be good for them?

The Views of other Appropriate People are Relevant to Best Interests[290]

Furthermore, the type of information that a doctor is required to consider does not fall within the boundaries of medical expertise and experience. Consequently, doctors are encouraged to consult those closest to the patient in order to gain information that may be relevant to a treatment decision where the interests of the patient would not be adversely affected by any subsequent delay.[291]

Indeed contact with the next of kin has an added advantage in that it may reveal that the patient has made an anticipatory choice which if clearly established and applicable in the circumstances would bind the practitioner.[292] However, Lord Donaldson has stated that:

> *"Neither the personal circumstances of the patient nor a speculative answer to the question 'what would the patient have chosen?' can bind the practitioner in his choice of whether or not to treat or how to treat or justify him in acting contrary to a clearly established anticipatory refusal to accept treatment but they are factors to be taken into account by him in*

---

[288] Ibid, para. 4.150/1

[289] *Airedale NHS Trust v Bland [1993] 1 All ER 821 HL*, Lord Goff

[290] Mason, J.K., McCall Smith, R.A., Laurie, G.T., Law and Medical Ethics, 2002, Sixth Edition, Butterworths, para. 10.36

[291] *Re T (Adult: Refusal of Treatment) [1992] 4 All ER 649 CA*, Lord Donaldson

[292] Ibid

forming a clinical judgment as to what is in the best interests of the patient. For example, if he learnt that the patient was a Jehovah's Witness, but had no evidence of a refusal to accept blood transfusions, he would avoid or postpone any blood transfusion as long as possible".[293]

The Past and Present Uncoerced Wishes and Feelings of the Person are Relevant[294]

The moral principle of autonomy emphasises the view that persons value being in control of their destiny and being able to decide how to live the good life.[295] On this basis it has been said that if the beliefs and values of the patient, though incomprehensible to others, are of long standing and have formed the basis for all the patient's decisions about his life, there is a strong argument to suggest that the doctor should respect and give affect to a patient's decision based on them.[296] To argue otherwise would effectively be to deny a patient the right to their own personality.[297] It is therefore a clearly established principle of law that the autonomously held values, beliefs and preferences of a formerly competent person may become binding at some future time when that person is deemed to be no longer competent to register a view about them.[298]

Nevertheless, Lord Donaldson has stated that a doctor is not bound to accept such information at face value when it has been obtained through consultation with the incompetent's friends and relatives, even when the information concerned is that pertaining to a person's religious beliefs.[299] Particular details of a patient's life should not in other words be considered in isolation of other relevant facts and this is especially true when a person's life is at stake.[300] Therefore, a doctor may presume that a state of affairs continues until evidence suggests that a person's expressed values, beliefs and preferences, no longer pertain.[301] The relevant question

---

[293] Ibid

[294] Mason, J.K., McCall Smith, R.A., Laurie, G.T., Law and Medical Ethics, 2002, Sixth Edition, Butterworths, para. 10.36

[295] Herring, Jonathan, Medical Law and Ethics, 2008, Second Edition, Oxford University Press, p.173

[296] Ibid

[297] Ibid

[298] *Re T (Adult: Refusal of Treatment) [1992] 4 All ER 649 CA*, Lord Donaldson

[299] Ibid

[300] Ibid

[301] Ibid

regarding past wishes and in particular their validity is whether the patient has evinced a settled continuous intention with regard to them.[302] In cases of doubt a persons present wishes and feelings may instead be a factor in any decision concerning what is in their best interests.

The Need to Permit and Encourage the Person to Participate as fully as possible in Decision-Making[303]

All adults are presumed to be competent and therefore to decide contemporaneously whether to accept or reject an offer of medical treatment. Consequently, unless a patient is unconscious a doctor may, in appropriate circumstances, first seek to assist a person to make a treatment decision on the spot. This is in keeping with the moral ideals emphasised by the moral principle of autonomy.

Best Interests are not Limited to what is in a Person's Best Medical Interests

The welfare appraisal itself suggests that assessment of what is in another's best interests should focus every bit as much on psychological health and well-being as on the person's physical health when deciding how to treat a patient and in this respect relationships with others, financial interests and moral or social obligations may also be relevant to the appraisal.[304]

This underpins the notion that decision-makers are responsible for an incompetent adult who previously had the capacity for self-determination and therefore had a life that was characterised by certain conventions, including engaging in transactions, managing things and people, and making and enforcing promises. Accordingly, the obligations owed can be reconciled with those pertaining to the situation of a competent patient who is free to choose to accept or reject a particular form of medical treatment on the basis of a belief or a commitment to someone or something other than themselves. A medical procedure may therefore be

---

[302] Ibid

[303] Mason, J.K., McCall Smith, R.A., Laurie, G.T., Law and Medical Ethics, 2002, Sixth Edition, Butterworths, para. 10.36

[304] Grubb, A., Principles of Medical Law, 2004, Second Edition, Oxford University Press, para. 4.160

rejected on religious grounds[305] such as happens when a Jehovah's Witness refuses a blood transfusion.

A Best Interests Treatment Decision must Confer an Advantage on the Patient[306]

A widely drawn welfare appraisal that encompasses medical, emotional, moral, ethical and social welfare issues is intended to ensure that a patient's best interests are not confined to best medical interests.[307] Neither must the statutory test be interpreted in a way that would make the patient the means to the end of any other. It is the patient's interests and not those of a third party that are paramount. However, it has proved possible to justify a procedure which is not medically indicated, serves no therapeutic purpose, and may even be attended with some medical risk or disadvantage, on the basis of some non-medical benefit which on balance outweighs any concern about whatever medical risks or disadvantages there may be.[308]

Test Criteria Support Decisions to Administer, Withhold or Withdraw Treatment or to Choose to Administer One Form of Treatment Instead of Another

The revised test of best interests established another important principle of law; that a mentally incompetent patient should not be denied necessary and appropriate medical treatment but neither must it be assumed that an incompetent patient can only have an interest in receiving necessary and appropriate medical treatment and care.[309]

This was a significant step forward for formerly competent patients who will have formed a world view and developed some sort of life plan that reflects their personally held values, beliefs and preferences.

---

[305] *Re T (Adult: Refusal of Treatment) [1992] 4 All ER 649 CA*

[306] Grubb, A., Principles of Medical Law, 2004, Second Edition, Oxford University Press, para. 4.158

[307] *Re MB (Adult: Medical Treatment) [1997] 2 FLR 426 CA*

[308] *Re Y (An Adult Patient) (Transplant: Bone Marrow) [1996] 4 Med LR 204*

[309] *Re T (Adult: Refusal of Treatment) [1992] 4 All ER 649 CA; Airedale NHS Trust v Bland [1993] 1 All ER 821 HL*

A Doctor must not, in considering whether Treatment is in the Best Interests of the Person, be Motivated to bring about their Death

Can a doctor legitimately withhold or withdraw life prolonging treatment and care in the best interests of a patient? In *Bland* Lord Goff stated that:

> *"I am of the opinion that there is ... no absolute obligation upon the doctor who has the patient in his care to prolong his life, regardless of the circumstances. Indeed, it would be most startling and could lead to the most adverse and cruel effects upon the patient, if any such absolute rule were held to exist. It is scarcely consistent with the primacy given to the principle of self-determination in those cases in which the patient of sound mind has declined to give his consent that the law should provide no means of enabling treatment to be withheld in appropriate circumstances where the patient is in no condition to indicate, if that was his wish, that he did not consent to it...*
>
> *I must however stress, at this point, that the law draws a crucial distinction between cases in which a doctor decides not to provide, or to continue to provide for his patient treatment or care which could or might prolong his life and those in which he decides, for example by administering a lethal drug, actively to bring his patient's life to an end... The former may be lawful, either because the doctor is giving effect to his patient's wishes by withholding the treatment and care, or even in certain circumstances in which the patient is incapacitated from stating whether or not he gives his consent. But it is not lawful for a doctor to administer a drug to his patient to bring about his death, even though that course is prompted by a humanitarian desire to end his suffering, however great that suffering may be".*[310]

The position in English law is that euthanasia is not lawful and Lord Goff believed that it could only be rendered lawful by legislation that expressed the 'democratic will' on the subject.[311] However, the law is inconsistent is distinguishing between a deliberate act that is intended to kill (active euthanasia) from an omission to act which allows the patient to die (passive euthanasia) on the basis that a doctor does not cause or is not the agent of death. [312] Instead, death is attributed to the patient's pre-existing

[310] *Airedale NHS Trust v Bland [1993] 1 All ER 821 HL*, Lord Goff
[311] Ibid
[312] Ibid

condition or underlying disease which is merely allowed to take its course.[313]

In upholding the acts and omissions distinction the law distinguishes a deliberate act that is intended to kill[314] from those where death is merely foreseen as an incidental outcome of a particular act.[315] The distinction is justified on basis of an important difference between intention and foresight or aiming to produce a result and being aware that a result is a possible result of one's actions.[316] As such the law holds to its qualified sanctity of life position in relation to mentally incapacitated patient and this means that a doctor is not placed under an absolute duty to prolong life, by any means available, regardless of the patient's quality of life.[317] In other words a doctor's duty to act in the best interests of the patient is similarly qualified.[318]

Therefore, a doctor who discontinues life support and allows the patient to die does not act unlawfully where there is no breach of duty to the patient.[319] And the courts have determined that a doctor will not be in breach of her duty to the patient where medical opinion determines that it is futile to continue with life support.[320] This is because no actual advantage is conferred by a decision to continue with the treatment. Similarly, a doctor is permitted, in accordance with the moral principle of double effect, to administer drugs intending to relieve intolerable pain even when death is foreseen as an incidental effect of treatment.[321]

Consequently, a doctor must not, in considering whether treatment is in the best interests of the person, be motivated to bring about their death.[322]

---

[313] Ibid

[314] *R v Cox [1991] 12 BMLR 38*

[315] *R v Bodkin Adams [1957] Crim LR 365*

[316] Herring, Jonathan, Medical Law and Ethics, 2008, Second Edition, Oxford University Press, p.487

[317] *Airedale NHS Trust v Bland [1993] 1 All ER 821 HL*, Lord Goff

[318] In accordance with the principles of non-maleficence and beneficence

[319] *Airedale NHS Trust v Bland [1993] 1 All ER 821 HL*

[320] Ibid

[321] *R v Bodkin Adams [1957] Crim LR 365*

[322] *R v Cox [1991] 12 BMLR 38; Airedale NHS Trust v Bland [1993] 1 All ER 821 HL*

The Best Interests Balancing Exercise

The favoured method of approach in evaluating what action to take in another's best interests is to draw up a balance sheet. Those factors in favour of a particular course of action should be recorded alongside any dis-benefits or disadvantages of treatment for the patient. A note should be made as to the viability of each such option and its likely effect on the patient and their enjoyment of life. Any likely benefit of the treatment has to be balanced and considered in the light of any additional suffering treatment might impose. Only if the account is in relatively significant credit will it be safe for a doctor to conclude that treatment is likely to advance the best interests of the patient.[323]

Treatment Information might be Assessed Subjectively by the Doctor

The wishes and preferences of the patient are relevant to best interests decision-making processes. On the assumption that these could reasonably be ascertained no indication is given about how the various factors that a doctor is being asked to consider should be weighted in order to determine which of them should assume priority. Neither does the test explain how conflicting or competing interests should be balanced where, for example, a incompetent patient was required to act as donor for a sibling but the procedure could endanger their future health and well-being. In the absence of such guidance it is possible for the decision-maker to assess information subjectively. As such the test remains uncertain in promoting the ascertained beliefs, values and preferences of a mentally incapacitated patient.

Estimating Benefits and Harms

In medical law, a decision to accord primacy to the moral principle of autonomy establishes that the views of a competent patient, rather than a beneficent doctor, should be made determinative of matters related to life, death and quality of life. In this way the law can be seen to be neutral in the face of legitimate moral diversity amongst members of society which in the light of advances in medical science now extends to decisions

---

[323] *Re MB (Adult: Medical Treatment) [1997] 2 FLR 426 CA*, Butler-Sloss LJ; *Re A (Mental Patient: Sterilisation) [2000] 1 FLR 549 CA*, Thorpe LJ

concerning life prolonging treatment.[324] Competent patients therefore have freedom to decide whether treatment might benefit or be harmful to them and that decision will have been formed by a process in which treatment information is used or applied to their own set of values, beliefs and preferences. It is therefore clear that people will differ in ranking the various harms that are to be avoided and benefits gained.

Moreover, persons differ in terms of estimating harmful or beneficial consequences of their action and this is linked to their attitudes to risk, in this instance to the risks inherent in medical treatment. These differences cannot be settled on empirical grounds as variation is more accurately accounted for by a person's nature and ideology. Personal estimations of the risks and benefits associated with treatment and non-treatment plausibly explain why someone with freedom to choose selects an option that others might think an unwise course of action.[325] This is because the process of estimating benefits and harms relies on human judgment and humans differ in their assessment of these things.

The fact that persons differ in prioritising harms and benefits and in estimating their propensity to arise in a given set of circumstances is beyond dispute. It is therefore regrettable that there is no prescribed process or method, other than the unifying principle or concept of best interests itself, to guide surrogate decision-makers when making decisions for others. Accordingly, mentally incapacitated patients are reliant upon the subjective deliberations of others with regard to the perceived benefits and burdens of treatment and may as a consequence be subjected to unwarranted and intrusive medical intervention in a way that a competent patient is not. This will be the case even when one can be confident that the values, beliefs and preferences of the patient have fully emerged because without a principled method for weighting the various factors that are being considered the task of ranking them is made virtually impossible which suggests that the values of the patient might inadvertently be overridden.

---

[324] *B v An NHS Trust Hospital [2002] 152 NLJ 470*

[325] *Re C (Adult: Refusal of Treatment) [1994] 1 All ER 819 CA*

Best Interests no longer tied to Best Medical Interests: On what Basis is a Doctor Qualified to Decide

The type of information that a doctor is required to consider does not fall within the boundaries of medical expertise and experience. Doctors are instead encouraged to consult those closest to the patient in order to gain information that may be relevant to a decision to administer, withhold or withdraw treatment or to choose to administer one form of treatment instead of another.

Best Interests: Trust in the Medical Profession

In practical terms a doctor exerts considerable influence and control over best interests decision-making processes and in the absence of a definitive welfare checklist and method emphasis is placed on the moral integrity of medical professionals in deciding. Yet circumstances have arisen where the treatment proposed was sterilisation to prevent pregnancy rather than to address problems associated with menstruation[326] and where the incompetent patient was to act as a donor to save the life of a sibling.[327] Consequently, it is relevant to consider the basis on which a doctor proposes to carry out non-therapeutic treatments or procedures when the factors that would legitimate such decisions do not naturally fit within an area of medical expertise or lie in exercising clinical judgment in accordance with the *Bolam* principle.

The Grounds for Deciding: The Welfare of the Patient should be the Overriding Consideration

An issue then in relation to a welfare appraisal that is cast in the widest possible terms is whether it is possible to justify treatment in the general public interest or based upon the interests of a third party. Andrew Grubb, for instance, raises the view that the general public interest and the moral and civic obligations of the patient can legitimately be taken into account in determining whether or not what is proposed is in the best interests of the patient. Of course as a matter of principle it is ultimately necessary to show some benefit or advantage to the patient from what is proposed.[328]

---

[326] *Re D (A Minor) (Wardship: Sterilisation) 1 All ER 326*

[327] *Re Y (An Adult Patient) (Transplant: Bone Marrow) [1996] 4 Med LR 204*

[328] Grubb, A., Principles of Medical Law, 2004, Second Edition, Oxford University Press, para. 4.166

Likewise in relation to third party interests the best interests in question are those of the incompetent patient and not those of the third party.[329] However, Stauch et al point out that *Bolam* determines that a doctor, who decides that what is proposed, is in the best interests of the incompetent patient, could if necessary find other doctors who were willing to endorse their view.[330] Although in this regard the courts and not medical professionals are the final arbiters of best interests. And an advantage of court proceedings is that there is an opportunity to discover and make explicit the grounds on which the decision is being made and therefore to decide that a responsible body of physicians would not accept that what was proposed, in another's best interests, was proper.[331]

Court Involvement in Decisions based on Best Interests: Inherent Jurisdiction of the High Court

In the absence of parens patriae jurisdiction the courts have no power to consent or to refuse medical treatment on behalf of a mentally incapacitated patient. However, the High Court may, in reliance on its inherent or discretionary jurisdiction,[332] issue a declaration to approve or disapprove a proposed operation on an adult patient who is believed to lack the capacity to decide the matter themselves.[333] This discretionary jurisdiction can be exercised whenever a person raises a real and not a hypothetical question of law.[334] The person raising the question must have a real interest in raising it such as would be the case if they were in dispute with another interested party who wished to oppose the declaration sought.[335] In other words a declaration must be sought on the basis of a proper argument. Consequently, a declaration when it is granted establishes, by judicial process, whether the proposed operation is in the best interests of the patient and therefore lawful.[336]

---

[329] Ibid, para. 4.161

[330] Stauch, Marc, Wheat, Kay, Tingle John, 2002, Second Edition, Sourcebook on Medical Law, Cavendish Publishing, p.215

[331] *Bolitho v City and Hackney HA [1997] 4 All ER 771 HL*

[332] Supreme Court Rule Ord. 15, r. 16

[333] *Re F (Mental Patient: Sterilisation) [1990] 2 AC 1 HL*, Lord Goff, p.81

[334] Ibid

[335] Ibid

[336] Ibid, Lord Brandon, p.63

A declaration does not however change anything.[337] The court is merely being asked to declare that had a course of action been taken without resort to the court, it would have been lawful anyway.[338] In other words the courts declaratory jurisdiction does not permit inquiry into what is in the actual best interests of the patient.

Another problem with the jurisdiction is that some incompetent patients may be without a true opposer to a proposed operation.

Reliance on Medical Experts

The court not the doctor is then the ultimate arbiter of what is in another's best interests. Nevertheless, the expert opinion of medical professionals will be sought in relation to what treatment the patient should receive. At the second stage, in best interests decision-making processes, medical opinion will also be influential because an assessment of medical risks and benefits is also a matter of clinical judgment. However, the judge must be satisfied that the body of medical opinion relied upon has a logical basis and that the experts have directed their minds to the question of comparative risks and benefits prior to forming a defensible conclusion on the matter.[339] And although the court reserves the right to decide that medical opinion is not supported by a responsible body of physicians[340] the court will not choose between different responsible bodies of opinion.[341]

It follows that a number of different courses may be lawful in any given case although courts may intervene when appropriate and, by a process of balancing the benefits and burdens of treatment, will determine which course to follow in the best interests of a mentally incapacitated patient having taken the requirements of the welfare appraisal into consideration.

---

337 Ibid, Lord Donaldson MR, p.20
338 Ibid, Lord Donaldson MR, p.20
339 *Bolitho v City and Hackney HA [1997] 4 All ER 771 HL*, Lord Browne-Wilkinson
340 Ibid
341 *Maynard v West Midlands RHA [1984] 1 WLR 634 HL*

Conclusion

Everybody enjoys a legally protected right to bodily inviolability. This fundamental right is however obtained through the right to self-determination. Persons must therefore be competent to have their choice, whether to accept or reject a medical treatment, respected by others. Earlier in this chapter I referred to the fact that autonomy allows persons to protect their own sense of well-being or happiness and also therefore serves to counter medical paternalism. A difficulty for legislators in drafting the legal framework in respect of mentally incapacitated patients is in striking a balance between the need to protect the medical welfare of those who are unable to accept or reject a medical treatment on their own behalf with respecting their right to self-determination. In this respect the MCA empowers medical professionals, amongst others, to interpret and then apply statutory and common law provisions which require them to give careful thought and detailed consideration to the patient's capacity because if a person is not capable of making a decision the 2005 Act determines that a doctor is required to make decisions in their best interests. Whilst all adults are presumed to have the requisite level of capacity to make decisions on their own behalf a capacity assessment may be sought in cases where there is reason to doubt the patient's capacity to make a particular decision. In this regard the MCA upholds a functional not outcome based test which means that part of the process of assessment is concerned with whether a patient can understand treatment information. Understanding is demonstrated when a patient can process or use information to arrive at a decision. Essentially a patient must be able to apply relevant facts about treatment to their values or own situation. However, the MCA cannot state what information will be relevant and so it becomes a matter that is left to the discretion of a doctor. The problem is that unless a doctor has knowledge of the patient, including their values and personality, there is a danger that a doctor may fail to adequately respect their right to make decisions for themselves. If the patient loses the right to make decisions about treatment a doctor is required to apply the inherently flexible best interests standard in relation to treatment decisions. Whereupon we find that any earlier failings may be compounded by the fact that the personality of the patient is not determinative of what should happen to them in their own best interests rather it is a factor that must be considered by surrogate decision-makers when making decisions and acting on their behalf.

CHAPTER FIVE

ADVANCE DECISIONS

To strengthen and preserve legally protected rights a competent person can elect to refuse treatment in advance and in anticipation of a time when a loss of decision-making capacity will prohibit them from choosing contemporaneously.[1] The nature and purpose of an advance decision is to therefore identify, preserve and give effect to the autonomous wishes of competent adults. As the Mental Capacity Act 2005, consistent with the common law before it, upholds the right of a competent person to self-determine matters related to their own body, life and life plan through this legal construct it is clear that the law seeks to avoid criticism for being inconsistent in respecting the legal rights and interests of competent and incompetent patients alike.

As a result an advance decision is treated, when it is given effect, as though it had been obtained in real time. This gives rise to two important and related features of the legal system. First, in prioritising the anticipatory choice of a formerly competent patient an advance decision is regarded in law as an exception to the principle that a doctor should act in the best interests of a mentally incapacitated patient. Moreover, in according priority to autonomy, not beneficence, a doctor is deemed to be acting on the instructions of a competent patient.

Nevertheless, decision-making and choosing between options can be a difficult exercise at the best of times. Prospective decision-making, where background facts must be forecast and ones response foreseen, will be even more demanding in placing a greater burden on one's decision-making capacity. Therefore, it is somewhat unsurprising to find that the law expects a person to be very competent when exercising the right to

[1] Mental Capacity Act 2005, ss.24-26; *Re T (Adult: Refusal of Treatment) [1992] 4 All ER 649 CA*, Lord Donaldson stated that: Contact with the next of kin … may reveal that the patient has made an anticipatory choice which, if clearly established and applicable in the circumstances … would bind the practitioner.

decide prospectively and in accordance with present values, beliefs and preferences. This is because the advance decision of a competent patient will be binding on them at a time when they are deemed incompetent to express a view about their earlier choice.[2] Thus legal provisions require doctors to be very certain about whether an anticipatory decision is valid[3] and applicable[4] in the circumstances that have arisen. In cases of doubt where a doctor is unable to satisfy themselves, adopting the civil standard, i.e. balance of probabilities, that an anticipatory choice is valid and/or applicable he will no longer be bound to respect it.[5] Although in these circumstances one may still be taken into consideration in determining what is in the patient's best interests.[6] Then, as previously stated, a doctor is merely required to have regard for the patient's decision, and/or its content, whereupon it is entirely possible that the wishes of the patient will be overridden in their best interests.

Indeed some say that the need to protect vulnerable persons and to care for them in their best interests should override their right to self-determination in these circumstances.[7] For this reason the situation of the incompetent patient has fuelled an ethical debate about whether it is entirely consistent with the right of self-determination to respect advance decisions. Philosophical and legal support for advance decisions is founded upon the individual right to bodily inviolability.[8] As this fundamental right is obtained through the right of self-determination it is clear that persons place a high value on individual control over present and future health care decisions.[9] So prior to examining the matter of whether an advance decision to refuse medical treatment will be treated as legally valid and

---

[2] Mental Capacity Act 2005, s.26(1); *Re T (Adult: Refusal of Treatment) [1992] 4 All ER 649 CA*

[3] Ibid, s.25(2); Ibid

[4] Ibid, s.25(4); Ibid, Lord Donaldson stated that: Just because adults have the right to choose, it does not follow that they have in fact exercised that right. Determining whether or not they have done so is a quite different and sometimes difficult matter, and if it is clear that they have exercised their right of choice, problems can still arise in determining what precisely they have chosen

[5] Mental Capacity Act 2005, s.26(2)

[6] Ibid, s.4(6)(a)

[7] Precommitment: A Misguided Strategy for Securing Death with Dignity – Rebecca Dresser – Texas Law Review, June 2003; 81 TXLR 1823

[8] *Re T (Adult: Refusal of Treatment) [1992] 4 All ER 649 CA*

[9] Ibid; Precommitment: A Misguided Strategy for Securing Death with Dignity – Rebecca Dresser – Texas Law Review, June 2003; 81 TXLR 1823, page 1828

applicable, and therefore binding on both doctors and patients, consideration will be given to some of the ethical arguments that arise when the right of self-determination is exercised prospectively.

Ethical Issues

Is it appropriate to pay heed to an advance directive?[10] What principal values or interests are at stake for the patient in whether they retain or lose this decisional authority?[11]

Principle of Respect for Autonomy

Kant intended persons to legislate according to values inherent in their own constitution. This means that each person is entitled to a life in which the subjectively held values, beliefs and preferences, of a particular individual, which do not infringe the interests of others, should be respected in matters related to personal welfare and for sustaining respect for more objective or universal moral laws that are concerned with protecting human welfare more generally.[12]

John Stuart Mill has also argued for the moral importance of respecting people's autonomy and similarly elaborated restrictions within this principle.[13]

> *"The sole end for which mankind are warranted, individually or collectively, in interfering with the liberty of action of any of their number, is self-protection. That is the only purpose for which power can rightfully be exercised over any member of a civilised community, against his will, is to prevent harm to others. His own good, either physical or moral, is not a sufficient warrant".*[14]

Whereas Kant claimed that respect for the autonomy of others was a necessary feature of rational agency itself and thus of any rational agent

[10] Herring, Jonathan, Medical Law and Ethics, 2008, Second Edition, Oxford University Press, p.182

[11] Brock Dan W., The Blackwell Guide to Medical Ethics, Edited by Rhodes, Rosamond, Francis, Leslie P., and Silvers, Anita, 2007, Blackwell Publishing, p.133

[12] Societal change may force an alteration in the application of values

[13] Gillon, Raanan, Philosophical Medical Ethics, 1986, John Wiley and Sons, p.63

[14] Ibid, p.65

Mill (subsequently) argued that respect for the autonomy of others was required to maximise overall human welfare provided such respect did not harm others.[15]

Autonomy and the Moral Right to Self-Determination

Accordingly, a patient has a principal interest in autonomy and in exercising their moral right to self-determination to promote personal welfare interests as Jonathan Herring has explained:

> *"Autonomy upholds the notion that people should be free to lead their lives as they wish and have control over their own bodies. People's decisions on how to live their lives deserve respect, even though other people might think them foolish. A person's decision is respected not because it is a good choice, but because it is their choice. To deny a person the respect for their views is the ultimate denial of respect for that person. Such respect is particularly important in relation to deeply personal or intimate issues such as when to die".*[16]

Dan Brock has described the right in similar terms but adds that:

> *"This is the interest of people in making significant decisions about their lives for themselves according to their own values or conception of a good life... The general requirement of informed consent is based on large part on recognition of this interest in ordinary people in self-determination. Sometimes the moral principle concerning self-determination is characterised as a right to self-determination, but whether characterised as a moral right or an interest, it is not absolute in the sense that it always trumps all other rights or interests. If it was, then in the context of consent to medical care, patients' choices would always have to be respected, whether or not they were competent to make those choices".* [17]

Right to Self-Determination and Medical Treatment

Consistent with the moral perspective we have observed that the law upholds the primacy of the principle of autonomy. The patient is thereby

---

[15] Ibid, p.63

[16] Herring, Jonathan, Medical Law and Ethics, 2008, Second Edition, Oxford University Press, p.466

[17] Brock Dan W., The Blackwell Guide to Medical Ethics, Edited by Rhodes, Rosamond, Francis, Leslie P., and Silvers, Anita, 2007, Blackwell Publishing, p.133

treated as the ultimate arbiter of what is in their own best medical interests in the knowledge that they will have had a reasonable opportunity to discuss and consider various treatment options and to have assessed these subjectively prior to registering a choice.[18] A competent patient therefore has the advantage of choosing, to consent or to refuse treatment, in the light of a welfare appraisal that has been specified in subjective terms to reflect the values, beliefs and preferences of the patient. These will be weighted and then balanced according to circumstance but will manifest the patient's attitude to risks and to the benefits and burdens of medical treatment.

The important point is that the subjective values and methods of a competent patient are prioritised by the law of consent. In view of the uncertainties inherent in the legal framework for mentally incapacitated patients, it is quite natural that a competent person might wish to seek to control events in the future when they are no longer competent to make a treatment decision contemporaneously.

Is it Consistent with the Right to Self-Determination to Respect an Advance Directive?

There are three main points to make. First, some claim that the person who makes an advance decision and the person who is subsequently incompetent are not the same person.[19] We will deal with this point in chapter six. Secondly, questions have been raised over whether it is possible for anybody to predict how they would like to be treated when incompetent.[20] Thirdly, it has been suggested that regardless of the weight to be given to the patient's wishes the primary obligation to the incompetent patient is to show compassion by acting in their best interests.[21]

---

[18] *Chester v Afshar 2004 WL 2289136*

[19] Herring, Jonathan, Medical Law and Ethics, 2008, Second Edition, Oxford University Press, p.182; Dresser, Rebecca, 1995, Dworkin on Dementia: Elegant Theory, Questionable Policy, Hastings Center Report; Nov, 25, 6; Dresser, Rebecca, 2003, Precommitment: A Misguided Strategy for Securing Death with Dignity, 81, Tex. L. Rev. 1823

[20] Herring, Jonathan, Medical Law and Ethics, 2008, Second Edition, Oxford University Press, p.183; Fagerlin, Angela, Schneider, Carl E., 2004, Enough The Failure of the Living Will, Hastings Center Report, March-April

[21] Herring, Jonathan, Medical Law and Ethics, 2008, Second Edition, Oxford University Press, p.183

Accurately Predicting Preferences

Competent persons have a right to autonomy, that is to say a right to self-determine matters related to their own body, life and life plan.[22] We respect the decisions of a competent patient based on arguments of rational agency itself[23] and/or because doing so is likely to do more good, and so promote human welfare, than would be the case if we interfered in the affairs of others.[24] Since persons have freedom to develop their own character and personality and to make decisions compatibly with it they generally know better than anyone else what is in their own best interests.[25] On this view the decisions of individuals are the best evidence we have of how autonomy is exercised in support of their own best interests to promote welfare.[26]

However, the evidentiary view of autonomy fails to sustain that argument.[27] People by their own admission do not always make decisions and act in their own best interests all things considered, think about someone who smokes.[28] Furthermore, people are not always the best judges of what their own best interests would be under circumstances they have never encountered and in which their preferences and desires may drastically have changed.[29]

Therefore, if we are to say that an advance decision should be recognised as an individual exercise of autonomy to promote welfare interests it is also reasonable to expect that persons can predict their preferences accurately.[30] An issue when autonomy is exercised prospectively is

---

[22] Dworkin, Ronald, Life's Dominion: An argument about Abortion and Euthanasia, Harper Collins, p.222

[23] This is what Kant proposed

[24] This is what Mill proposed

[25] Dworkin, Ronald, Life's Dominion: An argument about Abortion and Euthanasia, Harper Collins, p.223

[26] Ibid; Dresser, Rebecca, 1995, Dworkin on Dementia: Elegant Theory, Questionable Policy, Hastings Center Report; Nov, 25, 6, p.33

[27] Ibid

[28] Dworkin, Ronald, Life's Dominion: An argument about Abortion and Euthanasia, Harper Collins, p.223

[29] Dresser, Rebecca, 1995, Dworkin on Dementia: Elegant Theory, Questionable Policy, Hastings Center Report; Nov, 25, 6, p.33

[30] Fagerlin, Angela, Schneider, Carl E., 2004, Enough The Failure of the Living Will, Hastings Center Report 34, No 2, 30-42, p.33

whether anyone can accurately predict how they would like to be treated if they became incompetent.

Information

Did the patient have sufficient relevant information to make a choice? Here we may question whether people reliably know enough about illnesses and treatments to make prospective life-or-death decisions about them? On this Fagerlin and Schneider state that:

> *"Conventional legal and ethical wisdom insists that candidates for even a flu shot give a consent where the standards of disclosure have increasingly been raised. If we applied those standards to the information patients have before making the astonishing catalogue of momentous choices [advance directives] can embody, the conventional wisdom would be left shivering with indignation".*[31]

The consent of a competent patient who is informed about the nature and purpose of treatment is legally valid as a defence to a battery. It seems that a minimal amount of information is required to protect the patient's right to be maintained inviolate.[32] However, as patients are also entitled to be maintained free from bodily harms they would not consent to, doctors are required to obtain an informed consent.[33]

For that reason patients should be informed about the benefits and burdens of treatment, including information pertaining to potential risks and this information should be repeated to cover all relevant alternative options including non-treatment. [34] On this point Rebecca Dresser has commented that:

> *"The nature of advance treatment decision-making makes it difficult and often impossible to understand this information. Unless the person making a directive has a relatively clear prognosis and limited treatment options, there are too many potential situations to address. Most people simply cannot predict all the medical conditions that the future might bring, much*

---

[31] Ibid

[32] *Chatterton v Gerson [1981] QB 432*

[33] *Chester v Afshar 2004 WL 2289136*

[34] Ibid

less understand what would be the possible harms and benefits of interventions targeting those conditions".[35]

Consequently, it is unsurprising to find that empirical data suggests that people do not make informed decisions.[36] There is also evidence that some advance decisions will be based on misinformation.[37] Inconsistent statements tend to suggest that either the patient was misinformed or had failed to understand information relevant to their choice. For instance, a patient may say that whilst they will accept blood transfusions they would reject diagnostic procedures.[38] In many cases the patient's condition will determine that it is not possible to disassociate the two interventions.[39] The problem is that it is not altogether clear what circumstances were envisaged by the patient or indeed what they intended to happen. Someone who wanted a speedy death would reject both interventions whilst someone who wanted to live would consent to both.[40]

Stability of Preferences

Patient preferences must be reasonably stable in order for it to be a true expression of their will.[41] However, studies tend to show only moderate stability in relation to anticipatory decisions.[42] Moreover, when preferences had changed investigators found that decision-makers were often unaware of the fact and so were unlikely to change their statement of wishes.[43] These findings are especially concerning when anticipatory choices are being made in respect of life-sustaining treatment. For example, one cancer patient is quoted as saying that, '*by the time it has*

---

[35] Dresser, Rebecca, Precommitment: A Misguided Strategy for Securing Death with Dignity, 2003, Texas Law Review 1823, June, p.1833

[36] Ibid; Fagerlin, Angela, Schneider, Carl E., 2004, Enough The Failure of the Living Will, Hastings Center Report 34, No 2, 30-42

[37] Dresser, Rebecca, Precommitment: A Misguided Strategy for Securing Death with Dignity, 2003, Texas Law Review 1823, June, p.1834

[38] Ibid

[39] Ibid

[40] Ibid

[41] Fagerlin, Angela, Schneider, Carl E., 2004, Enough The Failure of the Living Will, Hastings Center Report, March-April, p.33

[42] Dresser, Rebecca, Precommitment: A Misguided Strategy for Securing Death with Dignity, 2003, Texas Law Review 1823, June, p.1834; Fagerlin, Angela, Schneider, Carl E., 2004, Enough The Failure of the Living Will, Hastings Center Report, March-April, p.33

[43] Ibid, p.1834/5; Ibid

tried to frighten you to death and threatened to take away your very existence, you'd be amazed at how little you're willing to settle for'.[44]

The instability of preferences substantiates the problem alluded to earlier, which is that people do a poor job of predicting their preferences in situations they have never experienced.[45] This view is supported by psychological research which indicates that in respect of choices among options that are important, complex, and unfamiliar preferences do not pre-exist but are constructed on the spot through a process that is heavily influenced by framing and contextual factors.[46] For example, investigators found that the preferences of patients after being hospitalised were different from those expressed in their advance directives. In general patient preference for life-sustaining treatment decreased amongst those recently hospitalized although many re-affirmed their advance decisions to receive treatment after a few months, presumably because they had adapted to life in hospital.[47] Therefore, it has been argued that people are unaware of the way they will respond to future health problems and do not know what they will want until they actually experience the situation.[48]

Can People Articulate what they Want?

Evidence suggests that when humans are asked to make a contemporary decision they often fail to gather all relevant information, possibly misunderstand and ignore what is gathered and lack well considered preferences to guide the decision-making process.[49] This leads to persons making ill considered choices which are inaccurately recorded.[50] As the information needs of those making anticipatory choices are likely to be

---

[44] Fagerlin, Angela, Schneider, Carl E., 2004, Enough The Failure of the Living Will, Hastings Center Report, March-April, p.34, see quote from Wilfred Sheed
[45] Dresser, Rebecca, Precommitment: A Misguided Strategy for Securing Death with Dignity, 2003, Texas Law Review 1823, June, p.1835
[46] Ibid
[47] Dresser, Rebecca, Precommitment: A Misguided Strategy for Securing Death with Dignity, 2003, Texas Law Review 1823, June, p.1835/6; Fagerlin, Angela, Schneider, Carl E., 2004, Enough The Failure of the Living Will, Hastings Center Report, March-April, p.34
[48] Dresser, Rebecca, Precommitment: A Misguided Strategy for Securing Death with Dignity, 2003, Texas Law Review 1823, June, p.1835
[49] Fagerlin, Angela, Schneider, Carl E., 2004, Enough The Failure of the Living Will, Hastings Center Report, March-April, p.33
[50] Ibid

more complex and thus more difficult to process it will be that much more difficult for us to make an anticipatory treatment choice for some unspecified future time which is attended with unidentifiable conditions with unpredictable treatments?[51]

Specificity is perhaps the most significant challenge in communicating wishes. An advance treatment refusal that is too specific may force patients to address more questions than they can comprehend, and in being definitive may even be of little practical use in the circumstances that have in fact arisen, whilst one that is too general may be insufficiently specific and insufficiently considered to be binding.[52] On this matter Fagerlin and Schneider have commented that:

> *"Writing complex instructions for the future is crushingly difficult. Statutes read horribly because their authors are struggling to (1) work out exactly what rule they want, (2) imagine all the circumstances in which it might apply, and (3) find language to specify all those but only those circumstances. Each task is ultimately impossible, which is why statutes explicitly or implicitly confide their enforcers with some discretion and why courts must interpret, rewrite?, statutes. However, these skills and resources are not available to physicians or surrogates".*[53]

Should Compassion be the Overriding Obligation?

Advance decisions possibly work optimally for those patients who choose to refuse life-preserving treatment after a long illness and close to the time of implementation. At least there is less reason in these circumstances to be hesitant about what is left to be achieved experientially and as the patient would not be under threat of a prolonged period of psychological disunity it seems reasonable to suggest that greater weight should be accorded to critical interests.[54] Moreover, the patient's decision is likely to be unambiguous, context specific and will not trigger concern, in any significant sense, that their welfare is under threat or may be compromised by any of the usual suspects, i.e. information, misinformation, stability of preferences and specification, as they will no doubt have had many conversations with carers and others prior to registering their choice.

---

[51] Ibid
[52] Ibid, p.35
[53] Ibid, p.34/5
[54] For example, in seeking a good death

However, it is also obvious that there will be situations where putting advance decisions into practice will not be easy for carers and others who have responsibility for maintaining patient welfare. This is most likely to arise when life-preserving treatment has previously been competently refused but the patient is now demented and appears to enjoy their life.[55] In these circumstances the patient's prior preferences appear to be in conflict with what is in their current best interests.[56] And in disagreeing with Dworkin, and others, Rebecca Dresser has argued that overriding the directive in such circumstances is the more defensible choice in furthering patient welfare.[57]

The question then is whether we should be led by the head or the heart in moral matters? In relation to the former Dresser might be inclined to chide that humans are complex but not particularly omniscient beings therefore access to truths about the self and one's motive in acting may be somewhat constrained or capable of being obscured from full view. If, however, we defer to the dictates of the heart, we must keep in mind the fact that there is no fixed idea about what good is, which means that one person will be placed in position to choose another's form of it in the absence of any meaningful feedback from them about whether what is being done makes a positive contribution to their life.[58]

Nevertheless, Dresser questions whether people can grasp what life would be like with dementia[59] and on this basis contends that there is a significant possibility that the advance refusal was either uninformed or an inaccurate account of the maker's true preferences, either of which justify her view.[60] If true, then of course the welfare of an incompetent patient may be at risk contrary to what was envisaged by theoretical strategists and policy makers who considered the patient was the best judge of what is in their own best interests.[61]

---

[55] Dresser, Rebecca, Precommitment: A Misguided Strategy for Securing Death with Dignity, 2003, Texas Law Review 1823, June, p.1837

[56] Ibid

[57] Ibid, p.1839

[58] Fellows, Lesley, K., Competency and Consent in Dementia, 1998, Journal of the American Geriatrics Society, Vol. 46; Part 7; 992-926, p.925

[59] Dresser, Rebecca, Precommitment: A Misguided Strategy for Securing Death with Dignity, 2003, Texas Law Review 1823, June, p.1836

[60] Ibid, p.1839

[61] Ibid, p.1836

Dresser acknowledges the high value that is placed on the right of an individual to make treatment decisions but draws on those ethical and legal principles, such as best interests, which support state intervention to shield vulnerable individuals from harm.[62] So, in cases where the capacity to appreciate critical interests is lost, experiential interests should take priority and the ethical and legal responsibilities to protect an incompetent patient ought not, on this account, to be suspended because someone has refused an intervention that now offers clear benefit.[63] Consequently, the decision to override would appear to depend on whether a surrogate decision-maker considers that a stay is warranted in the patient's best interests on account of the amount,[64] rather than quality,[65] of pleasure they currently derive from their life.

A substituted judgment standard is rejected on grounds that decision-makers are required to make the treatment choice the patient would make if capacity was momentarily restored so that they could perceive their condition and prognosis.[66] This decision-making standard, which focuses on the values of the patient when competent, has been criticised for being malleable enough to allow relatives and others to advance their own values and concerns in the guise of a decision that purports to be what the patient would want.[67]

When evidence of the patient's past values, beliefs and preferences is ambiguous or nonexistent the best interests standard is deemed to be more appropriate as the decision will be taken in accord with a perceived societal consensus, or the perspective of a reasonable person, choosing as most people would choose for themselves.[68] Therefore at the first stage a doctor is required to focus on the patient's current condition when considering various treatment options. At the second stage, the benefits and burdens of the proposed treatment are assessed in the light of community norms and attitudes towards treatment and what it would entail for a demented person, with the handicaps and disabilities of the patient

[62] Ibid, p.1838

[63] Ibid, p.1840

[64] Favours Bentham's hedonistic calculus

[65] Mill's qualitative approach by analogy does sit more favourably with Dworkin's view that people seek to advance their critical and experiential interests

[66] Dresser, Rebecca, Precommitment: A Misguided Strategy for Securing Death with Dignity, 2003, Texas Law Review 1823, June, p.1841

[67] Ibid, p.1842

[68] Ibid

taking into consideration their wishes and feelings, both past and present. However, adherence to an objective decision-making standard, unlike one that is subjective or individualistic, has the potential to shift the focus back to the patient's experience.[69]

Yet, a problem still exists with denying the subjectivity or personhood of a patient with dementia as who can identify with their experiences.[70] In this regard Lesley Fellows has stated that whatever the views of those around them the patient continues to experience the world they live in.[71] A patient may therefore be obliged to submit to the burdens of an intervention without having had input into whether the expected benefits bear any relevance to their current experience of life.[72]

Dresser approaches the problem by invoking an objective treatment standard whilst conceding that:

> *"The best interest standard is controversial because it requires healthy individuals to make quality of life judgments for vulnerable, impaired patients. Critics fear that social worth and economic considerations are too easily incorporated into best interests decision-making. These fears lead most scholars and legal authorities to regard the best interests standard as morally suspect. They see it as the least preferred treatment standard, the absolute last resort when no other standard will work.*
>
> *A desire to escape the dangers accompanying best interests judgments contributes to the general enthusiasm for advance directives. If treatment decisions appear to come from patients themselves, there is less cause to worry about inappropriate quality of life evaluations. At the same time, the dearth of advance directives and the shortcomings of the substituted judgment standard make the best interests standard central to most real cases. Because they have been preoccupied with advance directives,*

---

[69] Dresser, Rebecca, Precommitment: A Misguided Strategy for Securing Death with Dignity, 2003, Texas Law Review 1823, June, p.1842; Fellows, Lesley, K., Competency and Consent in Dementia, 1998, Journal of the American Geriatrics Society, Vol. 46; Part 7; 992-926, p.925

[70] Fellows, Lesley, K., Competency and Consent in Dementia, 1998, Journal of the American Geriatrics Society, Vol. 46; Part 7; 992-926, p.925

[71] Ibid

[72] Ibid

however, scholars and policy officials have neglected the best interests standard. As a result, the standard lacks precision and rigour".[73]

In the light of these concerns Fellows emphasises the importance of restoring a sense of the subjectivity of the demented patient and suggests that the attitude and approach of medical professionals and carers towards the patient is key to exploring the patient's perspective.[74] This was recognised by those exercising judgment on behalf of formerly competent patients within the terms of parens patriae doctrine.

Should the Right to Self-Determination prevail over the Sanctity of Life Principle?

The basic notion embedded in the principle of autonomy is that persons should be free to live their life in a way that seems good to them or in accord with their own conception of a good life provided no harm is done to the equal right of others.[75] Consequently, the right to freedom from physical interference and harm, i.e. to be maintained inviolate, is an essential pre-requisite to developing a life that is informed by one's own values, beliefs, and preferences.

Nonetheless, the right to be self-governing is not absolute in that it will always trump all other rights or interests. For instance, at stage one of a treatment decision-making process the right of self-determination is qualified by the need to respect the equal rights of others to medical care, treatment and resources.[76] Patients therefore have no right to insist on a particular form of treatment.[77] Instead, the obligations of physicians are limited to offering treatments that are consistent with professional standards of care taking into consideration principles of beneficence and justice to harmonise the competing interests of all.[78]

---

[73] Dresser, Rebecca, Precommitment: A Misguided Strategy for Securing Death with Dignity, 2003, Texas Law Review 1823, June, p.1843

[74] Lesley, K., Competency and Consent in Dementia, 1998, Journal of the American Geriatrics Society, Vol. 46; Part 7; 992-926, p.925

[75] Herring, Jonathan, Medical Law and Ethics, 2008, Second Edition, Oxford University Press, p.466

[76] Beauchamp, Tom L., Childress, James F., Principles of Biomedical Ethics, 2001, Fifth Edition, Oxford University Press, p.225

[77] *R (On the Application of Oliver Leslie Burke) v The General Medical Council [2005] EWCA Civ 1003 CA*

[78] Ibid;

The sanctity principle upholds the view that all human life is equally valuable and should not be intentionally destroyed.[79] Professional and legal standards thereby prohibit doctors from embarking on a course of action that is intended to kill a patient.[80] There is no right to die. A competent patient cannot consent to be killed but may choose to refuse life-preserving treatment.[81] In this way the sanctity of life principle is seen to yield to the patient's right of self-determination which preserves an autonomous choice.

Moreover, a doctor may withhold or withdraw life-preserving treatment from an incompetent patient by omission consistent with his or her obligation of non-maleficence.[82] Consequently the sanctity of life is not the sole guiding principle for medical professionals either. Instead a presumption exists that continued existence is in the best interests of the patient but that presumption is displaced where a doctor determines that continued existence would be intolerable[83] or that treatment would be futile.[84]

An intolerable life is one that is full of pain and suffering, in fact so experientially awful as to render life saving treatment inappropriate.[85] Clearly intolerability is a threshold test that is applied when the patient is incompetent but sufficiently sentient to experience the burdens that treatment would impose.[86] As a threshold test for medical intervention intolerability is contentious in requiring medical professionals to pass judgment on the quality of life of their patient. Judgment will be exercised on behalf of the patient in accordance with what a reasonable person would decide taking into consideration the nature of the patient's condition and degree of disability. On this point, you may remember that Rebecca Dresser questioned whether people can actually grasp things they have no

---

http://ww2.allina.com/anwim/GrandRounds/medicalfutility06/pages/slide38.html

[79] Herring, Jonathan, Medical Law and Ethics, 2008, Second Edition, Oxford University Press, p.466

[80] *Airedale NHS Trust v Bland [1993] 1 All ER 821 HL*

[81] *Re T (Adult: Refusal of Treatment) [1992] 4 All ER 649 CA*

[82] Ibid; *Airedale NHS Trust v Bland [1993] 1 All ER 821 HL*

[83] *Re J (A Minor) (Wardship: Medical Treatment) [1990] 3 All ER 930 CA*

[84] *Airedale NHS Trust v Bland [1993] 1 All ER 821 HL*

[85] *Re J (A Minor) (Wardship: Medical Treatment) [1990] 3 All ER 930 CA*; Grubb, A., Principles of Medical Law, 2004, Second Edition, Oxford University Press, para. 4.212

[86] Ibid

experience of. Is there any reason to suppose that the imagination of the doctor as decision-maker will be superior to that of any other, including the patient?

In contrast artificial nutrition and hydration has been withdrawn from a patient in a persistent vegetative state on the basis that it is futile to continue to provide life preserving treatment that cannot benefit an insentient patient.[87] Treatment that has a physiological effect is categorised as futile when it serves no therapeutic purpose of any kind that the patient can, or ever will, appreciate.[88] The fact that treatment would be futile, in that it could not fulfil its ultimate therapeutic purpose,[89] suggests that continued medical intervention can no longer be justified as being in the patient's best interests and this legitimises a doctor in withholding or withdrawing it.[90]

So whilst the sanctity principle yields to the doctor's obligation to act in the best interests of the patient the thresholds for futility and intolerability have purposefully been set quite high which fuels support for arguments in favour of euthanasia based on a commitment to personal ideas about human dignity. The question then is whether formerly competent patients should be permitted to pre-determine what happens to them at the end of life when incompetent and unable to decide the matter contemporaneously?

According to Kant the importance we attach to human life can be traced to an autonomous will which is treated as the morally significant feature of persons. Our sense of self is, according to Kant, derived from the human capacity to make use of reason to think critically or independently. John Harris has stated that in making autonomy central to personhood Kant might most reasonably be interpreted as requiring that it is autonomy that is protected and not physical life.[91]

---

[87] *Airedale NHS Trust v Bland [1993] 1 All ER 821 HL*; Grubb, A., Principles of Medical Law, 2004, Second Edition, Oxford University Press, para. 4.213

[88] Ibid; http://ww2.allina.com/anwim/GrandRounds/medicalfutility06/pages/slide37.html

[89] To restore the life, health or well-being of the patient

[90] *Airedale NHS Trust v Bland [1993] 1 All ER 821 HL*; Grubb, A., Principles of Medical Law, 2004, Second Edition, Oxford University Press, para. 4.213

[91] Harris, John, The Right to Die Lives! There is no Personhood Paradox, 2005, Medical Law Review, 13, Autumn, 386-92, p.388

Dworkin similarly attaches moral significance to human autonomy but is seemingly more interested in how freedom to choose has informed the shape of a person's life and in discovering which interests are critically important to it.[92] A person's critical interests are what make life important to the individual whose life it is.[93] About this Dworkin states that, '*someone's convictions about his own critical interests are opinions about what it means for his own human life to go well, and these convictions can therefore best be understood as a special application of his general commitment to the sanctity of life*'.[94] Thus a commitment to the integrity view of autonomy suggests that the interests that were critical to the shape of a person's life, when viewed as a whole, should not be sacrificed later simply because the patient is incompetent and unable to express a view.[95]

The relevant question according to Dworkin is not whether the sanctity of life should be required to yield to some other value, like humanity or compassion, but how life's sanctity should be understood and respected.[96] And on this opinions divide:

> *"Not because some people have contempt for values that others cherish, but, on the contrary, because the values in question are at the centre of everyone's lives, and no one can treat them as trivial enough to accept other people's orders about what they mean. Making someone die in a way that others approve, but he believes a horrifying contradiction of his life, is a devastating, odious form of tyranny".* [97]

Although Dworkin contends that the time and manner of a person's death should be determined by a person's critical interests Herring has an interesting postscript to add. He reports that not all supporters of autonomy are happy with Dworkin's analysis as it appears to leave the door open for someone to say to a person, who wished to invoke their critical interests to refuse life-preserving treatment, I know that you that

---

[92] Ibid, p.392

[93] Ibid

[94] Dworkin, Ronald, Life's Dominion: An argument about Abortion and Euthanasia, Harper Collins, p.215

[95] Ibid, p.216

[96] Ibid, p.217

[97] Ibid

are now saying you want to die, but a better fit with your life story (your critical interests) would be for you to live longer'.[98]

The Legal Framework for Advance Decisions

It is an established principle of law that a competent adult patient has a right to make their own health decisions.[99] When the right to self-determination is exercised prospectively the MCA states that where the decision of the patient is both legally valid and applicable in the circumstances a doctor would be bound to act in accordance with the patient's wishes.[100] Advance directives or decisions therefore preserve the patient's right to decide subjectively in accordance with their own values and methods whether the burdens or risks of treatment outweigh the benefits that it may bestow upon them. Consequently, a patient who outlines their wishes in advance retains control over their body as well as their life plan and gets round the problem that a doctor will weigh those interests objectively, in accordance with what a reasonable person would decide in the situation of the patient, with all its attendant uncertainties.

The purpose of this part of the chapter is then to examine the requirements of the Mental Capacity Act 2005 in relation to advance decisions.

General Requirements

As a doctor is acting on the instructions of the patient the considerations that apply to patient consent or refusals apply to an advance directive, i.e. an advance decision must similarly satisfy the general legal requirements that apply to ordinary consent.

Competent Choice

It is a clear requirement of the Mental Capacity Act that adults must have decision-making capacity at the time of making an advance decision to

---

[98] Herring, Jonathan, Medical Law and Ethics, 2008, Second Edition, Oxford University Press, p.467

[99] *Re F (Mental Patient: Sterilisation) [1990] 2 AC 1 HL; Re T (Adult: Refusal of Treatment) [1992] 4 All ER 649 CA*

[100] Mental Capacity Act 2005, ss.24-26; *Re T (Adult: Refusal of Treatment) [1992] 4 All ER 649 CA; Airedale NHS Trust v Bland [1993] 1 All ER 821 HL*

refuse medical treatment.[101] The MCA also establishes that the presumption in favour of capacity operates in respect of advance decisions[102] and that in cases of doubt a functional approach to capacity endures to safeguard persons against the repercussions of making a non-autonomous decision by placing emphasis on the way in which the decision was made rather than on the decision itself.[103]

The question is how are doctors to arrive at a safe conclusion in relation to competency on the evidence of a written document or the oral testimony of a third party particularly in circumstances where the patient was previously unknown to them? A patient may have been in severe pain, tired or fatigued, depressed or unduly stressed; they might also have been under the influence of drugs or alcohol which temporarily reduced their capacity to decide to refuse a particular form of medical treatment at the time the decision was made.[104] The patient's ability to understand or retain information may not have been significantly impaired but the ability to use or weigh information might have been and this would have a bearing on their judgment. By analogy this is the reason why the vehicles of long distance lorry drivers are fitted with a tachograph. Its purpose is to enforce drivers to take regular breaks and thus to prevent them from becoming a hazard to themselves, pedestrians and other road users through the effects of tiredness or fatigue. Alcohol is known to affect judgment consequently the public interest demands that a relatively low level of alcohol consumption is necessary to fail a breathalyser test. Direct communication with the patient aids doctors in deciding whether their patient is fully competent to decide the matter under consideration but indications of incompetency might be altogether too subtle to detect in the case of an anticipatory refusal.

It is perhaps for this reason that Lord Donaldson MR has previously stated that:

> *"Doctors faced with a refusal of consent have to give very careful and detailed consideration to the patient's capacity to decide at the time when the decision was made. It may not be the simple case of the patient having no capacity because, for example, at that time he had hallucinations. It*

[101] Mental Capacity Act 2005, s.24(1)
[102] Mental Capacity Act 2005, s.1(2)
[103] Mental Capacity Act 2005, s.1(4)
[104] Medical Law – Kennedy & Grubb – Third Edition – Butterworths – Chapter 5, page 642

> *may be the more difficult case of a temporarily reduced capacity at the time when his decision was made. What matters is that the doctors should consider whether at that time he had a capacity which was commensurate with the gravity of the decision which he purported to make. The more serious the decision, the greater the capacity required".*[105]

As the right to refuse medical treatment exists even where it may lead to the patient's death what link might there be between capacity and the effects of a decision.[106] Perhaps Lord Donaldson is claiming that a greater level of capacity is required to refuse medical treatment. However, it has been suggested that the link is not made on the basis of the patient displaying greater reasoning powers but rather that they should be able to understand more information the more serious their decision and for that reason the decision-making process will be subject to greater scrutiny in such circumstances.[107] This reasoning is compatible with the adoption of a functional based test to anticipatory decision-making. Indeed concerns with establishing capacity are ameliorated by the requirement that an advance directive should be both valid and applicable in the circumstances that have in fact arisen and to the special requirements that apply to decisions to refuse life-sustaining treatment.[108] Therefore, it is open to question whether a functional test for capacity, which appears to be fitted towards contemporaneous decision-making, can always be as safely relied upon in relation to anticipatory treatment decisions since appearances suggest that the effects of a decision may be the only real reason there is to query the competency of the person in question, whatever other name we may choose to attach to it.[109]

Free from Undue Influence

The effects of undue influence or coercion invalidate a refusal of medical treatment.[110] This is because the will of the patient has been acted upon and therefore the decision of the patient cannot be a true expression of

---

[105] *Re T (Adult: Refusal of Treatment) [1992] 4 All ER 649 CA*

[106] Mental Capacity Act 2005, s25(5); *Re T (Adult: Refusal of Treatment) [1992] 4 All ER 649 CA*

[107] Medical Law – Kennedy & Grubb – Third Edition – Butterworths, Chapter 5, page 627

[108] Mental Capacity Act 2005, s.25

[109] Ibid, s.25(2)©;s.25(4)©; s.25(5)(a)

[110] *Re T (Adult: Refusal of Treatment) [1992] 4 All ER 649 CA*

their wishes.[111] On the other hand persuasion of whatever force will not invalidate a refusal so long as the patient reached the decision to refuse independently.[112] That is to say they were persuaded of something through the merits of the reasons advanced by a third party.[113]

Can appeals to reason be easily distinguished from appeals to emotions?[114] Moreover, will it be possible to detect and measure the strength of an external influence?[115] When applied to the case before them the court in *Re T* concluded that a patient in a weakened medical condition, in pain and under the influence of drugs, that had been administered to assist her, had succumbed to pressure from her mother. In reaching their conclusion the courts were able to draw upon a catalogue of events that spanned a period of some two weeks whilst the patient was hospitalised. How should a doctor determine whether or not a patient's will has been overborne in relation to an advance decision? Relevant background information may not always be available and when the influence of others may be subtle[116] its presence may be relatively undetectable by those who are charged with ensuring the patients' right of self-determination.

Was the Patient Adequately Informed about the effects of a Choice?

What is required is that a patient knew in broad terms the nature and effect of the procedure to which their refusal is given.[117] Whilst there is also a duty to appropriately inform the patient as to the likely risks, including any special risks, attaching to the proposed treatment[118] in this instance treatment is being refused rather than consented to so a doctor must be satisfied that the patient was adequately informed about the risks of non-treatment.[119] How should the goals of informed consent be interpreted to

---

[111] Ibid
[112] Ibid
[113] Beauchamp, Tom L., Childress, James F., Principles of Biomedical Ethics, 2001, Fifth Edition, Oxford University Press, p.94; *Re T (Adult: Refusal of Treatment) [1992] 4 All ER 649 CA*
[114] Ibid
[115] Ibid
[116] note the distinction between persuasion and undue influence
[117] *Chatterton v Gerson [1981] QB 432*
[118] *Chester v Afshar 2004 WL 2289136*
[119] *Re T (Adult: Refusal of Treatment) [1992] 4 All ER 649 CA*

protect the inviolability of patients who choose to register an anticipatory treatment refusal?

Case law suggests that a doctor should consider whether the patient may have been misinformed about the nature and effects of treatment, or whether such information had been withheld.[120] Either way, the nature of the patient's choice and the manner of its expression will in most instances be the only method by which a doctor may be alerted to the possibility that the patient's choice was not adequately informed.[121] As to whether the patient was adequately informed about the risks of non-treatment[122] a safety net exists as the decision of the patient is not applicable to life-sustaining treatment unless the patient specifies otherwise.[123]

Recognition of Advance Refusals

An advance decision enables an adult while still capable to refuse specified medical treatment for a time in the future when they may lack the capacity to consent to or to refuse that treatment.[124] This position was challenged by Mr Burke who suffered from a progressively degenerative brain condition that follows a similar course to multiple sclerosis.[125] By reason of his condition the time would come when he would be entirely dependent on others for his care and indeed for his survival.[126] He was concerned that a doctor might decide to withdraw treatment, in this case artificial nutrition and hydration, because his life was no longer worth living even though death was not imminent.[127]

In the case of *Bland* the House of Lords had determined that doctors should ordinarily seek a declaration from the court prior to withdrawing artificial nutrition and hydration from an insentient patient in a persistent vegetative state on the basis that treatment was futile. However, guidance of the General Medical Council was to the effect that, '*where death is not imminent, it usually will be appropriate to provide artificial nutrition or*

---

[120] Ibid
[121] Ibid
[122] Ibid
[123] Mental Capacity Act 2005, s.25(5)
[124] Mental Capacity Act 2005, Code of Practice, Chapter 9
[125] *R (On the Application of Oliver Leslie Burke) v The General Medical Council [2005] EWCA Civ 1003 CA*, para.3
[126] Ibid, para.4
[127] Ibid, para.5

hydration. However, circumstances may arise where you judge that a patient's condition is so severe, the prognosis so poor, that providing artificial nutrition or hydration may cause suffering or to be too burdensome in relation to the possible benefits'.[128] Mr Burke anticipated the progression of his condition would result in an increase in his suffering and worried that artificial nutrition and hydration may be withdrawn without recourse to the courts as there was no obligation to seek a declaration, on the part of the doctor, in circumstances where a doctor determined that continued existence with treatment would be intolerable for a sentient patient.[129]

Mr Burke therefore commenced proceedings with a view to obtaining a ruling that the GMC's advice was unlawful and that doctors would be required to comply with his competent request to receive artificial nutrition and hydration.[130]

The court ruled that:

> *"Autonomy and the right of self-determination do not entitle the patient to insist on receiving a particular medical treatment regardless of the nature of the treatment. Insofar as a doctor has a legal obligation to provide treatment this cannot be founded simply upon the fact that the patient demands it. The source of the duty lies elsewhere.*[131]
>
> *... Once a patient is accepted into a hospital, the medical staff come under a positive duty at common law to care for the patient... A fundamental aspect of this positive duty of care is a duty to take such steps as are reasonable to keep the patient alive. Where ANH is necessary to keep the patient alive, the duty of care will normally require the doctors to supply ANH... Where the competent patient makes it plain that he or she wishes to be kept alive by ANH, this will not be the source of the duty to provide it. The patient's wish will merely underscore that duty.* [132]
>
> *[In circumstances] where the patient is not competent and it is not considered to be in the best interests of the patient to be artificially kept alive ... [t]he courts have accepted that where life involves an extreme*

---

128 Ibid, para.6

129 Ibid; *Re J (A Minor) (Wardship: Medical Treatment) [1990] 3 All ER 930 CA*

130 *R (On the Application of Oliver Leslie Burke) v The General Medical Council [2005] EWCA Civ 1003 CA*, para.15

131 Ibid, para.31

132 Ibid, para.32

> *degree of pain, discomfort or indignity to a patient, who is sentient but not competent and who has manifested no wish to be kept alive, these circumstances may absolve the doctors of the positive duty to keep the patient alive. Equally, the courts have recognised that ... the facts of the individual case may make it difficult to decide whether the duty to keep the patient alive persists".*[133]

Consequently, the advice issued to doctors by the GMC was lawful.[134] Notwithstanding that fact the court went on to observe[135] that whilst an advance directive to refuse life-preserving must be respected[136] a patient who had expressed a wish to be kept alive would be taken into consideration by doctors when considering what is in the best interests of the patient.[137] Therefore, the situation may be summarised thus. An advance directive provides a competent patient with a right to refuse treatment after they have ceased to be competent.[138] It cannot be used to request treatment that the patient might consider to be in their own best interests although a statement of wishes would be taken into consideration by doctors in determining what should be done in the patient's best interests.[139] As this principle extends to life-sustaining treatment there is no right to life. Nevertheless, there may be circumstances in which it would be possible for a patient to use an advanced directive to refuse all but the preferred method of treatment.[140] However there are no guarantees that this would have the hoped for effect. Moreover, the patient would be required to understand and process a considerable amount of information and even if this could be accomplished a doctor might still invoke the *Bolam* principle on the basis that the desired treatment is not treatment that a responsible doctor would administer in the circumstances.

---

[133] Ibid, para.33
[134] Ibid, para.47
[135] Ibid, para.57
[136] Mental Capacity Act 2005, s.26
[137] Ibid, s.4(6)(a)
[138] *R (On the Application of Oliver Leslie Burke) v The General Medical Council [2005] EWCA Civ 1003 CA*, para. 2
[139] Ibid
[140] Jones, Richard, Mental Capacity Act Manual, 2008, Third Edition, Thomson, Sweet and Maxwell, p.91

Requirements that are Specific to Advance Decisions

Advance decisions are attractive because they allow people to plan ahead for a time in the future when they may no longer have the power to be autonomous and for that reason are unable to make decisions for themselves.[141] However, an advance decision to refuse treatment must be valid and applicable to the circumstances that have in fact arisen to have the same effect as a decision that is made by a person with capacity.[142]

Validity

An advance decision to refuse medical treatment will have legal effect only when the decision is, at the material time, valid.[143] Inter alia[144] an anticipatory decision is not valid if it has subsequently been revoked either because the patient has withdrawn the decision at a time when they still had capacity to do so[145] or else has done anything that is clearly inconsistent with the advance decision remaining his fixed decision.[146]

Withdrawal

A valid advance directive may be made orally or be in writing.[147] As there are no formal requirements to be observed in creating an advance decision there are no formal requirements for the revocation of an advance directive so that one that is made in writing may be revoked orally.[148] The point of anticipatory decision-making is to further patient autonomy. Consequently, any clause or condition that seeks to fetter this underlying objective, including the right to change one's mind, will be void in being contrary to public policy.[149]

---

[141] Mental Capacity Act 2005, Code of Practice, Foreword by Lord Falconer

[142] Ibid, Chapter Nine, Quick Summary

[143] Mental Capacity Act 2005, s.25(1)(a)

[144] I do not intend to cover the situation whereby a Lasting Power of Attorney is created after an the advance decision was made – see s.25(2)(b)

[145] Mental Capacity Act 2005, s.25(2)(a)

[146] Ibid, s.25(2)©

[147] *HE v A Hospital NHS Trust 2003 WL 21729346*, para.46

[148] Ibid

[149] Ibid

However, a previously expressed competent decision can only be revoked where the person retains decision-making capacity.[150] Accordingly, when a previously competent adult patient loses both the capacity to decide whether or not to accept medical treatment and any ability to express his wishes and feelings then a previously valid advance directive that has not been revoked will in effect become and potentially remain irrevocable.[151] The fact that '*exceptionally difficult moral, ethical and legal questions*' may have to be addressed when a previously competent patient is in the twilight position of having lost their decision-making capacity but otherwise remains able to express their wishes and feelings has already been raised.[152]

Inconsistent Acts

At common law it has been determined that an anticipatory choice might not survive a subsequent, or even an impending, change of faith by the patient.[153] The case of *HE*, reveals that the daughter was born and brought up as a Muslim.[154] Her parents separated and AE, the daughter, went to live with her mother.[155] Sometime later the mother became a Jehovah's Witness and as the daughter followed suit she was from that time onwards brought up as a Jehovah's Witness.[156] Unfortunately, AE suffered from a congenital heart problem which might need to be treated in the future. Yet, AE had made an advance directive to refuse blood transfusions and blood products and this decision was consistent with her religious belief and commitments. In it she had stipulated that the refusal should continue to apply even when such treatment was required to save or preserve her life.[157]

When the earlier advance decision came to be applied AE's mother and brother remained adamant that she would refuse blood products.[158] Her

---

[150] Ibid, para.38
[151] Ibid
[152] Ibid
[153] *Re T (Adult: Refusal of Medical Treatment) [1992] 4 All ER 649 CA; HE v A Hospital NHS Trust 2003 WL 21729346*
[154] *HE v A Hospital NHS Trust 2003 WL 21729346*, para.2
[155] Ibid
[156] Ibid
[157] Ibid, para.4
[158] Ibid, para.10

father, grandmother and fiancé contested this.[159] In particular, her father claimed that AE had said, in the presence of her brother and aunt, that she did not want to die.[160]

On this matter the presiding judge ruled that the earlier anticipatory statement of AE should not be relied upon. This was primarily because she had more recently become engaged to be married to a Turkish man and it was a condition of their marriage that AE should reject her faith and become a Muslim once more.[161] Her intention in this regard was demonstrated by the fact that she had not and was not currently actively pursuing her faith as a Jehovah's Witness.[162]

Thus the issue of whether or not an advance decision continues to be valid or has been revoked is treated as a question of fact to be determined by the evidence.[163] And since AE had not demonstrated a settled and continuing commitment to uphold the belief that was a source of her advance decision there was a real, rather than speculative, reason to doubt the continuing validity of an advance decision.[164] In this regard words said to have been spoken by the patient might warrant further investigation. The problem is that too greater willingness to accede to this type of evidence could be detrimental to patient autonomy. But on the basis that actions often speak louder than words such evidence might more readily constitute a real reason to doubt the continuing validity of an advance directive,[165] and when the entire substratum or the assumption on which the advance directive was based has been destroyed by subsequent events then the refusal will cease to be effective.[166]

Clearly medical professionals will, for the most part, be charged with the task of separating out real reasons from those that are merely speculative.

---

[159] Ibid
[160] Ibid, para.6
[161] Ibid, para.13
[162] Ibid
[163] Ibid, para.46
[164] Ibid, para.34
[165] Ibid, para.43
[166] Ibid, para.49

Applicability

The issue here is whether an advance decision is applicable to the situation in question and in the current circumstances.[167] An advance decision will not be applicable if at the material time a patient remains competent to express their current wishes with regard to treatment.[168] Accordingly, an anticipatory decision will not be applicable if at the material time a person retains capacity to give or refuse consent to the treatment in question.[169] Likewise, an anticipatory refusal is not applicable to the treatment if that treatment is not the treatment specified in the advance directive,[170] or any circumstances specified in the advance directive are absent[171] or there may be reasonable grounds for believing that circumstances exist that were not anticipated at the time of the advance directive and which would have affected the decision had they been anticipated.[172] Lastly, and most importantly, an advance directive is not applicable to life sustaining treatment unless it is specified to do so.[173]

Retaining Capacity

There is a presumption that all adults have capacity to consent to medical treatment.[174] Setting the barrier too high in relation to the level of capacity that is required for medical decision-making would preclude many from exercising their right of self-determination. It is therefore an aspect of respect for personal autonomy that every effort is made to assist even borderline patients to overcome their difficulties in making a contemporaneous medical treatment decision.[175] Essentially if the person has or gains capacity to make a medical treatment decision they can refuse the relevant treatment at the material time or may exercise their right to change their decision and consent to the treatment in question. Consequently advance directives are inherently revocable.[176]

---

[167] Mental Capacity Act 2005, Code of Practice, para.9.41

[168] Mental Capacity Act 2005, s.25(3); Mental Capacity Act 2005, Code of Practice, para.9.41

[169] Mental Capacity Act 2005, s.25(3)

[170] Ibid, s.25(4)(a)

[171] Ibid, s.25(4)(b)

[172] Ibid, s.25(4)©

[173] Ibid, s.25(5)

[174] Ibid, s.1(2)

[175] Ibid, s.1(3), s.3(2), s.25(3)

[176] *HE v A Hospital NHS Trust 2003 WL 21729346*

In an appropriate case a finding that a patient retains decision-making capacity opens the door for them to review their prior choice, which may have been expressed at a time when they were in full health, in the light of their current situation. The issue of whether or not a person has capacity is treated as a question of fact to be determined by a doctor with responsibility for the patient. A possible concern, in view of the evidence reviewed earlier in this chapter, is with the circumstances in which a patient may be found to retain decision-making capacity as it is difficult to eliminate the possibility of them feeling vulnerable as a result of their condition and afraid by what is entailed in their prior instructions and these are the very conditions which are known to engender a change of mind with a little persuasion.[177]

Specifying Treatment

Of course medical treatment may be of one type such as when a ventilator is used to compensate for the cardio-vascular system in keeping the patient alive. On the other hand patients who are unconscious or are otherwise disabled from taking food and water orally may be given artificial nutrition and hydration by naso-gastric tube[178] or by percutaneous gastrostomy tube.[179] Therefore, it is a problem associated with specifying a form of treatment that a doctor may still treat their patient just as effectively with an alternative form of medical treatment. Indeed the decision may be overtaken by subsequent advances in medical science and technology that create a range of treatment options, particularly where some time has elapsed between the creation and use of an advance directive. Moreover, consideration should be given to the fact that medicine promotes divergent practices in any event.[180] Accordingly, patients that have sought medical advice in the process of drafting their advance directive are less likely to find themselves overtaken by advances in medical science.[181]

There is also the problem that in making an advance directive a patient may have used terms that cloud the issue of what treatment they are

---

177 *Re T (Adult: Refusal of Medical Treatment) [1992] 4 All ER 649 CA*, Butler-Sloss LJ
178 *Airedale NHS Trust v Bland [1993] AC 789 HL*
179 *W Healthcare NHS Trust v KH 2004 WL 2458658*
180 *Bolam v Friern Hospital Management Committee [1957] 1 WLR 582*
181 Ibid, s.8.19

refusing.[182] For example, a patient might simply state that they do not want to be placed on life support.[183] However, kidney dialysis constitutes life support.[184] It has therefore been suggested that advance directives might be more useful if rather than specifying the treatment a patient specified their expectations, i.e. what degree of illness or incapacity they were prepared to live with.[185]

Absent Circumstances

On the basis that a patient's actions speak louder than words a material change of circumstances may decree an advance directive no longer applicable to the treatment in question. Thus it may be alleged that the patient no longer professes the faith which underlay the advance directive, or it may be said that the patient executed the advance directive because they were suffering from an illness which has since been cured, medical science may have moved on, or it may be said that the patient, having since married or had children, now has more compelling reasons to choose to live even a severely disadvantaged life.[186]

Unanticipated Circumstances

Advances in medical science and the development of new medications or other forms of treatment or therapies might extend the treatment options that are available to doctors and if these were not foreseen by the patient their anticipatory decision to refuse treatment may not be applicable. Equally there may have been changes in the patient's personal life which were not anticipated at the time when they made an advance decision. For example, the patient may now be pregnant or might recently have had children and their hopes and expectations may have been modified by these events. In these circumstances a doctor cannot conclude that if the patient still had the necessary capacity in the changed situation they would have reversed their decision but they can consider what was the true scope and basis of the patient's decision, i.e. whether at the time the decision was made it was intended by the patient to apply in the changed situation.[187]

---

[182] Inside the Ethics Committee, Radio Four
[183] Ibid
[184] Ibid
[185] Ibid
[186] *HE v A Hospital NHS Trust 2003 WL 21729346*, para 43
[187] *Re T (Adult: Refusal of Medical Treatment) [1992] 4 All ER 649 CA*, Lord Donaldson MR

In other words physicians must consider whether the refusal is unequivocal or of more limited scope. It will be of limited scope where, for example, a patient refuses a blood transfusion in the belief that there is an effective alternative treatment.[188] Consequently, if the factual situation falls outside the scope of the refusal or if the assumption on which it is based is falsified, the refusal ceases to be effective.[189] Therefore, treatment refusals that have been expressed in an advance directive should be subject to constant review and updated where necessary.

Life Sustaining Treatment

When a person intends that their anticipatory refusal should extend to life-sustaining treatment this must be explicitly stated in the advance directive. Thus the true scope of their decision must be made explicit.

Preliminary Summary

In summary an advance decision is not applicable to the treatment a doctor proposes to administer in the patient's best interests if the treatment is not the treatment specified in the advance decision or if any circumstances specified in the advance decision are absent or there are reasonable grounds for believing that circumstances exist which the patient did not anticipate at the time of the advance decision and which would have affected their decision had they been anticipated.[190] There is evidence, however, to suggest that all persons frequently encounter problems in writing with such precision.[191]

The Effect of an Advance Decision

An advance decision that is legally valid and applicable has the same effect as a contemporaneous decision to refuse treatment.[192] The result, according to Andrew Grubb, is that:

---

[188] *Re T (Adult: Refusal of Medical Treatment) [1992] 4 All ER 649 CA*

[189] Ibid

[190] Herring, Jonathan, Medical Law and Ethics, 2008, Second Edition, Oxford University Press, p.159

[191] Fagerlin, Angela, Schneider, Carl E., 2004, Enough The Failure of the Living Will, Hastings Center Report, March-April, p.34; Herring, Jonathan, Medical Law and Ethics, 2008, Second Edition, Oxford University Press, p.466

[192] Mental Capacity Act 2005, s.26(1)

"If a competent adult has expressed an unequivocal decision to refuse treatment, it is not for the doctor or the court to speculate as to the strength of the patient's personal or religious convictions or as to his reasons for refusing consent. Nor is it for the doctor or the court to speculate as to what the patient's decision might have been if he had been alive to the current crisis, or if he had been more fully informed, or if he had had more forcibly brought home to him all the implications of his refusal. If it is not possible to say what the patient's decision would have been if he had been given more information, his expressed decision, if he was competent to make it, is decisive, even if it was not made in contemplation of life-threatening circumstances".[193]

Determining what was the Scope and Basis of the Patient's Decision?

Even if a doctor considers that the patient had the capacity to decide and has exercised their right to do so, they still have to consider what is the true scope and basis of that decision.[194] So although an unambiguous advance decision which is being applied in unambiguous circumstances will be treated in the same way as if the patient had expressed an unequivocal decision to refuse treatment contemporaneously[195] a doctor may have reason to doubt that the decision remains operative or continues to be valid and applicable.[196]

For example, a doctor may be given conflicting accounts of the patient's wishes or beliefs.[197] And here we must bear in mind that as there are no formal requirements for a valid advance directive, in that an anticipatory decision need not be either in or evidenced by writing, there are similarly no formal requirements for the revocation of an anticipatory choice.[198]

---

[193] Grubb, A., Principles of Medical Law, 2004, Second Edition, Oxford University Press, para. 4.120; *Re T (Adult: Refusal of Medical Treatment) [1992] 4 All ER 649 CA*, Lord Donaldson MR

[194] *Re T (Adult: Refusal of Medical Treatment) [1992] 4 All ER 649 CA*, Lord Donaldson MR

[195] Mason, J.K., McCall Smith, R.A., Laurie, G.T., Law and Medical Ethics, 2002, Sixth Edition, Butterworths, para. 18.64

[196] *Re T (Adult: Refusal of Medical Treatment) [1992] 4 All ER 649 CA; HE v A Hospital NHS Trust 2003 WL 21729346*

[197] Ibid

[198] *HE v A Hospital NHS Trust 2003 WL 21729346*, para.46

Moreover, an advance directive is inherently revocable.[199] It may be words said to have been written or spoken by the patient.[200] It may be the patient's actions, for sometimes actions speak louder than words.[201] It may be some change in circumstances.[202] Thus it may be alleged that the patient no longer professes the faith which underlay the advance directive; it may be said that the patient executed the advance directive because he was suffering from an illness which has since been cured; it may be said that medical science has now moved on; it may be said that the patient, having since married or had children, now finds himself with more compelling reasons to choose to live even a severely disadvantaged life.[203] It may be suggested that the advance directive has been revoked, whether by express words or by conduct on the part of the patient which is inconsistent with its continued validity.[204] It may be suggested that, even though not revoked, the advance directive has not survived some material change of circumstances.[205] Anyone of these factors but most particularly the lack of a formal process for the creation and revocation of an anticipatory decision can work to the advantage of those who would seek to challenge its existence or continuing validity or applicability.[206]

The issue of whether or not an advance decision exists and continues to be valid and applicable is treated as a question of fact to be determined, initially at least, by a doctor who cannot simply deny the patient's right of decision.[207] Instead a doctor is required to have some reason to doubt that the anticipatory choice remains operative and where doubt exists the burden of proof, in each case, is on those who seek to establish the existence or continuing validity and applicability of an advance directive.[208] Commenting on the doctor's position Justice Munby has stated that:

---

[199] *Re T (Adult: Refusal of Medical Treatment) [1992] 4 All ER 649 CA; HE v A Hospital NHS Trust 2003 WL 21729346*, para.46
[200] *HE v A Hospital NHS Trust 2003 WL 21729346*, para.43
[201] Ibid
[202] Ibid
[203] Ibid
[204] Ibid
[205] Ibid
[206] *Re T (Adult: Refusal of Medical Treatment) [1992] 4 All ER 649 CA; HE v A Hospital NHS Trust 2003 WL 21729346*
[207] Ibid; Ibid, para.46
[208] Ibid

> *"Whether there is some real reason to doubt, whether the doubt is a real or only some speculative or fanciful doubt, will inevitably depend on the circumstances. Holding the balance involves awesome responsibility. Too ready a submission to speculative or merely fanciful doubts will rob advance directives of their utility and may condemn those who in truth do not want to be treated to what they would see as indignity or worse... Too sceptical a reaction to well-founded suggestions that circumstances have changed may turn an advance directive into a death warrant for a patient who in truth wants to be treated.*[209]
>
> *At the end of the day, and however unhelpful for hard pressed doctors this seeming platitude may be, it must all depend on the facts. All I would add is that the longer the time has elapsed since an advance directive was made, and the greater the apparent changes in the patient's circumstances since then, the more doubt there is likely to be as to its continuing validity and applicability. There will be cases in which there will need to be especially close, rigorous and anxious scrutiny".*[210]

Doctors are required, in cases where life is at stake, to scrutinise the evidence as to the existence and continuing validity and applicability of an advance refusal with especial care to ensure that it is clear, convincing and inherently reliable and if there is reason to doubt that doubt falls to be resolved in favour of the preservation of life.[211] Once it has been determined that an advance directive cannot be relied upon a doctor will be required to exercise judgment in accordance with a best interests treatment standard on behalf of the patient.[212] Where the evidence relied upon by the doctor is contested an application to court can be made for a declaration as to the existence, validity or applicability of an advance decision.[213] Consequently, the court is the ultimate arbiter of whether an advance decision exists that is valid and applicable to a treatment.[214] In the interim period a doctor may provide treatment to sustain life or to prevent a serious deterioration in the patient's health.[215]

---

[209] *HE v A Hospital NHS Trust 2003 WL 21729346*, para.44
[210] Ibid, para.45
[211] Ibid, para.46
[212] Ibid, para.43
[213] Mental Capacity Act 2005, s.26(4)
[214] *Re T (Adult: Refusal of Medical Treatment) [1992] 4 All ER 649 CA; HE v A Hospital NHS Trust 2003 WL 21729346*
[215] Mental Capacity Act 2005, s.26(5)

Alerting Doctors to the Presence of an Advance Directive

A doctor who wishes to avoid liability for a battery is required to obtain a legally valid and applicable consent from their competent patient prior to administering medical treatment.[216] Medical professionals do not however incur liability for carrying out or continuing with treatment in their patient's best interests unless, at the time, the physician is satisfied that an advance directive exists which is valid and applicable to the treatment in question.[217] In other words, patients bear the responsibility for bringing their advance directive to the doctor's attention. An issue in this regard is the lack of a central system of registration in England and Wales. This is surprising in view of the legislative objective to empower patients and to place them at the centre of decision-making processes concerning them.

Consequently, this defence enables doctors to act in the patient's best medical interests in an emergency. In these situations the patient may be unknown and circumstances may dictate that the requirement to consult relatives cannot be fulfilled because one cannot reasonably be found in time. Therefore, it is presumed that all patients would wish to receive medical treatment and care, including life preserving treatment. In cases of doubt that doubt falls to be resolved in favour of the preservation of life.[218] So we can all rest assured that we will not be turned away from the accident and emergency department for want of a 'request for treatment' card.[219]

It is also apparent that treatment may be withheld or, more importantly in this context, subsequently withdrawn after it has been initiated, and a person does not incur liability for the consequences of doing so if at the time they reasonably believe that the patient has made an advance decision which is valid and applicable to the treatment in question.[220] This provision, in prioritising autonomy over beneficence, importantly restores moral neutrality in the law related to mentally incapacitated patients.

How likely is it, in these circumstances, that an advance directive will reach medical professionals who are responsible for the care of the

---

[216] *Re F (Mental Patient: Sterilisation) [1990] 2 AC 1 HL*
[217] Mental Capacity Act 2005, s.26(2)
[218] *Airedale NHS Trust v Bland [1993] 1 All ER 821*, Lord Keith
[219] Mason, J.K., McCall Smith, R.A., Laurie, G.T., Law and Medical Ethics, 2002, Sixth Edition, Butterworths, para. 18.68
[220] Mental Capacity Act 2005, s.26(3)

incompetent patient?[221] American research suggests that for a variety of reasons often they do not.[222] The time span between the creation and use of an advance directive is often critical as the greater the time that has elapsed the more likely it is that the existence and location of the advance directive will have faded from the memory.[223] Secondly, because of potential difficulties in drafting an advance directive many people enlist the help of lawyers and unfortunately research shows that a majority[224] of patients do not give their advance directive to their doctor.[225] Another reason why advance directives do not come to the attention of physicians is that on admission to hospital patients are often too anxious to recall and mention their advance directive and that those dealing with the patient's admission to hospital might be too busy, neglectful or just loath to ask awkward questions.[226] It's a little like a host asking his guests on arrival how long they intend to stay.

It may therefore be argued that if advance directives are to have any utility at all some consideration should be given to developing a central registry. Unconscious patients are at a particular disadvantage when the only people who can alert doctors as to the existence of an advance decision are friends or relatives and they may have an interest in not doing so if they disagree with its contents. They might also be concerned at being perceived as hard hearted in seeking to prevent treatment being administered to someone they supposedly care about. A central registry might also ensure that a patient is treated consistently with their advance directive should they have an accident or fall ill outside of their own general locality. Crucially, a central system for registering advance directives is an essential facility if we seriously intend to respect the patients' right to self-determination with regard to their own body, life and life plan.

---

[221] Fagerlin, Angela, Schneider, Carl E., 2004, Enough The Failure of the Living Will, Hastings Center Report, March-April, p.35

[222] Ibid

[223] Ibid

[224] 62%

[225] Fagerlin, Angela, Schneider, Carl E., 2004, Enough The Failure of the Living Will, Hastings Center Report, March-April, p.35

[226] Ibid

Conclusion

The moral ideal of autonomy points to the fact that welfare promoting incentives are born out of self-interest.[227] Indeed the rise in the popularity of autonomy in human affairs suggests that people value having control of themselves and their affairs. As the primacy of the principle of autonomy has been established by the law of consent a competent person is able to decide whether to consent to or refuse to consent to medical treatment by reference to their own values if they so choose.[228] It is also an established principle of law that the former values, beliefs and preferences of a competent person can be binding on physicians if at some future date that person is a patient and is deemed to be mentally incompetent.[229] Consistent with this principle the law makes provision for competent persons to record an advance decision to refuse a particular form of medical treatment in a living will or an advance directive.[230]

An advance directive allows a patient to be pro-active in settling what they want to happen in the future at a time when they are no longer competent to decide. In the same way persons customarily set out their wishes in a will to determine what shall happen to their estate upon their demise. The patient has time to consider things and to talk them over with family, friends and possibly medical professionals and/or carers as well as to consider the consequences of their decision. Ultimately the patient communicates their decision to refuse a particular form of medical treatment in a living will, living because it takes effect whilst the patient is still alive. To that extent the patient has an opportunity to maximise decision-making capacity and to thereby protect an autonomous choice.

In order for the decision to be binding the requirement is that it must be legally valid and applicable in the situation and circumstances that have arisen.[231] There is no defined form that an advance decision must take

---

[227] Kant, I, Groundwork of the Metaphysics of Morals, Edited by Mary Gregor, 2006, Cambridge University Press, p.47; Hill, Thomas E. Jr., Human Welfare and Moral Worth, 2002, Oxford University Press, p.33

[228] *Re T (Adult: Refusal of Medical Treatment) [1992] 4 All ER 649 CA*

[229] Ibid

[230] Mental Capacity Act 2005, ss.24-26; *Re T (Adult: Refusal of Medical Treatment) [1992] 4 All ER 649 CA*

[231] Mental Capacity Act 2005, ss.24-26; *Re T (Adult: Refusal of Medical Treatment) [1992] 4 All ER 649 CA; HE v A Hospital NHS Trust 2003 WL 21729346*

rather the law lays down criteria which a doctor is required to apply to the decision before them. As advance decisions, consistent with the right of self-determination, are inherently revocable legal validity is particularly concerned with whether the decision may subsequently have been withdrawn either by word or by deed.[232] Legal applicability is more directly concerned with what the true scope and basis of the patient's decision is in focusing more particularly on the choice the patient has made and the way in which it has been articulated. There are however, many practical problems and obstacles associated with making and drafting or articulating an anticipatory choice and as the law requires persons to be very clear about what they have decided specificity is one of the most difficult obstacles to overcome. One may either have said too much or too little. Alternatively, terms may have used that have clouded the issue of what the patient intended to happen. Additionally, there may have been a change in personal circumstances which may be reason enough to question the continuing applicability of a treatment decision.

In summary, validity and applicability are difficult standards to meet in seeming to require a patient to be very competent and/or to record a decision close to the time that it will come into effect when in all probability they will have had an opportunity to consult a physician about their decision. Essentially criteria establish that doctors must be very certain about what the patient intended. Consequently, there is a danger that in all other circumstances the values, beliefs and preferences that informed the treatment decision of the patient will be overridden in their best interests.

---

[232] *Re T (Adult: Refusal of Medical Treatment) [1992] 4 All ER 649 CA; HE v A Hospital NHS Trust 2003 WL 21729346*

CHAPTER SIX

PATIENTS' VALUES AND VALUE SYSTEMS

This dissertation has been building to this point of seeking to determine whether it is possible to reliably determine the values and value system of a competent person which if disclosed in a living will could then be used by another, as a relevant written statement of the patient, to inform a best interests decision-making process in the knowledge that particular weight should be given to it.[1] In theory, at least, it is entirely possible that a personal value system could be used in this way as competent patients customarily rely on their own values, beliefs and preferences when deciding whether to accept an offer of medical treatment, or to choose one treatment instead of another, or to reject all forms of medical treatment.

So the idea of using a value system to inform a treatment decision-making process is that it should be in all relevant respects as if the patient had made their decision to consent or to refuse to consent to treatment contemporaneously. In order to achieve this it is essential that a value system should be capable of yielding the choice the patient would make if competent to decide, or, to at least point towards a choice that is most consistent with the values, beliefs and preferences that were disclosed. And if a doctor could determine what should happen in someone's actual best interests there is some justification in saying that it should be possible to treat patients who suffer from a loss of decision-making capacity compatibly with the wishes of their former competent self.

The question is whether, and if so how, the values and value system of a competent person can be reliably identified and recorded, as a relevant written statement of the patient, so that particular weight should be accorded to it in determining what is in their best interests.[2] Therefore, in this chapter we will analyse the concepts of 'values' and of a value

---

[1] Mental Capacity Act 2005, s.4(6)(a); *Re T (Adult: Refusal of Medical Treatment) [1992] 4 All ER 649 CA; HE v A Hospital NHS Trust 2003 WL 21729346*
[2] Ibid

system; consider whether patient values should be paramount in decision-making; reflect on statutory and common law provisions to ensure that patient values are prioritised; propose methods for identifying, articulating and testing a value system to ensure that it is an inherently functional, coherent, clear and reliable source of information about their values; finally, we will explore whether certain values or value systems would not be upheld by the courts on the ground that it is against public policy.

A Personal Value System

We live in an era where medical scientific and technological advances increasingly place medical professionals in a position to satisfy medicine's overriding objective which is to preserve the life, health and well-being of patients. What is more medical science has not only succeeded in identifying new ways to treat illness and disease but has in addition brought forward the possibility of finding alternative treatments or ways of treating the various conditions that afflict mankind. Medical innovation has then brought us to a stage where doctors have the resources to prevent illness, cure ailments, restore health and well-being, alleviate symptoms or suffering, prevent death and prolong life in non-natural ways.

A professional ethical code ensures that medical knowledge and skills are used to benefit patients. The prescription is simple enough. Nevertheless effective medical treatments also carry with them certain inherent risks. Prescribed medicines, even more benign over the counter preparations, typically come with a list of possible risks and side-effects to health and well-being as well as instances of when it is appropriate to seek urgent medical attention. Risk is then an inherent feature of most medical treatments. The problem is that no one can predict with any degree of certainty whether, and if so in what circumstances, a particular risk will materialise.[3] Instead one is required to balance the benefits of treatment against the burdens of it, including its inherent risks.[4]

Decision-making might be relatively straightforward if the purpose of the evaluative process was to objectively appraise whether a course of action was more likely than not to produce a beneficial outcome whereby 'benefit' equated to a/the desired medical outome of treatment or non-treatment. A value system is clearly important to evaluation and eventual

[3] *Chester v Afshar 2004 WL 2289136*

[4] Ibid

judgment. One provides a framework within which someone can ascertain not only what is relevant to consider but to also assess and judge the worth of any proposed course of action.

In this regard the general framework for evaluation and decision determines that above all else human life should not be dishonoured, violated or be subject to injury. Thus all patients enjoy the right to be maintained inviolate and free from bodily harm. As the administration of a medical treatment not only interferes with the bodily integrity of the patient but also exposes them to the risk of harmful consequences materialising, the decision whether to favour one form of treatment over another, or to simply reject treatment, which at the end of life might involve withholding or withdrawing life prolonging treatment, engages self-interest in a way that such decisions should ordinarily reside with the patient.[5]

Here it is relevant to consider that cultural diversity and value pluralism are also part of contemporary life in which there is no definitive idea about what is good or about what is the best way for humans to live. Thus the process of deciding, whether to accept or reject treatment or to choose one treatment in preference to another, should ideally be informed by the patients own philosophical ideas about what a good life for them entails, i.e. what they value and the way in which they value those things. Or, the preferable and essential activities and interests that contribute to their good, since whatever promotes a sense of well-being will also be the source of their suffering,[6] as well as their own attitude to risk. As such some divergence in the responses of people similarly situated is to be expected.

Ethically and legally it has been decided that generalisations about human kind and human nature are an insufficient guide to what will be of interest and value to all individuals. For we have no clue about what makes a person's life good, i.e. what is valuable to them as an individual. The capacity to be rational, which is fundamental to the freedom we enjoy and take for granted, has not served to make humans entirely predictable when exercising their personal freedom. A measure of predictability arises out of the fact that the purpose of all living things is to survive and thrive and most rational persons do have a naturally strong desire for life and for their

---

[5] *Chatterton v Gerson [1981] QB 432; Chester v Afshar 2004 WL 2289136*

[6] Ibid

continued survival. Those who unexpectedly brush shoulders with death will tell you of this and they will tell you that in these circumstances the desire to survive is very powerful. One has only to consider what has been done in the name of survival to appreciate the potency of its force, for it has inclined one person to eat another when faced with hostile conditions, inadequate food supplies and an uncertain prospect of recovery, for it seems that hunger alone could not have been the motivation when the starving populations of Africa refrain from such acts of cannibalism. The desire to reproduce can similarly be attributed to this base instinct as it is through this process that our genetic make-up is passed on and if strong enough will form part of the gene pool of the next generation and as part of the genetic heritage of mankind.

Consequently, we can say, if not assume, that the will to live is an instinctive feature of our nature and explains why most rational individuals would rank death, in representing the ultimate human harm, as a harm that they would most wish to avoid. Persons are then predictable in that sense. But we cannot go further and say that persons only have an interest in their continued survival, as that is to misunderstand what complex beings we are. The desire to flourish or to lead a good life is equally pervasive and there are circumstances in which some individuals might consider that continued life is no longer a benefit to them.[7] Health has no real substitute so poor physical health is inclined to invoke sentiments of this kind since it imposes restriction not choice. It is the fight against preventable forms of restraint that may explain why there is a greater tendency for people of all ages to take regular exercise and to eat healthful foods. Government departments, advertising campaigns and health gurus also advise us to lose weight, to stop smoking and to reduce stress by improving our work-life balance. In other words we are being invited to look at and reconsider our life-style choices from a variety of sources in order to remind us of the need to look after our health and to inform us of the consequences of not doing so.

However, it is impossible to define good health in terms that are solely related to good physical health. A person's mental health status is equally important to their ability to survive and thrive, if not more so. So an arthritic hip or knee joint might prevent the sports enthusiast from participating in sporting activities that they enjoy various capacities,

---

[7] *Re B (Consent to Treatment: Capacity) [2002] EWHC 429; Airedale NHS Trust v Bland [1993] 1 All ER 821*

reasoning and sensual, will eventually succeed in pointing them towards other ways of pursuing a good life. In contrast, a person who suffers an injury to, or impairment in the functioning of, their brain will often have to contend with a more diverse range of issues in relation to the continued pursuit of what was formerly valuable to them. And when good mental health has been unduly or irretrievably compromised, as a result of an accident or disease, the values and interests that previously contributed to their good cannot be substituted. So it is at this point tempting to say that a good life is one of conscious awareness as we can then pursue those things that are valuable to us.

Perhaps that is right, but harmful physiological processes that are adverse to or destroy our vitality can also detrimentally impact upon the natural desire for continued life. A cancer patient who is terminally ill might be willing to relinquish whatever life is left in them in order to be free of continuous and intolerable pain. Similarly, patients who suffer from debilitating illnesses such as Motor Neurone Disease and Multiple Sclerosis, who often experience a gradual but nevertheless relentless physical decline, may eventually be overwhelmed by the indignities they must endure and would prefer to be spared them on grounds of mental intolerability. So whilst the desire to survive is a potent force within most rational persons when good physical and/or mental health has been irretrievably and detrimentally compromised, it may not, on every occasion, be entirely irrational for some people to view an earlier death as being preferable to a continued life of intolerable mental or physical pain, indignity and restricted freedom. Now we see that a good life is one where persons have freedom to pursue whatever is of value to them.

Persons are then generally predictable in the sense that they value life yet it is impossible to predict, with a similar degree of certainty, what a good life for them is or of how what is valuable might affect medical treatment decision-making processes. For example, a sports enthusiast might, in a situation where a choice of treatments exist, prefer to experiment with more conservative approaches to treating discomfort in a joint if more radical treatment posed a small but nonetheless potentially potent threat to their ability to continue with an activity that at one extreme defines them and at another simply provides a considerable degree of pleasure. Alternatively, quality of life considerations can also motivate some persons to pursue forms of treatment that carry with them known risks and/or at the very least unpleasant side-effects. Consider women who must resort to IVF treatment in order to become pregnant. These women must administer themselves with large doses of female hormone in order to stimulate egg production and must endure a surgical procedure for the recovery of those eggs. However, doubts about the burdens of treatment, which include the risks associated with taking excessive doses of the female hormone oestrogen together with the general risks associated with any surgical procedure, to say nothing of the mental anguish that must form a part of an ordeal where the risk that the procedure will fail to yield any positive outcome is known at the outset to be quite high, are all offset by a potential benefit; the prospect of an enjoyable family life which includes having and raising a child of one's own. Quality of life considerations are not therefore simply negative expressions of the harms we wish to avoid but also foretell something about the values, beliefs, interests and preferences that inform our conception of what a good life is and of the type of things that make a positive contribution to our experience of life or that are intrinsically or critically valuable to it.

A personal value system should capture these values and organise them so that they can be understood by others to impart information that is most relevant or fundamental to medical treatment decision-making processes that are concerned with the subjective value life has for the person whose life it is.[8]

Gaining Insight into the Personal Value of One's Own Life

To assist others to understand our view of what is good and bad and therefore what is right and wrong conduct with regard to us a personal value system must not only disclose one's values but must also facilitate decision-making that is taken consistently with the values, beliefs and preferences that previously assumed priority in life. Consistent decision-making, in accordance with adopted values, relies upon the availability of statements concerning the practical application of those values in terms of which values were relevant, how they were weighted and so forth. Other circumstantial evidence could be equally invaluable, particularly where it exposes differences in the ranking and balancing process in various and contrasting situations. For example, a cautious person might prefer to reject medication for a skin complaint that poses a small risk to the health of their liver preferring instead to invest in over-the-counter topical preparations that are benign but also relatively ineffective. However, if

[8] Dworkin, Ronald, Life's Dominion: An argument about Abortion and Euthanasia, Harper Collins, p.73

the way this person looks came to assume greater importance in their life then it is possible that a condition that was at one time tolerated could no longer be so that the small risk of incurring damage to their liver was diminished by the perceived advantages of having an unblemished skin.

The links that are made possible by the disclosed value or values and by the information that is given in support of them should ensure that a value system can be relied on to provide adequate justification for others in deciding matters one way rather than another in the various circumstances and situations that might prevail in the future. Clearly a value system that is limited to a single medical treatment refusal will be constrained by that factor.[9] For example, one of the problems associated with advance decisions is that in the circumstances arising necessitating decision there is likely to be more than one treatment decision that needs to be made. You might also recall from the previous chapter that legal applicability is a difficult standard to meet because doctors might be able to choose an alternative form of treatment that has not been refused or some difference in the prevailing circumstances suggest that the decision of the patient is not applicable. An account of a single belief might on the other hand apply in a multitude of situations. Take for example, a Jehovah's Witness who would in every situation refuse blood; changed circumstances would not elicit, from them, a different choice. Maintaining that religious belief absolutely and without the advantage of a caveat is what is valued and is not outweighed by the benefits of receiving blood. Consequently, a woman who had just given birth to a child that she desperately wanted and would otherwise be devoted to would refuse blood even when her life was at stake.

A more developed or sophisticated value system might put forward an abstract principle that is to be applied to the many and varied situations and circumstances that could arise in the future. Such a principle, in being suitably abstract, increases the likelihood that one can explain or justify a decision on the basis of its terms even when it might not always be obvious how the value system should be applied in practice. For example, let us say that a person is disposed to be a little philosophic and adopts as fundamental the principle that they would seek never to harm the interests of third parties. They were able to illustrate how fundamental this principle was to them and how it had informed their life by providing

[9] *Re T (Adult: Refusal of Medical Treatment) [1992] 4 All ER 649 CA; HE v A Hospital NHS Trust 2003 WL 21729346*

instances of where it had assumed priority over all other personal considerations including one's own financial or professional interests. However, occasion demanded that this principle should be considered in the context of medical treatment, for the person was in urgent need of a donor kidney and a sibling had stepped forward as a willing donor. Is this a clear case where the donation would not go ahead or might someone reason that the value had not previously been applied in a situation where life was at stake and that these circumstances, where it could not be shown that the person exhibited a settled commitment to it, should be treated as an exception that proves the rule. How might the situation be changed if the donated material was bone marrow or blood? Moreover, what should happen in circumstances where access to treatment, such as dialysis, was limited because demand outstripped supply?

When several prima facie principles are presented for consideration, in a single value system, it may be assumed that the difficulties associated with application and adequacy of justification will increase proportionately; at least there is evidence to this effect.[10]

Values

Whilst all persons have values recognising what they are and identifying their true significance might require a little reflective thought. We can use a company by way of analogy to help the process along because businesses like people wish to survive and prosper. Moreover, companies, like people, do not exist in a vacuum isolated from all external contact rather a business must integrate its activities alongside other similar enterprises within a community. So whereas people express themselves through speech and conduct one way in which a business finds expression in the outside world is through its products, services, mission statements, logos, branding, premises, advertisements, staff etc. These activities enable commercial enterprises to raise awareness of their values and ends and gather support for their goods. In general this is achieved by aligning their products or services with a particular consumer group. This is done by correlating the values of the company, product or service with those of the individuals they are seeking to appeal to. The process is successful when the messages that are projected are widely understood and are generally perceived to be true. So if we think of Roll Royce we think of

[10] Beauchamp, Tom L., Childress, James F., Principles of Biomedical Ethics, 2001, Fifth Edition, Oxford University Press, chapter 9

luxury cars that are driven by people who appreciate stateliness, quality and craftsmanship but if we think of Ferrari we are more likely to think of very fast cars driven by playboys and when we think of Ford we think of cars that are driven by a family man.

As profit making organisations, companies are generally careful to maintain positive links with established values, particularly those that are fundamental or critically important to the way in which the business has evolved. Consequently, anything inconsistent that has the potential to detrimentally impact upon the reputation and integrity of their brand in the minds of the public is taken very seriously. To illustrate the point, in 2006, we saw that Kate Moss lost modelling contracts and advertising campaigns with Chanel, Burberry and H&M following allegations in the press that she was taking drugs. In other words these companies considered, at that time that the values expressed by this alleged form of conduct were incompatible with those expressed by their brand names and therefore so too of the particular market they were appealing to.

People tend to think of personal values in similar ways particularly those that play a critical role in shaping that life. Persons co-exist alongside one another and therefore harmonious co-existence relies upon some integration of values, e.g. bodily inviolability and respect for autonomy. Otherwise persons have freedom to develop themselves and their skills and to promote those self-interests through a range of enterprising activities based on a partial account of what a good life is and on what is considered to be of value in human life. In other words persons construct their lives around activities that they like, or that they are good at, or that challenge them and in doing so will either adopt principles that serve their purposes, based on instrumental reasoning, or that assume some importance in establishing how things must be done, i.e. I want to achieve great things but not at any price because how you get there is important.

Essentially, persons determine what a good life is by selecting from the various forms of pleasures and pains that this world has to offer those which they will adopt as their own having noted how these affect personal well-being either positively or negatively and to what degree and by establishing rules for how a life will be lived, or to put the matter another way, those occasions when the will is freely exercised to intervene and triumph over the thoughts and activities of the inclination.

The Intrinsic Value of a Life being a Certain Way is reflected through Critical Values

The circumstances and situations in which we impose our will give us a more complete account of what we actually think is intrinsically good or bad. Moreover, it is in observing whether, when, how and why we exercise our will in relation to our desires and inclinations that we gain insight into how we value things or what is right and wrong conduct in relation to our goods, since we will have tapped into the beliefs and values that play a critical role in informing our life.

Integrity view of Autonomy and Critical Values[11]

Frequently we note the fickle nature of values. The values of companies, institutions, professions and persons change, adapt or are relinquished in favour of others. Reforms may be justified by the need to survive or to flourish in an ever changing world. So under commercial pressure a company, whose mission statement places priority on the value of customer service will, in the interests of their cost/income ratio, make the move away from decentralised switchboard operations in favour of a call centre, which are perceived by many customers as being impersonal and inefficient.

Conscious awareness of one's values enable persons to find ways of managing change on terms that are conducive to them and if personal values withstand the various pressures for change that will inevitably be put upon them, even when recognising that one might be out of step with others, then it is more likely that these values are truly meaningful in determining what a good life, for them, is built upon. And it might be particularly important to declare and make explicit values and beliefs that could on occasion be challenged because they appear to be in conflict with those of others that are more generally held, such as can happen when a practicing Jehovah's Witness wishes to refuse a particular form of medical treatment that could save their life as well as restore them to full health.[12]

---

[11] Dworkin, Ronald, Life's Dominion: An argument about Abortion and Euthanasia, Harper Collins, p.224

[12] *Re T (Adult: Refusal of Medical Treatment) [1992] 4 All ER 649 CA; HE v A Hospital NHS Trust 2003 WL 21729346*

The Consequences of not informing a Decision with Personal Values

The most obvious problem is that a decision that is not informed by personal values may stand out as being irrational, inconsistent or inauthentic when considered in the light of the overall shape of their life.[13] A model, for example, will presumably consider that a good life is one that entails becoming a designer's muse and will value striding decorously down a catwalk wearing that designer's latest creations. They will recognise that they must remain slim, toned and healthy if they desire to have and maintain a successful career. Consequently, decisions to take drugs or to regularly consume vast quantities of alcohol, or food for that matter, are all incompatible with the values associated with being a model.

A competent person also has freedom to change their mind.[14] Autonomy does not entail the notion that persons should be enslaved or controlled by their values, beliefs and preferences. If it were otherwise persons could never even contemplate changing their religious faith and yet many people adopt alternative religious convictions when they marry a person of a different faith. Similarly, a person might find reason to question a settled commitment to an existing religious belief following a recent experience or perhaps even a trip abroad. So values, beliefs and preferences of whatever kind and no matter how fundamental may be revised or relinquished in favour of new and presumably more important ones in the lifetime of a person.[15]

Rational reflection can assist a person to identify changes in attitude toward their beliefs and values and to discover whether the mind has moved in a different direction necessitating some revision of values to be made in conformity with it; alternatively this reflective process can also help to re-affirm values in their current format. The point, however, is to emphasise the importance of keeping values under review and to make any revision of critical values and beliefs known so that in the future a decision may not be challenged because it appears to others to be inconsistent with former decisions and ideas.[16]

---

[13] Ibid

[14] Ibid

[15] Ibid

[16] Mental Capacity Act 2005, s.25(2)©; *Re T (Adult: Refusal of Medical Treatment) [1992] 4 All ER 649 CA; HE v A Hospital NHS Trust 2003 WL 21729346*

Implications in Respect of Medical Treatment

A decision to refuse medical treatment that would, as a consequence, lead to the patient's death may appear to medical professionals to be inconsistent with common opinion about the value of human life particularly when treatment would not only prevent death but would also restore health.[17] This type of situation is exemplified by a woman who has just given birth having lost a lot blood but who now refuses to consent to a blood transfusion that will save her life. Arguably, a choice that would lead to this person's death would appear to be similarly inconsistent with the decision to have a child which is essentially a pro-life choice for it speaks of optimism and hope and of promise for the future and of playing a role in nurturing the talents and interests of a person as a member of a future generation. Crucially it is implicit in the decision to have a child that one accepts the responsibilities of that choice and all that it entails. So a decision to have a child, who is dependent on the actions of its parents, indicates a willingness to accept obligations of selflessness and sacrifice rather than self-indulgence, at least until the child is of age. Consequently, there are grounds to challenge, as irrational, a decision to refuse life-saving treatment. That is unless it was also known that this person was a Jehovah's Witness as then the decision to refuse such treatment would be rational, if not regrettable, in being consistent with their wider beliefs.

The beliefs and values we adopt as our own are then an important source of information about us and when understood by others explain and justify forms of conduct that might otherwise be considered irrational, inconsistent or inauthentic. As a consequence it is essential that a value system is maintained to accurately reflect current beliefs, values and preferences. Otherwise the risk is that upon becoming mentally incapacitated a person will be treated inconsistently with them and the consequences may be irreversible when life is at stake and treatment that would ordinarily save life is withheld.[18] Similarly, where the values, beliefs and preferences of an incapacitated patient are unknown a treatment decision may be imposed with the values that persons are commonly assumed to hold or which reflect the values of the decision-maker.

---

[17] Mental Capacity Act 2005, s.4(5) and 25(5); *Re T (Adult: Refusal of Medical Treatment) [1992] 4 All ER 649 CA; HE v A Hospital NHS Trust 2003 WL 21729346*

[18] Mental Capacity Act 2005, ss.24-26

Voluntariness: Do Persons Willingly Accede to the Values of Others?

Evidence suggests that persons are willing to fight for personal freedom in exercising their own free will. This much we know from observing the conflicts in Ireland and now Iraq which have been attributed to differences in the beliefs and values of the people of these geographic communities. Distrust feeds the conflict because one section of the community does not trust the other to protect their freedom to maintain beliefs and values that are one of the principal causes of the conflict. Consequently, one faction seeks domination over another and the aggressor makes use of military and political tactics to steal an advantage in overbearing the will of those they seek to govern.

So given the importance we appear to attach to autonomy it could be argued that it is against human nature to willingly accede to a situation in which the values, beliefs and preferences of others are imposed upon us particularly if we think that these are likely to be incompatible or conflict with our own. Is this not why accomplices, accessories or those who aid, abet or procure crime are considered to be parties to the crime whilst those whose will was overborne can claim the defence of duress and walk free?[19] Willing acceptance of the imposition of values can therefore also be made out to be a form of self-abuse as the practice denigrates one's rational nature and signals the start of a very slippery slope. When apathy or weakness of the will get a hold we are inclined to get washed along with the tide for we cannot resist the corruptive values of others as we are without means to critique what they have to say or do. At the very least we are vulnerable to being manipulated into forms of conduct we might otherwise have the strength to resist when we have values and beliefs that we defend and are willing to fight for.

Alternatively, we could say that those who aid and abet crime are ill disciplined in the exercise of their free will. For what is demonstrated is irresponsible use of one's rational nature to incite those that are preyed upon to act in ways that are not conducive to their ends. So, what appears to emerge from this discussion is that persons will fight for the right to live in accordance with their own beliefs and values but must at the same time

---

[19] *R v Howe [1987] AC 417 HL*

respect others who may have different ideas about what a good life is.[20] Therefore, harmonious co-existence would seem to rely on taking a disciplined approach to the exercise of our free will in order to temper the demands of the inclination, particularly in situations where the interests of others are engaged.[21]

Is this pure idealism; how realistic is it to suppose that persons will always show sufficient strength of character to both empower and temper the will as occasion demands when history demonstrates humankinds susceptibility to weakness of the will when subjected to various external[22] and internal[23] pressures to do otherwise? This surely explains why society is justified in creating a legal system with recourse to sanctions in respect of forms of conduct that fail to meet widely accepted standards of conduct. Then the question is from what considerations do we derive our ideas about right and wrong human conduct, i.e. what should be the aim of a legal system and from what source should a legal system derive its authority? Remember there is no universal agreement about what good is or of what a good life for humans should entail.

However, in common with Kant most people believe that adult humans are moral creatures who are capable of abstracting from personal differences in moral matters. Indeed many[24] go further and claim that our humanity is most vividly captured and expressed by those who evince a good will or see reason for why we should adopt an attitude of respectful friendship toward others. This capacity, to act in accordance with a reasoned set of principles or rules,[25] rather than from instinct or inclination, can be traced to our rational nature. Therefore should our legal system seek to impose a particular view of what is the right way for humans to live or is it more important that it should remain neutral on the matter and if so how should

---

[20] Mill and Kant anticipated or advocated that persons were capable of abstracting from personal differences in determining what action to take

[21] See Kants comments in respect of moral duty and the value of a good will

[22] Pressures exerted from various third parties perhaps as a result of particular social, economic or political conventions

[23] Inclination or desires, e.g. people pleasing on the basis that person are essentially pleasure seeking beings who wish to avoid pain

[24] God encouraged us to love our neighbour as we love ourselves; Kant claimed that there is nothing so good as a good will; Maslow claims that self-actualisation can only be realised by those who are sufficiently enlightened to see that biases and prejudices of any kind do not serve humanity well

[25] To engender moral respect and equality

this be achieved? Should it be validated purely in facts of nature and human nature in particular because respect for moral laws will be implicit within it or should scope also be given in a political democracy to social conventions, political discourse and in particular (objective) scientific facts, accepting that these may or may not have been correctly established, falsified or contested, particularly if some sort of moral approach can be formulated to these subjects that tells us whether a political order is just or unjust in its relationship to the people it governs.[26] This latter point is important because there exists a hidden opportunity for influential others to impose their views about the form of the good others are due and to therefore influence our thoughts about what is right and wrong human conduct in respect of those goods.

Can free will be directed and controlled in indirect ways by others that are ultimately counterproductive to personal interests and ends? Persons generally dislike any attempt to restrict freedom of the mind or body which might explain why imprisonment is considered to be a punishment. But do we always recognise when that freedom has been invaded? As individuals we are generally secure in feeling that others will respect our physical integrity and that we will respect theirs. This reciprocal arrangement is formed out of recognition for the fact that in life all persons exist in bodily form and consequently depend upon its safe passage for continued survival. Moreover, we learn to recognise situations and circumstances that may lead to direct physical violations and we are therefore increasingly able to take steps to protect ourselves against them. But is there such a thing as an indirect physical violation? Consider the situation of all patients who do not share the knowledge of their general practitioner or physician and do not therefore possess the means to assess the factors considered in the decision-making process or the way in which judgment was exercised in a particular case by these medical professionals.

Take as an example, a person who consults their doctor about recurring medical problems. The symptoms of these conditions are relatively minor and can be treated and managed as and when they arise but the patient is seeking to ascertain the underlying cause of the problems and to determine

---

[26] McGee, Glenn and Bjarnadottir, Dyrleif, Abuses of Science in Medical Ethics, Medical Ethics, 2007, Blackwell Publishing, Chapter 16, p.289; Epstein, Richard, A., The not so Minimum Content of Natural Law, 2005, Oxford Journal of Legal Studies, pp.219-55, p.224

whether these, seemingly unrelated issues can be cured or prevented from returning. Clearly this person relies on the doctor's superior knowledge in these matters. The doctor attributes the problems to life-style choices explaining that they are commonplace and that they are lucky not to be troubled more frequently by them in the way that many other patients are. Much later on however, this person discovers that an alternative body of opinion holds that the problems are related and that they do have an underlying cause for which treatment exists only the costs associated with this measure are greater. Could it be said of such a situation that the doctor steals an advantage, through his superior knowledge, in overbearing the will of the patient?

Should Patient Values be Paramount in Decision-Making?

The question is do persons have values that they live by or do they merely respond to events as they arise and make decisions accordingly which is what Dresser suggests.[27] Let us consider the position of infants who are brought into the world by loving parents. They accept the responsibilities of parenthood and as good parents wish that their child continues to survive and flourish, i.e. has a good life or at least one that they find satisfying. Of course the parent is not a passive bystander waiting patiently for their child's eighteenth birthday to arrive in the hope that everything will come together in accordance with their former wishes. The ideal parent puts to one side any self-interested notions of raising a child with the least possible effort on their part or of raising a child in their own image or of seeking to frustrate the passage to independence by inculcating the impression that the primary obligation of a good son or daughter is to look after their parents in old age. Instead, their child is given space to develop its own personality and to form their own ideas about the world so that the transition to adulthood, when normatively one has freedom to pursue a personal life plan, is unremarkable. The parent-child relationship so construed appears to have been embraced in law since a child's right to autonomy has frequently outweighed their parent's right to determine what is in the best interests of their child.[28] Consequently,

---

[27] Dresser, Rebecca, Dworkin on Dementia: Elegant Theory, Questionable Policy, Hastings Center Report, 1995, November-December, 25, 6, page 36

[28] *Gillick v West Norfolk and Wisbech AHA [1985] 3 All ER 402 HL*, see in particular the judgment of Lord Scarman; Family Law Reform Act 1969, s.8; Mental Capacity Act 2005, Code of Practice, p.1.2; see also *Re A (Children) (Conjoined Twins: Surgical Separation) [2001] Fam 147* a case that highlighted the importance of physical integrity as a pre-condition of autonomy

the law is consistent in its approach to welfare issues of discouraging those who are involved in caring for someone from being overly restrictive or controlling.

From What Source do Values Flow?

What is interesting about this question, if we relate matters back to infants and to legal recognition of their growing autonomy, is that an infant has no concept of the world and therefore no concepts with which to understand the world, its people or what a good life for them should entail. Imagine what sort of a world it would be if it were otherwise and there was a facility to automatically upload a programme that was both neutral and familiar to other users as the common platform on which the A-Z of knowledge and its various uses was built, stored and retrieved. Instead it is in the nature of persons to be curious and to have the capacity to process and store acquired information so that it can be used later on to reason with as a prelude to arriving at a decision or judgment. But persons are also unique and complex beings. So what we have is a situation where the human intellect is augmented by knowledge of concepts which accumulate over time however initial impressions can become modified through various pathways, intellectual, sensory or perceptual, which similarly affect reasoning processes and ultimately judgments.

However, the formative years of a child's life are shaped primarily by its parents. Initially at least family members and friends of the parents will be contributing to the manner of the child's development. Though the likelihood is that their contributions will be in conformity with those of the parents on the basis that persons quite often choose to mix with others who are like them or because anxious parents may wish to ensure that what others say and do conforms to their ideas about the type of experiences and information the child's mind should be exposed to.

The radius of influence increases markedly however when the child attends school and engages in other extra curricular or recreational pastimes and eventually has a social life of their own, attending birthday parties and so on. Nevertheless all of this takes place under the watchful eye of parents who therefore continue to exert an ever present and powerful influence over the social conditions under which their child lives. And this is entirely consistent with the notion that all parents have their child's best interests at heart but it is also possible to argue that by exposing their child to particular social practices the parent seeks to influence their child's evaluative experiences both in terms of what they value and the way it values those things.[29] Nurturing through social practices is a way to instil particular values and in a sense substitutes for having a child that has been genetically engineered to have certain natural attributes, i.e. genetically modified to be a gifted ballet dancer, musician or mathematician, for instance.

This is significant because the argument that social practices can shape our activities as valuers challenges the notion that nature, including above all human nature, determines that persons are the source of values.[30]

Are People or Values the Sources of Normative Claims?[31]

When persons talk about values they are more generally referring to states of affairs, objects or activities that are valuable to them. However it has been said that:

> *"Many of the objects and activities that we esteem would not so much as exist in the absence of various contingent and historical conditions. We could hardly be said to value philosophy, or romantic comedy, or textiles of the Art and Crafts movement, in a social world that did not contain the quite distinctive forms of human activity necessary to produce instances of these genres. More generally, the ways in which we relate to valuable objects and undertakings, and the significance they have for our lives, themselves depend crucially on the social conditions under which we live. The beauty of a beautiful sunset may not depend on the contingent practices of human communities. But our access to this form of value is shaped by our culture, including the conceptual resources it makes available for thinking about the aesthetic dimensions of the natural world. Furthermore, the significance of natural beauty for human lives depends on its connection to a range of concrete cultural practices, such as those of romantic painting and poetry".*[32]

It is against this background that Joseph Raz argues that most human values are socially dependent in one way or another because they can only come into being and exist if there are, or were in the past, social practices

[29] Raz, Joseph, The Practice of Value, 2003, Oxford University Press, p.1
[30] Ibid, p.2
[31] Korsgaard, Christine M., in Raz, Joseph, The Practice of Value, 2003, Oxford University Press, p.67
[32] Wallace, R. Jay, in Raz, Joseph, The Practice of Value, 2003, Oxford University Press, p.1

that sustained them.[33] Most human values are accounted for on the basis that more general useful or instrumental values are put into practice through some more specific or intrinsic ones, i.e. what is objectively valuable such as creating the greatest good or amount of human happiness whilst also respecting principles of justice.[34] And a sustaining practice is according to Raz a necessary condition for the existence of intrinsic values, i.e. that many people value a particular good or form of the good.[35] This ensures that values are not explained on the basis of 'brute' fact alone.[36] Instead of which the social dependence of value can be explained in two ways.[37] First, there may be a historical explanation for the emergence and fate of the sustaining practices.[38] Alternatively, there will be a normative explanation of why a particular form of the good is a genuine form of it.[39]

Raz justifies his theory that most human values are socially dependent on the basis that (1) it offers a promising route towards an explanation of the existence of values (2) it points to a ready explanation of how we can know about them (3) it accounts for the deeply entrenched common belief that there is no point to value without valuers and most importantly (4) it fits the basic structure of our evaluative thinking about questions of value, choice and judgment which is an inherently reflective process.[40] However, the fundamental thought is that values depend on valuers because the value of things is inert with no influence except through being recognised.[41]

Whilst we can all recognise some truths in this account of value my concern is that it tends to portray persons as being led along their lives either by more influential others or by popular culture at the other extreme. This is a situation that not even Mill countenanced. A comment often passed about older horses that have spent many years in a riding school is that they exhibit little or no personality. Their character or spirit seemingly crushed by a life spent conforming to the ideals and standards demanded of them by an external authority which in this case determines

---

[33] Raz, Joseph, The Practice of Value, 2003, Oxford University Press, p.19
[34] Ibid, p.21
[35] Ibid, p.25/6
[36] Ibid, p.25/6
[37] Ibid, p.26
[38] Ibid, p.26
[39] Ibid, p.26
[40] Ibid, p.27
[41] Ibid, p.27/9

that their form of the good consists of a regime completing many circuits over many days, weeks and years following the horse in front into walk, trot and canter. Indeed, a rider's skills can be tested quite simply by asking the horse, using hands and legs, to circle away from the pack to complete a random series of movements on an inside track going anticlockwise or against the general flow of the traffic.

A danger then in an account of values that undermines the independence of valuers is that the practice of certain other values might fall into decline or become redundant through unthinking adherence to a particular form of the good, or heteronomy in Kantian terms. Indeed Raz himself acknowledges that it is sometimes thought that social dependence is a normatively or ethically conservative thesis but insists that it is not.[42] He states that:

> *"The existence of a sustaining practice is merely a necessary, not a sufficient condition for the existence of some kinds of values. The special thesis does not in any way privilege the point of view of any group or culture. It allows one full recourse to the whole of one's conceptual armoury, information, and powers of argumentation in reaching conclusions as to which practices sustain goods and which sustain evil, or worthless things, which are, perhaps, taken to be good by a population. Of course, deficiency in our conceptual, informational, and argumentational powers may well make us blind to some goods, or lead us to accept some evils. But that must be true in any case. The special dependence thesis would be to blame only if it denied that such limitations lead to mistakes, and privileged the concepts or information of some group or culture. But that it does not do".*[43]

That may be so but elsewhere Raz has stated that a value comes into being at a particular point in time, but that once a value exists it bears on everything without restriction.[44] Korsgaard has remarked that this does in some ways undercut the thesis that values are socially dependent.[45] And we have observed that in relationships where an imbalance of power exists between the parties, i.e. parent and child or doctor and patient, how conceptual, informational and argumentational powers can uphold the

---

[42] Ibid, p.22
[43] Ibid, p.25
[44] Ibid, p.22
[45] Korsgaard, Christine, M., Raz, Joseph, The Practice of Value, 2003, Oxford University Press, p.64

values of those who hold a position of influence within the relationship should they have reason to wish to constrain, or fail to take into consideration, the situation, circumstances and values of the more vulnerable party.[46]

However, Korsgaard, in contrast to Raz, argues that values are not the contingent products of culture and historical events rather their existence more naturally depends on nature or more specifically human nature.[47] Korsgaard accepts the structure of Raz's basic idea, that a value comes into being at a particular time, but once it comes into existence it bears on everything, and recognises the truth of the claim but in relation to people. So, once a person exists, and it is contingent which ones exist, they become the source of objective normative claims, the right to bodily inviolability and self-determination for instance, which bear on everything without restriction.[48] Consequently, persons normatively considered are bearers of rights and sources of reasons.[49] Values are then referable to human nature and ultimately to the nature of a particular person. About this Korsgaard states that:

> *"[O]ne of the most important attributes of humanity is our nearly bottomless capacity for finding sources of delight and interest in nearly anything, and so for conferring value on almost anything. This very fact about human nature is part of what makes it so essential that our relations to one another – both moral and political – should not be mediated by our values. It is not because of our shared values that we should accord consideration to one another but because of our shared capacity for conferring value. In other words, that fact about human nature is part of what makes liberal democratic forms of the state the right ones".*[50]

This, I think, is the point being made by Mill when he says that respect for autonomy is consistent with the creation of the greatest amount of good for the greatest number, i.e. in order to maximise human welfare. All of which tends to focus attention on to the moral integrity of valuers who are involved in caring for vulnerable others. Doctors, for example, are

---

46 For example, *Chester v Afshar 2004 WL 2289136*

47 Korsgaard, Christine, M., Raz, Joseph, The Practice of Value, 2003, Oxford University Press, p.65

48 Ibid, p.65/7

49 Ibid, p.65/7

50 Ibid, p.73

empowered professionally[51] and legally[52] to act in the best interests of their mentally incapacitated patients without also being required to make explicit the grounds on which those decisions are being made when it is known at the outset that a potential conflict with autonomy might arise and that not all person can be relied upon to conduct themselves appropriately towards others.

Is it Consistent with the Right to Self-Determination for an Incompetent Person to be governed by the Values of their Former Competent Selves?

The question is raised because Dresser has argued that the person who makes advance provisions and the person who is subsequently incompetent are not the same person.[53] Therefore, it is her opinion that regardless of the weight to be given to the patient's wishes the primary obligation to the incompetent patient is to show compassion by acting in their best interests.[54]

Precedent Autonomy and Identity

Should our competent self have control over what happens to their incompetent self? Is the person the same individual at the later time as the person who exercised authority sometime earlier? Rebecca Dresser contends that personal identity theory provides another basis for questioning the moral and legal authority of precedent autonomy.[55] According to personal identity theory substantial memory loss and other psychological changes, such as occur with Dementia, may produce a new person.[56] The claim in these circumstances is that the incompetent person has no real

---

[51] The Hippocratic Oath instructs doctors to act in the patient's best interests in accordance with the moral principles of non-maleficence and beneficence

[52] Mental Capacity Act 2005, s.4

[53] Herring, Jonathan, Medical Law and Ethics, 2008, Second Edition, Oxford University Press, p.182; Dresser, Rebecca, 1995, Dworkin on Dementia: Elegant Theory, Questionable Policy, Hastings Center Report; Nov, 25, 6; Dresser, Rebecca, 2003, Precommitment: A Misguided Strategy for Securing Death with Dignity, 81, Tex. L. Rev. 1823

[54] Herring, Jonathan, Medical Law and Ethics, 2008, Second Edition, Oxford University Press, p.183

[55] Dresser, Rebecca, 1995, Dworkin on Dementia: Elegant Theory, Questionable Policy, Hastings Center Report; Nov, 25, 6, p.35

[56] Ibid

connection with their former competent self due to these shortcomings.[57] In effect there has been such a substantial change in personality and personhood that the competent person is no longer empowered to speak on behalf of the incompetent person.[58] Dresser therefore argues that an incompetent patient's current wishes and feelings, which are by their very nature experientially valid, should be morally and legally authoritative and challenges the view that we should always respect precedent autonomy on the basis that personhood does not always persist over time.[59]

Dworkin, on the other hand, contends that our lives are guided by the desire to advance two kinds of interests; experiential[60] and critical.[61] In giving content and definition to these terms he has this to say:

> *"Most of us have only ramshackle ideas, not philosophical theories, about what kinds of lives are good ones. We almost all think material comfort well worth having. Dedicated ascetics aside, and all else equal, we consider a life of pain or poverty much worse than a comfortable one, and many people's picture of the most satisfactory life for them includes very great wealth. But even for them, material comfort is only part of the story. For many people, for example, achievement also plays an important part. We want (as people often say) to do something with our lives, to leave the world a better place for our having been in it. There are grand forms of that ambition: people aim to invent or discover something marvellous, write great music or poetry or philosophy, liberate a nation or make one just. There are less grand forms: many people want nothing more than to play their part in a cooperative enterprise like a family or a farm or a team, to have contributed to something important rather than to have done it all themselves. Some people think "experience" an important component in a good life: they want to have travelled, perhaps to exotic places, to have lived in different ways, to have tried everything. Others take pride in rootedness, in belonging to a place, and to national or ethnic or religious traditions into which they believe they have been born, traditions of faith or humour or food or culture. Almost everyone thinks family and friends are an important part of a good life: that a life without special and intense concerns for particular people would lack something crucial.*

---

[57] Ibid

[58] Herring, Jonathan, Medical Law and Ethics, 2008, Second Edition, Oxford University Press, p.182

[59] Dresser, Rebecca, 1995, Dworkin on Dementia: Elegant Theory, Questionable Policy, Hastings Center Report; Nov, 25, 6, p.35

[60] Dworkin, Ronald, Life's Dominion: An argument about Abortion and Euthanasia, Harper Collins, p.201-4

[61] Ibid, p.210-16

Most of these different ideas about a good life we hold intuitively and in the background; we do not re-examine them except in moments of special crisis or drama. But these background ideas are always there, guiding decisions and choices that may seem to us automatic, and accounting for at least some part of the exhilaration or boredom or shame or sadness we find ourselves feeling, from time to time, about the way our lives are going. It is absolutely crucial to notice, however, that these various opinions and convictions, however inarticulate or submerged, are critical in the sense that they concern what makes a life successful rather than unsuccessful – when someone has made something of his life, not just wasted it. They are not, that is, opinions only about how to make life pleasant or enjoyable minute by minute, day by day.

I want to capture that difference by pointing out a distinction between two kinds of reasons people have for wanting their lives to go one way rather than another. First, everyone has what I shall call experiential interests. We all do things because we like the experience of doing them: playing softball, perhaps, or cooking or eating well, or watching football ... or just working hard at something. Pleasures like these are essential to a good life – a life with nothing that is marvellous only because of how it feels would not be pure but preposterous. But the value of these experiences, judged one by one, depends precisely on the fact that we do find them pleasurable or exciting as experiences...

Of course, a great many things are bad as experiences, too: pain, nausea, and listening to most politicians. We take pains to avoid these experiences, and sometimes we dread them...

But most people think that they have what I shall call critical interests: interests that it does make their life genuinely better to satisfy, interests they would be mistaken, and genuinely worse off, if they did not recognise. Convictions about what helps to make a life good on the whole are convictions about those more important interests. They represent critical judgments rather than just experiential preferences.

I do not mean that experiential interests are characteristically frivolous or critical interests inevitably profound... Nor am I trying to contrast supposedly elite, reflective, philosophical lives with more ordinary or mundane ones. I mean to identify what is elite, in the sense of aspirational, within most lives. ... even people whose lives feel unplanned are nevertheless often guided by a sense of the general style they think appropriate, of what choices strike them as not only good at the moment but in character for them.

We need the distinction between experiential and critical interests to understand many of our convictions about how people should be treated. We need it, for example, to explain why we think that mind-changing drugs or other forms of brainwashing that produce long-lasting pleasure and contentment are not in their victims' interests; we mean they are not in their critical interests. Understanding the difference between experiential and critical interests is also essential to understanding a certain kind of tragedy, in life as well as in fiction. It is tragic when someone looks back on his life, near the end, and finds it wasted, empty of any real significance, with nothing in which he can take any pride at all".[62]

Experiential interests are those things we like to do for the pleasures they bring, such as eating our favourite foods, being pampered and spending time with those we like or feel affectionate towards.[63] Consequently, experiential interests are something we have in common with all sentient creatures.[64] A person's critical interests are by contrast what make life important to the individual whose life it is. These are the interests or ends we possess and seek to satisfy, such as having an enjoyable family life, achieving some success in our working life and/or projects. They are critically important because these, do in addition, give our lives a sense of meaning and coherence. Maslow would argue that these ends are significant because they reflect the human need for self-actualisation or are intrinsic to our particular purpose in life, i.e. who we are and what we become. Dworkin argues that a person's critical interests form a narrative that reflects the way in which a person wants or has chosen to live.[65]

Accordingly, certain, i.e. critical, interests of a competent person survive the problems posed by psychological disunity and even beyond that. It is on this basis that he argues that even if there is some validity in the claim that the person has changed, since developing Dementia for instance, their critical interests remain.[66] This is because critical interests are those things that are fundamental to our life story and for this reason greater moral authority should be given to them.[67]

---

[62] Ibid, p.201-3

[63] Dresser, Rebecca, 1995, Dworkin on Dementia: Elegant Theory, Questionable Policy, Hastings Center Report; Nov, 25, 6, p.33

[64] Ibid

[65] Ibid

[66] Herring, Jonathan, Medical Law and Ethics, 2008, Second Edition, Oxford University Press, p.182

[67] Ibid

Buchanan and Brock are sympathetic to this view. They refer to 'performative acts of will' to distinguish commitments that are based upon deliberate choice, which are sturdy enough to survive becoming incompetent, dying or becoming a non-person, from mere preferences.[68] In attempting to provide an account of identity that will accommodate the notion of surviving interests they point out that an incompetent patient will either be the same person who existed when competent, if a low threshold is set for psychological connectedness, or may not be considered a person at all because they fail to satisfy the normal criteria for personhood[69], i.e. the ability to function cognitively.[70] Thus any apparent conflict in the interests of a competent and incompetent self are eliminated as the conscious incompetent patient's interests are not limited to those that are present and experiential in nature whilst the permanently unconscious patient is not a person at all, and therefore the former may legitimately exercise their authority to control events in respect of the latter on either count.

Dworkin acknowledges that his view may be resisted by others, like Dresser, on the basis that persons would be fated to never be able to change their minds. Their view is that the right to autonomy must be contemporary and that present wishes and feelings, where these can be expressed, should govern what happens to the patient.[71]

What then is the Force of Past Decisions?

Dworkin differentiates between experiential and critical interests and makes the claim that greater moral authority should be attributed to the latter over the former which does appear to contrast with our

---

[68] Kuczewski, Mark G., Whose Will is it, Anyway? A Discussion of Advance Directives, Personal Identity, and Consensus in Medical Ethics, 1994, Bioethics, Volume 8, Number 1, p.34

[69] (a) The ability to be conscious of oneself as existing over time – as having a past and a future, as well as a present; (b) The ability to appreciate reasons for or against acting; being (sometimes) able to inhibit impulses or inclinations when one judges that it would be better not to act on them; (c) The ability to engage in purposive sequences of actions.

[70] Kuczewski, Mark G., Whose Will is it, Anyway? A Discussion of Advance Directives, Personal Identity, and Consensus in Medical Ethics, 1994, Bioethics, Volume 8, Number 1, p.33

[71] Dworkin, Ronald, Life's Dominion: An argument about Abortion and Euthanasia, Harper Collins, p.226/7

understanding of the point or purpose of autonomy. However, Dworkin illustrates his point by distinguishing between an evidentiary and integrity view of autonomy. An evidentiary view of autonomy entails the notion that we should respect the wishes of a competent patient, even when their choice may be regarded by others as imprudent, simply because they know better than anyone else what is in their own best interests.[72] This is a point that Mill made before about the value of autonomy: '*the only purpose for which power can rightly be exercised over any member of a civilised society, against his will, is to prevent harm to others*'.[73] However, Dworkin goes on to explain that as persons act in ways that even they would agree is not in their own best interests the explanation of the right to autonomy cannot simply be that it promotes the welfare of people making the apparently imprudent decision. This is what he has to say:

> *"Though we often think that someone has made a mistake in judging what is in his own interests, experience teaches us that in most cases we are wrong to think this. So we do better, in the long run, to recognise a general right to autonomy, which we always respect, than by reserving the right to interfere with other people's lives whenever we think they have made a mistake.*
>
> *If we accepted this evidentiary account of autonomy, we would not extend the right of autonomy to decisions made by the seriously demented, who, having altogether lost the power to appreciate and engage in reasoning and argument, cannot possibly know what is in their own best interests as well as trained specialists, like doctors, can. In some cases, any presumption that demented people know their own interests best would be incoherent: when, for example, as is often the case, their wishes and decisions change radically from one bout of lucidity to another.*
>
> *But in fact the evidentiary view of autonomy is very far from compelling. For autonomy requires us to allow someone to run his own life even when he behaves in a way that he himself would accept as not all in his interests. This is sometimes a matter of what philosophers call 'weakness of the will'. Many people who smoke know that smoking, all things considered, is not in their best interests, but they smoke anyway. If we believe, as we do, that respecting their autonomy means allowing them to act in this way, we cannot accept that the point of autonomy is to protect an agent's welfare. And there are more admirable reasons for acting against what*

[72] Ibid, p.223

[73] Stauch, Marc, Wheat, Kay, Tingle John, 2002, Second Edition, Sourcebook on Medical Law, Cavendish Publishing, p.103

one believes to be in one's own best interests. Some people refuse needed medical treatment because they believe that other people, who would then have to go without it, need it more. Such people act out of convictions we admire, even if we do not act the same way, and autonomy requires us to respect their decisions. Once again, the supposed explanation of the right to autonomy – that it promotes the welfare of people making apparently imprudent decisions - fails to account for our convictions about when people have that right. All this suggests that the point of autonomy must be, at least to some degree, independent of the claim that a person generally knows his own best interests better than anyone else".[74]

An integrity view of autonomy offers a more plausible account of the point of autonomy and of the right of a competent person to make decisions on behalf of their incompetent self.[75] According to Dworkin autonomy encourages people to lead their lives in their own distinctive way and an integrity view of autonomy places emphasis on this rather than on the welfare of the choosing agent.[76] He goes on to state that:

"The value of autonomy, on this view, derives from the capacity it protects: the capacity to express one's own character – values, commitments, convictions, and critical as well as experiential interests – in the life one leads. Recognising an individual right of autonomy makes self-creation possible. It allows each of us to be responsible for shaping our lives according to our own coherent or incoherent – but, in any case, distinctive – personality. It allows us to lead our own lives rather than be led along them, so that each of us can be, to the extent a scheme of rights can make possible, what we have made of ourselves. We allow someone to choose death over radical amputation or a blood transfusion, if that is his informed wish, because we acknowledge his right to a life structured by his own values.

The integrity view of autonomy does not assume that competent people have consistent values or always make consistent choices, or that they always lead structured, reflective lives. It recognises that people often make choices that reflect weakness, indecision, caprice or plain irrationality – that some people otherwise fanatical about their health continue to smoke, for example. Any plausible integrity-based theory of autonomy must distinguish between the general point or value of autonomy and its consequences for a particular person on a particular occasion.

74 Dworkin, Ronald, Life's Dominion: An argument about Abortion and Euthanasia, Harper Collins, p.223/4

75 Ibid, p.224

76 Ibid

> *Autonomy encourages and protects people's general capacity to lead their lives out of a distinctive sense of their own character, a sense of what is important to and for them. Perhaps one principal value of that capacity is realised only when a life does in fact display a general, overall integrity and authenticity. But the right to autonomy protects and encourages the capacity in any event, by allowing people who have it to choose how far and in what form they will seek to realise that aim".*[77]

So Dworkin has argued that the evidentiary view of autonomy presents a weak case for respecting a person's past wishes simply because people are not the best judges of what their own best interests would be under circumstances they have never encountered and in which their preferences and desires may drastically have changed.[78] Whereas the integrity view of autonomy does by contrast support the conclusion that the past wishes of a patient must be respected.[79] A competent person making a living will providing for his treatment if he becomes mentally incapacitated is making exactly the kind of judgment that autonomy, on the integrity view, most respects: a judgment about the overall shape of the kind of life the person wants to have led.[80]

The integrity view of autonomy[81] therefore supports a doctrine of precedent autonomy and this means that a patient's past wishes should be respected even if they contradict their current experiential wishes and feelings about medical treatment.[82] Here Dworkin argues that in relation to a person's past and present wishes and feelings a decision to honour the latter over the former should be based entirely on whether the person is currently competent to make a decision.[83] In recognising that a paternalistic[84] response might be considered, particularly where the incompetent patient experiences distress by what is entailed in their former

---

[77] Ibid

[78] Ibid, p.226

[79] Ibid, p.226

[80] Ibid, p.226

[81] Rebecca Dresser contends that this model assigns moral significance to the individual's critical, as opposed to experiential interests – see Dresser, Rebecca, 1995, Dworkin on Dementia: Elegant Theory, Questionable Policy, Hastings Center Report; Nov, 25, 6, p.33

[82] Dworkin, Ronald, Life's Dominion: An argument about Abortion and Euthanasia, Harper Collins, p.228

[83] Ibid

[84] The principle of Beneficence

instructions, Dworkin maintains that to accede to the patient's wishes in these circumstances would be to violate their autonomy.[85]

Death's Meaning Attributed to Critical Interests

Should the manner and timing of one's death be determined by one's critical interests? Consider for a moment how often persons have gone ahead with critically important projects, such as to sit an examination, turn up for an interview for a job or watched their child perform in the school play, when they might otherwise have preferred to be absent due to a current bout of ill health, for example. Indeed most schools, colleges and universities recognise that persons commonly prioritise matters that are critically important from those that are currently experientially valid when determining what to do in their own best interests and will take steps in appropriate cases to mediate the effects of a poor performance at examination by rendering results as coherent as possible with a student's previous work.

It is on this basis that Dworkin claims that we cannot think about whether death is in someone's best interests unless we understand their critical interests.[86] He claims that it would be easy to decide what was in someone's best interests if we were only concerned with a person's experiential interests such as the principles of medical futility and intolerability tend to encourage.[87] Dworkin cites the case of *Bland* and notes that several members of the House of Lords assumed that only experiential interests mattered. He quotes Lord Mustill who considered and rejected the argument that it was against Bland's interests that his body was full of tubes to no point or that his family's happy recollections of him were being replaced by horrific ones or that his situation was causing them great misery; that cannot be so, Mustill said, because '*he does not know what is happening to his body and cannot be affronted by it; he does not know of his family's continuing sorrow. The distressing truth which must not be shirked is that discontinuing life support is not in the best interests of Anthony Bland, for he has no best interests of any kind*'.[88] The comments of Lord Goff in that case should also be

---

[85] Dworkin, Ronald, Life's Dominion: An argument about Abortion and Euthanasia, Harper Collins, p.227

[86] Ibid, p.208

[87] Ibid

[88] *Airedale NHS Trust v Bland [1993] 1 All ER 821 HL*; Dworkin, Ronald, Life's Dominion: An argument about Abortion and Euthanasia, Harper Collins, p.208

considered. There he suggested that the best interests test should comprise of something more than purely professional appraisal of a person's medical welfare.[89] To confine the test in this way, he said, would be inconsistent with the primacy given to the principle of self-determination and would '*downgrade the status of the incompetent person by placing a lesser value on [their] intrinsic worth and vitality*'.[90] Similar arguments would seem to apply to confining best interests assessments to purely experiential interests. Dworkin adds that:

> *"If we accept this view that only experiential interests count, we can make no sense of the widespread, near universal, view I described; that decisions like those we have been reviewing are often personally problematic and racking. We agonise about these decisions, for ourselves when we are contemplating living wills, or for relatives and friends, only or mainly because we take our and their critical interests into account. We must therefore begin by asking: how does it matter to the critical success of our whole life how we die? We should distinguish between two different ways that it might matter: because death is the far boundary of life, and every part of our life, including the very last, is important: and because death is special, a peculiarly significant event in the narrative of our lives, like the final scene of a play, with everything about it intensified, under a special spotlight. In the first sense when we die is important because of what will happen to us if we die later, in the second, how we die matters because it is how we die.*
>
> *Let us begin with the first, less theatrical, of these ideas. Sometimes people want to live on, even though in pain or dreadfully crippled, in order to do something they believe important to have done. They want to finish a job, for example, or to learn something they have always wanted to know...*
>
> *On the other hand, people often think they have strong reasons of a comparable kind for not staying alive. The badness of the experiences that lie ahead is one: terrible pain or constant nausea or the horror of intubation or the confusion of sedation... But people's reasons for wanting to die include critical reasons as well; many people, as I said, think it undignified or bad in some other way to live under certain conditions, however they might feel if they feel at all. Many people do not want to be remembered living in those circumstances; others think it degrading to be wholly dependent, or to be the object of continuing anguish. These feelings ... may be just as strong when the burden of physical care is imposed on professionals whose career is precisely in providing such care, and when*

[89] *Airedale NHS Trust v Bland [1993] 1 All ER 821 HL*
[90] Ibid

the financial burdens fall on a public eager to bear it. At least a part of what people fear about dependence is its impact not on those responsible for their care, but on their own dignity.

I must emphasise that this is not a belief that every kind of dependent life under severe handicaps is not worth living... It is however, plausible, and to many people compelling, that total dependence is in itself a very bad thing quite apart from the pain or discomfort it often but not invariably entails. Total or near total dependence with nothing positive to redeem it may seem not only to add nothing to the overall quality of a life but to take something important from it.

When patients remain conscious, their sense of integrity and of the coherence of their lives crucially affects their judgment about whether it is in their best interests to continue to live. Athletes, or others whose physical activity was at the centre of their self-conception, are more likely to find a paraplegic's life intolerable... for such people, a life without the power of motion is unacceptable, not for reasons explicable in experiential terms, but because it is stunningly inadequate to the conception of self around which their own lives have so far been constructed. Adding decades of immobility to a life formerly organised around action will for them leave a narrative wreck, with no structure or sense, a life worse than one that ends when its activity ends.[91]

So people's views about how to live colour their convictions about when to die, and the impact is intensified when it engages the second way in which people think death is important. There is no doubt that most people treat the manner of their deaths as of special, symbolic importance: they want their deaths, if possible, to express and in that way vividly to confirm the values they believe most important to their lives. ... The idea of a good (or less bad) death is not exhausted by how one dies – whether in battle or in bed – but includes timing as well. It explains the premium people often put on living to 'see' some particular event, after which the idea of their own death seems less tragic to them".[92]

So being able to determine how the final chapter of our life is played out, if we become incompetent, is a critical interest and therefore, we should, through advance directives, be able to restrict how we are treated if

[91] Dworkin, Ronald, Life's Dominion: An argument about Abortion and Euthanasia, 1993, Harper Collins, Chapter 7, p.209/11
[92] Ibid, p.211

incompetent.[93] Consequently, a person who wishes to live a life that is structured by their own values should seek to ascertain and express the values, interests and convictions that have played a critical role in shaping that life.[94]

Ensuring Patient Values are Prioritised

However, if beneficence is not to override autonomy it is also necessary to consider how a value system, which is insufficiently determinate to meet the legal standard of applicability, might still be considered a sufficiently robust an expression of intent that it constitutes a valid advance decision. In this regard statutory and common law provisions suggest that in order for priority to be accorded to a value system one would have to be clearly established and applicable[95] in the circumstances arising for decision.[96] Moreover, the integrity with which personal decisions have been made to accord with one's values, beliefs and preferences would seem to be an important factor in establishing that it is an inherently reliable and credible statement of intent, i.e. has the patient evinced a settled and continuing intention to honour the values, beliefs and preferences that were the source of previous decisions such that these factors may be regarded as being determinative of what should happen in their best interests in the future when they are no longer competent to express a view.[97] The important point is that the values statement must constitute trustworthy evidence of the patient's preferences in order for a limited objective best interests standard to be applied bringing best interests closer to the standards and practices of substituted judgment. This is to safeguard patients from the consequences of erroneous applications and judgments by surrogates which was the focus in the USA case of *Cruzan*.[98] Consequently, let us now look at ways in which someone can construct their value system to make it functional, coherent and an inherently clear, convincing and reliable source of information about the personal value of their own life.

---

[93] Herring, Jonathan, Medical Law and Ethics, 2008, Second Edition, Oxford University Press, p.182

[94] Dworkin, Ronald, Life's Dominion: An argument about Abortion and Euthanasia, 1993, Harper Collins, Chapter 7, p.224

[95] For example, the patient was not competent to decide contemporaneously

[96] *Re T (Adult: Refusal of Medical Treatment) [1992] 4 All ER 649 CA; HE v A Hospital NHS Trust 2003 WL 21729346*

[97] Ibid

[98] *Cruzan vs Director, Missouri Dept. of Health 110 S.Ct. 2841*

Constructing a Personal Value System

Whilst some people might be horrified at the idea of disclosing their values because of the autobiographical nature of the enterprise many individuals do nevertheless write their life story. And many others are interested to read them and make judgments as well as draw certain conclusions about the person and their life. In that sense stories are just a long hand version of the application of values because values are implicit within the story. For others a compelling feature of a value system is that it may be looked upon as an autobiographical record of your life because it represents your account of why the values, beliefs and preferences of the past are relevant to your present good.[99] Disclosing one's value system can be considered autobiographical in another respect for it also presents an opportunity to set the record straight.[100] To correct assumptions that people may have made about you, your conduct, and your ideas, what you said and what you chose not to say and about what you did and what you did not do and why.[101] A value system is therefore impressed with corrective powers that weigh against inferences that others may have drawn about you as a result of inadequate information.[102] As a definitive source of information, a personal value system, explains personal conduct, speech and ideas and gives evidence in support of all of that by providing insight into the reasons for it by reference to the values contained within it.[103]

A value system is then, in essence, a statement about the values that a person would use to inform a decision about whether to consent to an offer of medical treatment. But in disclosing their values, in this formal sense, a person is seeking to explain the basis on which their decision would be made ahead of being told what treatment is on offer. Dresser has of course questioned whether all persons have values that they live by or whether they merely respond to events as they arise and make decisions accordingly. Her viewpoint is likely to meet with some general agreement as it is doubtful that the vast majority of persons will have a detailed life plan, and even those we would count as being organised, disciplined, ambitious and determined will probably have plans that exist only in some

[99] *Re T (Adult: Refusal of Medical Treatment) [1992] 4 All ER 649 CA; HE v A Hospital NHS Trust 2003 WL 21729346*

[100] Ibid; *Cruzan vs Director, Missouri Dept. of Health 110 S.Ct. 2841*

[101] Ibid

[102] Ibid

[103] Ibid

sort of vague sense. And anyway life rarely turns out the way we planned it despite our best efforts. Nevertheless, everyone has moral values if only because they have an interest in their own survival and ability to flourish and self-interestedness will ensure that non-moral values take these factors into account. Dworkin refers to '*the dominating grip of the idea that human life has intrinsic as well as personal importance for human beings*'.[104] So for example, some people might object to medications that are notoriously toxic because they believe the body will repair itself given the right form of help or assistance. Likewise, self-knowledge informs our decisions about which types of environments, people and conditions are most likely to enable us to thrive or to lead a flourishing life.

Identifying Personal Values

The term 'values' is not here used in an exclusionary sense as the aim is to capture and classify as a value any relevant form of wish, feeling, belief, value, interest or preference that has informed a person's life. Consequently, a value system may be as simple as registering a wish to refuse a particular form of medical treatment.[105] For example, a person who is very old and frail might wish to refuse any attempt to resuscitate them in the event that they should suffer from heart failure. Similarly, persons who subscribe to a religious faith that prohibits them from accepting some forms of medical treatment would want their religious belief to be known to medical professionals. As knowledge that a patient is a practicing Jehovah's Witness would alert a medical professional to the fact that blood or blood products must not form a part of their treatment as the patient would refuse blood in all circumstances even when their life was a stake.

More generally however, the idea is that a value system should be sufficiently comprehensive that it can speak on behalf of the patient in a variety of circumstances and situations. Take a man who is married, has a young family, a career, is a committed member of the Territorial Army, likes to play golf with his friends on a Sunday and is passionate about art, both his own and that of others. He is unfortunately involved in a car accident in which he sustains multiple injuries and upon arrival at hospital he remains in an unconscious state. What should the doctor do? It is

[104] Dworkin, Ronald, Life's Dominion: An argument about Abortion and Euthanasia, Harper Collins, p.237

[105] *Cruzan vs Director, Missouri Dept. of Health 110 S.Ct. 2841*

possible that the doctor's hands are tied due to the severity of the injuries. On the other hand where a choice exists, it is clear that a doctor should choose to take that course of action that is least restrictive of the person's future rights and freedom of action.[106] But on what basis should the doctor make such a decision if the patient is unconscious and without representation? For there is no general agreement about what a good life is or about what is of value in life.[107] This is where comprehensive knowledge of a patient's values, interests and so on can usefully support the treatment decision-making process, enabling doctors to choose an option that least restricts the patient's future choices or that would allow the patient the most freedom to pursue their former goals or ends.

On the basis that persons wish to not only survive but to have a good or flourishing life it seems likely that their personal conception of what a good life is will have increasingly informed the pattern of that life so that particular objectives and/or principles will become apparent within it as time goes on. So an idea worth pursuing in this regard is that of Ronald Dworkin who has claimed that persons have critical as well as experiential interests.

The Core Features of a Value System: Critical and Experiential Interests

In distinguishing between two types of interest Dworkin claims that experiential interests are those things that people like to do for the pleasures they bring but argues that a person's critical interests are more relevant to the subjective value a life has for the person whose life it is, its personal value, because we judge that our life would be poorer without these things in it.[108] Therefore, Dworkin concludes that what makes a good life can be ascertained from a process that seeks to differentiate between those experiences that create the greatest amount of personal pleasure or happiness from those that are more self-defining; things that form part of a person's life because of the challenges they bring or just because they are deemed to be critically important to it as well as possibly pleasurable. The project is significant in requiring persons to identify and set apart what is intrinsically valuable from the value of experience which

---

[106] Mental Capacity Act 2005, s.1(6)

[107] Consider the contrasting positions of Kant and Mill

[108] Dworkin, Ronald, Life's Dominion: An argument about Abortion and Euthanasia, Harper Collins, p.73

is not deemed to be a source of intrinsic value. We are invited, in other words, to set out what we feel and act out of a sense of duty towards from those affairs that we show no settled commitment to,[109] as well as from those things we do from pure inclination.

Systematising Values: Is there a simple way of distinguishing between critical and experiential interests?

Dworkin has commented that people think it important not just that their life contain a variety of the right experiences, achievements, and connections, but that it have a structure that expresses a coherent choice among these.[110] He puts forward the view that a person's critical interests are what give their life this coherent narrative and in that sense they differ from experiential interests which are more likely to fluctuate over time.[111]

It is probably true to say that whatever is of value experientially will fluctuate over time. For example, our tastes or preferences can and do change. So perhaps caramel flavoured ice-cream is now preferred to vanilla and Japanese sushi is chosen over more traditional lunchtime snacks. Quite often natural, cultural and social circumstances are important precursors for changes of this sort.[112] When we look at old photographs it is often in horror at our clothes and hair and this is because society has embraced new ideas and ways to style ourselves so what was once considered de rigueur is now regarded as passé. So we may say that cultural and societal innovations broaden our range of experience and can

---

[109] When personal commitment is somewhat lacking inclination determines that we merely go through the motions of respecting and valuing something whose grip we have not quite managed to dislodge. For example, quite often employers require employees to give them notice of their intention to leave and during the notice period employees often feel less committed to the ends of their employer. Similarly we might think quite badly of a person who goes through the motions of a relationship with their boyfriend or girlfriend until something better comes along in the knowledge that they are depriving their partner of an opportunity to find or locate their good elsewhere. We regret the lost opportunity or in economic terms the opportunity cost.

[110] Dworkin, Ronald, Life's Dominion: An argument about Abortion and Euthanasia, 1993, Harper Collins, Chapter 7, p.205; Dresser, Rebecca, Dworkin on Dementia: Elegant Theory, Questionable Policy, Hastings Center Report, 1995, November-December, 25, 6, page 35

[111] Ibid

[112] Dresser, Rebecca, Dworkin on Dementia: Elegant Theory, Questionable Policy, Hastings Center Report, 1995, November-December, 25, 6, page 36

alter our perspectives about the things we value.[113] The motivation for change is however less clear. It is true that we live in a technological era which increasingly defers to the merits of computerisation by finding ever more sophisticated uses for technology that one can pre-programme. Sciences provide insight, though not necessarily truths, about many features of life. Last, but by no means least, commercialism has gained a considerable foothold in society and the practices associated with it, particularly that of managing perceptions, appears to have been developed into an art form to such a degree that we often find out retrospectively that change has been advocated on an empty promise of something new, or improved and therefore better, and more exciting.

So there is nodding agreement for the fact that experiential interests or preferences can and do change naturally but that we can be induced to introduce change to our lives also. Can the same be said about critical interests? Let's look at someone who values family life and the relationship they have with their children. This person has a career, which is important to them, though priority is given to their family life. Time passes by and the children, a boy and a girl, are now teenagers and like to spend time with their friends. However, this has become a source of conflict within the household because the girl is apt to be a little wayward in her choice of friends who are seen to be detrimentally influencing her attitudes and behaviour. Relationships suffer and deteriorate further when communication becomes strained, difficult even. Around this time the parent receives a boost at work when they are recommended for promotion. The ego is bolstered further when at interview the MD appears to see virtue in their ability and talent for the undertaking. They are subsequently drilled about commitment to the job and about the MD's vision to expand operations into untapped markets. Consequently, the role will involve a considerable amount of travel which means spending time away from home and working longer hours, perhaps even weekends. Having a presence at corporate events and a willingness to wine and dine prestigious clients as and when the need arises also form part of the job description. So what the parent chooses to do in these circumstances will reveal a great deal about their continued commitment to existing critical interests.

There is no refuting the possibility that a person's critical interests can and do change naturally, such as when a single person with an established

[113] Raz, Joseph, The Practice of Value, 2003, Oxford University Press, p.19

career decides to marry and have a family in their late thirties. But we can also be induced to make changes that will ultimately constrain our freedom to pursue our ideas about what a good life is and to seek out whatever else is thought valuable in life. Consequently, there is some difficulty in maintaining a distinction between critical and experiential interests based on notions of a coherent narrative alone. A point that is taken up by Dresser who questions whether people actually think as Dworkin says they do. She states that:

> *"If I were to play psychologist, my guess would be that many people take life one day at a time. The goal of establishing a coherent narrative may be a less common life theme than the simple effort to accept and adjust to the changing natural and social circumstances that characterise a person's life".*[114]

No Clear Means/Ends Distinction

Dresser draws attention to the fact that it is not always possible to draw a sharp line between experiential and critical interests. Her claim is that people often choose critical projects because of the rewarding experiences they provide and that at certain times in our lives experiential interests may be of greater value to us than critical projects.[115] Doubtless we all recognise the truth of the claim when persons generally have a tendency to gravitate towards those things that give pleasure or that they are good at but are interesting to them as well. For example, we would not expect to find that a person had successfully established themselves in a career that they did not also enjoy. This is because boredom, dislike, disinterest, unhappiness and indifference are unlikely to drive an enduring will to succeed. Relationships, which are another fundamental feature of life, similarly appear to succeed on the basis of pleasure and interest.

Integrity of Personal Convictions relevant to Critical Interests

However, Dworkin explains critical interests by reference to the integrity with which important self-defining decisions are made to accord with our more abstract ambition to lead a good life.[116] He demonstrates his point

---

[114] Dresser, Rebecca, Dworkin on Dementia: Elegant Theory, Questionable Policy, Hastings Center Report, 1995, November-December, 25, 6, page 36

[115] Ibid

[116] Dworkin, Ronald, Life's Dominion: An argument about Abortion and Euthanasia, 1993, Harper Collins, Chapter 7, p.204/5

by inviting us to face an important self-defining decision. Our example is a woman with a chance to begin a demanding career that intrigues her, but which would also require that she sacrifice some of the time spent with her children. He states that:

> "*People think it important not just that their life contain a variety of the right experiences, achievements, and connections, but that it have a structure that expresses a coherent choice among these – for some, that it display a steady, self-defining commitment to a vision of character or achievement that the life as a whole, seen as an integral creative narrative, illustrates and expresses. Of course, this ideal of integrity does not itself define a way to live: it presupposes substantive convictions*'.[117]

Integrity is here tied to our convictions about how life should be lived and to our future commitment to honour that chosen path.[118] This suggests that there is a mark of duality in the notion of integrity for the convictions that were the causes of our past choices argue that they establish a precedent that should be maintained for the future.[119] Rather like the tail wagging the dog only here power would reside in values that had been adopted on some previous occasion to dictate the terms of our future life. Would this be inconsistent with our notion of persons as rational creatures who do, as a consequence, have freedom of the mind and body?

Convictions, values, beliefs or critical interests, call them what you will in this context, can and do appear to have a constraining effect on personal freedom. For example, the man or woman who values family life might choose not to pursue a career opportunity that required them to spend time away from their family. It would also be entirely rational for a person who valued their family but demonstrated this through the fruits of their labour to consider the ways in which the terms and conditions of the job could be adapted to suit their ends. Values are then capable of pervading all areas of a person's life so that the life as a whole becomes one of recurring themes, i.e. once a value exists it bears on everything without exception. So the man who values his family to the point of sacrificing his career prospects is perhaps more likely to devote the majority of his spare time to his family forsaking interests and activities that would exclude them.

---

[117] Ibid, p.205

[118] Ibid, p.206

[119] Ibid; see also Dresser, Rebecca, Dworkin on Dementia: Elegant Theory, Questionable Policy, Hastings Center Report, 1995, November-December, 25, 6, page 34

Similarly the person who relies on material gain to demonstrate their affections is perhaps more likely to be a willing accomplice to a money making undertaking that requires some sacrifice of their spare time.

Dworkin's point is then that an individual right to autonomy makes self-creation possible which allows each of us to live our lives in accordance with our own unique personality or out of a sense of what is important to us.[120] As autonomy allows people who have it to choose how far and in what form they will seek to realise that aim an integrity based view of autonomy is essential to considerations about what the personal consequences of this are for the person concerned.[121]

Critical Interests and End of Life Treatment Decisions

Persons who have substantive convictions about what a good life is for them may feel a great deal of concern about how they will be treated at the end of life when they may no longer be competent to decide what shall happen contemporaneously.[122] They may fear that the underlying creative process that was entailed in building that life will be undermined or destroyed by decisions that fail to properly take into consideration the values, beliefs and preferences that were critically important in shaping it that way.[123]

Such a person wants to be maintained in a condition where genuine self-respect is possible and that means that they want to be maintained in a manner that is befitting with what has gone before.[124] Crucially they care about their own dignity and what is a dignified life for them is most

---

[120] Dworkin, Ronald, Life's Dominion: An argument about Abortion and Euthanasia, 1993, Harper Collins, Chapter 7, p.224

[121] Ibid

[122] *R (On the Application of Oliver Leslie Burke) v The General Medical Council [2005] EWCA Civ 1003 CA; Cruzan vs Director, Missouri Dept. of Health 110 S.Ct. 2841*

[123] See the dissenting judgment of Justice Stevens in the US case of *Cruzan vs Director, Missouri Dept. of Health 110 S.Ct. 2841* at p.2885/6 in which he states that 'it may, in fact, be impossible to live for anything without being prepared to die for something'.

[124] Dworkin, Ronald, Life's Dominion: An argument about Abortion and Euthanasia, 1993, Harper Collins, Chapter 7, p.233; see also the dissenting judgment of Justice Stevens in the US case of *Cruzan vs Director, Missouri Dept. of Health 110 S.Ct. 2841* at p.2885/6

vividly illustrated by the critical interests that have played a significant role in it.[125]

A Functional Value System

As a person may in the future be bound by the contents of their value system the issue here is to identify a method of reasoning that will assist persons to reliably conclude, and perhaps also specify, which values, beliefs, preferences or interests are experiential and which should be considered critical to a treatment decision-making process.[126]

Casuistry

Casuistical reasoning involves concentrating on a particular case or event to see what account of values, beliefs, preferences and interests can be constructed from it.[127] This paradigm or model case is then compared to other similar cases to see whether initial ideas withstand further scrutiny under different lights. The reasoning process is therefore enhanced when comparative cases are sought out with a view to noting similarities and differences in the application of values.[128] Casuistry is then a case based model of reasoning that relies on human intuition to interpret the relevant information and to formulate certain generalisations as well as more specific observations from it about what is the true source of a person's experiential and critical interests.[129]

Values and interests are therefore established within the context of a particular factual situation.[130] Thus what can be known about them is potentially limited to the number of similar factual situations that have

---

[125] Ibid, p.237

[126] Beauchamp, Tom L., Childress, James F., Principles of Biomedical Ethics, 2001, Fifth Edition, Oxford University Press, p.385

[127] Gert, Bernard, Culver, Charles M., Clouser, K. Danner, Bioethics: A Systematic Approach, 2006, Second Edition, Oxford University Press, p.254; Beauchamp, Tom L., Childress, James F., Principles of Biomedical Ethics, 2001, Fifth Edition, Oxford University Press, p.392/7

[128] Gert, Bernard, Culver, Charles M., Clouser, K. Danner, Bioethics: A Systematic Approach, 2006, Second Edition, Oxford University Press, p.254

[129] Beauchamp, Tom L., Childress, James F., Principles of Biomedical Ethics, 2001, Fifth Edition, Oxford University Press, p.397

[130] Herring, Jonathan, Medical Law and Ethics, 2008, Second Edition, Oxford University Press, p.27

arisen in which a particular value was both relevant but also tested. That a perceived value should have been subjected to a process of falsification aids confidence in a procedure that draws on a supposed inferior source for acquiring knowledge. A car manufacturer, for example, that wishes to road test their latest concept car will not necessarily acquire meaningful data from a test run that is conducted at moderate speed on a deserted air strip.

Neither, it seems, can casuistry explain in a particular case why there is a discrepancy in the application of established values, unless the availability of other similar cases to it support a line of reasoning that would enable a person to specify their values with greater precision or in greater detail.[131]

In summary casuists rely on case-comparison and analogies to draw conclusions about their beliefs, values and interests.[132] As casuistry does not proceed from a position of pre-theoretical beliefs and norms, instead these are intuited or discovered in the data, this method of reasoning brings forward the problem that there may be insufficient meaningful data to support a statement that seeks to establish a settled commitment to one's critical interests.[133] For example, a person might more recently have turned to religion or changed their religion. Moreover Beauchamp and Childress point out that reasoning by analogy suffers from the drawback that it never warrants a claim of truth, which is exactly what is illustrated by the game of Japanese Whispers. They state that:

> *"It is true enough that we reason by analogy every day, and we are often confident in our conclusions. For example, if we feel better after using a certain medicine, then we feel comfortable in recommending it to other persons, in the expectation that they too will feel more comfortable. A logical form is present in all analogy: If some person or thing has one property associated with a second property, and another person or thing also has the first property, we may feel justified in inferring that the second person or thing also has the second property. However, such analogies often fail: Our friends may not feel better after they take our favoured medicine. Analogies never warrant a claim of truth, and we often do not know something by analogy that we think we know. The method of*

[131] Gert, Bernard, Culver, Charles M., Clouser, K. Danner, Bioethics: A Systematic Approach, 2006, Second Edition, Oxford University Press, p.254
[132] Beauchamp, Tom L., Childress, James F., Principles of Biomedical Ethics, 2001, Fifth Edition, Oxford University Press, p.395
[133] Ibid; The alleged problem in *Cruzan vs Director, Missouri Dept. of Health 110 S.Ct. 2841*

casuistry leaves us in precisely this position: No matter how many properties one case and another share, our inference to yet another property in the second case may mislead or produce false statements". [134]

The danger with a method that relies on analogies is that they may evolve in the wrong way.[135] This could happen because relevant information was improperly analysed or processed at the outset and one cannot ignore the possibility that false beliefs, personal biases or prejudices may have infected individual judgments.[136] These problems, i.e. the potential for distorting effects to arise and become manifest within a value system that distinguishes between experiential and critical interests, raise questions about its reliability and thus whether a person could ever be justified in placing their full trust in it.[137]

Coherence Theory: Reflection

Whilst a coherence theory of knowledge and justification has detractors[138] supporters[139] would argue that persons are at least presented with an opportunity to subject their beliefs about values to a form of reflective testing to see whether those beliefs cohere with what happens in reality. Do the states of affairs, i.e. what happens on a day-to-day basis, provide evidence that is sufficiently strong to justify the claims that have been made? The purpose of reflective testing is then to prevent personal biases and prejudices from infecting deliberative processes whilst seeking interpretive equilibrium between pre-analytic assumptions and what happens in reality.[140] Coherence theory therefore accepts that humans operate under certain constraints when reasoning and in doing so aims to safeguard individuals against falling into arbitrariness.[141]

---

[134] Beauchamp, Tom L., Childress, James F., Principles of Biomedical Ethics, 2001, Fifth Edition, Oxford University Press, p.396

[135] Ibid, p.395

[136] Ibid

[137] Ibid

[138] For example, Bertrand Russell argued that if coherence was the objective that it was perfectly possible for false beliefs to outweigh true ones during the reflective process and that one would be forced to conclude that it was truth. This possibility cannot be totally eliminated in constructing a personal value system, partly because persons are not omniscient and cannot always be objective about themselves.

[139] For example, John Rawls and Kant presumably

[140] Dworkin Ronald, Justice in Robes, 2006, The Belknap Press of Harvard University Press, Rawls and the Law, p.250/1

[141] Ibid, p.250

According to coherence theory a person who wishes to develop a comprehensive theory about what a good life for them is and of what is critically important within it should start by examining their considered or paradigm judgments on the subject.[142] Our considered judgments are those that have acquired a rich history in experience.[143] Considered judgments are not therefore mere matters of individual intuition instead they are credible and trustworthy beliefs, norms or action guiding principles because time demonstrates a personal commitment to them. This information, where it exists, is reliable because it exhibits the lowest level of personal bias about what our true ends are.[144] Similarly, displays that signify a continued commitment to those convictions may be perceived as ones where our capacities were displayed without distortion.[145]

For instance, a person might say that they have built a life around their family. Let's say that this person was a female with young children who were just about to go to school. Once the children had settled into their new routines she planned to obtain part-time work so that the family could have an annual holiday abroad as well as other treats and trips out that would broaden their horizons and perspectives about the world. Her sole aim was to create a good life for the family but most particularly to ensure that the children had a secure and happy childhood in which they were given opportunities to develop as individuals and to form their own character. To this end employment opportunities that are unlikely to conflict with her critical interest in having an enjoyable family life are sought. Six months later she starts work as a receptionist at the local doctors' surgery. She gets on well with the other females she works alongside and goes to an exercise class with one of her co-workers one evening a week and once a month they all get together over lunch at a local pub. Another year passes and the surgery is looking to recruit a new practice manager and whilst not in a position to make that sort of transition the job appeals to her. Everyone at home is settled and reasonably contented and so she resolves to start a programme of re-education that will help her to acquire the sort of skills and qualifications that would enable her to apply for a job like that in the future.

---

[142]Beauchamp, Tom L., Childress, James F., Principles of Biomedical Ethics, 2001, Fifth Edition, Oxford University Press, p.398

[143] Ibid, p.400

[144] Ibid, p.398/400

[145] Ibid, p.398

Coherence theory invites this person, who wishes to articulate a personal value system, to subject their considered judgments to a form of reflective testing.[146] This process raises the level of self-knowledge or conscious awareness about whether the end moral or non-moral value is really what is valued when taking our conduct and reasoning into consideration which enables persons to not only construct a general account of what they value but also to specify their values more comprehensively.[147] The requirement is by analogy rather like the job of the defence in a courtroom drama which is to gather witness accounts of events that converge or are consistent with the claims of the accused to give their story credibility and to engender the requisite level of trust in it by an independent jury.[148] And the reflective process continues indefinitely or for as long as a person remains committed to the goal of bringing their convictions about their experiential and critical interests into a state of coherence.[149]

However, the ethicists, Beauchamp and Childress, point out that the method is not entirely clear about how coherence can be achieved or how we can know when we have successfully completed the task.[150] As a value system may later become binding one suggestion is that persons focus on ascertaining the truth about what is intrinsically valuable to them. To be determined to locate their real rather than perceived interests which are identified through the process of rational reflection. It is possible that this could be secured by acquiring the ability to suspend belief and delay judgment pending a review of the evidence. Rather like a member of a jury who does not hold onto the desire for a particular outcome but remains open to what the evidence suggests. And we should be particularly receptive to what we can learn from those occasions where free will has endorsed or intervened in the activities of the inclination since this sort of information would tend to lean towards that of a character reference in identifying what is in one's experiential and critical interests. Transparency regarding the factors that were considered as well as assumptions that were made will assist in establishing a credible personal account of what is critically valuable. In personal matters the requisite level of objectivity can be achieved when there is some distance between the time of an event and the onset of the reflective process which coherence theory tends to encourage.

---

[146] Ibid
[147] Ibid
[148] Ibid, p.400
[149] Ibid, p.398
[150] Ibid, p.401

On the other hand, persons, as mere mortals, are not omniscient which places some limit on self-knowledge. For instance, what can be known about external events in the outside world challenges our ability to get to the truth of anything but information that is withheld or that one has no access to could have the effect of changing events and of facilitating a different kind of history.[151] In that respect perhaps Dresser is right because people can only respond to events as they perceive them to be. So the woman in the example above may not embark on a career that interferes with family life because she believes that she has freedom to choose to wait until the children are a little older.

How feasible is it that the process will ever be perfected? Beauchamp and Childress emphasise the ideal, although not the Utopian, character of this procedure.[152] They state that:

> *"We should assume that we face a never-ending search for incoherence, for counter-examples to our beliefs, and for novel situations that challenge our moral framework. From this perspective, moral thinking is analogous to hypotheses in science that we test, modify, or reject through experience and experimental thinking".*[153]

A Value System Must Explain and Justify Treatment Decisions

The lack of any formalities associated with an advance directive that is drafted conventionally, i.e. to refuse a particular treatment, tends to lull persons into a false sense of security. They know what they mean when they say that if they were demented they would wish to refuse life-preserving treatment but do others? A lack of formality tends to promote ideas about treatment at the end of life that might never have been fully aired and therefore the decision to refuse treatment suffers from the defect that it has not been subjected to more rigorous testing to ensure that it will withstand critical appraisal from others.[154] If a personal value system is intended to function reliably as a patient's personal messenger in the future, it should not suffer from the same defect.

---

[151] *Chester v Afshar 2004 WL 2289136*

[152] Beauchamp, Tom L., Childress, James F., Principles of Biomedical Ethics, 2001, Fifth Edition, Oxford University Press, p.399

[153] Ibid

[154] *Re T (Adult: Refusal of Medical Treatment) [1992] 4 All ER 649 CA; HE v A Hospital NHS Trust 2003 WL 21729346*; see also the USA case of *Cruzan vs Director, Missouri Dept. of Health 110 S.Ct. 2841*

Medical professionals are called upon to make treatment decisions on behalf of mentally incapacitated patients in a wide variety of situations and circumstances, not just those at the end of life. The lives of patients who suffer from conditions such as Dementia, for example, extend long after the initial diagnosis. So a value system must have the capacity to provide an explanation and justification for a wide variety of treatment decisions.[155]

The issue then is whether the framework for decision can meet this requirement of it. Can an independent third party understand and use the value system to inform a treatment decision-making process in a manner that is consistent with what was intended?[156] Accordingly, there is a need to test any resultant action guide to see if it yields a result that is incoherent or inconsistent with one's personal conception of what a good life is.[157] In this regard Beauchamp and Childress propose that the adequacy of any theory can be ascertained from eight conditions or benchmarks and these are clarity, coherence, completeness and comprehensiveness, simplicity, explanatory power, justificatory power, output power and practicability.[158]

Clarity

The framework for decision must be set out clearly to reflect the values that should be used to inform a treatment decision-making process. A little like following a recipe where the ingredients are listed separately from instructions about how to assemble the various components. Indeed

---

155 According to USA case *Re Guardianship of Estelle M. Browning, 568 So.2d 4* when a patient has taken time and trouble to specifically express their wishes for future health care in event of later incapacity, surrogate appointed after patient has become incompetent need not obtain prior judicial approval to carry out those wishes (para.15). In instances where a patient has left instructions for future health care a patient may designate decision-maker who is to carry out those instructions but a patient need not do so (para.16).

156 The importance of testing a value system cannot be over emphasized when the principle of self-determination, not beneficence, is to be prioritised as it was stated in the USA case of *Re Guardianship of Estelle M. Browning, 568 So.2d 4* that a written declaration, as opposed to an oral statement made by a competent patient, in the absence of any evidence of intent to the contrary, can establish a rebuttable presumption that constitutes clear and convincing evidence of the patient's wishes

157 Beauchamp, Tom L., Childress, James F., Principles of Biomedical Ethics, 2001, Fifth Edition, Oxford University Press, p.398

158 Ibid, Criteria for Theory Construction, p.338/40

recent legislation follows a similar pattern.[159] Therefore, any embellishments that add meaning to vague terms of reference should be placed within a separate 'Code of Practice' which should be given equal legal status.[160]

Coherence

In order to establish a value system that is both valid and reliable persons must engage in an interpretative exercise of sorts. The idea is to set out ones values in a general way and to subject these to a form of reflective testing which aims to bring initial ideas about values into a state of equilibrium with concrete judgments.[161] Values exist on many levels. Some may be more fundamental and thus more enduring than others whilst others change with circumstances, i.e. the crucial difference between critical and experiential interests. However, even when these have been identified and then specified as such a person's values may not always be consistent with each other, for example someone may value being in good health and yet continue to smoke. Alternatively, it may be impossible to draw a rational link between someone's personal ideology or worldview, where identified and disclosed, or maybe their attitude to risk and their values. A coherent value system then is one where conceptual inconsistencies and contradictory statements, which has been discussed above, have been eliminated.[162] In cases of difficulty it may be necessary to establish an order of precedence between various values or else a rule or theory that could be used by a surrogate decision-maker to help them decide which value to accord priority to when weighing all of the various factors they are required to consider. When a value system has been constructed in this way it is possible to explain ones character and values more precisely. It is also possible to embed within the value system truth conditions from a variety of sources, including the practice of value, which

---

[159] Mental Capacity Act 2005 and it accompanying Code of Practice which is given statutory force

[160] According to USA case *Re Guardianship of Estelle M. Browning, 568 So.2d 4* a surrogate must take great care in exercising incompetent patient's right to self-determination in particular when authorising withholding of medical treatment and must be able to support their decision with clear and convincing evidence (para.18)

[161] Dworkin Ronald, Justice in Robes, 2006, The Belknap Press of Harvard University Press, Rawls and the Law, p.246

[162] Beauchamp, Tom L., Childress, James F., Principles of Biomedical Ethics, 2001, Fifth Edition, Oxford University Press, Criteria for Theory Construction, p.339

supersede the pre-analytic assumptions of the individual whose value system it is.[163]

Completeness and Comprehensiveness

A comprehensive value system is one that gives a general as well as a more specific account of all moral and non-moral values that have informed the overall shape of a person's life. This information should be contained in a code of practice. The completeness of the system would be assessed against its ability to explain and justify a range of treatment and non-treatment decisions, including a decision to withdraw or withhold treatment at the end of life. Doctors must be able to determine from a patient's values whether the benefits of treatment would outweigh the burdens it would impose on them. The evaluative process would focus on a person's critical interest in leading a good life that preserves their sense of dignity. Thus patient values must be considered in the context of their attitude to risk since this would affect evaluation and judgment about whether to accept or reject medical treatment.

An assessment of this kind might be facilitated by the nature of the values themselves. For example, a person whose experiential interests included paragliding might not be considered risk adverse. However, it should not be assumed to be the case so an alternative proposal is to require persons who wish to be treated in accordance with their values to list health as a critical interest which they are required to give both a general and more specific account of. A person's general attitude to risk in this context may be ascertained from previous treatment decisions. The idea is that previous treatment decisions and the factors that were considered would provide relevant insight, as would experimental thinking exercises, simply because one is required to bring interests into a state of coherence.

Simplicity

Beauchamp and Childress state that:

> *"If a theory with a few basic norms generates sufficient moral content, then that theory is preferable to a theory with more norms but no additional content. A theory should have no more norms than are*

---

[163] Dworkin Ronald, Justice in Robes, 2006, The Belknap Press of Harvard University Press, Rawls and the Law, p.246

necessary, and no more than people can use without confusion. However, morality is complicated and any comprehensive moral theory will be complex".[164]

What is necessary and sufficient for a system of values, beliefs and preferences to constitute a simple decision-making devise? Act utilitarianism, for instance, takes a single unifying principle, the principle of utility, to create the greatest good for the greatest number. The instruction is simple enough but disagreement exists about what good is and by what method we can arrive at judgments concerning what is good as well as about whose interests should rightfully be considered in any assessment where the primary concern is to benefit the greatest number. Similarly, a single treatment decision is a simple expression of wishes that typically seeks to reflect the values of the patient which is intended to have limited application and yet specificity, the act of instituting a simple instruction, is proven, yet again, to be the formidable obstacle that one has to overcome.[165]

According to Dworkin autonomy encourages people's general capacity to lead their lives in their own distinctive way and an integrity view of autonomy places emphasis on this rather than on the welfare of the choosing agent.[166] Consequently, a person who wishes to continue to live a life that is structured by their own values should seek to ascertain and express the values, interests and convictions that have played a critical role in shaping that life.[167] The answer to the question of whether that sense of self can transcend the page through a series of simple statements is what is being facilitated by this process of testing particularly if one can gain critical input from an independent third party.

Explanatory Power

You should at this stage recall Herrings comment from the previous chapter, that not all supporters of autonomy are happy with Dworkins analysis of how that principle should be understood when someone suffers a loss of decision-making capacity. Their contention primarily arises out

---

[164] Ibid

[165] *Re T (Adult: Refusal of Medical Treatment) [1992] 4 All ER 649 CA; HE v A Hospital NHS Trust 2003 WL 21729346*

[166] Dworkin, Ronald, Life's Dominion: An argument about Abortion and Euthanasia, 1993, Harper Collins, Chapter 7, p.224

[167] Ibid

of the fact that human judgment cannot be eliminated from the decision-making process consequently there is scope for a decision-maker with knowledge of a person's critical interests to use or weigh that information in a way that is inconsistent with what was intended. With that in mind the aim here is to provide sufficient insight into the person, their life, reasoning processes and so on so as to facilitate the notion that someone else will continue on after them with a line of decisions that will leave that heritage undisturbed.[168] It's a little like training someone to do a job where the creative input has been pre-determined. In this regard think of a dot-to-dot picture and then of actors who are required to interpret the words on the page. In regard to the former we join the dots to complete the picture as we were intended to do. But an actor will typically set out to identify with the character they are intended to portray to give their performance integrity, credibility, authenticity call it what you will. What matters to them is that they should get the characterisation right. Indeed many develop an intimate relationship with the nature of the individual characters they play on screen or stage to a point where they might consider that they know better than the writer, who was responsible for creating that individuality, what this person should say or do next.[169]

Justificatory Power

In creating a personal value system a person is seeking to stay in control of their body and life by laying down the foundations of their decision-making processes, i.e. they are disclosing their values to assist others to determine what ought to happen in the future based on a personal account of what their good is.[170] The project is given a foundation by Dworkin

[168] The situation is very similar in the USA which favours the substituted judgment decision-making standard. In the case of *Re Guardianship of Estelle M. Browning, 568 So.2d 4*, for example, the court stated that, 'it is important for the surrogate decision-maker to fully appreciate that he or she makes the decision which the patient would personally choose. In this state, we have adopted a concept of 'substituted judgment'. One does not exercise another's right of self-determination or fulfil that person's right of privacy by making a decision which the state, the family, or public opinion would prefer. The surrogate decision-maker must be confident that he or she can and is voicing the patient's decision'.

[169] See Herring, Chapter Five

[170] See the USA case *Re Guardianship of Estelle M. Browning, 568 So.2d 4, p.2* which states that; 'The issue involves a patient's right to self-determination and does not involve what is thought to be in the patient's best interests. More is involved in respect for self-determination than just the belief that each person knows what's best for him or herself … Even if it could be shown that an expert

who claims that a person's life is informed by two types of interests, experiential and critical. However, the integrity view of autonomy holds that what persons have most reason to pursue is ultimately determined by their critical interests. This is because critical interests are explained by reference to the integrity with which important self-defining decisions are made to accord with our more abstract ambition to lead a good life.[171] Thus a person's critical interests have the power within them to provide greater insight into the personal disposition of the individual whose life it is. The issue is whether imperatives to guide judgments on some future occasion can safely be derived, and later relied upon, from the facts of our individual decisions.

Now it may be assumed that self-interest should be sufficient to validate personal judgments about which ends one has most reason to pursue. However, there is a danger that persons might fail to be sufficiently objective about what is critically important in their life. Take for example a young man whose family are ardent supporters of a particular football club. As season ticket holders they regularly attend home matches and also endeavour to support their team when they play away. The problem is that the young man has now been selected to go onto a trainee manager programme at work and following a short romance has recently become engaged to be married. Quite naturally these developments place some additional pressure on his spare time but finds that the change in lifestyle suits him quite well. Nevertheless he feels some pressure from his father to maintain existing family ties and traditions. So this is a situation where someone might experience conflict about which values they are most committed to.

Therefore, some form of reasoning process is required to help persons to objectively validate their critical interests or those things that they feel obligated to do as this will prevent them from giving a merely descriptive account of what exists in their world and how it may be understood by others. A value system will have justificatory power in this sense if, the person whose value system it is, gives grounds for justified belief which

---

(or a computer) could do the job better, the worth of the individual, as acknowledged in Western ethical traditions and especially American law, provides an independent and more important ground for recognising self-determination as a basic principle in human relations, particularly when matters as important as those raised by health care are at stake

[171] Dworkin, Ronald, Life's Dominion: An argument about Abortion and Euthanasia, 1993, Harper Collins, Chapter 7, p.204/5

entails something more than merely reformulating the beliefs they already possess.[172] Accordingly, persons who develop a coherent narrative of their life story which is supported by evidence of a settled commitment to that particular end would go some way to satisfying this particular requirement. This is because personal values will have been subjected to a form of empirical testing during which time a person may have had an opportunity to question and maybe even revise their values. Consequently, a value system that can capture the essence of the person through moments of weakness or self-doubt may have more credibility and inspire more confidence in it than one which portrays absolute and unyielding rigidity. Empirical testing therefore renders self-knowledge an inherently valid and reliable source of information for others who may be required to justify what should happen in the person's best interests on some future occasion.

Output Power

A value system should not operate in the way that a decision to refuse a medical treatment does since in those instances a person is merely recording an instruction which they intend to take effect in a particular set of circumstances. The idea is that a treatment refusal should be specific to engender trust and confidence that it represented a settled decision and not an off-hand comment.[173] To have output power a personal value system must generate an explanation and justification in new and novel situations that may not have been contemplated or considered by the person whose value system it is. Hopefully persons will have used experimental thinking exercises to test their beliefs and values in a medical context as a decision by the surrogate decision-maker must be rendered coherent with the prior considered judgments of the patient.

Practicality

A doctor or carer would be required to have regard to the contents of a value system, where these were reasonably ascertainable. This means that surrogates must be informed that a value system exists and that it should be made reasonably accessible to all concerned. Equally, it would be unacceptable if a value system was of a length or was composed in such a

---

[172] Beauchamp, Tom L., Childress, James F., Principles of Biomedical Ethics, 2001, Fifth Edition, Oxford University Press, Criteria for Theory Construction, p.340

[173] *Cruzan vs Director, Missouri Dept. of Health 110 S.Ct. 2841*

style or amount of detail that information could not reasonably be understood by others in the time available.

Personal Value Systems and Public Policy

Coherence alone is not a sufficient justification for being treated in accordance with a personal value system. Beauchamp and Childress have, for instance, previously commented that a body of principles that cohere could be morally unsatisfactory and for that very reason may not be upheld on grounds of public policy.[174] So what is public policy and how is it relevant to personal value systems when the primacy of autonomy is firmly established in law?

The process of determining what public policy is or should be originates out of controversial problems or issues concerning human morality and welfare. To settle policy issues it is necessary to determine what policy should be pursued and why. This last point is significant given that the choice that is made will have consequences for human and civil life in circumstances where no actual public consultation will take place. What factors then, in the absence of public debate and scrutiny, are relevant to formulating policy? Well in this regard the theoretical perspectives of moral and legal philosophers have a significant role to play in view of the interests that are at stake.[175] Yet, in highlighting the complexity of issues that must be considered Beauchamp and Childress claim that policy formation and criticism involve more complex forms of judgment than ethical principles and rules can handle on their own.[176] This is what they have to say:

> *"Public policy is often formulated in contexts that are marked by profound social disagreements, uncertainties, and different interpretations of history. No body of abstract moral principles and rules can determine policy in such circumstances, because it cannot contain enough specific information or provide direct and discerning guidance. The specification and implementation of moral principles and rules must take account of problems of feasibility, efficiency, cultural pluralism, political procedures,*

---

[174] Beauchamp, Tom L., Childress, James F., Principles of Biomedical Ethics, 2001, Fifth Edition, Oxford University Press, p.400

[175] *Chester v Afshar 2004 WL 2289136; Airedale NHS Trust v Bland [1993] 1 All ER 821*

[176] Beauchamp, Tom L., Childress, James F., Principles of Biomedical Ethics, 2001, Fifth Edition, Oxford University Press, p.8

uncertainty about risk, non-compliance by patients and the like. Principles and rules provide the moral background for policy evaluation, but a policy must also be shaped by empirical data and by information available in fields such as medicine, nursing, economics, law and psychology".[177]

Accordingly policy could be developed on the basis of contributions from think tanks, empirical data and relevant interest groups. The factors that create pressure for change, how these are perceptible and when it is appropriate to mark a change from one set of ideas to another are therefore embedded within the notion of public policy. Yet what is in the public interest may be unknowable, indeed hidden values and motivations may become manifest within it, because there are so many potential and competing factors to be considered. Furthermore, the fact that the law has to be practical as well as moral means that we cannot move with certainty from moral principles or rules to laws and to what is public policy in particular.[178] In other words we cannot necessarily move from what is morally right or wrong to imply what should or should not be permitted in law.[179] Consequently, a person who has disclosed their values and value system in a living will should not assume that those values ought on every occasion to inform decisions regarding what should be done in their medical welfare and other interests.

Public Policy Issues

On some occasions conflicting moral principles and rules create dilemmas. A most obvious example, within the context of this thesis, is that of autonomy and best interests where the only way to comply with one obligation is to contravene another.[180] Clearly, patients who have disclosed their wishes or values in a living will may not be immune from this problem. In which case a doctor or judge will be required to decide which obligation is overriding.[181]

---

[177] Ibid, p.8/9
[178] Ibid, p.9
[179] Ibid, p.9
[180] Ibid, p.10
[181] Mental Capacity Act 2005, ss.24-26; *Re T (Adult: Refusal of Medical Treatment) [1992] 4 All ER 649 CA; HE v A Hospital NHS Trust 2003 WL 21729346*

Another example arises out of a situation where the patient expresses a preference for a particular form of treatment.[182] In these circumstances it has been determined in law that the form of treatment that it is in the patient's best interests to receive should be determined by a doctor, i.e. someone who is expert in medical matters and who is able to more fully appreciate the implications of that decision for the general medical welfare of all patients including, one assumes, potential patients.

You might also remember from previous discussions that human life has intrinsic value and in upholding the sanctity principle it is a crime for any person to bring about the death of another.[183] Hence, euthanasia is not lawful at common law.[184] Nevertheless, Lord Goff recognised that many responsible members of society thought that euthanasia should be legalised.[185] In this regard he believed that it could only be rendered lawful by an act of Parliament that expressed the 'democratic will' on the subject.[186] However, we have also observed, in relation to treatment decisions at the end of life, that a distinction is maintained in law between acts and omissions and therefore between active and passive forms of euthanasia. In holding to its qualified sanctity position the law seeks to draw a distinction between deliberate acts that are intended to kill[187] from those where death is merely foreseen as an incidental outcome of an act that is intended to benefit the patient.[188] Whilst a patient cannot consent to be killed a doctor may, in accordance with the moral doctrine of double effect, for example, lawfully administer morphine for pain relief in the knowledge that this will advance the impending death of the patient.[189] Similarly, a doctor, though not a relative or lay person, may flick the switch of a life-support machine knowing that this will hasten the person's death, which will be attributed to their underlying condition, and in law the decision to withdraw medical treatment is in some circumstances regarded as an omission to treat.[190]

---

[182] *R (On the Application of Oliver Leslie Burke) v The General Medical Council [2005] EWCA Civ 1003 CA*

[183] *Airedale NHS Trust v Bland [1993] 1 All ER 821 HL*

[184] Ibid, see Lord Goff

[185] Ibid

[186] Ibid

[187] *R v Cox [1991] 12 BMLR 38*

[188] *R v Bodkin Adams [1957] Crim LR 365*

[189] Ibid

[190] *Airedale NHS Trust v Bland [1993] 1 All ER 821 HL*

Essentially, a doctor who discontinues life support and allows the patient to die does not act unlawfully where there is no breach of duty to the patient.[191] And it has been determined that a doctor will not be in breach of their duty to the patient where medical opinion determines that it is futile[192] to continue with life support.[193] This is because no actual advantage is conferred by a decision to continue with the treatment in these circumstances. Similarly, a doctor is permitted, in accordance with the moral principle of double effect, to administer drugs intending to relieve intolerable pain even when death is foreseen as an incidental effect of treatment.[194] In sum therefore, a doctor must not, in considering whether treatment is in the best interests of the person, be motivated to bring about their death.[195]

Some have argued that the law is morally inconsistent as a result of maintaining the acts and omissions distinction.[196] The opposing argument is that the law maintains a qualified sanctity of life position which means that a doctor is not placed under an absolute duty to prolong life, by any means available, regardless of the patient's quality of life and dignity.[197] In other words a doctor's duty to act in the best interests of the patient is similarly qualified.[198]

Recent clarification of the law of assisted suicide,[199] which places emphasis on the motivation of culprits, leaves unaltered the basic principle in respect of patients who are not terminally ill, or though dying are not in pain, that doctors should refrain from engaging in activities that directly shorten life as this will be treated as an assisted suicide contrary to s.2 of the Suicide Act 1961.

---

[191] Ibid

[192] In the sense that the overall purpose of treatment cannot be fulfilled

[193] Ibid

[194] *R v Bodkin Adams [1957] Crim LR 365*

[195] *R v Cox [1991] 12 BMLR 38; Airedale NHS Trust v Bland [1993] 1 All ER 821 HL*

[196] For instance see Keown, J., Restoring Moral and Intellectual Shape to the Law after Bland, 1997, The Law Quarterly Review Journal, Vol 113, pp.481-503

[197] *Airedale NHS Trust v Bland [1993] 1 All ER 821 HL*, Lord Goff

[198] In accordance with the principles of non-maleficence and beneficence

[199] See the Director of Public Prosecutions statement on Assisted Suicide at the Crown Prosecution Service website

Within what Limits should Personal Values be taken into Consideration?[200]

Beauchamp and Childress commented that a body of principles that cohere could be morally unsatisfactory and for that very reason may not be upheld on grounds of public policy.[201] Of course public opinion will reflect divergent viewpoints on most moral matters.[202] Yet laws are likely to be most effective when they are consistent with accepted societal norms and therefore reflect the common or collective morality of society. In this regard it is possible to witness a move towards autonomy and therefore away from paternalism in medical law and this change has become more deeply entrenched within the legal system over time as confidence increases in the underlying policy considerations that gave way to it.[203]

Members of the judiciary are familiar with the problems presented by a conflict of interests and know that if they comply with one obligation in such situations, i.e. to respect an autonomous refusal of life preserving medical treatment, that another will or may be contravened, i.e. sanctity of life. In these circumstances decision-makers have to determine which obligation is overriding. However, in some contexts in matters that are of greatest concern to individuals, in this context those affecting the right of a competent patient to self-determine what shall happen to their body in a medical context and therefore of how they should live and die, the exercise of that right might still be considered controversial when set against the values, beliefs and interests of the wider community.

So as matters of public policy tend to arise where there is conflict between what is in the interests of the individual and society members more generally should a value system have to be morally sound? Are there some ingredients that all value systems should have regardless of the wishes of the person, for example, some form of other regarding principle?

---

200 Hill, Thomas E. Jr., Human Welfare and Moral Worth: Kantian Perspectives, 2002, Oxford University Press, p.244

201 Beauchamp, Tom L., Childress, James F., Principles of Biomedical Ethics, 2001, Fifth Edition, Oxford University Press, p.400

202 This is because there is no consistent view about what good is and therefore of what a good life should entail. Human psychology renders us predictable to some degree as Maslow points out however if we take a basic need of humans such as security we see that persons differ about how this should be pursued.

203 *Chester v Afshar 2004 WL 2289136*

Well a Kantian could be expected to voluntarily will that their imperative of action was capable of being applied without contradiction. Thus Kant sought to ensure that personal autonomy was not bought at too high a price to principles of equality, fairness, justice and social and economic responsibility. Mill, similarly argued that '*the only purpose for which power can rightfully be exercised over any member of a civilised community, against his will, is to prevent harm to others*'. Both sought to encourage persons to reason and act ethically rather than purely self-interestedly.

Certainly case law suggests that in order for a value system to be respected due regard must be had for the sensibilities of others. For example, the opinion of the majority in the case of *R v Brown* determined that there is a limit to the amount of harm that one can consent to. Essentially a particular act or form of activity must in itself be lawful for consent to operate as a defence.[204] Accordingly the scope for autonomous choice is limited by the need to ensure that a particular practice is not dangerous and injurious and that if allowed and extended would not be harmful to society generally in that it does not offend against the principle of maximising human welfare more specifically. This must be born in mind when thinking about Dworkin's argument about the point of autonomy, which he claims is not the maximisation of one's own welfare necessarily but to be given sufficient scope to develop one's own character and personality and to live and die in a manner that is consistent with that creative legacy.

Consequently, a person, let's say a sadomasochist, whose values reflected a desire to remain alive for a prolonged period in a state of, what for most would be, intolerable pain could not expect their values to be respected for public policy reasons.[205] Similarly, a person who is religious and a Catholic should not expect to be maintained in a pvs indefinitely simply on the basis of their faith.[206] An anorexic who prefers to starve rather than eat could not expect to find that food and water would be withheld.[207] Contrarily, *Burke* informs us that a person who is afraid that they may be starved to death cannot insist upon receiving basic care such as artificial food and water.[208] Moreover, it is possible to infer from *Bland* that a

---

[204] *R v Brown [1993] 2 All ER 75,* see Lord Templeman
[205] Ibid
[206] *Airedale NHS Trust v Bland [1993] 1 All ER 821 HL*
[207] *Re W (A Minor) (Medical Treatment) [1992] 4 All ER 627 CA*
[208] *R (On the Application of Oliver Leslie Burke) v The General Medical Council [2005] EWCA Civ 1003 CA*

tramp who values living rough cannot refuse basic care that might cover such things as basic hygiene.[209]

The question however was whether some sort of other regarding principle should be explicit within a value system. Well we saw in chapter one that other than in limited circumstances persons have no general obligation to be beneficent; general beneficence is supererogatory, nice to do but not wrong to omit. If, for example, we examine the legal system there is no real expectation that people should report wrongs and bring cases against those that are perceived to have transgressed against the interests of others. Negligence is a case in point where the difficulties associated with bringing a case to court and of succeeding with it are widely accepted, rape is perhaps another instance. We are apparently unconcerned about the consequences of this for the individuals concerned as well as for the general welfare of citizens now and in the future. This is curious when we consider the comment made by Raz that values can have a cultural or historical origin but once a value comes into existence it bears on everything without exception.

Still we have witnessed the emergence of an Organ Donation (Presumed Consent) Bill. One assumes that if such a Bill is passed and becomes legislation that society would be in favour of such a principle and might be inclined to infer one when it is not present. Alternatively, it is possible that some sort of other regarding principle be inferred from one's values. Take someone who is a proud communitarian but who had made no provision to donate their organs for the benefit of others on their death? If we take *Re Y* as an example we see that merely because a non-therapeutic treatment or procedure is not in the medical best interests of someone it should not be assumed that it cannot be in their welfare interests when welfare is more widely conceived. A medical treatment or procedure must however confer some advantage and in this case a non-therapeutic procedure which was intended to benefit a third party, in this case a close relative, was held to be in the best interests of the patient because it could be presumed, from her conduct, that the undertaking would confer an emotional advantage on the patient. This suggests that it might be presumed that someone who took their civic duties seriously would consent to donate body tissue and organs for the benefit of others generally, rather than members of their immediate family, on the basis of their former values.

---

[209] *Airedale NHS Trust v Bland [1993] 1 All ER 821 HL*

Consider also the role that many ordinary competent persons play in advancing the causes of medical science through clinical trials for example. Or, of those that donate body tissue so that unknown others can conceive a child. Should mentally incapacitated patients play an equal role in advancing the causes of medical research? In this regard we must remember that mentally incapacitated patients play as big a role in advancing medical science and therefore the general welfare of the population as do most other members of society. They will be given medicines, treatments and procedures when the occasion arises and can be monitored for side effects as well as for the efficacy of treatment and surgeons have an opportunity to perfect and develop their skills when they are being operated on. Moreover, if we examine the case of *Simms* in which highly experimental treatment based on research conducted in Japan was given to mentally incompetent patients suffering from variant Creutzfeldt-Jakob disease then incapacity in that case arguably justified a decision to administer a form of treatment that would advance medical knowledge about that condition and its prognosis which would benefit patients in the future.[210] Herring reports on this case and states that:

> *"Butler-Sloss P. held that it was lawful to administer the treatment and that it would be in their best interests also. This was because there was no responsible body of opinion which thought it irresponsible to provide the proposed treatment referring to the Bolam test. Although there was a 5 per cent chance of haemorrhage as a result of this procedure, this was within the reasonable bounds of risk given the situation the patients were in. The proposed treatment was of benefit to the patients even if there was no hope of recovery, and the hope was that the treatment would slow down deterioration or prolong life. Even though the chance of improvement was slight it was a risk worth taking. As she pointed out:*
>
> *The concept of 'benefit' to a patient suffering from v-CJD does encompass an improvement from the state of illness, or a continuation of the existing state of illness, without deterioration for a longer period than might otherwise have occurred.*
>
> *Here the condition was fatal and progressive; it was therefore reasonable to attempt experimental treatment with unknown risks and benefits. She stated:*

[210] *Simms v Simms [2003] 1 All ER 669 CA*

> *A patient who is not able to consent to pioneering treatment ought not to be deprived of the chance in circumstances where he would have been likely to consent if he had been competent.*
>
> *When considering what was in the patients' best interests their futures with and without treatment, as well as the views of their families should be taken into account. The parents' support of this proposed treatment was said to carry 'considerable weight'.*[211]

The case of *Simms* can be contrasted with that of *R v Cambridge Health Authority, ex parte B*.[212] In that case a child aged ten was suffering from non-Hodgkins lymphoma with common acute lymphoblastic leukaemia and received chemotherapy and treatment which was initially successful. Some time later the child developed acute myeloid leukaemia and was once again treated with a course of chemotherapy and underwent a course of total body irradiation which prepares the body for a bone marrow transplant or stem cell therapy but medical opinion was that this form of treatment should be undertaken only once. It appeared once again that treatment had been successful. Unfortunately some months later B suffered a further relapse.

Everything possible had been done by the child's family to secure the best possible treatment for her and up until that point no apparent disagreement existed between the family and the doctors who were responsible for treating B. However, that was to change. Medical opinion was now that the child had a very short period to live, perhaps six to eight weeks, and doctors considered that as further treatment could not usefully be administered she should be allowed to die. Further treatment would involve a further course of chemotherapy which if successful would be followed by a second bone-marrow transplant operation. A second opinion was sought which affirmed the opinion of the doctor who was treating B.

At this point B's father decided to seek out the opinion of doctors in America and was encouraged to find that certain doctors believed that there was a substantial chance of further treatment being successful. Yet treatment was prohibitively expensive in America. Therefore, B's father

---

[211] Herring, Jonathan, Medical Law and Ethics, 2008, Second Edition, Oxford University Press, p.564

[212] *R v Cambridge Health Authority, ex parte B [1995] 2 All ER 129 CA*

returned to England to seek out a medical professional who was sympathetic to the views expressed by the American doctors, i.e. an alternative body of medical opinion. In this regard a notable expert in that particular field of medicine was willing to recommend to the treating doctors that it was reasonable to compromise in this instance and try a further course of chemotherapy with the hope of achieving a complete remission. He also recommended the use of a particular drug that was less toxic with fewer side effects so that if complete remission was achieved it might be possible to contemplate a second bone marrow transplant. This doctor assessed the chances of success as being less than 20 per cent and as the doctor's so far responsible for B's care were not keen to administer further treatment he suggested the name of another practitioner who would be willing to do so.

The health authority that was required to fund the treatment contacted B's father and explained that a decision not to fund further treatment had been taken on clinical not financial grounds. As treatment was at variance with majority medical opinion it could be categorised as experimental rather than therapeutic treatment. The cost of treatment had been estimated to be £15000 for chemotherapy and a possible £60,000 for a bone marrow transplant which may or may not be necessary. In his affidavit to the court the officer stated that:

> *"Having considered all the medical opinions put before me I decided to accept the clinical judgment of ... that a further course of intensive chemotherapy with a view to a second transplant operation was not in the best interests of B. I have also been influenced in my decision by the consistent advice and directions of the Department of Health with regard to the funding of treatments which have not been proven to be of benefit. The ethical use of resources demands that new and expensive treatments are evaluated before they are transferred to the NHS for service funding. The doctors to whom I spoke were consistent in their advice that the proposed treatment was neither standard nor had been formally evaluated. I also considered that the substantial expenditure on treatment with such small prospect of success would not be an effective use of resources. The amount of funds available for health care are not limitless. The authority has a responsibility to ensure that sufficient funds are available from their limited resources for the provision of treatment for other patients which is likely to be effective".*

Clearly the officer showed scant regard for the wishes of the family which seemed to play a considerable role in the decision reached by Butler-Sloss

P. in *Simms*. Moreover, the track record of the treatment appears to have been an overriding factor in his decision which of course in *Simms* had not even been established. Speaking on behalf of the Appeal Court, Sir Thomas Bingham MR, reiterated that our society is one in which a very high value is placed on human life and that although decisions affecting human life should be regarded with great seriousness, the courts are not arbiters as to the merits of cases of this kind in which judgments about the effectiveness of a medical treatment are necessary. The constitutional role of the court is to rule upon the lawfulness of decisions.

At first instance the judge had said that the Health Authority '*must do more than toll the bell of tight resources ... they must explain the priorities that have led them to decline to fund the treatment*'. On this matter Sir Thomas Bingham MR, stated that:

> *"I have no doubt that in a perfect world any treatment which a patient, or a patient's family, sought would be provided if doctors were willing to give it, no matter how much it cost, particularly when a life was potentially at stake. It would however, in my view, be shutting one's eyes to the real world if the court were to proceed on the basis that we do live in such a world. It is common knowledge that health authorities of all kinds are constantly pressed to make ends meet... Difficult and agonising judgments have to be made as to how a limited budget is best allocated to the maximum advantage of the maximum number of patients. That is not a judgment which the court can make. In my judgment, it is not something that a health authority can be fairly criticised for not advancing before the court".*

Accordingly, the court extended sympathy to B and her family but ultimately determined that this was not a matter in which it was possible to make any decision in their favour.

CHAPTER SEVEN

HOW USEFUL IS THE MCA IN PROMOTING AUTONOMY THROUGH ADVANCE DECISION-MAKING AND DECISIONS MADE IN PATIENT'S BEST INTERESTS?

In the case of *Bland* it was suggested by Lord Goff that the best interests test should comprise of something more than purely professional appraisal of a person's medical welfare.[1] To confine the test in this way, he said, would be inconsistent with the primacy given to the principle of self-determination and would '*downgrade the status of the incompetent person by placing a lesser value on [their] intrinsic worth and vitality*'.[2] Approximately twelve years later in the foreword to the Mental Capacity Act 2005 Lord Falconer has stated that:

> *"The Mental Capacity Act 2005 is a vitally important piece of legislation, and one that will make a real difference to the lives of people who may lack mental capacity. It will empower people to make decisions for themselves wherever possible, and protect people who lack capacity by providing a flexible framework that places individuals at the very heart of the decision-making process. It will ensure that they participate as much as possible in any decisions made on their behalf, and that these are made in their best interests. It also allows people to plan ahead for a time in the future when they might lack the capacity, for any number of reasons, to make decisions for themselves".*[3]

The primary purpose of the 2005 Act is to determine who, in the doctor-patient relationship, should decide and what criteria and standards are relevant to decision-making processes concerning mentally incompetent patients. And as a contemporary piece of legislation the Mental Capacity

---

[1] *Airedale NHS Trust v Bland [1993] 1 All ER 821 HL*

[2] Ibid

[3] Mental Capacity Act 2005, Code of Practice, Foreword by Lord Falconer

Act enshrines current thinking about the role that patient autonomy and medical paternalism should play in relation to this patient group.

What is interesting is that enactment of the 2005 Act took place at a time when the common law had established that the primacy accorded to the moral principle of autonomy was derivative of the patient's fundamental right to bodily inviolability. As a consequence doctors have a legal obligation to obtain patient consent prior to administering a medical treatment. Moreover, the law had also determined that in order for a patient consent to be legally valid it must be informed also to safeguard patient welfare and autonomy.[4] Accordingly, a competent patient must be placed in a position to make an informed decision about whether to accept or reject an offer of medical treatment and be maintained inviolate.[5] As personal autonomy means being one's own person without constraints being imposed by another's action a doctor's legal obligations have increasingly been tailored to meet the needs of patients leaving little scope to invoke professional privilege to justify what the patient was or was not told.[6] Neither should a doctor's legal obligations be mediated by any psychological or physical limitations of their patients.[7]

It is then perhaps unsurprising that the scope of the patient's right to self-determination in law should be extended to include advance directives or an advance treatment decision of a competent patient. These, as a matter of principle the common law determines, must be respected in the same way as if the decision of the patient had been made contemporaneously.[8] As this common law doctrine has been incorporated within the Mental Capacity Act there is now statutory recognition of the primacy that should be accorded to the moral principle of autonomy in relation to decisions concerning formerly competent patients.[9] In law, at least, the incompetent person is deemed to retain psychological continuity with their former competent self. This amounts to legal recognition of the idea that a person's values and method for arriving at judgments of value when they are competent are the best indication we have of what should happen in the future when they are incompetent, i.e. the values that underpinned their

[4] Berg, Jessica W., Appelbaum, Paul S., Lidz Charles W., Parker, Lisa S., Informed Consent, 2001, Second Edition, Oxford University Press, p.94

[5] For example, *Chester v Afshar 2004 WL 2289136*

[6] Ibid

[7] Mental Capacity Act 2005, s.1

[8] *Re T (Adult: Refusal of Treatment) [1992] 4 All ER 649 CA*

[9] Mental Capacity Act 2005, ss.24-26

decisions as a competent persons should continue to play a determinative role in decisions, in this context medical treatment decisions, that will affect the patient now and in the future. Consequently, respect for the principle of autonomy in medical law can more generally be understood to mean that a doctor's primary obligation is to ascertain and respond to the values of the patient, howsoever expressed, in deciding whether to administer a medical treatment. So, when autonomy is respected persons, competent and incompetent alike, not only have dominion over their life plan but also their body and lifespan.

Disclosing a value system in a living will promotes patient autonomy because decision-makers will have relevant knowledge and insight about the values that were most important in the life of a particular person.[10] Still, its format, as discussed in chapter six, would mean that it did not amount to an advance decision where the values of the patient are merely implicit in their choice. As a prior written statement of the patient it would instead be considered,[11] alongside other factors, as part of a best interests balancing exercise.[12] Considering that the decision-maker in a 'patient centred' best interests standard is someone other than the patient the possibility exists that any decision affecting them may not entirely coincide with what they would themselves have decided. Primarily this is because the past wishes of the patient, i.e. that the values that had informed their earlier life should continue to inform their future life, need not necessarily be made determinative of what should happen by a third party decision-maker.[13]

Consequently, the 'patient-centred' best interests standard that is being upheld by the Mental Capacity Act continues to provide considerable scope for patient autonomy to be undermined, even when the values and value system of the patient have been disclosed in a living will. This, in part, is due to the uncertain nature of the medical treatment decision-making standard itself. The fact that the test has not been fully defined, perhaps because it is incapable of being fully defined, consigns it to a

[10] Dworkin, Ronald, Life's Dominion: An argument about Abortion and Euthanasia, 1993, Harper Collins, Chapter 7, p.201-3, A value system confirms persons' critical and experiential interests

[11] There is no process for determining what is in another's best interests and nor does the MCA establish the precise weight that a prior statement of the patient should be accorded only that it should have some weight

[12] Mental Capacity Act 2005, s.4(6)(a)

[13] Ibid, s.4(6)&(7)

reputation of indeterminacy. Yet it is the lack of a decision-making method that is possibly of greatest significance in this context since there is no instruction about the weight that should be given to a prior relevant written statement of the patient. Either way personal or medical professional values, non-maleficence and beneficence, will ultimately be relied upon to fill the gaps left vacant by the legal test of best interests. A situation which the law has on various occasions sought to avoid not only in relation to competent patients[14] but also in respect of those who were formerly competent through, for example, the use of advance decisions.[15]

Nonetheless guidance within the Code of Practice claims that this legislation is intended to be enabling and supportive of people who lack capacity, not restricting or controlling of their lives.[16] Accordingly, this chapter is focused on suggesting ways in which the sentiment underlying the Act might reasonably be made a reality. At least for those who are competent to disclose their value system in a living will and who clearly wish to have what happens to them as an incompetent patient determined by an appropriate application of their former personal values.

Consequently, the purpose of this final chapter is to determine whether, and if so how, the values of a competent person, when they are understood by others, can play a role in medical treatment decision-making under the Mental Capacity Act 2005 at a time when that person is no longer capable of making their own decisions.

This chapter will now divide into four parts. The first section will focus on whether the idea proposed in the previous chapter will uphold patient autonomy when assessed in the light of the MCA, i.e. whether a value system that had been disclosed in a living will could play a key role in decision-making. On the basis that the legal test of best interests accords no particular weight to the prior values of a former competent person in the second part of the chapter we will go on to explore the issue of how respect for values could fit in with the doctor's ethical obligations of non-maleficence and beneficence. Next we move on to consider what practical problems might still arise if respect for patient autonomy, i.e. for their

---

[14] For example, *Chester v Afshar 2004 WL 2289136*

[15] Mental Capacity Act 2005, ss.24-26; *Re T (Adult: Refusal of Treatment) [1992] 4 All ER 649 CA*; Rich, Ben A., The Values History: A New Standard of Care, 1991, Emory Law Journal, 40, p.1127

[16] Mental Capacity Act 2005, Code of Practice, Chapter Two

values, beliefs and preferences, was incorporated within the ethical framework of the medical profession. In particular there is a need to explore the possibility that a doctor may override a patient's value system, not wilfully perhaps, but, due to the subconscious imposition of the doctor's value system and to identify possible grounds for doing so.[17] The fourth and final section will consider whether reform of the Mental Capacity Act 2005 will be necessary to uphold patient values.

Patient Values and the MCA

In chapter four we discovered that the Mental Capacity Act 2005 provides a flexible framework for decision-making on behalf of persons who are no longer capable of making their own decisions. This ensures that its provisions can be applied flexibly to meet a wide variety of situations and circumstances including those arising from the potentially different demands of never competent and formerly competent patients which this thesis is so obviously concerned with.

The MCA, unlike the statute De Prerogativa Regis, does in other words attempt to be all things to all people who are mentally incompetent. However, its inherent flexibility places doctors as surrogate decision-makers in a position of having to determine whether the source of authority or legal justification for beneficent intervention, or acting in another's best interests, is protection, in which case medical welfare might be the paramount consideration, or whether it should instead be respect for precedent autonomy.[18]

It was also clear from our discussions in the previous chapter that public policy has a role to play in determining what health behaviours to encourage. In *Bland*, for example, Lord Goff appeared to be saying that the right to beneficence should not be in conflict with the right to autonomy but what can be gleaned from the 2005 Act in that regard? Well the tone is set by Lord Falconer, the former Lord Chancellor, in the foreword to the MCA. There he speaks in positive terms about the Act and proudly boasts that this legislation has been constructed to empower people to make their own decisions wherever possible but also to protect

[17] Raz, Joseph, The Practice of Value, 2003, Oxford University Press, p.21 – values are open to re-interpretation

[18] Dworkin, Ronald, Life's Dominion: An argument about Abortion and Euthanasia, Harper Collins, p.229

those who lack capacity by providing a flexible framework that places individuals at the heart of a best interests decision-making process.[19] He goes on to state that it also allows people to plan ahead for a time in the future when they might lack the capacity, for any number of reasons, to make decision for themselves.

As we will be talking about the authority of precedent autonomy we must keep in mind the distinction between experiential and critical interests on the basis that the latter should assume greater moral authority because of the integrity with which important self-defining decisions are made to accord with them. Clearly, a previous statement of a competent patient that has been written with this distinction in mind may be of particular significance in safeguarding precedent autonomy. The question then is whether the MCA will support an integrity,[20] not evidentiary,[21] view of autonomy in circumstances where a person has chosen to disclose their value system in a living will rather than attempt to make an advance treatment decision.

Does the MCA Support the use of a Statement of Values?

The claim made by Lord Falconer that the MCA allows people to plan ahead for a time in the future when they might lack the capacity, for any number of reasons, to make decisions themselves would seem to be a direct reference to advance decisions which the Act supports.[22] An advance decision that is not legally valid and/or applicable might still be regarded as an expression of the person's wishes and must therefore be considered by doctors when working out their best interests.[23] In addition any relevant written statement made by the patient when they had capacity is one of the factors to be considered in any best interests determination.[24]

---

[19] Mental Capacity Act 2005, s.1(5)

[20] An integrity view of autonomy places emphasis on the right of a competent person to lead their lives in their own distinctive way rather than on the welfare of the agent

[21] The point of autonomy on the evidentiary view is to enable persons to safeguard their own personal welfare, i.e. to make decisions and act in their own best interests. An evidentiary view presents a weak case for respecting a person's past wishes because people are not always the best judge of what their own best interests are in new and novel circumstances

[22] Mental Capacity Act 2005, ss.24-26

[23] Ibid, Code of Practice, Chapter 9, Quick summary

[24] Mental Capacity Act 2005, s.4(6)(a)

However, it is somewhat less obvious that the person who discloses their values has a critical interest in ensuring that their future is governed by them including in situations where a doctor seeks to ascertain whether they have or might lack capacity to make a treatment decision contemporaneously.

Living Wills

Advance decisions have their appeal in the fact that they by-pass the application of best interests criterion, in which the past and present wishes of a formerly competent patient may be given equal consideration by a surrogate decision-maker, and instead absolute priority is accorded to precedent autonomy. Thus the patient retains control over what shall happen to their body in a medical context.[25] Crucially a legally valid and applicable advance decision takes effect in the same way as if the patient had contemporaneously refused to consent to a treatment or procedure that a doctor proposed to administer in their (medical) best interests.[26] Consequently, a failure to respect a valid and applicable advance directive can result in a claim for battery being made against the treating clinician.[27] This is because a doctor is not acting for or on behalf of someone who lacks capacity but on the instructions of a capacitated individual.[28]

The question then is whether a statement of values contains relevant and clear instructions so that it might reasonably constitute an advance decision to refuse a medical treatment or procedure. Given the fact that an advance decision may not only be made in writing but orally as well one might have more reason to regard a values statement that was capable of yielding the choice the patient would make if competent to decide as an advance decision than an oral advance decision. Richard Jones has, for instance, written about how difficult it can be for a treating doctor to have confidence in an oral advance directive bearing in mind that it will not be the patient but a third party who will be making the case on behalf of the patient that an advance directive exists that is both valid and applicable in the circumstances arising for decision.[29] Very briefly it is possible that the

---

[25] Ibid, s.26(1); *Re T (Adult: Refusal of Treatment) [1992] 4 All ER 649 CA*
[26] Ibid
[27] *Airedale NHS Trust v Bland [1993] 1 All ER 821 HL*; Jones, Richard, Mental Capacity Act Manual, 2008, Third Edition, Sweet and Maxwell, p.90, para.1-211
[28] Jones, Richard, Mental Capacity Act Manual, 2008, Third Edition, Sweet and Maxwell, p.102, para.1-235
[29] Ibid, p.91, para.1-212

person may have held similar conversations with others over a considerable period of time and their mood on various occasions may have elicited a different response or approach to the subject. Doubts might arise about the competency of the patient at the time the alleged decision was made i.e. was this a situation where open conversation had led to a particular statement being made that represented their fixed view on the matter or had the conversation taken place against the backdrop of an unsettled period during which spirits had been wrought low? Perhaps the decision to refuse a particular form of treatment was a response to something they had witnessed that had happened to someone else and had not been informed by recent advances in medical science. Had the person been coerced or unduly influenced into making their decision? Finally, a doctor might be inclined to question whether the purported advance decision is applicable to the proposed treatment and was intended to apply in the circumstances that have arisen.[30] It must surely be unusual for someone other than a medical professional to hold a casual conversation with an acquaintance, friend or relative which was sufficiently specific in every detail. Furthermore, it must be equally questionable that anyone should be able to recall those details with complete accuracy. Isn't this why those who witness a crime are required to make a statement before leaving the crime scene and prior to talking to others, including other witnesses who were at the scene, about what had taken place. Accordingly, Richard Jones considers that few oral statements made by patients to lay people that are said to constitute advance decisions would survive such scrutiny, especially if the statements were made a considerable time ago.[31]

Isn't the more likely scenario, in relation to oral advance decisions, that the discussion was one about values, e.g. I value my freedom far too much to enjoy a life being dependent on others and it's not living to be hooked up to a machine. Aren't these the type of things that people typically say? Consequently, if we genuinely believe that persons do not exist apart, or can be isolated, from their values, and provisions of the MCA are supportive of that view, then there would appear to be fewer reasons to be concerned about those background conditions of whether a patient was competent when deciding, whether their decision was informed and whether it was entered into voluntarily when a doctor is invited to make a treatment decision that is coherent with a patient's

[30] Ibid, p.102, para.1-236
[31] Ibid, p.102, para.1-236

experiential and critical values as well as with previous decisions, which is so crucial to preserving the integrity of the patient's creative legacy. As to whether confidence in a statement of values may be misplaced Eric Cassell has written that:

"A person's values, both negative and positive, are apparent in the things that are important to them: Their interests, concerns, what they respond to, and the relative weights they apply in making choices. Since people constantly make choices, live in a world shaped by their choices, act on their interests and concerns with varying degrees of intensity, and cannot, in fact, be totally neutral to their world for even a moment, it follows that people constantly display their values in every facet of their existence. But are these their 'true' values? It could not be otherwise, since even a consciously fabricated set of values must bear some relation to the person's values – otherwise why the choice of one set of counterfeit values over another? Furthermore, since values are displayed in every moment of existence, it is inconceivable that they could all be under conscious control. It is the case, however, that persons' values may not always be consistent with each other, that values exist on many levels, that some are more enduring than others, and that they may change with circumstances.

These realities, that values can be so changeable and may be inconsistent give rise to the belief that information about values is of limited utility. In clinical medicine this issue surfaces when patients express a desire not to be resuscitated in the event of a cardiac arrest. Should such patients later lose consciousness or be otherwise unable to express their wishes, doctors often believe they should be resuscitated despite their earlier wish, 'in case they changed their mind'. It is true that there are things about which we change our minds – tastes change. And it's also true that when illness is severe, people often discover what is really important to them – another way of saying that values change or change in priority. Because of this it would be foolhardy to believe that because one knows a person's values, the knowledge is eternal and unchanging. Since the body also changes, physicians understand the importance of keeping abreast of the changes with up-to-date test results and repeated examinations. Yet most people do not think of the changes in the body as transitory in the same way that values are believed to vary. There are surface phenomena, such as skin temperature, and physiologic parameters, such as blood pressure, which change from minute to minute or day to day, but there are other bodily features, such as bone structure, which change very slowly. The same with values: some superficial likes and dislikes are as changeable as the wind, while basic personality, expressed by values, is remarkably constant.
People, in their presentation to the world, do display their values for others to see and know. Furthermore, information about values should be considered in the same light as information about the body. Some of it is

> *rock solid, some inconstant, but none of it is merely random variation unrelated to the person as a whole or the entire spectrum of the person's values. Here, as in all our other dimensions, we are of a piece".*[32]

Legal validity and applicability are though tough tests to surmount in requiring those who must implement the patient's instructions to be in no doubt about what was intended to happen. As you will remember the former is concerned with revocation and the latter specificity.[33] In relation to legal validity it is arguable that in disclosing a value system in a living will a person has made a decision, when they had capacity to do so, to set out the values that are critically important to their treatment preferences, those values being perfectly capable of assessment for legal validity, i.e. has the person withdrawn their decision to disclose those values;[34] have they, since declaring their values conferred authority on an LPA to give or refuse consent in accordance with them[35] or have they done anything that is clearly inconsistent with the notion of that or those values remaining critically important in shaping their life.[36]

Unfortunately, it is less easy to argue that a value system that had been disclosed in a living will should pass the test for legal applicability. Essentially, the Act requires persons to specify the treatment they would wish to refuse[37] and for the removal of doubt they are invited to specify the circumstances under which that treatment would be refused,[38] i.e. I would not want to be given antibiotics if I was in a persistent vegetative state. This is to avoid the situation where a generally written decision was applied in unintended circumstances.[39] Legal certainty should not easily be forsaken in circumstances where life, health and well-being are at stake. Therefore, legislators make no provision for someone to interpret and apply a value system to see whether a particular form of treatment would be refused in the circumstances arising for decision. That said, interpretation does form part of the legislative scheme and not just in

---

[32] Cassell, Eric J., The Nature of Suffering and the Goals of Medicine, Second Edition, 2004, Oxford University Press, p.178

[33] Mental Capacity Act 2005, s.25(2)

[34] Ibid, s.25(2)(a)

[35] Ibid, s.25(2)(b)

[36] Ibid, s.25(2)(c)

[37] Ibid, s.25(4)(a)

[38] Ibid, s.25(4)(b) & s.25(5)

[39] *Re T (Adult: Refusal of Treatment) [1992] 4 All ER 649 CA; HE v A Hospital NHS Trust 2003 WL 21729346*

relation to oral advance decisions. This is because doctors are invited to exercise their interpretative powers when considering whether there are reasonable grounds for believing that circumstances exist, which their patient had not anticipated at the time of making their advance decision, and which would have affected their decision.[40]

Might a particular or individual critical value constitute an advance decision? Bear in mind that, with the exception of life-sustaining treatment,[41] the Act does not establish any procedures or formalities that must be followed for an advance decision to be made.[42] Moreover, it anticipates that decisions will have been made by persons who are not medical professionals with the consequence that lay language and terminology may have been used to express a decision which must be interpreted and then applied to the facts of the situation.[43] In taking these factors into account the MCA foresees the problem that designated persons are likely to place different interpretations on the information they receive and therefore in cases of doubt the court has jurisdiction to make a declaration as to whether an advance decision exists[44] and if it does whether it is also either or both valid[45] and applicable.[46]

So now consider a person who claims to have a critical interest in departing from this world with the same limbs and organs they were born with. Their statement was evidenced by a previous medical decision in which they refused to consent to have their gangrenous foot amputated against medical advice preferring instead to continue with more conventional forms of therapy which was in fact successful. Is it reasonable to conclude from this statement and the evidence given in support of it that this person has made an advance decision to refuse to consent at any time in the future to receive a donor kidney, for example?

Case law certainly suggests that the use of lay terms is permissible provided it does not lead to any ambiguity about the identity of the

---

[40] Mental Capacity Act 2005, s.25(4)(c)

[41] Ibid, s25(5)

[42] Jones, Richard, Mental Capacity Act Manual, 2008, Third Edition, Sweet and Maxwell, p.91, para.1-212

[43] Ibid

[44] *Mental Capacity Act 2005, s.26(4)(a); Re T (Adult: Refusal of Treatment) [1992] 4 All ER 649 CA; HE v A Hospital NHS Trust 2003 WL 21729346*

[45] Ibid, s.26(4)(b); Ibid; Ibid

[46] Ibid, s.26(4)(c); Ibid; Ibid

treatment that is being refused.[47] Consequently, a court has held that if a patient makes a valid advance directive stating that they are not to be resuscitated if they are found in an unconscious state following an attempt to commit suicide then the directive must be respected.[48] By contrast a suicide note written by a capable person that fails to specify a treatment they would refuse in the event of a suicide attempt cannot be an advance decision. However, recently a doctor who believed that his patient, Kerrie Wolltorton, had made a valid and applicable advance decision to be allowed to die, i.e. no intervention, refused to take any action to save her life and therefore respected her decision to commit suicide.[49] This was despite the fact that after having taken a noxious substance she rang the emergency services for assistance.[50]

Let us take this example a step further and say that legislation has been passed, in accordance with the democratic will, to the effect that all persons should be presumed to consent to donate their organs on their death. Is it clear that their critical interest in being maintained as nature intended would constitute an advance decision to register their intention to opt out of the proposed scheme?

Alternatively, a person might take great pride in being a member of their local community and this is demonstrated by generously donating their time and energy to helping out the old folk with shopping, transporting them to the local hospital for appointments whenever the need arises and then organising events at the local community centre that will appeal to the aged and that they hope will make their lives more pleasant and enjoyable. So there is ample evidence to suggest that this person is a strong communitarian who takes their civic duties very seriously, particularly with regard to the elderly. Now whilst it is clear that persons cannot use advance directives to request treatment in their own best interests[51] could this critical interest be construed as an advance decision, on the part of the

---

[47] *W Healthcare NHS Trust v H [2004] EWCA Civ 1324*; Jones, Richard, Mental Capacity Act Manual, 2008, Third Edition, Sweet and Maxwell, p.96, para.1-217
[48] Ibid; Ibid, p.90, para.1-211;
[49] http://news.bbc.co.uk/1/hi/England/Norfolk/8284728.stm
[50] Ibid
[51] *R (On the Application of Oliver Leslie Burke) v The General Medical Council [2005] EWCA Civ 1003 CA*; Jones, Richard, Mental Capacity Act Manual, 2008, Third Edition, Sweet and Maxwell, p.95, para.1-216

patient, to consent to taking part in a clinical trial, for example, for a new drug for Alzheimer's disease?[52]

The more likely response is that neither a value system nor any of its individual component parts would be regarded as an advance decision. This is because a value system provides evidence of a patient's wishes but its form means that the evidence is unclear or indecisive of them. The strict standards imposed by legal validity and applicability appear to be aimed at avoiding the problem of an advance decision being applied in unintended circumstances.[53]

Best Interests

Could a value system be used by a medical professional to determine what should happen in the actual best interests of a patient when they are no longer capable of deciding the matter contemporaneously?[54] Now a person who discloses their values in a living will has a right to inviolability and displays a critical interest in doctors prioritising precedent autonomy over their current wishes when making decisions and acting in their best interests. Let us now focus on the weight a doctor is legally required to give such a statement in determining what is in a patient's best interests.

Best Interests takes Subjective Factors into Consideration

Only one course of action can be in the best interests of a mentally incapacitated patient.[55] At stage one of any treatment decision a doctor is given responsibility and authority to decide what form of treatment is necessary and appropriate to a patient's condition.[56] What though should doctors have in mind when exercising their discretionary powers to make a judgment on behalf of an incompetent patient? Well in recent years there

[52] Even though the patient is incompetent it might helpfully demonstrate whether certain physiological processes that were intended to occur did so either immediately or over time

[53] Brock, Dan W., Medical Ethics, 2007, Blackwell Publishing, Chapter 7, p.139

[54] Mental Capacity Act 2005, s.4(6)(a)

[55] Jones, Richard, Mental Capacity Act Manual, 2008, Third Edition, Sweet and Maxwell, p.26, para.1-042

[56] *R (On the Application of Oliver Leslie Burke) v The General Medical Council [2005] EWCA Civ 1003 CA*

has been a general improvement in the education of the public through a media who disseminate information about advances in medicine as well as the ethical and legal dilemmas those advances produce.[57] As a result the public are aware that the decisions doctors make in the use of medical knowledge can make a vast difference to their lives and that those decisions increasingly involve value choices.[58] So a doctor should be thinking about how the unprecedented expansion of medical technological capability has expanded enormously the range and complexity of clinical and policy decisions in health care.[59] Therefore, it would seem relevant for a health professional to think carefully about the entry of economic considerations as primary forces in individual and policy decisions regarding health and medical care.[60] The question is how these activities should be viewed in the case of mentally incompetent patients. This patient group have no opportunity to research their own health problems or to obtain a second opinion or just to place themselves in a position to ask their medical adviser informed questions about their health and future prospects as well as about alternative forms of treatment (*Bolam*) or of making a comparison between treatments and their respective advantages and disadvantages.[61]

Consequently, if the shift in the locus of decision-making from paternalism to autonomy is to be recognised in relation to formerly competent patients then the test of best interests must be capable of taking into consideration and giving appropriate weight to those subjective factors the patient would themselves have considered when a doctor sets out to determine whether the treatment they propose to administer is in the actual best interests of the patient.[62] This level of consideration is necessary if we are to establish equality of interest, between competent and formerly competent patients,

---

[57] Pellegrino, Edmund D., Thomasma, David C., The Conflict between Autonomy and Beneficence in Medical Ethics: Proposal for a Resolution, 1987, Journal of Contemporary Health Law and Policy, Volume 3, p.23-46, p.24

[58] Ibid, p.25

[59] Ibid, p.23; *Airedale NHS Trust v Bland [1993] 1 All ER 821 HL; Chester v Afshar 2004 WL 2289136*

[60] Pellegrino, Edmund D., Thomasma, David C., The Conflict between Autonomy and Beneficence in Medical Ethics: Proposal for a Resolution, 1987, Journal of Contemporary Health Law and Policy, Volume 3, p.23-46, p.23

[61] *Chester v Afshar 2004 WL 2289136*

[62] Pellegrino, Edmund D., Thomasma, David C., The Conflict between Autonomy and Beneficence in Medical Ethics: Proposal for a Resolution, 1987, Journal of Contemporary Health Law and Policy, Volume 3, p.23-46, p.23

to refuse medical intervention preferring instead to be maintained inviolate, if only for the period necessary to obtain a second opinion.[63]

Best interests should therefore invite a doctor to consider whether the treatment they propose to administer is in the medical best interests of the patient as well as in the actual rather than the overall best interests of the patient all things considered.

Best Interests not Substituted Judgment

The substituted judgment principle applies in situations where no advance directive exists with clear and convincing instructions about the decision at hand. Nevertheless a surrogate decision-maker who has sufficient relevant knowledge of the patient and/or of their values must attempt to make the decision the patient would make in the circumstances if competent to decide.[64] Therefore, a values statement brings forward the possibility that a doctor could make a substituted judgment on behalf of the patient and therefore autonomy not paternalism would be the prevailing ethical consideration.

However, in accordance with the common law the propriety of a medical treatment or procedure to be administered to an incompetent adult was to be judged by reference to what is in the patient's best interests and not therefore by the application of a substituted judgment.[65] In the case of *Re T* Lord Donaldson M.R. commented that whilst next of kin have no legal right to consent or to refuse to consent to a medical treatment it is a desirable practice for doctors to consult them when practicable. This was because:

> *"[C]ontact with the next of kind may reveal that the patient has made an anticipatory choice which, if clearly established and applicable in the circumstances – two major ifs – would bind the practitioner. Consultation with the next of kin has a further advantage in that it may reveal information as to the personal circumstances of the patient and as to the*

---

[63] *Chester v Afshar 2004 WL 2289136*

[64] *Airedale NHS Trust v Bland [1993] 1 All ER 821 HL* see Lord Goff; Brock, Dan W., Medical Ethics, 2007, Blackwell Publishing, Chapter 7, p.137/8

[65] *Re T (Adult: Refusal of Treatment) [1992] 4 All ER 649 CA; Airedale NHS Trust v Bland [1993] 1 All ER 821 HL*; Grubb, A., Principles of Medical Law, 2004, Second Edition, Oxford University Press, para. 4.147

choice which the patient might have made, if he or she had been in a position to make it. Neither the personal circumstances of the patient nor a speculative answer to the question "what would the patient have chosen?" can bind the practitioner in his choice of whether or not to treat or how to treat or justify him in acting contrary to a clearly established anticipatory refusal to accept treatment but they are factors to be taken into account by him in forming a clinical judgment as to what is in the best interests of the patient".[66]

In *Bland* Lord Goff made the following comments in relation to the test of substituted judgment:

"I do not consider that any such test forms part of English law in relation to incompetent adults, on whose behalf nobody has power to give consent to medical treatment... Of course, consistent with the best interests test, anything relevant to the application of the test may be taken into account; and, if the personality of the patient is relevant to the application of the test (as it may be in cases where the various relevant factors have to be weighed), it may be taken into account".[67]

Today the Mental Capacity Act 2005 is the primary source of law governing the treatment of mentally incapacitated patients and it is clear from its provisions that the law continues to adopt the test of best interests in relation to incompetent adults who have not made an advance decision, '*one of the key principles of the Act is that any act done, or any decision made on behalf of a person who lacks capacity must be done, or made, in that person's best interests*'.[68] Acting in another's best interests requires decision-makers to take into account all relevant factors that it would be reasonable for them to consider and not just those they think are important. You may remember this was raised as a contention in relation to those appointed to accept or reject a medical treatment on behalf of an incompetent by way of a Lasting Power of Attorney, i.e. the motivation to appoint someone in that capacity must surely be related to the ability of an Attorney to apply and when necessary prioritise knowledge attributable to the personality and character of the patient, i.e. to former values, beliefs and preferences, when making decisions on their behalf.

---

[66] *Re T (Adult: Refusal of Treatment) [1993] Fam. 95 CA*, p.103

[67] *Airedale NHS Trust v Bland [1993] 1 All ER 821*, p.872; Stauch, Marc, Wheat, Kay, Tingle John, 2002, Second Edition, Sourcebook on Medical Law, Cavendish Publishing, p.204

[68] Mental Capacity Act 2005, s.1(5); Code of Practice, Chapter Five

Objective Best Interests

As a surrogate decision-maker is not required to attempt to make the decision the incompetent patient would make, if they were competent to decide, the test of best interests is objective and therefore guides decision-makers to make the decision that a reasonable person would make in the circumstances.[69] A difficulty with an objective standard is in knowing how to access such knowledge. This is important because we need to know or be assured about whether the required standard has been met. A move away from traditional beliefs about God and God's judgment towards a culture in which rights have a more significant role to play tends to encourage each one of us to believe that our values, beliefs and preferences are as reasonable as those of anybody else. However, the imbalance in knowledge between doctors and lay persons when coupled with the sort of professionalism engendered by Hippocrates, i.e. use your skill and judgment for the benefit of your patients, would also tend to encourage the notion that doctors are in a better position to know what is reasonable in the circumstances than anyone else.

Therefore, it seems reasonable to question whether an objective test leads to decision-makers infecting the decision-making process with their own values. In *Bland*, for instance, Lord Goff referred to the possibility that a doctor may well be influenced by his own attitudes and values in reaching a decision about whether to withhold life-preserving medical treatment.[70] However, in that case Lord Goff thought the possibility was more theoretical than real suspecting that it was unlikely to arise in practice '*if only because the solution could be found in a change of medical practitioner*' whilst adding that it is enough to state that the best interests test is broad and flexible in the sense that room must be allowed for the exercise of judgment by the doctor ...[71] Of course it is open to question whether Lord Goff had in mind the fact that this inherent flexibility means that no two doctors need necessarily come to the same conclusion as to what is in someone's best interests.

---

[69] Ibid, s.4; Ibid, Chapter Five, para.5.13; Grubb, A., Principles of Medical Law, 2004, Second Edition, Oxford University Press, para. 4.150; Brock, Dan W., Medical Ethics, 2007, Blackwell Publishing, Chapter 7, p.138

[70] *Airedale NHS Trust v Bland [1993] 1 All ER 821*

[71] Ibid

Has the MCA improved upon the common law in this regard bearing in mind the particular personality of the patient is a factor that can be taken into account in deciding what is in someone's best interests? The problem is that best interests has not been fully defined in the Act simply because of the wide variation in the circumstances of people similarly situated, including never competent patients.[72] Section four of the MCA therefore contains a checklist of common factors that must always be considered by a surrogate decision-maker when trying to work out what is in another's best interests.[73] Decision-makers are in addition required to consider any other factors the patient would be likely to consider if they were able to do so.[74] Furthermore, the Code of Practice appears anxious to dispel the notion that gaps in the legislative test provide some scope for decision-makers to allow their own particular biases or prejudices to dominate the decision-making process. It confirms that decision-makers must take into account all relevant factors not just those that they think are important and in particular they must not act or make a decision based on what they would want to do if they were the person who lacked capacity.[75]

Consequently, surrogates are concerned with the question, what is in the best interests of this particular patient but they are required to consider the matter objectively which means that they must consider information not from the point of view of an ordinary or normal fit person but from the assumed point of view of a person suffering the handicaps of a particular patient.[76] As a value system should provide actual knowledge of the patient's point of view about what a good life for them is based upon would best interests be subjectively appraised or objectively assessed in relation to such a patient?[77]

Best Interests and the Past and Present Wishes and Feelings of the Patient

I have previously argued that persons are the source of human values and therefore autonomy requires us to respect people as particular individuals whose identity is bound up with particular projects and traditions as a

[72] Mental Capacity Act 2005, Code of Practice, Chapter Five, para 5.5
[73] Ibid, para 5.6
[74] Mental Capacity Act 2005, s.4(6)©
[75] Mental Capacity Act 2005, Code of Practice, Chapter Five, para.5.7
[76] Grubb, A., Principles of Medical Law, 2004, Second Edition, Oxford University Press, para.4.150
[77] Idea taken from my supervisor Professor Michael Gunn

constraint against paternalism.[78] The question then is whether special emphasis would be placed on a prior written statement of a formerly competent patient. i.e. would it be treated as an indispensable source of information about the values, beliefs and preferences that should be used to inform a treatment decision based on the patient's right to inviolability which they share with others.

Well it is entirely feasible that section 4 of the MCA can accommodate a values based approach to decision-making if the practical effect of sub-section 6 is to ascertain whether a treatment that a doctor proposes to administer in an incompetent patient's medical best interests is also in their actual best interests, after taking into consideration various critical and experiential interests. Of course, then one might expect that particular weight should be accorded to the past wishes of a formerly competent patient.[79]

Indeed first impressions suggest that the preferences of a former competent patient are taken very seriously as even when a patient has requested a specific treatment, which is generally thought to be relevant at stage one of a treatment decision, decision-maker's are urged to give serious consideration to such requests.[80] This requirement is however qualified by the fact that a doctor would not be bound to follow such a request if they considered that the specific treatment would be clinically unnecessary or was not appropriate to their condition and so could not be in their best interests.[81] Consequently, the right of a medical professional to determine, in accordance with the *Bolam* principle, what form of treatment is in the best interests of any particular patient is preserved.[82]

In determining whether what is proposed is in the actual best interests of the patient decision-makers are reminded that everybody's values and beliefs influence the decisions they make and may become especially important later on in their lives when progressive illness, such as

---

[78] Hill, Thomas E. Jr., Respect, Pluralism and Justice: Kantian Perspectives, 2003, Oxford University Press, p.77-9

[79] Jones, Richard, Mental Capacity Act Manual, 2008, Third Edition, Sweet and Maxwell, p.26, para.1-042

[80] Mental Capacity Act 2005, s.4(6)(a); Code of Practice, Chapter Five, para.5.44

[81] Ibid

[82] *R (On the Application of Oliver Leslie Burke) v The General Medical Council [2005] EWCA Civ 1003 CA*

dementia, denies them the chance to make decisions in accordance with them due to a lack of decision-making capacity. With that thought in mind the Code of Practice acknowledges that some people will choose to set out their values while they still have capacity to do so.[83] Decision-makers are therefore advised to consider written statements carefully[84] out of recognition for the fact that persons may have held strong views in the past that are relevant to their future care.[85]

However, the prospects of a formerly competent patient continuing to exert influence over their bodies and life plans through a values statement are, to coin Lord Goff's phrase, more theoretical than real. As although the character and personality of the patient, which is expressed through their wishes and feeling, is made a very relevant factor in ascertaining best interests,[86] the Act fails to adequately distinguish between the force of a person's past and present wishes and therefore to the weight that should be accorded to each.[87]

Accordingly, the current wishes and feelings or emotional responses of an incompetent but conscious patient, i.e. someone with dementia, which are experientially though not critically valid, may properly be regarded by a decision-maker as being objectively relevant, perhaps more so because they are the current wishes of the patient, to a best interests decision-making process. In which case priority will have been accorded to protecting the patient's current preferences and interests even though these may be uninformed as well as unstable and beneficence will be in conflict with autonomy. Should precedent autonomy be an illusory concept in relation to incompetent but conscious patients? This is what Ronald Dworkin has to say:

> *"Suppose a patient is incompetent in the general, overall sense but that years ago, when perfectly competent, he executed a living will providing for what he plainly does not want now. Suppose, for example, that years ago, when fully competent, [the patient] had executed a formal document directing that if [they] should develop Alzheimer's disease, [they] should not receive treatment for any other serious, life-threatening disease [they]*

---

[83] Mental Capacity Act 2005, s.4(6)(a); Code of Practice, Chapter Five, para.5.46
[84] Ibid; Ibid, para.5.43
[85] Ibid; Ibid, para.5.41
[86] Grubb, A., Principles of Medical Law, 2004, Second Edition, Oxford University Press, para.4.151
[87] Mental Capacity Act 2005, s.4(6)(a); Code of Practice, Chapter Five, para.5.40

might contract. Or even that in that event [they] should be killed as soon and as painlessly as possible. If [they] had expressed any of those wishes when [they were] competent, would autonomy then require that they be respected now by those in charge of [their] care, even though [they] seem perfectly happy ...?

If we had accepted the evidentiary view of autonomy, we would find the case for respecting [their] past directions very weak. People are not the best judges of what their own best interests would be under circumstances they have never encountered and in which their preferences and desires may drastically have changed. But if we accept the integrity view, we will be drawn to the view that [their] past wishes must be respected. A competent person making a living will providing for his treatment if he becomes demented is making exactly the kind of judgment that autonomy, on the integrity view, most respects: a judgment about the overall shape of the kind of life he wants to have led.

This conclusion is troubling, however, even shocking, and someone might want to resist it by insisting that the right to autonomy is necessarily contemporary: that a person's right to autonomy is only a right that his present decisions, not past ones that he has since disowned, be respected. Certainly this is the normal force of recognising autonomy. Suppose that a Jehovah's Witness has signed a formal document stipulating that he is not to receive blood transfusions even if out of weakness of will he requests one when he would otherwise die. He wants, like Ulysses, to be tied to the mast of his faith. But when the moment comes, and he needs a transfusion, he pleads for it. We would not think ourselves required out of respect for his autonomy, to disregard his contemporary plea.

We can interpret that example in different ways, though, and the difference is crucial for our present problem. We might say, first, that the Witness's later plea countermanded his original decision because it expressed a more contemporary desire. That presumes that it is only right to defer to past decisions when we have reason to believe that the agent still wishes what he wanted then. On that view, precedent autonomy is an illusion: we treat a person's past decision as important only because it is normally evidence of his present wishes, and we disregard it entirely when we know that it is not. On the other hand, we might say that the Witness's later plea countermanded his original decision because it was a fresh exercise of his autonomy, and that disregarding it would be treating him as no longer in charge of his own life. The difference between these two views about the force of precedent autonomy is crucial when someone changes his mind after he has become incompetent, that is, when the conditions of autonomy no longer hold. Suppose that the same accident that made a transfusion medically necessary for the Witness also deranged him, and that while still plainly deranged he demands the transfusion. On the first view, we would not violate his autonomy by administering it, but on the second we would.

Which of the two views about the force of past decisions is more persuasive? Suppose we were confident that the deranged Witness, were he to receive the transfusion and live, would become competent again and be appalled at having had a treatment he believed worse for him than dying. In those circumstances, I believe, we would violate his autonomy by giving him the transfusion. That argues for the second view about the force of past decisions, the view that endorses precedent autonomy as genuine. We refuse to give the deranged Witness a transfusion not because we think he really continues to want what he wanted before, this is not like a case in which someone who objects to a given treatment is unconscious when he needs it, but because he lacks the necessary capacity for a fresh exercise of autonomy. His former decision remains in force because no new decision by a person capable of autonomy has annulled it.

What makes the difference, when we are deciding whether to honour someone's plea even though it contradicts his past deep convictions, is whether he is now competent to make a decision of that character, not whether he will regret making it later.

The argument has very troubling consequences however... Should we really deny a person [who is happy] ... routine medical care needed to keep [them] alive? Could we ever conceivably kill [them]? We might consider it morally unforgivable not to try to save the life of someone who plainly enjoys [their] life, no matter how demented [they are], and we might think it beyond imagining that we should actually kill [them]. We might hate living in a community whose officials might make or license either of those decisions. We might have other good reasons for treating [a patient as they now wish], rather than as, [they once asked]. But still, that violates rather than respects [their] autonomy".[88]

Must we uphold the distinction between critical and experiential interests to understand our convictions about how people should be treated at the end of life? A commitment to the integrity view of autonomy suggests that a loss of decision-making capacity should not be used as an excuse for overriding what is an essential element of the right to autonomy, i.e. to refuse a medical treatment or procedure that a doctor considers is in someone's best medical interests, even when that treatment is life preserving.[89]

---

[88] Dworkin, Ronald, Life's Dominion: An argument about Abortion and Euthanasia, Harper Collins, p.226-9

[89] Idea taken from my supervisor Ms Kay Wheat

However, Dworkin has noted that in the case of *Bland* several members of the House of Lords assumed that only experiential interests mattered in this context.[90] His view is that it would be easy to decide what was in someone's best interests if we were only concerned with a person's experiential interests such as the principles of medical futility and intolerability tend to encourage.[91] Nonetheless, when the case was considered by the Court of Appeal Lord Justice Hoffmann, who was influenced by the thoughts of Dworkin, considered that as dignity[92] is an aspect of autonomy priority should be accorded to a person's critical interests instead.

Consequently, Hoffmann LJ was of the mind that persons should be able to determine how the final chapter of their life is played out and would presumably condone the use of a values statement to restrict how we are treated if incompetent.[93] Lord Goff, did by contrast, acknowledge why it is important that the test of best interests should comprise of something more than purely professional appraisal of a person's medical welfare, as to confine the test in this way, he said, '*would be inconsistent with the primacy that is accorded to the principle of self-determination and would 'downgrade the status of the incompetent person by placing a lesser value on [their] intrinsic worth and vitality*' but then failed to be tied to the mast of his own convictions.[94]

So if the interests that were critical to the shape of a person's life, when viewed as a whole, should not be sacrificed later, simply because the patient is incompetent and unable to express a view, does the MCA

---

[90] *Airedale NHS Trust v Bland [1993] 1 All ER 821 HL*; Dworkin, Ronald, Life's Dominion: An argument about Abortion and Euthanasia, Harper Collins, p.208

[91] Dworkin, Ronald, Life's Dominion: An argument about Abortion and Euthanasia, Harper Collins, p.208

[92] A person who cares about the inherent value of their own life will want to live in conditions in which genuine self-respect is possible which means in a manner that is most befitting with what has gone before. In accordance with the distinction between experiential and critical interests what is a dignified life for them will be most vividly illustrated by the critical interests that were significant in it

[93] Herring, Jonathan, Medical Law and Ethics, 2008, Second Edition, Oxford University Press, p.182

[94] *Airedale NHS Trust v Bland [1993] 1 All ER 821 HL*

improve upon the focus of the common law in relation to decisions about withholding or withdrawing life-sustaining treatment.[95]

First things first, the sanctity of life principle is a fundamental value of the MCA. Thus anyone who is deciding whether or not life-sustaining treatment is in the best interests of someone who lacks capacity to consent or to refuse such treatment must not be motivated by a desire to bring about the person's death.[96] Whether a treatment is in fact life-sustaining depends not only on the type of treatment that is being considered but also on the particular circumstances in which it is being prescribed.[97] So whereas antibiotics can be used to treat non life-threatening conditions in some circumstances, such as when someone is in PVS or has MRSA, administering antibiotics may be life-sustaining.[98] So clearly at the first stage of a best interests decision-making process medical professional opinion, formed in accordance with the standard proposed in *Bolam*, will inform a decision as to whether a particular treatment is life-sustaining taking the circumstances into consideration.[99]

As that same rule cannot be interpreted to mean that doctors are under an obligation to provide, or to continue to provide, life-sustaining treatment where that treatment is not in the best interests of the person, even where the person's death is foreseen, the MCA can be seen to uphold the acts and omissions doctrine thus maintaining a qualified sanctity position. Consequently, the MCA incorporates the decisions in *Bland* and *Burke*.[100] As previously mentioned in this chapter legislators were aware that persons might be tempted to exercise their autonomy by making a written statement requesting a specific form of treatment. However, such a statement will merely be taken into account in deciding what is in a person's best interests as a doctor must consider all relevant circumstances prior to exercising judgment.[101] The prior written statement of a patient requesting a specific form of treatment will therefore be considered

---

[95] Dworkin, Ronald, Life's Dominion: An argument about Abortion and Euthanasia, Harper Collins, p.216

[96] Mental Capacity Act 2005, s.4(5); Code of Practice, Chapter Five, para.5.29

[97] Ibid, s.4(10); Ibid, para.5.30

[98] Ibid

[99] Mental Capacity Act 2005, s.4(10); Code of Practice, Chapter Five, para.5.30

[100] *R (On the Application of Oliver Leslie Burke) v The General Medical Council [2005] EWCA Civ 1003 CA*

[101] Mental Capacity Act 2005, s.4(2)

alongside all other relevant factors in deciding whether to provide or to continue to provide life-sustaining treatment.[102]

At the second stage of a treatment decision the presumption in favour of life is maintained as all reasonable steps which are in the person's best interests should be taken to prolong their life. Clearly a doctor's obligation of non-maleficence is upheld by the MCA. So on what basis can the presumption be rebutted? Well the 2005 Act requires decision-makers to consider and weigh in the balance all relevant circumstances[103] of which they are aware[104] and which it would be reasonable for them to regard as relevant.[105] In this regard a doctor must consider those factors in the welfare checklist, including the past and present wishes and feelings of the patient and in particular any relevant written statement that was made by them when they had capacity.[106] These provisions serve to remind surrogate decision-makers that the character and personality of the patient should be regarded by them as being relevant to a best interests determination. The problem, as previously stated, is that the MCA fails to provide relevant insight as to why a person's past wishes may be relevant to their present situation and therefore omits to state which particular characteristics decision-makers should attribute the greatest amount of significance to in deciding. Essentially the Act fails to distinguish adequately enough between the different considerations that might apply in respect of formerly and never competent persons. It is also possible that legislators, through the concept of advance decisions, have attempted to influence the activities and evaluative experience of valuers who subscribe to the integrity view of autonomy and therefore wish to have what happens to them at the end of life determined by their critical interests. However, in the absence of a legally valid and applicable advance decision the best interests principle will apply and the Act enshrines a privilege that doctors exercise to decide which of the various circumstances they are aware of it would be most reasonable to regard as relevant. If we think back to the last chapter and to the benchmarks Beauchamp and Childress proposed to check the adequacy of any theory it is possible to observe that the MCA might score quite highly in respect of practicability and output power. However, the conditions that would tend to provide coherence, clarity and

[102] Ibid, s.4(6)(a); Code of Practice, Chapter Five, para.5.34
[103] Mental Capacity Act 2005, s.4(2)
[104] Ibid, s.4(11)(a)
[105] Ibid, s.4(11)(b)
[106] Ibid, s.4(6)(a)

certainty in the law relating to formerly competent patients are absent. Thus there is a danger that doctors, albeit somewhat understandably, will be more likely to protect their patients medical welfare rather than their right to self-determination and in this regard the Code of Practice states that:

> *"There will be a limited number of cases where treatment is futile, overly burdensome to the patient or where there is no prospect of recovery. In circumstances such as these, it may be that an assessment of best interests leads to the conclusion that it would be in the best interests of the patient to withdraw or withhold life-sustaining treatment, even if this may result in the person's death. The decision-maker must make a decision based on the best interests of the person who lacks capacity. They must not be motivated by a desire to bring about the person's death for whatever reason, even if this is from a sense of compassion".*[107]

Consequently, the MCA, like the House of Lords in *Bland*, assumes that only experiential interests matter which leads me to conclude that in relation to an advance statement of values, as opposed to an advance treatment decision, there is reason to suppose that beneficence can be in conflict with autonomy when a doctor seeks to determine whether life-sustaining treatment should be withheld or withdrawn in the patient's best interests.

Assessing Capacity

The right to self-determination flows from legal capacity and so the best interests principle will not apply to someone who has sufficient capacity to make a treatment decision for themselves.[108] Capacity assessments are therefore important events because a patient either retains or loses the right to make decisions about treatment for themselves and in accordance with their own values, beliefs and preferences or critical and experiential interests.

As the primacy of autonomy has been established in law it is therefore reasonable to suggest that a patient's values and value system should be most relevant to this evaluative process. Moreover, the potential conflict between capacity and values suggests the need to underpin capacity assessments with coherence theory. However, the MCA does not establish

---

[107] Code of Practice, Chapter Five, para.5.31

[108] Mental Capacity Act 2005, s.1(2); Code of Practice, Chapter Five, para.5.3

a formal procedure for the assessment of capacity and no statutory form confirming incapacity needs to be completed. Furthermore, the person who is required to assess another's capacity will be a member of the medical profession upon whom the MCA also confers authority to make decisions and act in the best interests of their mentally incapacitated patients. This state of affairs does lead to the obvious concern that a doctor may say that a patient is competent to give consent to treatment when the patient is compliant with medical expert opinion and conversely to claim that the patient is not competent to decide if they raise objections or refuse a necessary and appropriate treatment or procedure. In this regard the Act requires decision-makers to take reasonable steps to determine whether a person lacks capacity to decide.[109] However, where an assessor reasonably believes[110] the person lacks capacity to make the decision in question,[111] and they act in their best interests,[112] they will not incur liability in relation to that act.[113] Still decision-makers may be held to account for their decisions. In this regard guidance contained within the Code of Practice confirms that anyone who believes that a person lacks capacity should be able to prove their case[114] by giving reasons and providing objective evidence in support of their belief.[115] Therefore a decision to restrict autonomy requires a clear and convincing assessment that a patient's decision regarding care was non-autonomous and could result in unintended, irreparable harm to them.[116]

Harm is difficult to define in this context because what is deemed harmful varies from one person and set of circumstances to another. Persons also differ in estimating the likely harm that will ensue from their decisions and actions. However, if autonomy not harm is the dominant consideration then potential decision-makers should have at the forefront of their mind the patient's right to refuse necessary and appropriate treatment, including life-preserving treatment. Contrarily, if harm were the dominant principle then what is in one's medical best interests would become the overriding consideration which an outcome based test for capacity would capture.

[109] Mental Capacity Act 2005, s.5(1)(a)
[110] Ibid, s.5(1)(b)
[111] Ibid, s.5(1)(b)(i)
[112] Ibid, s.5(1)(b)(ii)
[113] Ibid, s.5(2)
[114] Mental Capacity Act 2005, Code of Practice, Chapter 2, para 2.5
[115] Ibid, Chapter 4, para 4.63
[116] Tunzi, Marc, Can the Patient Decide? Evaluating Patient Capacity in Practice, 2001, American Family Physician, Vol.64 No.2, p.301

As the MCA adopts a functional test for capacity[117] assessors will be more concerned with whether an impairment or disturbance of the mind or brain does in fact prevent a patient from making a decision.[118] A person is unable to make a decision for themselves if they are unable to understand the information that is relevant to a treatment decision;[119] to retain it;[120] to use it or weigh it as part of the process of making the decision;[121] or to communicate their decision.[122] Accordingly, someone can be deemed non-autonomous when an impairment of the mind or brain leads to a problem with mental functioning. What information is relevant and must be understood by the patient so that they can apply it to their situation prior to registering a choice? The law of consent determines that doctors are required to inform patients as to the nature and purpose of a medical treatment or procedure so that they know what will happen to them if the treatment is provided and of what the likely consequences will be if treatment is not provided in order to escape liability for a battery.[123] To avoid liability in negligence a doctor must also inform their patient of the inherent risks and side effects of a treatment.[124] Accordingly, the distinction between battery and negligence is somewhat artificial when information about risks will be relevant to the way in which a patient exercises their right to decide whether to accept or reject a medical treatment and be maintained inviolate. This possibly explains why the House of Lords have more recently determined that no gap should exist between beneficence and autonomy when disclosing information about the risks of treatment, i.e. what is custom and practice within the medical profession should no longer be used to justify what the patient should be told.[125] The scope of the doctor's duty should instead be more closely equated with the patient's need for information and the right to decide upon its materiality.[126] Consequently, knowledge of the patient and their values should mark the designated starting point for a discussion on

---

[117] Mental Capacity Act 2005, s.1(4)

[118] Ibid, s.2(1); Code of Practice, Chapter Four, para.4.3

[119] Mental Capacity Act 2005, s.3(1)(a)

[120] Ibid, s.3(1)(b)

[121] Ibid, s.3(1)(c)

[122] Ibid, s.3(1)(d)

[123] *Chatterton v Gerson [1981] QB 432*; Jones, Richard, Mental Capacity Act Manual, 2008, Third Edition, Sweet and Maxwell, p.22, para.1-034

[124] *Chester v Afshar 2004 WL 2289136*; Jones, Richard, Mental Capacity Act Manual, 2008, Third Edition, Sweet and Maxwell, p.22, para.1-034

[125] *Bolam v Friern Hospital Management Committee [1957] 1 WLR 582*

[126] *Chester v Afshar 2004 WL 2289136*, para.55

capacity if we genuinely believe that the right to bodily inviolability is so fundamental that a decision to restrict autonomy requires a clear and convincing assessment that a decision was non-autonomous and could result in them suffering unintended, irreparable harm. This is because an absence of such knowledge might leave doctors unsure of which goal, autonomy or protection, to pursue when assessing whether the patient is competent to decide. Moreover, different doctors might come to different conclusions about the patient's ability to decide.

Therefore, assessing capacity in relation to subjective rather than objective factors, i.e. in accordance with a values statement, has the potential to introduce coherence in an area of law where currently there is none. The result should be that a doctor may no longer be free to say that a patient is competent to give consent to treatment merely because the patient is compliant with medical expert opinion and conversely to claim that the patient is not competent to decide if they raise objections or refuse a necessary and appropriate treatment or procedure. Moreover, the practicable steps that are taken to help someone to make a decision would be governed by the subjective standards set by the patient rather than their doctor.[127]

So, will the provisions of the MCA safeguard patients against an incorrect assessment of decision-making capacity when someone has made their wishes known in a living will? Is it possible for decision-making capacity to be assessed in accordance with a person's value system? Does a value system present an assessor with an open invitation to make a finding of incompetence?

Clearly the person who has compiled and then disclosed their value system wishes to ensure that future decisions are rendered coherent with the values, beliefs and preferences that were responsible for their past choices. So on the assumption that a patient would wish to share this information with a medical professional when consulting with them a value system would appear to have two obvious functions; it would act as an aide-memoire for the patient and it would provide the treating doctor with an opportunity to consider how best to respect the patient's right to self-determination.

[127] Mental Capacity Act 2005, s.1(3)

Might a person's value system trigger an assessment for decision-making capacity or provide grounds for a doctor to reasonably believe that the person does lack capacity to make the decision in hand? The evidence is to an extent equivocal. Consider the case of an elderly chronic schizophrenic who was resident at the Broadmoor high security hospital. He had a gangrenous foot and medical professional opinion was that without amputation he may die and the risk of this was estimated to be in the region of eighty five per cent.[128] The fact that he might die without an amputation was accepted the problem was that he refused to accept medical opinion that his foot should be amputated because he held certain beliefs. These were that God did not want him to have an amputation and that he was a great and gifted doctor with an ability to cure damaged limbs hence he preferred to accept a more conventional form of medical treatment, i.e. antibiotics.[129] Therefore, this person has a critical interest in departing from this world with the same limbs and organs that he was born with. Is there a danger, in these circumstances, that a doctor might be inclined or tempted to work backwards and assume from a person's somewhat irrational beliefs that they have an impairment or disturbance of the mind or brain and that this prevents them from exercising their autonomy when making a decision?

The synopsis above is taken from the case of *Re C* and in that case the court determined that C was competent to refuse to have an amputation.[130] This case gave rise to an important principle of incapacity law; that even when a patient is suffering from a mental disorder or disability there is still a presumption of competence.[131] The position at common law is that a competent patient has a right to accept or reject a medical treatment based

---

[128] *Re C (Adult: Refusal of Treatment) [1994] 1 All ER 819*; Stauch, Marc, Wheat, Kay, Tingle John, 2002, Second Edition, Sourcebook on Medical Law, Cavendish Publishing, p.121; Maclean, Alasdair, Briefcase on Medical Law, 2004, Second Edition, Cavendish Publishing, p.18

[129] Ibid; Ibid, p.204; Ibid

[130] Maclean, Alasdair, Briefcase on Medical Law, 2004, Second Edition, Cavendish Publishing, p.18

[131] Mental Capacity Act 2005, s.1(2); *Re C (Adult: Refusal of Treatment) [1994] 1 All ER 819*; Stauch, Marc, Wheat, Kay, Tingle John, 2002, Second Edition, Sourcebook on Medical Law, Cavendish Publishing, p.121; Maclean, Alasdair, Briefcase on Medical Law, 2004, Second Edition, Cavendish Publishing, p.18; Grubb, A., Principles of Medical Law, 2004, Second Edition, Oxford University Press, para. 3.69

upon reasons that are rational, irrational, unknown or even non-existent.[132] Provisions of the MCA are compatible with this view; it is a principle of the MCA that a person must be assumed to have capacity unless it is established that they lack capacity.[133] It is also a principle of that Act that a person should not be treated as unable to make a decision merely because they make an unwise decision.[134] The sole reason for restricting autonomy is that an impairment or disturbance in the patient's mental functioning prevents them from being able to understand, retain and weigh or use treatment information to make a decision which they can communicate.[135] Assessment of legal capacity to consent or to refuse treatment cannot therefore rest on or be established merely upon a person's age[136] or status[137] or an aspect of their behaviour which might lead others to make unjustified assumptions about their capacity to decide.[138] Furthermore, the Code of Practice reminds decision-makers that everybody has their own values, beliefs, preferences and attitudes.[139] Thus assessors should not make unjustified assumptions about a person's capacity to decide based on the contents of their value system also, even though it does not stipulate this as such.

Thus a religious belief that would lead a patient to refuse life preserving medical treatment that would restore them to full health does not indicate that they lack the capacity to make that decision however irrational their decision may appear to others.[140] In relation to the law's position on religious beliefs Andrew Grubb explains that:

> *"There are two explanations of the law's position here. First, the law defers to religiously based decisions made by adults, though not those made by children, as a matter of social tolerance. Providing the person understands what is entailed in their decision, there is no reason for the*

[132] *Re C (Adult: Refusal of Treatment) [1994] 1 All ER 819; Re T (Adult: Refusal of Treatment) [1992] 4 All ER 649 CA*
[133] Mental Capacity Act 2005, s.1(2)
[134] Ibid, s.1(4)
[135] Mental Capacity Act 2005, s.3(1); Grubb, A., Principles of Medical Law, 2004, Second Edition, Oxford University Press, para.3.83
[136] Ibid, s.2(3)(a)
[137] Ibid, s.2(3)(b)
[138] Ibid, s.2(3)(b)
[139] Mental Capacity Act 2005; Code of Practice, Chapter Two, para.2.10
[140] Grubb, A., Principles of Medical Law, 2004, Second Edition, Oxford University Press, para.3.83

> *law to deprive the individual of decision-making power. It would be an act of unjustified state interference to override decisions made on religious grounds. Secondly, and perhaps of more general importance for medical law, such decisions do not stem from any mental disability or mental malfunctioning on the part of the patient. Apart from situations where the patient is unable to communicate his decision, a necessary condition for depriving an individual of decision-making power, and justifying state intervention in his 'best interests', is that the patient is suffering from a mental malfunctioning having a pathological or psychological etiology. It is the impairment or disturbance in the patient's mental ability to understand which potentially renders him, in law, incompetent".*[141]

Consequently, an irrational belief, value or preference which would affect or influence a patient's judgment about medical treatment can lead to a finding of incompetence if it is also possible to infer from it that the patient is suffering from a mental disability.[142] And there have been circumstances in which the irrationality of the patient's decision has led to the conclusion that a patient lacks the capacity to make that particular treatment decision.[143] In this context the case of *Re MB* is instructive. The case concerned a young pregnant woman who was advised to have a Caesarean operation for the safe delivery of her child.[144] This was because the baby was in a breech position and there was a risk that the baby, though not herself, would be seriously injured, a fifty per cent likelihood, if delivered conventionally.[145] She consented to the operation but due to her needle phobia she refused to consent to the anaesthesia.[146] Initially she agreed to inhalation anaesthesia but subsequently withdrew her consent when she saw the mask.[147] The hospital therefore sought a declaration from the court that it would be lawful to operate.[148] At first instance the declaration was granted on the basis that the needle phobia had rendered the patient temporarily incompetent to decide but MB appealed against the decision.[149] This was dismissed in the Court of Appeal and the decision of the first instance judge was upheld.

---

[141] Ibid

[142] Ibid, para.3.84

[143] *Re MB (Adult: Medical Treatment) [1997] 2 FLR 426 CA*

[144] Ibid; Alasdair, Briefcase on Medical Law, 2004, Second Edition, Cavendish Publishing, p.18

[145] Ibid

[146] Ibid

[147] Ibid

[148] Ibid

[149] Ibid

Lady Justice Butler-Sloss said that a person who has capacity to decide can, for rational or irrational reasons or for no reason at all, choose to refuse medical intervention even where to do so will lead to their death or that of their child.[150] She defined an irrational decision in that case as one that is so outrageous in its defiance of logic or accepted moral standards that no sensible person who had applied their mind to the question to be decided could have arrived at it.[151]

Must decisions or values be moral and rational? To respect a person as an autonomous being is to regard them as forming part of the moral community in which members typically do not intend, by their decisions and actions, to cause harm to fellow members of that community. Consequently, in cases where the interests of an individual clash or conflict with those of the society in which they are situated the law has to balance the point or role of autonomy against the utility[152] or its consequences for the wider community. In this way the law can be seen to take a paternalistic attitude towards what is good and bad for one in the interests of maintaining social harmony. Thus a value system should have some sort of moral integrity in order for it to command respect from others as a matter of public policy, i.e. should not be morally or ethically offensive.

To respect a person as an autonomous being means that it is also reasonable to presume that they can reason and be rational always accepting that each person is a unique individual, on the basis that created co-creators are all made to be just that little bit different, with a life that has personal value.[153] When these ethical considerations are translated into laws we see that a presumption operates in favour of decision-making capacity[154] that should not be undermined by the fact that someone makes an unwise decision.[155] It is consistent with that notion that a test for decision-making capacity should focus on whether or not a person suffers

[150] *Re MB (Adult: Medical Treatment) [1997] 2 FLR 426 CA*; Alasdair, Briefcase on Medical Law, 2004, Second Edition, Cavendish Publishing, p.19

[151] Ibid; Grubb, A., Principles of Medical Law, 2004, Second Edition, Oxford University Press, para.3.84

[152] What is the greatest good

[153] Dworkin, Ronald, Life's Dominion: An argument about Abortion and Euthanasia, Harper Collins, p.73

[154] Mental Capacity Act 2005, s.1(2)

[155] Ibid, s.1(4)

from some form of cognitive impairment or disturbance that prevents them from being able to reason and to be rational because this might affect their ability to make a decision in conformity with their own personality or constitution.[156]

Accordingly, a skewed and indefensible view of the world is not sufficient to render someone incompetent in law to make a decision unless it results from mental malfunctioning.[157] So even if an irrational decision or value triggers an assessment of decision-making capacity the law requires an assessor to consider whether it is attributable to the personality and character of the patient or to something pathological, i.e. a mental illness, or psychological, i.e. a fear or phobia, that acted on the mind so as to paralyse the will and thus destroy the capacity to make a decision.[158]

So it would not be proper to find someone incompetent merely because their decision or values appear irrational to others unless it results from an inference that the patient is also suffering from a mental disability.[159] Consequently, if the seeds of the decision or value are the product of distorted or deluded perceptions that resulted from some sort of organic mental malfunctioning, i.e. were based on a misperception of reality or resulted from compulsive or driven behaviour or was induced by an external factor, i.e. pain, shock, medication, fatigue or general confusion, there may be reason to question whether these factors have affected someone' ability to understand, retain and to use and weigh information that is relevant to making a fully autonomous decision or choice.[160]

The difficulty for an assessor lies in determining whether an irrational value or decision results from any such inability. Thus it is essential for a person who wishes to be nailed to the mast of their own convictions to make sure that their value system functions in this way; that their considered judgments have been subjected to a form of reflective testing so that the end moral and non-moral values have been rendered coherent with what is valued having taken into consideration past conduct and reasoning. In this way it should be possible for decision-making capacity

---

[156] Ibid, s.2

[157] Grubb, A., Principles of Medical Law, 2004, Second Edition, Oxford University Press, para.3.86

[158] Ibid

[159] Ibid, para.3.84

[160] Ibid, para.3.84-91

to be assessed in accordance with the degree to which a person's wishes or preferences are coterminous with or are expressive of the particular personality or constitution of the individual valuer and decision-maker.

Let us now return to the main event. Will that value system safeguard the patient against an incorrect finding of incapacity? What matters in this regard is that the patient's ability to carry out the processes involved in making a decision should be assessed in the light of their own values and subjective standard of decision-making, i.e. is the patient able to understand, retain and use or weigh relevant treatment information to make a decision that is consistent with the facts and values of this case.

Careful scrutiny of the Code of Practice leads me to believe that a statement of values could be used in this sense. The obvious reason is that anyone assessing capacity must not assume that someone lacks capacity because they have a particular condition[161] but must have proof that the condition affects their ability to make a decision when it needs to be made.[162] Furthermore, assessors are advised to take certain practical steps when assessing capacity.[163] For example, assessors should make sure that they understand the nature and effect of the decision to be made themselves and in this regard the Code stipulates that they may need access to relevant documents and background information.[164] Has the principle established in *Chester v Afshar* that the patient's right to bodily inviolability determines that no gap should exist between beneficence and autonomy in relation to decisions concerning the life, health and welfare of patients become enshrined within the Act?

Let us first consider whether at stage one of a treatment decision-making process a patient with a value system can be said to have pre-empted the right of a medical professional to determine what constitutes necessary and appropriate treatment given the patient's medical condition.[165] For instance, the Code of Practice states that providing relevant information is essential in all decision-making. Thereafter, it reads, '*to make a choice about what they want for breakfast, people need to know what food is*

[161] Mental Capacity Act 2005, s.2(3)
[162] Ibid, s.3(1)
[163] Mental Capacity Act 2005; Code of Practice, Chapter Four, para.4.49
[164] Ibid
[165] *R (On the Application of Oliver Leslie Burke) v The General Medical Council [2005] EWCA Civ 1003 CA*

available'.[166] In this context you may recall those references above to the dissemination of information by the media about medical advances which has led to a general improvement in public awareness of the 'can do' of medicine and correlatively that the decisions doctors make in the use of medical knowledge can make a vast difference to their lives and that those decisions increasingly involve value choices.[167] It is also relevant to consider dictum in the case of *Chester v Afshar* which alludes to the doctor's duty to not only inform patients about risks but to answer their questions candidly and to respect their rights, including (where they so choose) to postpone medical procedures and to go elsewhere for treatment.[168] These considerations are relevant when a patient has disclosed their value system in a living will as even if a doctor is not committed, as a matter of policy, by the patient's wishes about treatment, he or she is being invited and has the necessary means at their disposal to consider and make transparent the various options for treatment that exist and which should be recommended in the patient's medical best interests having reflected more specifically on the reasons that support their choice.

Yet it remains part of a doctor's duty to determine what necessary and appropriate medical treatment is and to offer to treat a patient in their medical best interests in the knowledge that patients have a legal right to accept or reject a medical treatment in accordance with their own values, beliefs and preferences. So in relation to making an assessment of decision-making capacity the concern at the second stage of a treatment decision-making process is the degree to which the information the patient is required to understand would be driven by the value system of the patient.[169] And in this context it would seem to be of the utmost importance to the patient that their capacity to decide, about whether to accept or to refuse treatment, and to thereby maintain bodily integrity, should be measured against their ability to make decisions in accordance with their pre-existing values, beliefs and preferences.

A problem for the law related to incapacity is that if respect for self-determination not protection is the primary consideration then its requirements should not be set so high or be so onerous as to exclude a

---

[166] Mental Capacity Act 2005, Code of Practice, Chapter Three, para.3.7
[167] Pellegrino, Edmund D., Thomasma, David C., The Conflict between Autonomy and Beneficence in Medical Ethics: Proposal for a Resolution, 1987, Journal of Contemporary Health Law and Policy, Volume 3, p.23-46, p.25
[168] *Chester v Afshar 2004 WL 2289136*, see Lord Hope, para.76
[169] Mental Capacity Act 2005 2005, s.3(1)(a)

majority of persons from exercising their own free will about whether to accept or reject an offer of medical treatment. Clearly, a patient who chooses to disclose their value system wishes to continue to live a life that is structured by their pre-existing values. They want to be able to understand, retain and manipulate treatment information in way that is relevant to their former values. In particular, this person does not want whatever seems experientially valid[170]at the time the decision needs to be made, induced perhaps by fear, uncertainty or (false) happiness, to undermine the integrity with which self-defining decisions are made to accord with their critical interests as that would violate their autonomy. Consequently, an assessor who focuses on the patient's capacity to decide in conformity with their critical interests will be respecting their autonomy as well as making decisions and acting in their welfare interests.

What Information must the Patient Understand?

In this context it is important to note that the MCA is primarily concerned with whether someone is unable to make a treatment decision rather than with informed consent.[171] Naturally there will be overlapping considerations because the consent of a patient who has the capacity to decide must be real or informed.[172] However, in cases where there is reason to doubt a doctor will, at least initially, be guided by statutory not common law provisions.

So in accordance with the provisions of the MCA a person is unable to make a decision themselves if they are unable to understand the information that is relevant to the decision they need to make.[173] Relevant information includes that pertaining to the nature of the decision, the reason why the decision is needed, i.e. the nature and purpose of the medical treatment, and the reasonably foreseeable consequences of deciding one way or another[174] or of making no decision at all, i.e. the inherent risks of treatment and of non-treatment.[175] That information should be repeated to cover each treatment in cases where various treatment options are open to be considered.

---

[170] As you may remember experience is not the source of intrinsic value

[171] Ibid, s.3

[172] *Chester v Afshar 2004 WL 2289136*

[173] Mental Capacity Act 2005, s.3(1)(a)

[174] Ibid, s.3(4)(a)

[175] Mental Capacity Act 2005, s.3(4)(b); Code of Practice, Chapter Four, para.4.16

Supplementary guidance within the Code of Practice confirms that whilst the Act cannot state exactly what information will be relevant in each case it is important that a person has access to all the information they need to make an informed decision.[176] Where a choice of treatments exist information about each of them should be presented in a balanced way and it is appreciated that there will be instances in which the patient may need access to independent or specialist advice to help them to make a decision.[177] It is equally important that persons are not given more information than they need as this might confuse them and so in some cases a simple broad explanation will be enough.[178]

Of course imparting information regarding the nature and purpose of a medical treatment in broad terms takes into consideration the ability of the ordinary lay person to be able to compute more technical and detailed scientific data and/or knowledge. Imagine the amount of detail that a doctor would have to convey in respect of chemotherapy, for example, if it were otherwise? So as autonomy is the primary value in medical law it is practical to work backwards and to require medical professionals to disclose information pertaining to the risks and/or side-effects of a treatment or procedure. As in theory once a patient is in possession of this information they are in a position to not only apply those facts about the risks of treatment to their values but to also personally evaluate or estimate the likelihood of those risks arising in their particular case which is a factor that is likely to influence the way in which they exercise their choice.[179]

In respect of the amount of information the patient should be given the MCA merely requires doctors to disclose information about those risks

---

[176] Mental Capacity Act 2005, Code of Practice, Chapter Three, para.3.9

[177] Ibid

[178] Ibid

[179] There is a danger with this particular course. For example, we all have feet and buy shoes to protect them against general wear and tear and injury. Various styles and forms of footwear exist taking into consideration the purpose to which they will be put, i.e. jogging, climbing a mountain, horse-riding or they may be designed with a more decorative purpose in mind, i.e. attending a ball. Yet we also know that even when footwear has been designed for a specific purpose that some manufacturers produce better products than others when assessed against a range of relevant criteria. The same is true in medicine however patients have no way of knowing or accessing this information and therefore of knowing whether their doctor has been appropriately beneficent.

that are reasonably foreseeable. As the Act cannot state what information will be relevant to the patient's decision it appears that doctors will instead determine what the patient should be told in accordance with the prudent doctor standard[180] proposed in *Sidaway*.[181] An objective standard is potentially problematic because the privilege to decide on the relevance or materiality of treatment information would be that of the doctor whereas the principal reason for imposing the higher prudent patient standard in *Chester v Afshar* was to promote the patient's decision-making autonomy.[182] Therefore, appearances suggest that the MCA will fail to safeguard a patient who has disclosed their value system in a living will against an incorrect finding of incapacity.

Nonetheless, *Chester v Afshar* alludes to the doctor's duty to not only inform patients about risks, i.e. the information a doctor is required to voluntarily disclose by law, but to answer their questions candidly and to respect their rights, including (where they so choose) to postpone medical procedures and to go elsewhere for treatment.[183] A similar point was made in *Sidaway* by Lord Diplock who stated that:

> *"It may be that most patients, though not necessarily all, have a vague knowledge that there may be some risk in any form of medical treatment: but it is flying in the face of reality to assume that all patients from the highest to the lowest standard of education or intelligence are aware of the extent and nature of the risks which, notwithstanding, the exercise of skill and care in carrying out the treatment, are inevitably involved in medical treatment of whatever kind it be but particularly surgical...*
>
> *But when if comes to warning about risks, the kind of training and experience that a judge will have undergone at the Bar makes it natural for him to say (correctly) it is my right to decide whether any particular thing is done to my body, and I want to be fully informed of any risks there may be involved of which I am not already aware from my general knowledge as a highly educated man of experience, so that I may form my own judgment as to whether to refuse the advised treatment or not.*

---

[180] To disclose those risks that are so obviously necessary, or material to the decision to be made that no reasonably prudent doctor would fail to mention them

[181] *Sidaway v Board of the Bethlem Royal Hospital and the Maudsley Hospital and Others [1985] AC 871*

[182] *Chester v Afshar 2004 WL 2289136*, para.77

[183] Ibid, see Lord Hope, para.76

> *No doubt if the patient in fact manifested this attitude by means of questioning, the doctor would tell him whatever it was the patient wanted to know: but we are concerned here with volunteering unsought information about risks of the proposed treatment..."*[184]

Could a patient with a value system be said to have manifested such an attitude?

Functional not Outcome Based Test

A patient with a value system wishes to make decisions that are broadly coherent with their pre-existing values and choices. Taking into consideration the standard for disclosure of risks is the right to autonomy necessarily contemporary in the sense that an assessor will be more concerned with present not past decisions?

Perhaps the first point to make about a functional approach to capacity is the underlying expectation that a competent patient should be able to understand and retain treatment information so that it can be applied to their own situation, in particular its significance and potential effects with regard to their existing values, beliefs and preferences, in order that their decisions are (roughly)[185] coherent[186] with their pre-existing values and thus with their previous choices and convictions or to at least appreciate that their decision entails a departure from them. Crucially a patient must demonstrate their continued ability to bring values and decisions into a state of coherence. Therefore, it is essential that a value system is functional in this sense in that it must explain and justify treatment decisions, i.e. an independent third party must be able to understand and use the value system in order to be able to ascertain whether the decision of the patient is consistent with the facts and values of the case as well as with their previous decisions.[187]

As a doctor will determine whether or not a decision is autonomous it is especially important to the person who has disclosed their value system

---

[184] *Sidaway v Board of the Bethlem Royal Hospital and the Maudsley Hospital and Others [1985] AC 871*, p.894/5

[185] If the law in *Sidaway* applies

[186] If the law in *Chester v Afshar* applies

[187] *Re MB (Adult: Medical Treatment) [1997] 2 FLR 426 CA*

that the assessment should not rely on the subjectivity of the assessor, i.e. their impressions, intuitions or standards.[188] Andrew Grubb explains why:

> *"[C]aution must be exercised in applying the third stage of the ... test [for capacity]. It is potentially an open invitation to make a finding of incompetence because the doctor (or court) finds the patient's decision difficult to understand. This is not what the courts intend. That a patient must have the ability to 'weigh' information does not mean that every incongruous decision is an incompetent one. The court is not entitled simply to re-weigh the factors relevant to the patient's decision and because it would come to a different decision, treat the patient as incompetent. It is the patient's ability to weigh, rather than the actual weight given to particular factors, which is at the core of the third stage of the test. A patient may have the ability to weigh the information but, for reasons particular to him, reach a decision that the doctor (or court) would not. That is the patient's choice and the decision may be based upon the patient's own perception of the world or values providing it is not the product of distorted or deluded perceptions stemming from mental malfunctioning, in particular the very mental disorder for which treatment is needed. To do otherwise, would be to introduce a test of unreasonableness or irrationality which the courts have rejected".*[189]

A functional based test for capacity is then less concerned with the outcome of the deliberative process and thus with whether the patient has made a wise or actually competent choice.[190] From this I conclude that a functional approach to decision-making capacity is somewhat deceptive because it suggests that as patients are not expected to demonstrate their ability to arrive at a choice that is actually wise or competent, when assessed in the light of their values, beliefs and preferences, that an assessor, who is in possession of their patient's value system, should not be unduly concerned with the outcome of a deliberative process and therefore with whether the patient has actually understood treatment information. However, the fact that patients must demonstrate understanding through an ability to apply facts to values and to make a decision that is in some way coherent with their past decisions and choices

---

[188] Mental Capacity Act 2005, Code of Practice, Chapter

[189] Grubb, A., Principles of Medical Law, 2004, Second Edition, Oxford University Press, para.3.89

[190] Although note Butler-Sloss LJ in *Re MB (Adult: Medical Treatment) [1997] 2 FLR 426 CA*

means that patients must actually be able to understand, retain and use or weigh the information that is relevant to their decision.[191]

There is then a difference between unwise decisions which a person has the right to make,[192] which is so obviously important to preserving the patient's right to make a decision that goes against expert medical opinion,[193] and decisions based on a lack of understanding of risks or inability to weigh up the information about a decision.[194] Accordingly, information about decisions the person has made based on a lack of understanding of risks or inability to weigh up the information can form part of a capacity assessment particularly if someone repeatedly makes unwise decisions that put them at risk or result in harm to them or someone else[195] or makes a particular decision that is obviously irrational or out of character for them.[196] It is therefore somewhat ironic that it might be possible for a doctor to determine the information that is material to a decision independently of the patient's value system which may in turn be used to make the claim that their decision is so obviously irrational or out of character for them, when considered in the light of their past decisions and choices, that they may be treated as incompetent.

On the other hand it is also a principle of the MCA that a person is not to be treated as unable to make a decision unless all practicable steps to help him to do so have been taken without success.[197] As autonomy is the primary value in medical law then it is consistent with respect for that principle that a doctor should seek to restore patient autonomy by developing their capacity to make a decision in accordance with personally held values with the aim of preventing unnecessary intervention in the lives of their patients.[198] However, in this regard Pellegrino and Thomasma have stated that:

---

[191] Mental Capacity Act 2005, Code of Practice, Chapter Two, para.2.11
[192] Mental Capacity Act 2005, s.1(3)
[193] *Re C (Adult: Refusal of Treatment) [1994] 1 All ER 819*
[194] Mental Capacity Act 2005, Code of Practice, Chapter Four, para.4.30; *Re MB (Adult: Medical Treatment) [1997] 2 FLR 426 CA*
[195] Mental Capacity Act 2005, Code of Practice, Chapter Four, para.4.30
[196] Mental Capacity Act 2005, Code of Practice, Chapter Two, para.2.11; *Re MB (Adult: Medical Treatment) [1997] 2 FLR 426 CA*
[197] Mental Capacity Act 2005, s.1(3)
[198] Intervention in the absence of consent ordinarily constitutes a battery

> *"[O]ne cannot assume that autonomy is fully restorable or preservable in cases of serious illness. Patricia Bradley formulates a telling objection to the position of Robert Veatch, one of the most prominent ethicists arguing for the patient autonomy model. According to Bradley,*
>
> > *'Veatch argues that the relationship between doctor and patient is an equal one, ignoring the fact of illness which places the patient in a potentially vulnerable relationship with his physician. Based as it is on a wrong assumption, this model must be rejected when applied to the traditional doctor-patient relationship'.*
>
> *Even the briefest experience with illness shows that ill persons often can become so anxious, guilty, angry, fearful or hostile that they make judgments they may not make in calmer times. Patients become preoccupied with their diseases and their bodies. The patient may see his body as an object that failed him. Patients are forced to reassess their values and goals. These primary characteristics of illness alter personal wholeness to a profound degree. They change some of our assumptions about the operation of personal autonomy in the one who is ill".*[199]

The fact that one cannot assume that autonomy is fully restorable or preservable in cases of serious illness underscores the importance of coherence theory when helping someone to make decisions. In this regard some emphasis is placed on the importance of explaining information using the most effective form of communication for that person in order to help them to remember important facts.[200] Since the idea is to get decision-makers to connect with patients more effectively and to help people to remember important facts a value system would appear to have an obvious advantage over most other forms of communication. This is because a doctor will have access to information that enables him or her to meet the needs and circumstances of the patient who broadly speaking wants to be helped to make an informed treatment decision the corollary of which is that they want a doctor to safeguard them against the effects of making a non-autonomous decision when judged in relation to subjective rather than objective factors. In this regard a doctor will be in a better position to determine how to treat the patient in their medical best interests and to determine what treatment information it is relevant to disclose and which the patient must understand, retain and use or weigh.

---

[199] Pellegrino, Edmund D., Thomasma, David C., The Conflict between Autonomy and Beneficence in Medical Ethics: Proposal for a Resolution, 1987, Journal of Contemporary Health Law and Policy, Volume 3, p.23-46, p.27-8

[200] Mental Capacity Act 2005, Code of Practice, Chapter Four, para.4.17

For patients a value system does in a sense act as a memory stick or at least it has the capacity to act as such if it enables them to make a decision in conformity with their existing values or to appreciate that their current decision entails a departure from them. In other cases it might act as little more than a prompt. I say this because a person will have become engaged intellectually and emotionally when constructing their value system and because of that it is possible that details of it will reside in the mind thereafter at various levels of consciousness, i.e. intellectual and emotional, therefore it might be possible for a doctor to access the mind in various ways in order to elicit a decision from them.[201] Otherwise it provides the framework upon which the patient must demonstrate their ability to use or weigh treatment information and to arrive at a decision that does at the very least keep faith with their critical interests. As the value system becomes the focus for discussion and decision it should also safeguard patients against the effects of undue influence when deliberating and making decisions, i.e. the decision is the actual decision of the patient. These factors taken together would tend to diminish the concern that a doctor may say a patient is competent to consent to treatment when they are compliant with medical opinion and conversely to claim that the patient is not competent to decide if they raise objections or refuse a necessary and appropriate treatment or procedure.

It is therefore unfortunate that in relation to information about risks doctors are merely advised to describe any foreseeable consequences of making the decision and of not making any decision at all.[202] In this respect it is important to note that information must be tailored to an individual's needs, circumstances[203] and abilities.[204] So whilst it is important that a person has access to treatment information that information can presumably be presented in broad or simple terms to aid their understanding of it whereupon there is a danger that the true meaning and significance of it might get lost in translation.[205] This of course means that if the patient fails to understand the true significance of the

[201] Think of music and its capacity to reach deep inside, rather like a firework lights up the night sky, which triggers various intellectual as well as sensual responses, emotions and feelings

[202] Mental Capacity Act 2005, Chapter Three, para.3.9

[203] Mental Capacity Act 2005, Code of Practice, Chapter Four, para.4.17

[204] Ibid, Chapter Three, para.3.8

[205] Ibid, Chapter Three, para.3.9

information they are given then they will also be unable to apply it meaningfully to their own situation.[206]

So is the right to autonomy contemporary? Yes and no. Yes, because a doctor is concerned with whether someone has capacity to make a particular decision, i.e. the decision in hand. No, because in order to demonstrate their ability to make a decision a person must be able to understand, retain and use or weigh the relevant information and to make a decision that is coherent or broadly consistent with their past decisions and choices.

In this regard you may remember that the general legal framework that applies to decisions concerning a medical treatment in respect of a competent patient incorporates two standards. A physician will escape liability for a battery whenever a patient is informed about the broad nature and purpose of a medical treatment or procedure so that they know what would happen to them if the treatment is provided, as well as the likely consequences to the patient if treatment is not provided.[207] Disclosures in relation to risks inherent in medical treatment, which may or may not materialise, are dealt with under the law of negligence in spite of the fact that the harms envisaged may be material to the way in which a patient chooses to exercise their right to self-determination. An issue of particular relevance in this context is that non-disclosure of such risks would effectively deny patients the opportunity to refuse medical treatment and to exercise their right to maintain bodily integrity.

To summarise, the duty to obtain a patient's consent is protected by the tort of battery, however the duty to ensure that a patient has been given enough information (whatever that might mean) is part of the doctor's ordinary duty of care to act in the best interests of their patients, meaning that a failure to offer sufficient information might ground an action in negligence.[208] In relation to this latter point the House of Lords, in the case of *Chester v Afshar*, have more recently determined that no gap should exist between beneficence and autonomy, i.e. custom and practice

---

[206] *Chester v Afshar 2004 WL 2289136*

[207] *Chatterton v Gerson [1981] QB 432*; Jones, Richard, Mental Capacity Act Manual, 2008, Third Edition, Sweet and Maxwell, p.22, para.1-034 – what a patient should be told in order for a doctor to escape liability for a battery

[208] Jackson, Emily, First Do No Harm, edited by Sheila McLean, 2006, Ashgate Publishing, Chapter 17, p.273

within the medical profession should no longer be used to inform the law about what the patient should be told.[209] Instead the scope of the doctor's duty has been more closely equated with the patient's need for information and the right to decide upon its materiality. In that case Miss Chester claimed that:

> *"She told Mr Afshar that she had heard a lot of horror stories about surgery and that she wanted to know about the risks, but that none of this was explained to her. She did not mention paralysis specifically as one of the risks that she wanted to be told about, and this was not mentioned as a risk of surgery by Mr Afshar. The rely she got from him as a throw away line, was that he had not crippled anybody yet. She agreed to the surgery because he made it all sound so simple"...*[210]

Accordingly, Lord Hope accepted the trial judge's findings and said that:

> *"As has been recognised in many cases (including Sidaway...) it is often a difficult and delicate matter for a consultant to advise a patient about what he regards as comparatively minor risks, particularly when that patient is already suffering from stress, pain and anxiety. He will naturally be anxious to avoid alarming or confusing the patient unnecessarily. In the present case, as the defendant indicated in his evidence, he clearly thought that the risk of damage to the claimant was extremely small. Furthermore, he knew that he personally had never caused any nerve damage in the many hundreds of operations he had carried out over 20 to 25 years. It may well be that he considered the claimant to be over-anxious or over-preoccupied with 'horror stories' and the possibility of being crippled. In these circumstances I do not find it improbable that, in an attempt to reassure, he deflected her inquiries by answering them in the light hearted terms which she has described – and which he accepts that he may have used at some stage. However understandable such a response may have been in psychological terms, it was not an adequate response in legal terms, as Lord Templeman indicated in Sidaway...*[211]
>
> *Thus the right to make the final decision and the duty of the doctor to inform the patient if the treatment may have special disadvantages or dangers go hand in hand. In this case there is no dispute that Mr Afshar owed a duty to Miss Chester to inform her of the risks that were inherent in the proposed surgery, including the risk of paralysis. The duty was owed to her so that she could make her own decision as to whether or not she*

---

[209] *Bolam v Friern Hospital Management Committee [1957] 1 WLR 582*
[210] *Chester v Afshar 2004 WL 2289136*, para.44
[211] Ibid, para.50

> *should undergo the particular course of surgery which he was proposing to carry out. That was the scope of the duty, the existence of which gave effect to her right to be informed before she consented to it. It was unaffected in its scope by the response which Miss Chester would have given had she been told of these risks".* [212]

Here it is relevant to reflect on the fact that the law follows morality in determining that people rather than social customs and practices are the sources of values. Consequently, people are the sources of their own rights to bodily inviolability from which the right to self-determination is derived and because these interests are so fundamental in human life, indeed to the future prosperity of humankind, they are made the source of any normative claims that we may have on others.

Significantly, a legal standard of disclosure has now been established that is unaffected in its scope by a professional privilege to withhold information that might alarm a patient.[213] Indeed taking into consideration the circumstances of the case[214] one could be forgiven for thinking that Lord Hope had given effect to the court's equitable jurisdiction in order to resolve a dispute in favour of the patient that was related to the doctor's failure to disclose relevant treatment information.[215] Consequently, the law of negligence in this case seemed closer to that of battery.

Having set the scene let us once again consider the protestations of both Lord Goff in *Bland* and Lord Falconer in the Foreword to the MCA because the rights and interests of persons who lack capacity are considered in accordance with one standard not two; the standard proposed by the ordinary law of negligence or the reasonable person standard which

[212] Ibid, para.55

[213] Ibid, para.55

[214] The risk that the doctor had failed to warn the patient about materialised and as a result they suffered injury. However, the patient was unable to say that had she been adequately warned of the risk that she would never have consented to the operation. She claimed instead that she would have postponed her decision until later. Consequently an application of the all or nothing 'but for' test of causation, i.e. but for the doctor's failure to warn, the patient would have declined treatment and would not have incurred injury, would have left her without a remedy. On policy grounds therefore Lord Hope held that the test of causation had been satisfied in this case.

[215] *Chester v Afshar 2004 WL 2289136*, para.87

is an objective standard.[216] Consequently, a doctor who acts in someone's best interests and exercises care and skill in the performance of their duty does not incur liability for doing the act which a competent patient must consent to if they reasonably believe that their patient lacks capacity to make that particular decision.[217] In relation to a patient with borderline or fluctuating capacity a doctor must follow the steps to establish whether a person has capacity in order to form a reasonable belief that the patient does lack capacity in relation to the matter.[218] The problem is that the MCA upholds the standard proposed in *Sidaway*, the prudent doctor standard. It therefore appears that a professional privilege to withhold treatment information has been maintained in respect of those to whom this legislation applies.

For this reason it is somewhat disingenuous of the current law to fail to more effectively recognise the different considerations that should apply to formerly competent patients, and in particular those who might choose to disclose their value system in a living will, and others or never competent patients as the statute De Prerogativa Regis 1324 did, in terms of applying the higher prudent patient standard in respect of the former patient group though perhaps not the latter. As otherwise the right to autonomy is indeed contemporary and because the MCA would fail to fully safeguard the patient who has disclosed their value system against an incorrect finding of incapacity a doctor is free to say that a patient is competent to give consent to treatment when the patient is compliant with medical expert opinion and conversely to claim that the patient is not competent to decide if they raise objections or refuse a necessary and appropriate treatment or procedure.

So far we have considered the situation in relation to patients where doubt exists about someone's capacity to make decisions and act autonomously. What about patients who have disclosed their value system in a living will but are in urgent need of treatment or are unconscious and in need of emergency treatment? Does the medical welfare of these patients assume priority over respect for the patient's right to self-determination in these circumstances? In this regard the Code of Practice states that:

---

[216] Mental Capacity Act 2005, s.5(1);
[217] Ibid, s.5(2)
[218] Ibid, s.5(1)(a)

> *"[I]n emergency medical situations (for example, where a person collapses with a heart attack or for some unknown reason and is brought unconscious into a hospital), urgent decisions will have to be made and immediate action taken in the person's best interests. In these situations, it may not be practical or appropriate to delay the treatment while trying to help the person to make their own decisions, or to consult with any known attorneys or deputies. However, even in emergency situations, healthcare staff should try to continue to communicate with the person and keep them informed of what is happening".*[219]

Whilst it may not be practical or appropriate to delay treatment in these circumstances the principle of finding the least restrictive alternative appears to have considerable bite, i.e. before an act is done, or the decision is made, regard must be had to whether the purpose for which it is needed can be as effectively achieved in a way that is less restrictive of the person's rights and freedom of action.[220] As autonomy allows each of us to develop a life in conformity with our own character and personality this principle suggests that the values, beliefs and preferences of formerly competent patients, where these are known and understood by others, should be relevant to best interests. In this regard guidance within the Code of Practice confirms that finding the least restrictive option includes considering whether there is a need to act or make a decision at all and goes on to state that:

> *"Where there is more than one option, it is important to explore ways that would be less restrictive or allow the most freedom for a person who lacks capacity to make the decision in question. However, the final decision must always allow the original purpose of the decision or act to be achieved.*
>
> *Any decision or action must still be in the best interests of the person who lacks capacity. So sometimes it may be necessary to choose an option that is not the least restrictive alternative if that option is in the person's best interests. In practice, the process of choosing a less restrictive option and deciding what is in the person's best interests will be combined. But both principles must be applied each time a decision or action may be taken on behalf of a person who lacks capacity to make the relevant decision".*[221]

---

[219] Mental Capacity Act 2005, Code of Practice, Chapter Three, para.3.6
[220] Mental Capacity Act 2005, s.1(6)
[221] Mental Capacity Act 2005, Code of Practice, Chapter Two, para.2.16

The principle attempts to reduce the potential for conflict to exist between beneficence and autonomy when a doctor sets out to determine what is in someone's best interests. However, the underlying aim of this principle can only be achieved in an emergency situation when a doctor has access to the patient's value system. Although even in these circumstances it should be noted that this principle does at the same time retain a doctor's right to make decisions and act in another's best medical interests, as only 'regard' must be had to this principle so an option that is not the least restrictive option can still be in a person's best interests.[222] Accordingly, the principle merely serves to constrain the worst effects of medical paternalism, i.e. to prevent doctors from overriding the patient's value system, when it is known and can be understood by others, in order to protect their medical welfare. In other words the principle serves to remind doctors that what is in someone's medical best interests, as they judge them to be, may not also be in their overall or actual best interests all things considered.

This principle, like so much else about the MCA tantalises – it promises something, transformation if you will, but that potential is frustrated rather than fulfilled possibly because the Act fails to adequately distinguish between the circumstances of people similarly situated as the statute De Prerogativa Regis 1324 did or maybe just fails to be tied to the mast of its own convictions. In any event as with many of its other provisions the scope to be something different in this respect remains.

Making the case for a form of Autonomous Decision-Making

In general a commitment to the fundamental principle of bodily inviolability as well as to a patient interest in exercising their right to self-determination seldom allows scope for paternalism to emerge in the doctor-patient relationship as was illustrated by the case of *Chester v Afshar*. So we can say that doctors are both morally, professionally and legally required to assist their patients to maximise their autonomy and act immorally, unprofessionally and illegally whenever they deprive patients of their autonomy.[223] Beneficence cannot override autonomy.[224] The value of

[222] Jones, Richard, Mental Capacity Act Manual, 2008, Third Edition, Sweet and Maxwell, p.12, para.1-017

[223] *Chester v Afshar 2004 WL 2289136*; Mental Capacity Act 2005, s.1

[224] Ibid

autonomy does in other words carry far greater weight than the value of beneficence does. Sometimes however, people suffer a loss of decision-making capacity and are then incompetent to exercise autonomy. In these circumstances, when one person is entrusted into the care of another they have a right to beneficence, i.e. a right that the latter make decisions and act in the former's best interests.[225]

An issue in respect of incapacity is that the best interests of the patient might override the choices or wishes of a formerly competent patient. This is due in no small part to the selection and subsequent application of a test for evaluating decision-making capacity and best interests which permits physicians to exercise their discretion to limit a patient's right to autonomy to reflect the physician's primary commitment to the patient's physical welfare. Consequently, there is a need to identify a physician-patient decision-making model that can remove the conflict between beneficence and autonomy.

In this way there is no advantage in a doctor saying that a patient is competent to give consent to treatment merely because the patient is compliant with medical expert opinion and conversely to claim that the patient is not competent to decide if they raise objections or refuse a necessary and appropriate treatment or procedure. This is because the doctor would in any event be bound to make decisions and act in conformity with the values, beliefs and preferences of the patient where these could be known and understood. Consequently, in this part of the chapter we will be exploring the issue of how respect for values could fit in with the doctor's ethical obligations of non-maleficence and beneficence.

Re-examining the Nature of the Doctor-Patient Relationship

The doctor-patient relationship has been characterised in various ways and this is achieved by emphasising a particular characteristic of that relationship which may or may not hold true when considered in different contexts. An issue of some magnitude in this context is how that relationship should be defined to be compatible with our notions of inviolability and respect for persons, i.e. that persons have moral worth and dignity.

---

225 Dworkin, Ronald, Life's Dominion: An argument about Abortion and Euthanasia, Harper Collins, p.229

The Paternalistic Model

The paternalistic model sought justification in a doctor's professionalism. A doctor is someone who has knowledge and expertise in medical matters and is also bound to act ethically in accordance with the principles of non-maleficence and beneficence. These factors suggest that physicians should be trusted to be in control of the relationship and to decide what is best for their patients.[226]

This model is however limited in various respects in seeming to suggest that a physician is both omnipotent as well as omniscient. The former is a fallacy as the profession itself recognises, i.e. that various practices may be considered proper, which takes due account of the fact that medicine is a science but its practice is an art. Consequently, only the crudest of practitioners will treat medical data as sacrosanct. Other medical concepts like differential diagnosis also point out the limitations of a doctor's expert powers as there may be many explanations for a malady and it is a question of working through things by a process of elimination or the most likely to the least likely cause.[227] Let us not also forget that no doctor has the ability to accurately work out what benefits and harms will result from a medical treatment or procedure in a particular case.[228] There is also the point that in a democracy society defines what benefits its citizens should be given and which medical benefits may be offered.[229] Finally, unless the physician is also omniscient the model tends to demand too much or too little according to your view of things. A doctor cannot determine what a good life for their patient is and what is in someone's welfare interests cannot be fully encapsulated by the goals of medicine. So in either of these respects there is an ever present risk of an affront to human dignity. Pellegrino and Thomasma put things in these terms:

> *"[A] physician often cannot heal a person just by curing a disease, especially if the physician systematically ignores or disregards the patient's view...*

---

[226] Herring, Jonathan, Medical Law and Ethics, 2008, Second Edition, Oxford University Press, p.184

[227] Pellegrino, Edmund D., Thomasma, David C., The Conflict between Autonomy and Beneficence in Medical Ethics: Proposal for a Resolution, 1987, Journal of Contemporary Health Law and Policy, Volume 3, p.23-46, p.37/8

[228] Ibid

[229] Ibid, p.38

Strong paternalism is objectionable because it violates the humanity of the patient. The obligation is owed rational beings to be free to decide about the conduct of their own lives. Indeed, such decisions are peculiarly human. To infringe on such a fundamental right clearly demands special justification. Medical paternalism fails because it overrides an essential element in deontological ethics, at the core of medicine, i.e. respect for persons. To violate the patient's autonomy is to deprive him of one essential component of his own good, and thus to violate medicine's promise to act for the good of the patient.

Many physicians hold that the patient's rights to autonomy should not get in the way of their medical needs, i.e. medical "indications" should dominate clinical decisions. But as we shall argue the case, the hierarchy of patient goods may not always place medical needs in the highest place. Lack of respect for such a hierarchy of values is a major cause of patient complaints about physician paternalism.

Like the autonomy model, medical paternalism can fail to distinguish contexts and their role in medical and ethical decision-making. As a consequence, medical paternalism tends to universalise a stance valid in one context but not necessarily in another. Generalisation of one experience, like "saving" one patient through paternalism, into a universal moral posture, is not valid.

Perhaps the biggest failure of medical paternalism is its assumption that medical values or medical good is the highest good, and that it has an absolute quality which overrides other values. Or, even less justifiably, a particular physician's preferences for one treatment among several may become an absolute. Some surgeons prefer radical mastectomy while others prefer limited resection and radiation for cancer of the breast. Some cardiologists prefer medical over surgical management in certain types of angina pectoris. Alternative procedures may lead to similar outcomes but with different risks and quality of life. Selection of one procedure over others depends as much on the patient's and the physician's values as on the scientific data. The patient, for reasons of great importance to him, may reject even the scientifically preferred therapy for one of lesser effectiveness.

Medical paternalism asserts that the physician unequivocally knows better than the patient what is "good" for him. It also subsumes all the patient's good under only one good – medical good. Other dimensions of the good of the patient must also be considered. One of these is surely the preservation of the fundamental human good of making one's own decisions about the kind of life one wants to lead, or the risks one wants to take".[230]

Autonomy Model

When autonomy is respected persons have dominion over their life path and also their bodies and life-spans. Consequently, the autonomy model preserves the patient's right to make a decision in accordance with their own character and personality to reject a beneficial medical treatment or procedure because they prefer instead to be maintained inviolate. In this way the autonomy model may be contrasted with the former, paternalistic model.

Whilst respect for autonomy is a normative condition of medical treatment decision-making an individual's interest in or right to autonomy can only be exercised by those with capacity to make decisions in accordance with their own values, beliefs and preferences. Yet it might not be possible to preserve[231] or to restore autonomy in every case due to the nature or severity of illness.[232] This fact has led Pellegrino and Thomasma to comment that:

> *"The effects of illness and disease on personal autonomy limit self-determination to variable degrees. That is why so many physicians report that patients really want them to make the decisions. On this view, autonomy ought not, therefore, to be taken as a starting point or absolute overriding principle in medicine. Rather it should be seen as part of the goal of treatment, one of the goods of the patient, to be promoted but not to the total exclusion of all other goods.*
>
> *If we take the impact of illness and disease seriously, we must modify the autonomy model. That model has four features: self-direction, establishing a life plan, deliberating about applying a life plan (reasoning and information), and acting on the basis of such deliberations.*
>
> *Becoming "sick" can modify each of these features. To "be" sick is to be subject to the patho-physiological effects of illness, pain, fear, and to the special professional and institutional environment in which decisions occur. Self-direction is marred by the way disease may disrupt the unity of the self, ego and the body. Life plans are threatened by the finitude of*

---

[230] Ibid, p.36/7; *B v An NHS Trust Hospital [2002] 152 NLJ 470*

[231] For example, dementia

[232] For example, persistent vegetative state

human life revealed in illness. Deliberation and application are impeded by the distractions of pain and fear, or by the process of institutionalisation. The extent to which the operations of autonomy can be impeded by being, and becoming, a patient is impressive.

Of course the autonomy of most patients is only mildly incapacitated by disease. We must not, therefore, use the autonomy limitation as an excuse for all sorts of paternalism. On the whole, patient's choices can, and should, be accepted. On the other hand, people who are incapacitated by disease or trauma should not be abandoned to their autonomy, but merely given the "facts" and asked to make a decision. This is a form of moral abandonment...

One might argue that we are merely talking about varying degrees of competence, and that the problem is one of determining competence. On this view the autonomy model would remain intact since incompetent patients could be treated paternalistically without violating the principles of autonomy. Such an interpretation would, however, offend those for whom autonomy has become an absolute principle of medical ethics".[233]

An obvious problem with this right is then that incompetent patients who have not left a legally valid and applicable advance decision will in the future have medical treatment decisions made for them by a surrogate decision-maker who will in normal circumstances be the patient's doctor. Now whilst we might reflect on certain facts, that the law recognises that competent[234] and incompetent[235] persons have an interest in refusing necessary and appropriate medical treatment, that there is also recognition that treatment refusals need not be motivated by particular medical facts such as that of being terminally ill or in an advanced stage of sickness,[236] there is an issue surrounding the uncertainty of the legal standards applicable to an incompetent patient who, in the context of this thesis, has disclosed their value system in a living will. As a consequence physicians may override the values of the patient, not wilfully perhaps but, in order to preserve their life, health or well-being.

---

[233] Pellegrino, Edmund D., Thomasma, David C., The Conflict between Autonomy and Beneficence in Medical Ethics: Proposal for a Resolution, 1987, Journal of Contemporary Health Law and Policy, Volume 3, p.23-46, p.31/2

[234] *Re C (Adult: Refusal of Treatment) [1994] 1 All ER 819*

[235] *Airedale NHS Trust v Bland [1993] 1 All ER 821 HL*

[236] *B v An NHS Trust Hospital [2002] 152 NLJ 470; Re T (Adult: Refusal of Treatment) [1992] 4 All ER 649 CA*; see also the recent case of Kerrie Wooltorton

Moral Conflict

Doctors are aware, through their medical training, that all living things seek their own survival. Personal experience, perhaps supplemented by training in medical ethics, should equally inform them that persons also desire to live a good life and do not therefore always pursue life to the point where it is empty of any real content. So patients should be informed about the benefits and potential harms of medical treatments and procedures to assist them to make a choice that is right for them. As the physician is a person of knowledge and skill in medical matters beneficence cannot be subverted by autonomy during this process. Consequently, it matters that patients feel able to trust their doctor especially in relation to the exercise of their duties.

In any case that contains elements of at least two competing values conflict will exist, e.g. autonomy versus utility; beneficence when construed as paternalism versus autonomy. Yet if we reflect on the fact that not a lot that is good in life is ever achieved by requiring one party to bow to the unreasonable needs or demands of another we will recognise that extreme positions of any kind tend to achieve very little in the end. Good relationships are by contrast sustained on the basis of give and take or mutual respect and understanding. Consequently, there is a need to think about the importance of maintaining standards that are for the benefit of all of us.

In this regard any apparent tension that is created between the principles of beneficence and autonomy is released by asserting that the doctor-patient relationship is of a fiduciary nature. When a doctor acts as a fiduciary he or she is placed under an obligation to respect the wishes of the patient on the basis that autonomy is made an essential element of beneficence. Thus a doctor is trusted to at least prioritise the dignity interests of the patient ahead of their own inclinations. So should autonomy be a more important value in healthcare than trust in one's physician taking into consideration the facts of incompetency?

Beneficence in Trust: A Fiduciary Model for Medical Decisions

What is the connection between trust and beneficence? Beneficence means to act on behalf of another. In relation to medical professionals beneficence translates into devotion, well a commitment at least, to the welfare of others.[237] As the patient is sick and does not have knowledge or expertise in the practice of medical science they must trust their doctor to apply a specialised body of information in a way that is most conducive to promoting their personal welfare and sense of well-being.[238] Therefore, beneficence is implied each time a doctor acts or takes up the responsibility to care for a patient based on the patient's trust.[239] It is also clear that to act on behalf of another in medicine no longer means to act only on behalf of the other's body or medical welfare.[240] About this Cassell writes that:

> *"The changes in the notions of person, of patienthood, and of the doctor-patient relationship that have occurred over these last decades emphasise that when the doctor acts for patients the action is meant to work towards the goals that the patients would choose if they could act on their own. What patients believe to be in their own best interests may well require the active participation of the physician to discover but can almost never be known without the patient's knowledgeable participation. [Beneficence] in medicine requires more than knowledge of medical science; it also requires understanding illness – its causes, course, and outcome – from the patient's viewpoint, and then acting on the knowledge. Above all, it requires knowing about sick persons".*[241]

Therefore it is implicit in this model that beneficence is the prime requirement for medicine and as a patient places their body and health in trust with the physician the patient's problems and needs become the

---

[237] Cassell, Eric J., The Nature of Suffering and the Goals of Medicine, Second Edition, 2004, Oxford University Press, p.73

[238] Ibid, p.71/2; Pellegrino, Edmund D., Thomasma, David C., The Conflict between Autonomy and Beneficence in Medical Ethics: Proposal for a Resolution, 1987, Journal of Contemporary Health Law and Policy, Volume 3, p.23-46, p.38-45; Rhodes, Rosamond, The Professional Responsibilities of Medicine, The Blackwell Guide to Medical Ethics, (2007, Blackwell Publishing); Hui, E.C., Doctors as Fiduciaries: a legal construct of the patient-physician relationship; 2005, Hong Kong Medical Journal, Vol. 11, No.6, pp.527-29; Beauchamp, Tom L., Childress, James F., Principles of Biomedical Ethics, 2001, Fifth Edition, Oxford University Press, p.64

[239] Cassell, Eric J., The Nature of Suffering and the Goals of Medicine, Second Edition, 2004, Oxford University Press, p.73

[240] Ibid; Mental Capacity Act 2005, s.4; *Chester v Afshar 2004 WL 2289136*

[241] Cassell, Eric J., The Nature of Suffering and the Goals of Medicine, Second Edition, 2004, Oxford University Press, p.73

physician's primary concern taking precedence over all other concerns.[242] In other words the physician must consider the wishes of the patient although ultimately it is they who must take responsibility for making treatment decisions.[243] So autonomy and paternalism are superseded by the prior obligation to act beneficently and the decision to foster autonomy or to act paternalistically should be based on what will benefit the patient most and not the personal idiosyncrasies or values and impulses of the medical professional.[244] The fact that there is no automatic ranking of values benefits the patient because each patient will be treated as an individual as Pellegrino and Thomasma now explain:

> *"Both the patient's autonomy and medical paternalism models emphasise single values which are always to be preferred. For example, the patient's right to autonomy is always to be preferred over other values in the patient's autonomy model. In the paternalism model, each patient must be treated as if he or she did not know what is best. By contrast, in the beneficent model, no such "automatic" ranking of values takes place. The elements of the beneficence model are not ranked in any pre-set hierarchy. Each patient must be handled individually not only for the medical but also for the moral implications. No ethical stance, other than acting for the patient's best interests, is applied beforehand. This model requires that patients and physicians become able to identify, rank, discuss, and negotiate values, and to define the particular good of a particular patient. This is not to say that general ethical axioms applied to more than one patient are invalid".*[245]

Core Features of a Fiduciary Relationship

How does this interpretation of beneficence differ to the one proposed by the MCA, for example, of acting on the principle of the least restrictive option? When the doctor-patient relationship is defined as a fiduciary relationship there is a distinct shift in emphasis away from the controlling

---

[242] Pellegrino, Edmund D., Thomasma, David C., The Conflict between Autonomy and Beneficence in Medical Ethics: Proposal for a Resolution, 1987, Journal of Contemporary Health Law and Policy, Volume 3, p.23-46, p.41; Maclean, Alasdair, Briefcase on Medical Law, 2004, Second Edition, Cavendish Publishing, p.12

[243] Ibid

[244] Ibid

[245] Pellegrino, Edmund D., Thomasma, David C., The Conflict between Autonomy and Beneficence in Medical Ethics: Proposal for a Resolution, 1987, Journal of Contemporary Health Law and Policy, Volume 3, p.23-46, p.43

influences of the paternalistic and autonomous models, i.e. either the physician makes the decision or the patient does, towards one in which a doctor's professionalism in carrying out his or her professional obligations is assessed in relation to the level of fidelity shown toward the patient.[246]

Fidelity is intrinsic to the doctor-patient relationship if we think, as Hippocrates apparently did, that the practice of medicine should be distinguished from ordinary business practices and that medical professionals should continue to be held to higher standards of morality than those traditionally found to exist in the market place and elsewhere. If it were otherwise there might be a need to consider placing a government health warning at the entrance to the doctor's surgery or maybe a 'buyer beware' notice according to whether one used private or public services. Instead of which the physician necessarily acts as trustee for the patient's medical welfare, which must surely have been what Hippocrates intended.[247]

If fidelity is the fundamental ethical principle regulating the medical profession how should it, fidelity, be defined when used in this context?[248] Well the paradigmatic fiduciary relationship is the one that exists between a trustee and beneficiary where the purpose of the relationship and the role and reason of one party is to promote the interests of the other.[249] In order to fulfil their role obligation and to act altruistically a trustee is required in law to relinquish their own self-interests and administer the trust in the

---

[246] Beauchamp, Tom L., Childress, James F., Principles of Biomedical Ethics, 2001, Fifth Edition, Oxford University Press, p.64; Rodwin, Marc. A., Strains in the Fiduciary Metaphor: Divided Physician Loyalties and Obligations in a Changing Health Care System; American Journal of Law & Medicine, 1995, Vol. XXI Nos. 2&3, pp.241-257, p.243; Hui, E.C., Doctors as Fiduciaries: a legal construct of the patient-physician relationship; 2005, Hong King Medical Journal, Vol. 11, No.6, pp.527-29, p.527

[247] Ibid, p.312; Hui, E.C., Doctors as Fiduciaries: a legal construct of the patient-physician relationship; 2005, Hong Kong Medical Journal, Vol. 11, No.6, pp.527-29, p.527

[248] Rodwin, Marc. A., Strains in the Fiduciary Metaphor: Divided Physician Loyalties and Obligations in a Changing Health Care System; American Journal of Law & Medicine, 1995, Vol. XXI Nos. 2&3, pp.241-257, p.243; Hui, E.C., Doctors as Fiduciaries: a legal construct of the patient-physician relationship; 2005, Hong Kong Medical Journal, Vol. 11, No.6, pp.527-29, p.527

[249] Ibid

sole interests of the beneficiary.[250] So ultimately, the relationship exists for the exclusive benefit of one party although of course the doctor is financially compensated for their services.[251]

A fiduciary is also someone who has power, i.e. specialised knowledge and skill, and/or property, i.e. has access to medicines, procedures and specialist practitioners, which may all be used for the benefit of their patient.[252] In the case of a paradigmatic relationship between trustee and beneficiary the beneficiary delegates discretionary power to the trustee in respect of the property of the trust and holds them to the highest, fiduciary, standard of conduct in the use of it.[253] By process of analogy, in relation to the doctor-patient relationship, a doctor has a delegated discretionary power in matters of health care, i.e. prescribing medicines and ordering tests etc, which is directly conferred on them by the individual patients they attend to, and indirectly by society as a whole, legitimately expecting that this knowledge will be used for the benefit of particular individuals and society.[254]

In this regard it is important to understand the social role of medicine and its ethics and to therefore recognise that the medical profession is a social artefact, or socially constructed body that was created to serve all of humankind.[255] Society in other words gave control over a set of knowledge, skills, powers and privileges, which in the wrong hands could do considerable harm, to a select few who are entrusted to provide their services for the good of those who are in need of them.[256] So the point is that this knowledge is not individually owned, and therefore ought not to

[250] Ibid
[251] Ibid
[252] Ibid
[253] Ibid
[254] Hui, E.C., Doctors as Fiduciaries: a legal construct of the patient-physician relationship; 2005, Hong Kong Medical Journal, Vol. 11, No.6, pp.527-29, p.527
[255] Rhodes, Rosamond, The Professional Responsibilities of Medicine, The Blackwell Guide to Medical Ethics, (2007, Blackwell Publishing), Chapter 4, p.83; Pellegrino, Edmund D., Thomasma, David C., The Conflict between Autonomy and Beneficence in Medical Ethics: Proposal for a Resolution, 1987, Journal of Contemporary Health Law and Policy, Volume 3, p.23-46, p.41
[256] Ibid

be used primarily for personal gain, prestige or power, rather medical professionals hold this knowledge in trust for the good of the sick.[257]

Let us not forget that in the course of treating 'a' patient 'a' doctor may expose their body as well as obtain information from them that they might otherwise choose to keep private.[258] So in this situation the patient chooses to forego privacy out of deference to the physician's medical knowledge in order to facilitate their health care.[259] Thus the aim of medicine is beneficent however, the knowledge of the physician, the knowledge and care that the patient seeks, is not proprietary by which I mean that it is not individually owned.[260] On this matter Pellegrino and Thomasma state that:

> *"Medicine as a human activity is of necessity a form of beneficence. It is a response to the need and plea of a sick person for help, without which the patient might die, or suffer unnecessary pain, or disability. The obligation to help the sick is a general one involving humans, even those who are not professed healers. It is grounded in the claim that comes from the vulnerability and suffering of a fellow human. One is impelled, even by the lesser degrees of beneficence [non-maleficence], not to harm, and even, to ease suffering.*
>
> *When one is a professed healer one possesses knowledge and skill society has permitted one to acquire precisely because it can benefit others. One also promises to help and to act on behalf of the good of the patient when one offers oneself to another as a healer. Further, without the special knowledge [pharmacology, for example] the healer has acquired others would suffer so that, in a sense, all the sick have some claim on all healers".*[261]

[257] Hui, E.C., Doctors as Fiduciaries: a legal construct of the patient-physician relationship; 2005, Hong Kong Medical Journal, Vol. 11, No.6, pp.527-29, p.527

[258] Ibid

[259] Ibid

[260] Ibid; Rhodes, Rosamond, The Professional Responsibilities of Medicine, The Blackwell Guide to Medical Ethics, (2007, Blackwell Publishing), Chapter 4, p.83; Pellegrino, Edmund D., Thomasma, David C., The Conflict between Autonomy and Beneficence in Medical Ethics: Proposal for a Resolution, 1987, Journal of Contemporary Health Law and Policy, Volume 3, p.23-46, p.41

[261] Pellegrino, Edmund D., Thomasma, David C., The Conflict between Autonomy and Beneficence in Medical Ethics: Proposal for a Resolution, 1987, Journal of Contemporary Health Law and Policy, Volume 3, p.23-46, p.41

Patients trust doctors on the basis of that understanding and not simply on the strength that their information will be kept confidential.[262] A problem is that doctors have acquired powers which put them at an advantage in the doctor-patient relationship. The relationship is, in other words, built on an inequality of influence and knowledge and these conditions provide doctors with an opportunity to exercise the power of discretion to the detriment of the patient.[263] Therefore, it is inherent in this relationship that a doctor might be susceptible to misusing or abusing the entrusted power and position either to promote his own interests or to undermine those of the patient, which may ultimately cause them harm.[264] Accordingly, fiduciary standards and safeguards are necessary to prevent such abuses.[265] While fiduciaries have specialised knowledge or expertise, that information has to be applied to the particular person and set of circumstances confronting them and so they must exercise judgment and discretion in order to fulfil their obligations.[266] Consequently, the more vulnerable party has no option other than to place their trust and confidence in that other person.[267] This is of course true of the doctor-patient relationship as patients are made more vulnerable by their conditions which brings forward the point as to whether dependence and vulnerability[268] or trust and loyalty are the real basis for treating a doctor as a fiduciary.[269]

---

262 Rhodes, Rosamond, The Professional Responsibilities of Medicine, The Blackwell Guide to Medical Ethics, (2007, Blackwell Publishing), Chapter 4, p.83

263 Hui, E.C., Doctors as Fiduciaries: a legal construct of the patient-physician relationship; 2005, Hong Kong Medical Journal, Vol. 11, No.6, pp.527-29, p.527

264 Ibid

265 Ibid

266 Ibid, p.527/8; Rodwin, Marc. A., Strains in the Fiduciary Metaphor: Divided Physician Loyalties and Obligations in a Changing Health Care System; American Journal of Law & Medicine, 1995, Vol. XXI Nos. 2&3, pp.241-257, p.244

267 Hui, E.C., Doctors as Fiduciaries: a legal construct of the patient-physician relationship; 2005, Hong Kong Medical Journal, Vol. 11, No.6, pp.527-29, p.528

268 The ascendancy of one party in a relationship means that the other is vulnerable to the formers exploitation and manipulation

269 Hui, E.C., Doctors as Fiduciaries: a legal construct of the patient-physician relationship; 2005, Hong Kong Medical Journal, Vol. 11, No.6, pp.527-29, p.528; Bartlett, Peter, Doctors as Fiduciaries: Equitable Regulation of the Doctor-Patient Relationship, 1997, Medical Law Review, No.5, pp.193-224

Should Doctors be Regarded as Fiduciaries?

The ethics of medicine has traditionally been based on the ordinary moral standards that people generally endorse. These universal standards of conduct apply to non-professionals as well as to persons in their private life. The question then is whether the doctor-patient relationship is sufficiently distinctive to justify us in marking it out for special consideration in terms of requiring medical professionals to conform to any higher standard of conduct than that commonly found to exist in the market place.

When we put things this way we are automatically drawn into examining a doctor's professional responsibilities. In medicine doctors and other health professionals are supposed to care about the general welfare of the population. We can observe this in terms of research that is carried out into all sorts of horrible diseases and conditions that pose a threat to human life or to someone's quality of life affecting as it does their ability to prosper or to live a good life. Public welfare also relies upon the ability of the medical profession to combat external agents that are the cause of sickness and disease. This may be through the implementation of policies that aim to preserve or improve standards of personal and public hygiene or through the development of drugs such as antibiotics to kill infections when these arise. Important immunisation programmes are also aimed at improving public health. These are example of what might be termed arms length medicine in that no particular relationship need come into being to know that these sorts of things are a common enemy of humankind and their ability to thrive.

Medical professionals also have a positive duty to beneficently respond to the needs of each patient and consequently to actively promote their good. Neither can we ignore the fact that members of society also value being maintained inviolate and free from bodily harm. This means that people are not only concerned about their susceptibility to disease but to injury also.[270] So with respect to their medical needs people want attention from skilled and knowledgeable practitioners who could cure disease, alleviate symptoms, restore function and ease suffering but are at the same time respectful toward them and their dignity interests.[271]

---

[270] Rhodes, Rosamond, The Professional Responsibilities of Medicine, The Blackwell Guide to Medical Ethics, (2007, Blackwell Publishing), Chapter 4, p.75

[271] Ibid

The problem is that there is no general conception of what good is or of what a good life entails. As there is no prior ordering of goods that a doctor can implement on behalf of the patient we arrive at the situation where beneficence must be defined in terms of those conditions that enable this particular patient to flourish. We also know that whatever is the source of our good will also be the source of our suffering. So when we talk about the possible advantages and risks of a medical treatment it is important to bear in mind the situation and circumstances of the patient. They typically know very little about medical science, of the possible causes of illnesses, how these can be treated and where a choice of treatments exists of the comparisons that can be made between them. As patients must accept the advice of their physician on these matters they need to be able to place their full trust in doctors. Their reliance and medicine's monopoly[272] over medical practice explains the importance of trust and of why medical professionals should be held to higher standards than those commonly found to exist in the market place.[273]

How Useful is it to regard Doctors as Fiduciaries?

Here we must bear in mind that an interested party must come forward to ask the court to become involved in the affairs of an incompetent adult.[274] Were that to happen the courts powers are to an extent constrained, in respect of this patient group, by the loss of its parens patriae jurisdiction. An interested party may however make an application for a declaration as to whether a person has or lacks capacity to make a decision. They may also question whether a treatment or procedure that has been or is proposed to be carried out is lawful and therefore in the best interests of an incompetent patient.[275]

Speaking in the case of *Bland*, where an application was made to the court by the hospital regarding the lawfulness of withholding or withdrawing

---

[272] Remember society as a whole prefers choice over monopoly situations as these typically provide grounds for the provider to exploit or abuse their position by advancing their own interests or those of a particular third party at some expense to the consumer

[273] Rhodes, Rosamond, The Professional Responsibilities of Medicine, The Blackwell Guide to Medical Ethics, (2007, Blackwell Publishing), Chapter 4, p.75

[274] *Re F (Mental Patient: Sterilisation) [1990] 2 AC 1 HL*, note Lord Griffiths p.70

[275] Mental Capacity Act 2005, s.15; *Re F (Mental Patient: Sterilisation) [1990] 2 AC 1 HL*, note Lord Griffiths p.70

life-preserving medical treatment from a patient in a permanent vegetative state, Lord Lowry expressed his opinion that:

> *"[T]he parens patriae jurisdiction over adults who are for whatever reason mentally incompetent was abolished by statute. I have never heard a rational, or indeed any, explanation for this step, which has placed under a further disadvantage a class of adults who are already handicapped... I sincerely hope that the parens patriae jurisdiction will soon be restored. The corresponding jurisdiction in wardship has continued to prove its value and it is most unfortunate that the court's armoury in relation to adults remains thus depleted. The prospect of restoration of this lost power is not controversial, since it does not conjure up the spectre of euthanasia; the decisions which can be made by the courts on behalf of incompetent persons would, as in wardship cases, be confined within lawful bounds.*
>
> *Procedurally I can see no present alternative to an application to the court... This view is reinforced for me when I reflect, against the background of your Lordship's conclusions of law, that, in the absence of an application, the doctor who proposes the cessation of life-supporting care and treatment on the ground that their continuance would not be in the patient's best interests will have reached that conclusion himself and will be judge in his own cause unless and until his chosen course of action is challenged in criminal or civil proceedings. A practical alternative may, however be evolved ... possibly [by] parliament through legislation, it will of course be understood that the court has no power to render lawful something which without the court's sanction would have been unlawful. When I take into account that the case now before your Lordships could not be clearer on its facts, I have to say that I am left with the feeling that the general position is not very satisfactory"*[276]

Of course some healthcare decisions are so serious[277] that the court must be asked to make a declaration and in these cases the NHS trust or other organisation responsible for the patient's care will usually make the application.[278] Other cases that may be referred to the court are those that present an ethical dilemma, perhaps because treatment is innovative and

---

[276] *Airedale NHS Trust v Bland [1993] 1 All ER 821 HL*

[277] Decisions about the proposed withholding or withdrawal of artificial nutrition and hydration from patients in a permanent vegetative state; cases involving the proposed non-therapeutic sterilisation (e.g. for contraceptive purposes) and cases involving organ or bone marrow donation of persons who lack capacity to consent to these treatments/procedures

[278] Mental Capacity Act 2005, Code of Practice, Chapter Eight, para.8.8

untested.[279] Beyond that the circumstances precipitating referral are likely to involve irresolvable conflicts between healthcare staff and family members or where it is unclear that a proposed serious and invasive treatment is likely to be in the best interests of the patient.[280]

Essentially, the court may only become involved in a case, other than in situations where the court must be asked to make a declaration, because someone opposes what a doctor proposes to do and feels sufficiently strongly about the matter to petition the court.[281] The problem is that not everyone will have someone they can depend upon to act in this way on their behalf. Consider that the person who has disclosed their value system in a living will did not create an LPA for a reason.

The better solution then is to base the doctor-patient relationship on principles of trust as once a fiduciary relationship is established fiduciary obligations are due and the patient as beneficiary is entitled to expect that the doctor will act in all good faith when carrying out their duties in respect of them. Acting in good faith means acting with honesty and integrity[282] and guidance, contained within the Mental Capacity Act's Code of Practice, for LPA's states that this generally means that a fiduciary must try to make sure that their decisions do not go against a decision the patient made while they still had capacity unless it is in their best interests to do so.[283]

Who Decides that a Relationship is a Fiduciary One, and on what Basis?

Whilst trust or dependence is necessary implied in many different types of relationship, for example, trustee and beneficiary, solicitor and client, parent and child, doctor and patient, tutor and student, not all are fiduciary

---

[279] Ibid, para.8.23; *Simms v Simms [2003] 1 All ER 669*

[280] Mental Capacity Act 2005, Code of Practice, Chapter Eight, para.8.24

[281] Ibid, para.8.12

[282] Rodwin, Marc. A., Strains in the Fiduciary Metaphor: Divided Physician Loyalties and Obligations in a Changing Health Care System; American Journal of Law & Medicine, 1995, Vol. XXI Nos. 2&3, pp.241-257, p.244; Hui, E.C., Doctors as Fiduciaries: a legal construct of the patient-physician relationship; 2005, Hong Kong Medical Journal, Vol. 11, No.6, pp.527-29, p.528

[283] Mental Capacity Act 2005, Code of Practice, Chapter Seven, para.7.63

relationships.[284] The issue of whether a relationship should be recognised in this way is determined by courts and by legislation rather than by the individual parties themselves.[285] Consequently, a decision to recognise the fiduciary nature of a relationship is a social and policy choice as well as a legal one.[286]

In this regard inspection of the MCA reveals that LPA's[287] and court-appointed deputies[288] act as the chosen agent of the patient under the law of agency and acquire fiduciary obligations but that doctors do not. As a court-appointed deputy is as much a stranger to the patient as is a doctor it appears that the law of incapacity emphasises that fidelity and loyalty, the absence of a conflict of interests, is the fundamental feature of a fiduciary relationship, not the dependence and vulnerability of the patient.

Doctors as Fiduciaries: Equitable Regulation of the Doctor-Patient Relationship - Revisited

Although doctors perform fiduciary like roles and claim to be fiduciaries in their ethical codes the law fails to recognise the fiduciary like status of the relationship. This presumably is attributable to the divided loyalties of doctors in the practice of modern medicine. The needs of other patients have to be considered. Then there are the institutional interests of the hospital as well as the interests of third parties in various contexts, and the impossibility of a doctor being able to serve each of them simultaneously.[289]

Should divided loyalties, conflict of interests be reason enough to question whether doctors can act as fiduciaries? The status of fidelity within the doctor-patient relationship is contested because it requires medical professionals to put their patient's interests ahead of all others including

[284] Rodwin, Marc. A., Strains in the Fiduciary Metaphor: Divided Physician Loyalties and Obligations in a Changing Health Care System; American Journal of Law & Medicine, 1995, Vol. XXI Nos. 2&3, pp.241-257, p.244

[285] Ibid

[286] Ibid, p.245

[287] Mental Capacity Act 2005, Code of Practice, Chapter Seven, para.7.60

[288] Ibid, Chapter Eight, para.8.58

[289] Rodwin, Marc. A., Strains in the Fiduciary Metaphor: Divided Physician Loyalties and Obligations in a Changing Health Care System; American Journal of Law & Medicine, 1995, Vol. XXI Nos. 2&3, pp.241-257, p.242

their own.[290] Yet it is arguable that trust in one's physician matters more in these circumstances not less. However, Rodwin observes that:

> *"Strains on the fiduciary metaphor may cause the law to adopt other metaphors through which to view physicians. There is already a growing scholarship which advocates dispensing with fiduciary obligations in favour of letting individuals determine their respective obligations by contract. Courts and other legal institutions may cease to consider physicians as fiduciaries or at least let individuals contract out of traditional fiduciary obligations the law imposes as default rules, provided that doctors have properly disclosed relevant information to patients. What are the prospects of this occurring?*
>
> *It seems unlikely that society will quickly abandon the fiduciary metaphor for physicians for a simple reason. Public policy and Market forces are creating pressures for greater physician and provider accountability. And accountability is the core of the fiduciary ideal.*
>
> *How else, besides abandonment, might the law respond to strains on the fiduciary metaphor? Courts and legislatures may work out ways to resolve the competing demands on physicians within a fiduciary framework. Fiduciaries, by definition, owe loyalty to the parties they serve, but the law can define precisely the limits of a fiduciary obligation or specify the interests of different parties for which the fiduciary works. Such definitions of the scope of fiduciary relationships and specification of how to balance interests the fiduciary must serve can provide a means to resolve or at least ease the strains fiduciaries experience.*
>
> *There is ample precedent for balancing competing interests within a fiduciary framework. To be sure, the simplest fiduciary relation is one of undivided loyalty to an individual. Many fiduciaries, however, have to balance the interests of competing individuals or groups. Corporate officers must serve the interest of different groups of stockholders. The trustee must serve the interests of the trust beneficiary and remainderman. Lawyers are expected to be zealous advocates for their clients while they serve as officers of the court and protect the integrity of the judicial system.*
>
> *Therefore, the fact that physicians have obligations to third parties does not mean that they cannot be fiduciaries for patients. Obligations to third parties may merely limit the scope of fiduciary obligation or indicate that physicians are fiduciaries for more than one party. It is only when*

[290] Hui, E.C., Doctors as Fiduciaries: a legal construct of the patient-physician relationship; 2005, Hong Kong Medical Journal, Vol. 11, No.6, pp.527-29, p.527

performing as a fiduciary for one party and working for another that creates too great a conflict and there are no adequate ways to resolve these conflicts that the law says performing both roles is incompatible with fiduciary obligations.

In short, the law may hold doctors to fiduciary standards yet also expect physicians to take adequate account of the interests of many patients or even parties other than patients. The law could hold doctors accountable to patients for specific goals while holding doctors accountable to other parties for other goals. As a result, physicians would be subject to greater oversight and more stringent standards of conduct. It is likely that both private and public sector controls will be used to oversee the conduct of physicians, and with institutional mechanics that are not traditionally used to supervise fiduciaries".[291]

In this respect it is interesting to note that the law distinguishes between status based and fact based fiduciary obligations.[292] With regard to the latter a significant change in the law has taken place regarding a physician's obligation to disclose relevant treatment information that may be useful to us now.[293] For example, in the case of *Sidaway*, the patient claimed that the doctor had failed to advise her about a small but potentially very serious inherent risk of neurosurgery that materialised in the course of the operation and that caused her injury.[294] Therefore, she claimed that in failing to disclose this information the doctor had acted in breach of his duty of care.[295] The House of Lords disagreed holding that what the patient should be told was a matter for a doctor to determine in accordance with the *Bolam* standard, i.e. a practice accepted as proper by a responsible body of medical opinion. Nevertheless their Lordships concluded that where the proposed treatment involved a substantial risk of harm a patient's right to be informed of it when deciding whether to consent was so obvious that no reasonably prudent doctor could fail to

[291] Rodwin, Marc. A., Strains in the Fiduciary Metaphor: Divided Physician Loyalties and Obligations in a Changing Health Care System; American Journal of Law & Medicine, 1995, Vol. XXI Nos. 2&3, pp.241-257, p.255/6

[292] Ibid, p.244; Stauch, Marc, Wheat, Kay with Tingle, John, Sourcebook on Medical Law, 2002, Second Edition, Cavendish Publishing, p.44; Bartlett, Peter, Doctors as Fiduciaries: Equitable Regulation of the Doctor-Patient Relationship, 1997, Medical Law Review, No.5, pp.193-224, p.195

[293] *Chester v Afshar 2004 WL 2289136*

[294] *Sidaway v Board of the Bethlem Royal Hospital and the Maudsley Hospital and Others [1985] AC 871*, p.871

[295] Ibid

mention it save in an emergency or for some other sound clinical reason.[296] Crucially, the law did not disturb the doctor's professional privilege to withhold treatment information that might alarm the patient and thus prevent them from consenting to a treatment or procedure that was on balance more likely to do good than to cause harm.

In the course of argument counsel for the appellant first attempted to persuade their Lordships that the patient had a right to be informed of the risks inherent in the medical treatment that was proposed by the doctor by invoking the doctrine of informed consent.[297] This was rejected because '*it would be deplorable to base the law in medical cases of this kind on the torts of assault and battery*'.[298] The second line of attack was to claim that the relationship between doctor and patient is of a fiduciary nature and to claim that the doctor had not been scrupulously honest with the patient.[299] That attempt also failed as '*there is no comparison to be made between the relationship of doctor and patient with that of solicitor and client, trustee [and beneficiary] or the other relationships treated in equity as of a fiduciary character*'.[300] Nevertheless, added Lord Scarman, '*the relationship of doctor and patient is a very special one, the patient putting his health and his life in the doctor's hands*'.[301]

So the time was not yet right to eliminate the potential for conflict to exist between autonomy and beneficence in terms of what a patient must be told in order for their consent to be regarded, in law at least, as real. But Lord Scarman held out a beacon of hope because he said that:

> *"[T]he circumstances that this House is now called upon to explore new ground is no reason why a rule of informed consent should not be recognised and developed by our courts. The common law is adaptable: it would not otherwise have survived over the centuries of its existence. The concept of negligence itself is a development of the law by the judges over the last hundred years or so. The legal ancestry of the tort of negligence is to be found in the use made by the judges of the action on the case. Damage is the gist of the action. The action on the case was sufficiently flexible to enable the judges to extend it to cover situations where damage*

---

[296] Ibid, p.872
[297] Ibid, p.883
[298] Ibid
[299] Ibid, p.884
[300] Ibid
[301] Ibid

was suffered in circumstances which they judged to call for a remedy. It would be irony indeed if a judicial development for which the opportunity was the presence in the law of a flexible remedy should result now in rigidly confining the law's remedy to situations and relationships already ruled upon by the judges".[302]

And so it came to pass as the more recent case of *Chester v Afshar* demonstrates that doctors should be held accountable to patients in respect of the specific goal of making an informed choice about whether to consent or to refuse to consent to a medical treatment or procedure.[303] This case was unusual because a causal connection could not be established, between the doctor's failure to warn the patient of a small but nonetheless serious inherent risk of surgery that materialised resulting in injury, using the usual causal principle or 'but for' test.[304] So the usual causal principle or 'but for' test was in this case overridden on policy grounds in order that the defendant doctor would bear the risk of the harm that they did not cause;[305] '*did the doctor's breach of duty cause the patient's injury? It would appear that this question can only be answered in the negative. He did nothing which increased the risk to the patient, or even altered it. It was a risk to which she was exposed anyway. It was the same risk, irrespective of when or at whose hands she had the operation*'.[306]

What may be concluded from this case? Well it seems reasonable to conclude that the court did not intend to fundamentally alter the nature of the doctor-patient relationship however if tortious relationships require the application of fiduciary principles, then the courts will impose them in informed consent cases as a means of protecting patient autonomy where such principles ensure a greater level of protection and a more satisfactory outcome in the event of a breach.[307]

---

302 Ibid, p.883/4
303 *Chester v Afshar 2004 WL 2289136*, para.58
304 Ibid, para.65
305 Ibid, para.80
306 Ibid, para.84
307 *Breen v Williams (1996) 186 CLR 71*; see also the USA case *Re Quinlan 70 N.J. 10* where Hughes CJ endorses the view, in this case in respect of an incompetent patient, that 'as part of the inherent power of equity, a Court of Equity, and in the UK all courts apply the common law and rules of equity, has full and complete jurisdiction over the persons of those who labour under any legal disability… The court's action in such a case is not limited by any narrow bounds, but it is empowered to stretch forth its arm in whatever direction its aid and

Where does this leave us in respect of an incompetent patient who has disclosed their value system in a living will? In the absence of fully defined test or method for deciding what is in the incompetent's best interests there is a need to regulate a doctor's approach to decision-making on behalf of a formerly competent patient where their actual wishes can be known and readily understood. In this respect the principle of the least restrictive option embraces many of the ideals of beneficence in trust if the MCA did at the same time distinguish between the circumstances of people similarly situated as the statute De Prerogativa Regis 1324 did by employing fiduciary obligations consistently with those proposed by *Chester v Afshar* to this fact based situation. As autonomy is made an essential element of beneficence a doctor is required to at least prioritise the dignity interests of the patient ahead of their own inclination to act paternalistically. Essentially a doctor is made the agent of an incompetent patient in this limited respect as a matter of necessity.

The Potential for Conflict between Professional and Patient Values

The advantage of casting the doctor-patient relationship in fiduciary terms is that beneficence in trust entails respect for autonomy which allows us to oust the paternalism-autonomy divide and to emphasise the point that medical professionals have an ethical and legal duty to act in the actual best interests of their patients. When beneficence is no longer in conflict with autonomy the only ethical requirement is that each patient must be handled and treated as an individual whose life has intrinsic and personal value.[308] This is why the fiduciary model might be particularly well suited to the situation of an incompetent patient who has disclosed their value system in a living will.[309]

---

protection may be needed. While this is indeed a special exercise of equity jurisdiction, it is beyond question that by virtue thereof the Court may pass upon purely personal rights'.

[308] Pellegrino, Edmund D., Thomasma, David C., The Conflict between Autonomy and Beneficence in Medical Ethics: Proposal for a Resolution, 1987, Journal of Contemporary Health Law and Policy, Volume 3, p.23-46, p.43

[309] Stauch, Marc, Wheat, Kay with Tingle, John, Sourcebook on Medical Law, 2002, Second Edition, Cavendish Publishing, p.44; Pellegrino, Edmund D., Thomasma, David C., The Conflict between Autonomy and Beneficence in Medical Ethics: Proposal for a Resolution, 1987, Journal of Contemporary Health Law and Policy, Volume 3, p.23-46, p.41; Maclean, Alasdair, Briefcase on Medical Law, 2004, Second Edition, Cavendish Publishing, p.12

Does a fiduciary model keep faith with the Kantian notion that persons are the sources of values?[310] In this regard Pellegrino and Thomasma have stated that both doctor and patient must be free to make informed decisions and to act fully as moral agents.[311] The values of both doctor and patient must be respected since each is a person deserving of respect as such.[312] Value consensus results only if each can, without coercion or deception, express their own values meaning that neither party should impose their values on the other just as they may not make use of the other for selfish ends and equally each must be free to withdraw from the relationship if value conflicts cannot be resolved satisfactorily.[313]

Respect for autonomy requires doctors to treat their patients as persons with interests of their own which preserves, rather than compromises, the integrity of the patient. Clearly, the integrity of the patient is compromised whenever they are required to follow the values of others. Moreover, performance of any action that is inconsistent with their critical values threatens their unified identity and thus the notion of integrity. Therefore, respect for autonomy presupposes respect for humanity generally and for each person as an individual and moral equal who has freedom to create a life of their own choosing. In respecting autonomy a fiduciary must respect the inherent value of that life and the choices that have informed it or have shaped it that way. Their purpose in so doing will be to maintain the authenticity of that creative legacy as something that is to be valued for its own sake rather like a skilled or sympathetic restorer of a architecturally significant building or painting would, retaining its lines, dimensions, artefacts or period features recognising that what was once significant about it should remain significant now.

Doctors must also be respected fully as moral agents with values and beliefs of their own. It could not be otherwise as it can hardly be credible to argue why something that is fundamental to all humanity should be true of only one party to a relationship. However, we must also be sufficiently realistic to take account of the facts of human nature and to recognise that

---

[310] Kant's formula for humanity is to the effect that persons should be treated as ends and never merely as the means to the end of any other

[311] Pellegrino, Edmund D., Thomasma, David C., The Conflict between Autonomy and Beneficence in Medical Ethics: Proposal for a Resolution, 1987, Journal of Contemporary Health Law and Policy, Volume 3, p.23-46, p.44

[312] Ibid

[313] Ibid

an imbalance of power in a relationship means that the more powerful party may abuse their position of power in respect of the weaker one. The idea that doctors should act as fiduciaries for their patients goes some way to addressing this particular problem.

Nevertheless, a doctor's values and beliefs are also likely to be the source of their own particular idiosyncrasies or biases and prejudices. These may or may not be problematic according to the degree to which they are allowed to affect or infect the way in which an individual doctor might approach their decision-making responsibilities in respect of an incompetent patient. In particular there is a need to examine the potential for decision-makers to override the values of the patient, not wilfully perhaps, but due to the subconscious imposition of the decision-makers own values.[314]

For instance, what is the place of personal morality or individual conscience when medicine is accounted for in fiduciary terms? This is what Rosamond Rhodes has to say on the subject:

> *"A frequently overlooked issue [in the practice of medicine] is the place of personal morality or individual conscience. Again the problem is not unique to the medical profession. In the military, soldiers owe obedience to the chain of command. Those in the military are not free to make their own judgments about which military actions are justified and how much force is appropriate. Instead they are obliged to follow the orders of higher ranking officers, who, in turn, must follow the direction of their political authorities. Similarly, lawyers and judges are not free to make decisions based on their own values and personal conscience. They are committed to following the rule of law even when their personal values dictate a different conclusion. Whereas the fact that professional responsibility overrides personal values is well accepted in other fields, those who write about the ethics of medicine typically ignore this element in their discussions, while some who consider the matter offer no justification but champion personal conscience over professional responsibility... The account of the ethics of medicine based on fiduciary responsibility and trust, leads, however, to the opposite conclusion.*
>
> *... [D]octors are primarily trusted because of their role. Patients and society expect doctors to act in accordance with the Ethical Standard of Care, and they rely upon them to meet that shared standard in all that they do... This means that medical practice is not a matter of private judgment.*

[314] The idea of my supervisor Ms Kay Wheat

Rather, medical decisions should be the ones that any competent physician facing a comparable clinical situation would endorse as a matter of professional judgment.

Just as disagreements over treatment decisions have to be resolved by turning to the available evidence and the standard of care, conflicts between principles of medical ethics that arise in individual cases have to be resolved in terms of principle related reasons that other medical professionals would also find compelling. Deviations from the Ethical Standard of Care have to be justified to peers in terms of principles of medical ethics or by special considerations about the patient's anatomy or values that colleagues from the profession would endorse as relevant reasons for a departure given the particular circumstances. In other words, we expect physicians to consult the clinical and ethical standards of care, rather than their individual heart or hearts in making medical decisions...

In other words, personal priorities and personal assessment of risk have no place in the response of the medical professional. Individuals who have committed themselves to uphold the professional responsibilities of medicine, have, in essence, endorsed the Ethical Standard of Care, rather than personal conscience as their principles for making medical decisions...

When a physician chooses to act on his own values instead of honouring his patient's, the physician puts his own interest in ease of conscience above the fiduciary responsibility that is the defining feature of the ethics of medicine. The doctor who chooses to avoid personal psychic distress, declares his willingness to impose burdens of time, inconvenience, financial costs, and rebuke on his patients so that he might feel pure. Someone who places his own interests above his patients' departs from medicine's standard of promoting the patient's good and violates a crucial tenet of medical ethics that every physician is duty bound to observe".[315]

The foregoing clearly emphasises the priority of professional ethics over personal morality. Though the extent to which this may safeguard the interests of incompetent patients against the vagaries of medical professional decision-making is to an extent unknown. This is because medical professionals have also entered into both a knowledge based and values based profession and whilst empiricism is emphasised in medical

---

[315] Rhodes, Rosamond, The Professional Responsibilities of Medicine, The Blackwell Guide to Medical Ethics, (2007, Blackwell Publishing), Chapter 4, p.83-5

doctrine it is still possible for medical knowledge to be interpreted and explained in different ways.[316] We acknowledge this by requiring physicians to be professionally competent in the performance of their duties. So doctors must make decisions and act in accordance with their profession's rules and standards but these too are sufficiently flexible to support the various interpretations that may be placed on medical knowledge.

So it may be no less difficult for medical professionals to carry out their fiduciary obligations in practice at either stage one or two of the medical treatment decision-making process. Here, as has been mentioned in other contexts, human judgment cannot be eliminated from treatment decision-making processes and so the mentally incapacitated patient is still reliant upon the subjective deliberations of a medical professional. In this regard Pellegrino and Thomasma have remarked that physicians must be persons of personal moral integrity. They go on to state that:

> *"The physician must have the capacity to make prudential judgments that factor in the particulars of each case, the general features of the disease and general moral principles. Ultimately, the good of the patient depends as much on the physician's character as his capacity to make these judgments. Furthermore, it depends on the extent to which he can be trusted to keep the good of the patient as his primary aim. In a morally pluralistic society, there is a tendency to downplay moral character in the education of the physician. However, there are qualities of moral judgment that should apply to all physicians and for this they will need to be educated. As Aristotle noted, "it is impossible, or not easy, to do noble acts without the proper equipment". Yet skills without moral integrity, will not suffice in those moments when no one is there to watch, thus the good of the patient hangs on the moral integrity of the physician".*[317]

How realistic is it then to suppose that medical professionals will act any differently from any other persons in always showing sufficient strength of character to both empower and temper the will as occasion demands when history demonstrates mankind's susceptibility to weakness of the will

---

[316] Objective and subjective value of science – empirical methods to test theories however truths can only be known within the context of a particular experiment – subjectively valuable because of the particular persuasions of an individual practitioner

[317] Pellegrino, Edmund D., Thomasma, David C., The Conflict between Autonomy and Beneficence in Medical Ethics: Proposal for a Resolution, 1987, Journal of Contemporary Health Law and Policy, Volume 3, p.23-46, p.44

when subjected to various external and internal pressures to do otherwise? Remember the ascendancy of any party in a relationship can mean that the ascendant's class interests are maintained at the expense of the other who is vulnerable to the former's exploitation and manipulation. How do we know, for example, whether a doctor has been negligent or has acted from morally indifferent or objectionable motives in deciding what ought to happen in their patient's best interests? Shouldn't we be as equally interested in a doctor's capacity to make decisions that are moral and rational at both stages of the treatment decision-making process?

Stage One of a Treatment Decision-making Process

The law upholds a professional's right to clinical freedom in determining what form of treatment is in the best interests of an individual patient.[318] A spiralling healthcare budget means that health policy now focuses on the population rather than individual patients.[319] Whilst on the one hand economic considerations are attributable to the success of modern medicine they have on the other hand given rise to a potential conflict which is as between individual and general well-being. So at the first stage of a treatment decision there is a continuing expectation that physicians should be just in their use of a valuable resource, i.e. medicines and so on. Hence the fact that the decisions doctors make can make a vast difference to the lives of patients and that those decisions often involve value choices. In other words a doctor will most often take account of resource issues when using his or her medical knowledge.

Clearly there is a need to be practical when funds are finite but a doctor's dual role in serving patients and also guarding NHS resources provides scope for hidden values to become manifest in clinical decisions concerning individual patients. As they cannot detach themselves from economic matters what interpretation should be given to beneficence in trust at stage one of a treatment decision-making process? Dworkin has explained that the right to beneficence is a right that doctors make decisions in their patient's best interests but that they, like a trustee, must work with what they have. It is not a right that particular resources be put at the disposal of the fiduciary. This means that the right only governs the

---

[318] *R (On the Application of Oliver Leslie Burke) v The General Medical Council [2005] EWCA Civ 1003*

[319] A doctor must be appropriately beneficent

use of whatever resources are in fact available for the beneficiary's care.[320] So should patients have a right to informed denial of care, for example? In this regard Newdick asks how should law and ethics respond?

Informed Denial of Care

"A strong pragmatic case can be made that there should be a duty to disclose the reasons for rationing treatment. Patients refused access to care on economic grounds for whom treatment could provide valuable medical benefit, ought to be able to consider arranging their finances so that it could be provided privately. They may be denied that opportunity unless the reasons for the decision not to treat are made clear. The patient might wish to modify the way in which the system of priorities has been set, organise a petition, or raise money through charity, or write to his or her MP.

Some patients may have their own resources for obtaining medical care. Others may choose to invest their energies in trying to change rationing policies rather than passively accepting them. In any event, many patients may have personal or professional priorities and commitments that would change in the light of full, truthful information about their medical conditions and treatment options. To deny such patients such information is to compromise the exercise of personal autonomy, the raison d'etre of the informed consent doctrine.

Also, as a matter of principle, the law of disclosure is intended to promote the relationship of trust and confidence between doctor and patient, based on a collaboration where "decisions are made through frank discussion, in which the doctor's clinical expertise and the patient's individual needs and preferences are shared, to select the best option". There is a risk that, unless medical decisions based on economic considerations are also disclosed to the patient, the relationship will be eroded".[321]

A Duty to Disclose

Bearing in mind that clinicians have specialised knowledge and skill and access to medicines, procedures or specialist advice they are in the best position to understand both the clinical merits of medical treatments and procedures and the needs of their patients so do doctors have a duty to

[320] Dworkin, Ronald, Life's Dominion: An argument about Abortion and Euthanasia, Harper Collins, p.229

[321] Newdick, Christopher, Who Should we Treat? 2005, Second Edition, Oxford University Press, p.160-1

disclose information of this nature?[322] Well the law of informed consent has developed out of the law of battery and it is concerned with the unlawful touching of another's body and no touching would arise in this instance.[323] The better alternative then is to stress the importance of trust and confidence in the doctor-patient relationship and to state that one of the purposes of this trust and confidence is to enable patients, to understand the choices and to make informed decisions for themselves.[324] This of course is entirely consistent with recent developments in the common law which has stripped away a doctor's professional privilege to withhold relevant treatment information that might alarm the patient.[325] Crucially what is custom and practice within the medical profession has to give way to the need to vindicate the moral rights of patients. As the law clearly respects that we are masters over our bodies with the right to determine what should happen to us it is a logical extension of that principle to argue that the right is not properly recognised if we are denied information we would wish to know to protect our health and well-being.[326]

Moreover, none of this need displace a doctor's clinical freedom as Newdick explains:

> *"Trust will never thrive if patients suspect there is a hidden rationing agenda dominating the doctor's decision-making process. So far as possible, decisions of this nature should not be taken covertly, at the bedside, by the doctor who happens to be on duty at the time, depending on his or her own perceptions and prejudices. They should be taken within a clear, consistent, and cogent priorities framework to which patients have free access. Thus, doctors' responsible clinical freedom should remain intact unless the proposed treatment is subject to guidance within the ethical framework. In this way, doctors can retain the trust of the patient and be open about the funding constraints imposed upon them. Such an approach is surely desirable in principle for supporting the doctor-patient relationship.*

---

[322] Ibid, p.164

[323] *Re F (Mental Patient: Sterilisation) [1990] 2 AC 1*; Newdick, Christopher, Who Should we Treat? 2005, Second Edition, Oxford University Press, p.161

[324] Newdick, Christopher, Who Should we Treat? 2005, Second Edition, Oxford University Press, p.161

[325] *Chester v Afshar 2004 WL 2289136*

[326] Newdick, Christopher, Who Should we Treat? 2005, Second Edition, Oxford University Press, p.161

Doctors obliged to make resource-sensitive decisions should be able to say to the patient:

(1) I will always act in your best interests.
(2) Sometimes, for reasons of NHS policy, treatment may be available only in limited circumstances. I will inform you of that policy.
(3) If you have experienced need for treatment which is not generally available I will inform you about it.
(4) In such a case I will, if you wish, advise the health authority of your special need and request that you be treated as an exceptional case.

In this way, in an environment which recognises the need for hard choices, patients could be reassured of the doctor's commitment to their best interests and of his or her willingness to act as their advocate in favour of exceptional care. Given the institutional constraints that may be imposed upon them, the commitment may fall short of a guarantee of treatment. Instead, it is to promote patients' best interests within the confines imposed by the system as a whole. A failure to commit to this principle and, instead, to encourage the mistaken belief that care will always be provided on the basis of patient need alone will surely hasten the erosion of patients' trust in doctors" ...[327]

It is a fact of life that demand outstrips supply and that we cannot always have things that we want or would like due to the equal claims of others. However, doctors do act as gatekeepers to what is a valuable resource. So what is important to the patient is that doctors should be open and transparent regarding the facts of their decision and any assumptions they may have made unless duty is to be a chimerical concept. Higher standards ought reasonably to be imposed to reflect the significance of the subject of their decision-making. Well at least it should if we are serious when we say that human life has intrinsic and personal value to the person whose life it is, and we must be otherwise what justifies IVF treatment and gene therapy for example. This engenders trust because the doctor is seem to maintain his independence and integrity as a member of the medical profession and the public understand more about what that entails. None of this should be seen as an affront to the dignity of doctors. If we think about state welfare benefits, for example, it is apparent that the state will seek to claw back what a person would otherwise be entitled to if they obtain an income from elsewhere. Those receiving benefits have a legal duty to report this otherwise they face a penalty, including possible

[327] Ibid, p.164

imprisonment, for defrauding the welfare office if they fail to comply. So the morality of not informing patients about cost issues, i.e. factors considered and dismissed, raises moral concerns that would have to be justified if the practice is to continue. Of course we don't want doctors reduced to reading out the sort of disclaimers made by those institutions that are regulated by the Financial Services Authority, the majority of which are fairly meaningless to most persons anyway, rather something of the ilk that Newdick proposes should serve us well enough. Though I would just add that perhaps the doctor should also ask him or herself the rhetorical question would I in these circumstances accept my advice; do I prescribe medications that I would not take myself or would I take alternative measures to protect my own life and well-being.

What I am getting at is that transparency at stage one is a necessary pre-requisite to establishing real autonomy within the democratic process, i.e. whereby the people can decide whether a practice is right or wrong based on its implications for human and civil life. Changing the conditions under which justice is dispensed in medicine should eventually lead to greater equality between patients because a doctor's practice would actually be regulated by this process. Remember bankers got drawn into taking ever greater risks as a consequence of the bonus culture and this has wide ranging implications for the rest of the population and the world economy and will continue to do so for years to come.

Stage Two of a Treatment Decision-making Process

Earlier on in this section I mentioned that a fiduciary model has the potential within it to remove the paternalism-autonomy divide and for that reason may be particularly well suited to the medical care of an incompetent patient who has disclosed their value system in a living will. A doctor's ethical duty is to act in a patient's best interests taking into consideration their values, beliefs and preferences or critical and experiential interests. The problem is that a patient and doctor may take a different view of the former's best interests. Consequently, the right of beneficence differs from the right to autonomy and may in some circumstances be in conflict with it, when for example, a demented patient's current best interests are at odds with their precedent autonomy when competent. Is that conflict genuine and which obligation is overriding?

Beneficence vs Precedent Autonomy

On this matter Dworkin has stated that:

"If it is then a person's present right to beneficence when demented, would be a reason to ignore their precedent autonomy, to make them happy now is spite of whatever the patient had directed before.

There is no reason to doubt that a demented person has a right to beneficence, but we face an obvious problem in considering the consequences of that right. What are the best interests of someone seriously and permanently demented? Previously I emphasised the distinction between what I called experiential and critical interests and that distinction is indispensable now.

Even a seriously demented person (unlike someone in a persistent vegetative state) has experiential interests. But by the time the dementia has become advanced, Alzheimer's victims have lost the capacity to think about how to make their lives more successful as a whole. They are ignorant of self, because they have no sense of a whole life, a past joined to a future, that could be the object of any evaluation or concern as a whole. They cannot have projects or plans of the kind that leading a critical life requires. They therefore have no contemporary opinion about their own critical interests.

Nevertheless they continue to have such interests [such as] when we consider how the fate of a demented person can affect the character of his life, we consider the patient's whole life, not just its sad final stages, and we consider his future in terms of how it affects the character of the whole.

In many respects the demented person is in the same position as an unconscious, persistently vegetative patient. But there is an important difference. If I am convinced that it would spoil my life to be kept alive for years as a vegetable, I can act on the conviction with no prospect of conflict, by signing a living will directing that I be allowed to die. But I know that if I become demented, I will probably want to go on living, and that I may then still be capable of primitive experiential pleasures ... Would it be in my best interests to go on living like that, or to die as soon as possible?

People disagree sharply about that excruciating question. Roughly half are repelled by the idea of living demented, totally dependent lives, speaking gibberish, incapable of understanding that there is a world beyond them, let alone of following its course. They do not think that the possible childish pleasures of dementia would redeem its curse; some think the capacity to enjoy such pleasures would be part of that curse. They would prefer not to live on. But half take the other view. They do not think that a demented life is worse than no life at all, and for them the meagre childish pleasures are better than nothing.

People in the first group may consider signing living wills stipulating that if they become permanently and seriously demented, and then develop a serious disease, they should not be given medical treatment except to avoid pain. Respect for their autonomy would be a reason for doing what they ask. But I raised the question whether there might be a conflict between respecting their autonomy and serving their best interests. Is there a conflict between respecting precedent autonomy if a living will has been signed and doing what would later be in her best interests? Is this like the case in which we have to choose between respecting a Jehovah's Witness's autonomy and giving him a lifesaving transfusion after he falls unconscious?

Of course there is a conflict between precedent autonomy and a person's contemporary experiential interests if that person is still enjoying their life, but there is no conflict with her critical interests as that person would themselves conceive them when competent or if competency could temporarily be restored. If I decide when I was competent that it would be best for me not to remain alive in a seriously and permanently demented state, then a fiduciary could contradict me only by exercising an unacceptable form of moral paternalism. Once we rule out that form of paternalism, once we accept that we must judge a person's critical interests as she did when competent to do so, then the conflict between autonomy and beneficence seems to disappear. If a person has asked not to be given medical care for life-threatening illnesses contracted after they had become demented, neither their right to autonomy nor their right to beneficence would give grounds for denying that request, even if the demented person is enjoying their life. We cannot say that we would be showing compassion for them if we refused to do what they wanted when they were competent, because that would not be compassionate toward the whole person, the person who tragically became demented. We might have other reasons for refusing to endorse the living will, we might find ourselves unable to deny medical help to anyone who is conscious and does not reject it, but we cannot claim to be acing for their sake.

It would be a mistake to resist this conclusion on the ground that letting them die in these circumstances would be irrevocable. After all both choices, to honour or not to honour a past request are irrevocable. But consider a different objection: that in the circumstances of dementia, critical interests become less important and experiential interests more so, so that fiduciaries may rightly ignore the former and concentrate on the latter. It is true, I said, that demented people have no sense of their own critical interests, but before that, when they were competent, they did, and we cannot disregard this or think it no longer matters. Persistently vegetative patients have no sense of their own critical interests, but that is not a good reason for ignoring their fate, and it is not a good reason for ignoring the demented either". [328]

Consequently, it is important that surrogate decision-makers are able to comprehend and appreciate the importance of the distinction between critical and experiential interests in order for them to understand which obligation is overriding and thus how people must be treated at the end of life. Indeed Dworkin uses this distinction to explain why a patient's right to dignity,[329] which is an essential element of autonomy, is thought to be more fundamental even than their right to beneficence.[330] Do the demented have a right to dignity?

Dignity vs Beneficence

"Self-respect like autonomy requires a degree of general competence and, especially, a sense of self-identity over time, which seriously demented people have lost. [331]

So on the experiential account of dignity, it seems dubious that the demented have any general right to dignity, and concern for their self-respect does seem only expensive sentimentality, like providing hairdressers for the comatose. Of course we may still think it important to maintain the demented in circumstances of dignity out of respect for the sensibilities of their relatives or others who might otherwise suffer outrage and guilt. But if the patient himself suffers no distinctive distress of indignity, his relatives might be led to see that their own indignation and guilt are misplaced. In any case, respect for the feelings of others does not require us to recognise a right of dignity for demented patients who have no relatives or friends.

This experiential account of indignity is unpersuasive, however, because it does not explain central features of our convictions about dignity...

What other account of the right to dignity can explain all this? Why is indignity a special kind of harm, whether self-inflicted or inflicted by

---

[328] Dworkin, Ronald, Life's Dominion: An argument about Abortion and Euthanasia, Harper Collins, p.229-32

[329] To live in conditions in which genuine self-respect is possible

[330] Dworkin, Ronald, Life's Dominion: An argument about Abortion and Euthanasia, Harper Collins, p.233

[331] Ibid, p.234

others, and why does it seem worse when the indignity is not recognised by its victims? I have been arguing that we not only have in common with all sensate creatures, experiential interests in the quality of our future experiences but also critical interests in the character and value of our lives as a whole. These critical interests are connected to our convictions about the intrinsic value, the sanctity or inviolability of our own lives. A person worries about his critical interests because he thinks it important what kind of a life he has led, important for its own sake and not simply for the experiential pleasure that leading a valuable life (or believing it valuable) might or might not have given him. A person's right to be treated with dignity, is the right that others acknowledge his genuine critical interests; that they acknowledge that he is the kind of creature, and has the moral standing, such that it is intrinsically, objectively important how his life goes. Dignity is a central aspect of the value we have in the intrinsic importance of human life.

Putting it this way explains how and why the right to dignity is different from the right to beneficence. We can acknowledge that it is important how someone's life goes without accepting any general positive obligation to make it go better. The distinction is necessary to explain the pervasiveness of our concern with dignity, why we insist, on the dignity even of prisoners. When we jail someone convicted of a crime in order to deter others, we do not treat him with beneficence, on the contrary we act against his interests for the general benefit. But we insist that he be treated with dignity in accordance with our understanding of what that requires, that he not be tortured, or humiliated, for example because we continue to regard him as a full human being, as someone whose fate we continue to treat as a matter of concern. Requiring his custodians to respect his dignity shows, among other things, that we appreciate the gravity of what we are doing; that we understand we are jailing a human being whose life matters, that our reasons for doing so are reasons we believe both require and justify this terrible injury, that we are not entitled to treat him as a mere object at the full disposal of our convenience, as if all that mattered was the usefulness, for the rest of us, of locking him up.[332] *(Understanding that dignity means recognising a person's critical interests, as distinct from advancing those interests, provides a useful reading of the Kantian principle that people should be treated as ends and never merely as means. That principle so understood does not require that people never be put at a disadvantage for the advantage of others, but rather that people never be treated in a way that denies the distinct importance of their own lives.) ...*

[332] Ibid, p.236

> *This general account of the meaning of dignity explains our sense that people care or should care for their own dignity. Someone who compromises his own dignity denies, in whatever language his community provides, a sense of himself as someone with critical interests, the value of whose life is important for its own sake. That is self-betrayal. And our account also explains why indignity is most serious when its victim no longer suffers from the indignity. For a person who accepts indignity accepts the classification implicit in it, and accepting that one's life lacks the critical importance of other lives, that it is less intrinsically important how it goes, is a great and sad defeat...*
>
> *Does a seriously demented person have a right to dignity in their custodial care? Yes. A person who has become demented retains his critical interests because what happens to him then affects the value or success of his life as a whole. That he remains a person, and that the overall value of his life continues to be intrinsically important, are decisive truths in favour of his right to dignity. Now we may complete the argument. We mark his continued moral standing and we affirm the importance of the life he has lived, by insisting that nothing be done to or for him that, in our community's vocabulary of respect, denies him dignity. Though dignity is different from beneficence it would be inconsistent to deny dignity while recognising the critical interests that it confirms. So here is yet more proof of the dominating grip of the idea that human life has intrinsic as well as personal importance for human beings, the complex but inescapable idea that it is, sacred".*[333]

Modelling the doctor-patient relationship along fiduciary lines keeps faith with the Kantian ideal of respect for persons, i.e. that persons have moral worth and dignity. Therefore, it is imperative in the moral life that persons should always be treated as an end and never solely as the means to the end of any other. Consequently, doctors who fail to recognise and act on the distinction between a person's experiential and critical interests would cause harm to the patient and be in breach of their obligation to be non-maleficent.

Finally, can we rely on the judgment of others? Bear in mind that substituted judgment does not form part of our law because it is a fallacy to suppose that anybody can think and act as the patient would. We saw evidence of this in relation to the ability to predict the preferences of those we are close to which will come as no surprise to those who are familiar with the game show Mr and Mrs. So we must return to Kant for guidance

[333] Ibid, p.238

because although a doctor cannot think like the patient he or she can reason and make decisions that cohere with rules, laws etc.[334] Still that does not necessarily address the problem of decision-makers infecting a decision-making process with their own biases and prejudices. In this regard Kant thought that persons who can by definition reason should be equally capable of abstracting from personal differences when acting under various constraints as a legislator in a kingdom of ends.[335] All gloriously theoretical, I know, but doctors are already doing this as they are morally and legally required to be appropriately beneficent, not paternalistic. Nevertheless, human judgment cannot be eliminated from the decision-making process and Kant determined that a person's attitude was critical to the way in which they interpreted their responsibilities to others. According to Kant only someone who has a good will[336] has the capacity to make decisions that are both moral and logical.

Kantian Good Will

Before we get to Kant let us return for a moment to Maslow's hierarchy of needs because he recognised that values differ in kind and in suggesting that there is a spiritual dimension to self-actualisation he clearly did not think that all values are commensurable or could be accounted for in terms of a single standard of measurement as Bentham had suggested. Human life, according to Maslow, should not be all about deciding what you want to become and then doing whatever you can to realise your goals. He claims that in order for each individual to become the best that they are capable of or to realise their true potential they must also have the capacity to transcend their sense of self and to instead think of others and their needs. By which he means that persons should seek to be more objective or to look beyond personal biases and prejudices, which simple toleration might preserve, in any situation where the interests of others are engaged. So we are on the road to enlightenment when we are willing to respect others and to regard their interests as equal to our own. Furthermore, in depicting a hierarchy of needs Maslow is suggesting that the individual

---

[334] Categorical imperatives, so act that your maxim of action does not permit of any contradictions, i.e. it can be universally applied

[335] A more ordinary way of putting this is to say that Kant determined that persons are capable of putting differences to one side when they come together to decide what is in the common good

[336] Kantian good will is a secular form of the biblical notion 'love thy neighbour as you love yourself', i.e. adopt an attitude of respectful friendship toward others or treat others as you would like to be treated yourself

decisions and activities of persons, though they may not recognise it as such, have an ultimate end that can be explained in rational terms on the basis of human psychology.[337]

Thus it is rational for persons to see that we all have similar needs that we will seek to satisfy in our various ways and so the rules of life apply equally well to all of us.[338] When a person is disposed to think in these terms they will also be motivated to act well toward others.[339] This, I think, is what Kant is trying to get at when he says that a person who does the right thing for the right reason evinces a good will and a good will is the only thing to which we should attribute unconditional worth.[340] A good will is good through its willing which means that it is only through actions that are expressive of it that we see this special value realised.[341]

So according to Kant, the moral worth of an action consists not in the consequences that flow from it, but in the intention from which the act is done. What matters is the motive, and the motive must be of a certain kind. What matters is doing the right thing because it's right, not for some ulterior motive.[342] Therefore what gives a morally good action its special value is the motivation behind it and if we can discover the principle on which it was chosen or in Kantian terms willed we will have knowledge of what principle a genuinely beneficent person such as a rescuer has acted upon and what makes them morally good.[343]

---

[337] Whilst there is no single view of what a good life entails some consider that humans are psychology disposed to seek to satisfy certain ends

[338] Kant, Mill, Bentham, Raz and Dworkin, for instance, all make this point but express it in different ways

[339] In a sense this is a secular version of the biblical principle 'love your neighbour as you love yourself'. This is the standard, according to that tradition, by which the decisions and actions of mankind should be measured. Thus one is made accountable for personal conduct in accordance with this ideal standard.

[340] Gregor, Mary (Editor), Korsgaard, Christine M. (Introduction), Kant: Groundwork of the Metaphysics of Morals, 2006, Cambridge University Press, p.xi

[341] Ibid

[342] Sandel, Michael J., Justice: What's the Right Thing To Do?, 2010, Penguin Books, Chapter Five, p.111

[343] Ibid

We must have a certain conception of the motives from which the person acted if we wish to attribute unconditional value to an action.[344] Although you may remember from chapter one that Jonathan Glover was there concerned about discovering the real facts through re-descriptions of acts and he thought that this made moral evaluation that much more difficult.

Kant was however more concerned with determining which actions are morally good as a means to discover what the moral law tells us to do.[345] As if to get around Glover's point Kant focuses on a particular class of morally good actions, those that are done from duty: duty because persons who perform their duty will do so under 'certain subjective limitations and hindrances, i.e. they have other motives which, in the absence of duty might have led them to avoid the action.[346] The point is that when a person acts on the principle of duty before self, not otherwise wanting to, we know that the thought of duty alone has produced the action rather than something that can be traced to some direct or indirect self-interested principle of action, such as inclination or desire.[347] Hence actions that are derived from self-interest lack moral worth because the action, however morally commendable, pleases them. Whereas the person who acts from duty makes it their maxim to help because they conceive that helping others is something that is required of them. In this way the person who acts from duty thinks that the needs of others make a claim on them that one has an obligation to respond to.[348]

Thus Korsgaard writes that:

> *"Kant thinks that performing an action because you regard the action or its end as one that is required of you is equivalent to being moved by the thought of the maxim of the action as a kind of law. The dutiful person*

---

[344] Gregor, Mary (Editor), Korsgaard, Christine M. (Introduction), Kant: Groundwork of the Metaphysics of Morals, 2006, Cambridge University Press, p.xii

[345] Ibid

[346] Ibid

[347] Gregor, Mary (Editor), Korsgaard, Christine M. (Introduction), Kant: Groundwork of the Metaphysics of Morals, 2006, Cambridge University Press, p.xiii; Sandel, Michael J., Justice: What's the Right Thing To Do?, 2010, Penguin Books, Chapter Five, p.112

[348] Gregor, Mary (Editor), Korsgaard, Christine M. (Introduction), Kant: Groundwork of the Metaphysics of Morals, 2006, Cambridge University Press, p.xiv

> *takes the maxim of helping others to express or embody a requirement, just as a law does. In Kant's terminology, she sees the maxim of helping others as having the form of a law. When we think that a certain maxim expresses a requirement, or has the form of a law, that thought itself is an incentive to perform the action. Kant calls this incentive 'respect for law'.*
>
> *We now know what gives actions done from duty their special moral worth. They get their moral worth from the fact that the person who does them acts from respect for law. A good person is moved by the thought that his or her maxim has the form of a law. The principle of a good will, therefore, is to do only those actions whose maxims can be conceived as having the form of a law. If there is such a thing as moral obligation, if, as Kant himself says, 'duty is not to be everywhere an empty delusion and a chimerical concept', then we must establish that our wills are governed by this principle: "I ought never to act except in such a way that I could also will that my maxim should become a universal law".* [349]

Therefore the Kantian view, like the consequentialist one, does not give rational priority to self-interest or satisfaction of one's own preferences.[350] Hill adds that:

> *"There is, as it were, a common rational source for both self-regarding and other-regarding requirements. Thus, on the Kantian view, though the question arises why is it really rational to follow the (self-regarding and other regarding) norms we call moral, the task of answering this question is not equated with showing that what is obviously rational (self-interest or preference satisfaction maximisation), despite appearances, really supports what was dubiously rational (moral regard for others). Whether the issue concerns one's own life or the life of another, the question to ask is whether reasonable, autonomous legislators, under the various Kantian constraints, can justify to each other the treatment that is proposed. In effect the Kantian idea of reasonable deliberation (like common sense) has built into it concern for the voice of every reasonable person.*[351]

Will Reform of the Mental Capacity Act 2005 be Necessary?

Surprisingly little needs to be done in this regard since most of what is needed is already in place. So it is more a question of how existing

---

[349] Ibid, p.xv

[350] Hill, Thomas E. Jr., Human Welfare and Moral Worth: Kantian Perspectives, 2002, Oxford University Press, p.159

[351] Ibid

provisions should be interpreted when someone has disclosed their values or value system in a living will. The principle of the least restrictive option recognises the fiduciary nature of the doctor-patient relationship. To that extent we have beneficence in trust. Moreover, that principle applies to all provisions of the MCA and therefore to every decision-making process under it. Accordingly, legal provisions must be interpreted consistently with that principle, including those related to capacity assessments. It is also apparent that a living will can be constituted by a value system or values but in cases where these do not amount to an advance decision one can take the form of a relevant written statement of the patient whereupon it should be accorded particular weight by third parties when making decisions and acting in the patient's best interests. In cases where patients have sought to separate their values into the essential and preferable factors that give their life personal meaning and purpose it is clear that where the patient is sentient but incompetent and there is a conflict between current and former interests that doctors should prioritise the former autonomous wishes or life choices of the patient over current experiential interests since the MCA, and relevant case law, suggests adherence to an integrity view of autonomy. Thereby the reasonable person or purely objective decision-making standard traditionally associated with best interests is displaced in favour of a limited objective approach that seeks to preserve the subjective standards of a formerly competent patient since the obligation is to be loyal to the wishes of the patient.

Three matters remain. The first concerns capacity assessments and the obligation to disclose relevant treatment information. This should be in accordance with the prudent patient standard proposed in *Chester v Afshar*. Secondly, a potential conflict of interests arises at the first stage of a treatment decision and an incompetent patient has the disadvantage of being unable to challenge the treatment decision of the doctor. Therefore, when doctors act as the agent of the patient it seems reasonable and proper for them to give an account of their decision. Lastly, to ensure that the patient's autonomous wishes are given full effect it is important to adopt a rational method when deciding what should happen in their best interests and in this regard I propose that doctors should seek to ensure that their decision coheres with the patient's values and past decisions. This way there will be no advantage in maintaining that a patient is competent to make a decision when they are compliant with medical opinion and conversely to claim that the patient is incompetent to decide when they raise objections to it because a doctor will be required to make a decision that is consistent with the values, beliefs and preferences of the patient.

How does a Doctor Differ from an LPA?

A fiduciary standard requires decision-makers to maximise the interests of the beneficiary and to exercise loyalty[352] and good faith in the performance of their duties.[353] As Sallyanne Payton suggested[354] there is an underlying concern with the agent's state of mind and a fiduciary standard requires the decision-maker to adopt an attitude of respectful friendship toward the incompetent person, just as though they were to be accountable to the person where they to recover their faculties and become competent once more.[355]

The notion of an accounting, which the MCA preserves,[356] is intended to promote honesty, transparency, fairness and an absence of intent to do harm when acting on behalf of an otherwise vulnerable person.[357] As a doctor could be required to give an account of decisions made and action taken this should narrow the scope for paternalistic tendencies to emerge, would prevent arbitrary and other misuse of executive powers and lead to certainty and confidence in surrogate decision-making processes, including in circumstances where a doctor is known to have torn loyalties.

The Need of a Central Registry

In common with the situation of those who make advance decisions those who disclose their value system in a living will currently have no way of knowing that their decisions or values will be respected in the future as we

---

[352] Mental Capacity Act 2005, Code of Practice, Chapter Seven, para.7.60

[353] Ibid, para.7.63; Payton S., The Concept of the Person in the Parens Patriae Jurisdiction over Previously Competent Persons, Journal of Medicine and Philosophy, 1992, December, 17(6), pp.605-45

[354] See Chapter Four

[355] Mental Capacity Act 2005, Code of Practice, Chapter Seven, para.7.63; Payton S., The Concept of the Person in the Parens Patriae Jurisdiction over Previously Competent Persons, Journal of Medicine and Philosophy, 1992, December, 17(6), pp.605-45

[356] Mental Capacity Act 2005, Code of Practice, Chapter Five, para.5.15

[357] The Concept of the Person in the Parens Patriae Jurisdiction over Previously Competent Persons, Journal of Medicine and Philosophy, 1992, December, 17(6), pp.605-45

have no facility with which to register and place these documents. Interestingly, this is not the fate of those who wish to appoint an LPA to manage their affairs when they are no longer competent to do so themselves as their documents must be registered at the office of the Public Guardian.[358] Perhaps this principle could be extended to include the situation of persons who have disclosed their value system in a living will. Alternatively, the NHS is currently undertaking to computerise health records and consequently it might be possible to register a value system that way.

What Implications flow from requiring Doctors to uphold a Fiduciary Standard of Care?

Earlier in this chapter I made reference to the fact that a doctor who fails to respect a valid and applicable advance directive can be found liable for a battery and that this was because they are not acting for or on behalf of someone who lacks capacity but on the instructions of a capacitated individual.[359] If dignity is an aspect of autonomy and a person cares about the inherent value of their own life that person will want to live in conditions in which genuine self-respect is possible[360] which means in a manner that is befitting with what has gone before.[361] Consequently, what is a dignified life for them will be most vividly illustrated by those critical interests that were significant in it.[362] As a person's critical interests are connected to our convictions about the intrinsic value, i.e. the sanctity or inviolability of our own life, then a person's right to be treated with dignity, Dworkin suggests, is the right that others acknowledge their genuine critical interests: that they acknowledge that they are the kind of creature, and has the moral standing, such that it is intrinsically important how their life goes.[363]

Therefore, my view is that a failure to respect a value system disclosed in a living will should result in a claim for battery being made against the

---

[358] Mental Capacity Act 2005, Code of Practice, Chapter Seven, Quick Summary

[359] Jones, Richard, Mental Capacity Act Manual, 2008, Third Edition, Sweet and Maxwell, p.102, para.1-235

[360] Dworkin, Ronald, Life's Dominion: An argument about Abortion and Euthanasia, Harper Collins, p.233

[361] Ibid, p.216

[362] Ibid, p.237

[363] Ibid, p.235/6

clinician. The doctor would in other words have acted in breach of a fundamental moral and legal duty in human life; respect for the bodily inviolability of others. Liability for failing to disclose relevant treatment information is judged by reference to the tort of negligence, but if a prudent patient standard is adopted the standard imposed on physicians can be more closely equated to that of the tort of battery which looks to the validity of the patient's consent to treatment.

I have previously stated that maintaining a distinction between battery and negligence is somewhat artificial when the right to bodily inviolability is derived through the right to self-determination. The problem is that humans are imperfect and even when acting with the best of intentions it is possible that they might end up causing harm to others. As a non-intentional tort negligence accepts this view of humanity but says that each of us must refrain from acting in ways that one could reasonably foresee might cause harm to others. My view therefore is that the principle established in *Chester* should apply to the amount of information a doctor is required to disclose when deciding how best to respect the patient's autonomy. However, because it is possible for individual decision-makers to weigh or use information differently even when attempting to bring values into a state of coherence an incorrect or contested application of values should continue to be assessed, at least for the time being, in accordance with a prudent doctor standard. Bearing in mind that we are interested in the application of facts to values we are interested in determining whether someone who holds themselves out as having specialist knowledge and a good will toward others could reasonably have arrived at the decision they claimed to make on behalf of the patient, as judged by the *Bolam* standard. Hopefully trust in the medical profession in this respect will not be misplaced.

Postscript

Taking into consideration the fundamental values of persons, i.e. the sanctity and inviolability of human life from which the right to autonomy is derived, are the changes proposed by this thesis necessary and appropriate to uphold them? Well one way to consider this question is to understand what may be the consequences for particular individuals of failing to consider reforms of this nature. Consider, for example, this story about the great evolutionist Charles Darwin who left London to live with his family at Down House in Downe a pretty Kent village. It was during his time there that he was inspired to write his theory of evolution; 'The

Origin of Species', which challenged traditional religious beliefs about God and creation. Darwin had for a time held back from committing his ideas to paper. This was partly because he knew that once the genie had been let out of the bottle there would be no turning back and he was wary about the conflict that would ensue between traditional and scientific values and beliefs. He was also aware that his wife was deeply religious and he did not wish to offend her or cause her any distress. However, he was eventually persuaded to commit his ideas to paper by those who, like him, believed that all earthly phenomenon could be explained in natural rather than non-natural terms.

It would nonetheless be a falsehood to try to define Darwin solely in terms of his contribution to natural science because he was also a committed family man who had several children, in whom he took great interest. Unfortunately two died in infancy and another, Annie, died during childhood. Her death devastated Darwin. The children were buried at the family plot in St Mary's churchyard in Downe, where Darwin's brother was also buried. When Darwin himself died, suddenly on the 19th April 1882, the family made arrangements for him to be buried, alongside his children at the family plot in St Mary's churchyard. However, William Spottiswoode, who was president of the Royal Society, which is this country's national academy for science, petitioned the Dean of Westminster Abbey to have his body buried there. His thinking, no doubt, was that if the church honoured Darwin this would help to popularise Darwinism leading to the introduction of an alternative set of concepts through which to view the world and its people and eventually to a sea-change in the activities and evaluative experiences of valuers. As his request was honoured Darwin's family reluctantly sent his body to be buried there.[364]

I rest my case.

---

[364] Various internet sources were used to compile this tale about Darwin

CONCLUSION

This study is concerned with the circumstances under which the Mental Capacity Act 2005 authorises the administration of a medical treatment in respect of formerly competent patients; to show why the law might fail to deliver what it promises in respect of this patient group and to make suggestions about how it might be made to work better.

The significance we attach to the human body and life is underpinned by the principle of bodily inviolability. Thus all persons enjoy a right to bodily inviolability. However, this fundamental right is derived through another, the right to self-determination. As autonomy is the primary principle of law this establishes that persons value being in control of their own person, life and life plan. Moreover, autonomy serves to counter medical paternalism.

An obvious difficulty arises when someone suffers a loss of decision-making capacity as a third party must make decisions and take action for and on behalf of the mentally incapacitated patient. The legislative problem, if we are not to downgrade the status of mentally incapacitated patients, is in determining whether, and, if so, how decisions concerning their medical welfare should be made to accord with their autonomously held wishes.

A decision to respect autonomy, not beneficence, in these circumstances must be to ensure that its underlying purposes are fulfilled not frustrated, i.e. to ensure that a decision to administer, withdraw or withhold a medical treatment is informed by the patient's prior right to make decisions concerning their welfare and other liberty interests in accordance with their own values, beliefs and preferences. This way the right to self-determination transcends the advent of mentally incapacity and formerly competent patients retain control over their body, life and life plan.

In this regard the legislative framework aims to promote and respect patient autonomy in respect of capacity assessments and advance decisions. And whilst the concept of precedent autonomy is embedded within the legislative framework, thereafter, the MCA adopts a patient-centred approach to decision-making in approving a best interests, not substituted judgment, decision-making standard. Essentially, the welfare appraisal makes the character and personality of the patient a very relevant factor that is to be considered, though this need not be made determinative of what should happen, by surrogate decision-makers.

The, not insubstantial, underlying concern of legislators is that in a civil society a vulnerable person should not be denied medical treatment merely because they cannot consent to it. With this in mind our legislature has determined that the patient's right to self-determination should be positively recognised through the concept of advance decisions. The idea is that a patient when competent seeks to maximise decision-making capacity by recording an anticipatory treatment decision in a living will. Crucially, a previous treatment decision of a competent patient must be respected in the way it would be if the patient had contemporaneously refused to consent to a treatment or procedure that a doctor proposed to administer in their (medical) best interests. Thus a formerly competent patient retains control over what happens to their body in a medical context.

As previously implied these are a device through which patient's may seek to refuse a particular form of medical treatment, most often at the end of life. However the evidential burden is on the patient to establish that an advance decision exists that is both legally valid and applicable in the circumstances arising for decision. As these are very difficult standards to meet it seems reasonable to conclude that if the patient's right to self-determination is to prevail over the State's interest in the sanctity of human life that legislation requires them to be very competent indeed when making a decision to refuse treatment. The justification for the legislative response is that patients often fail to gather information that is relevant to their decision and may even misunderstand the information they have gathered. Moreover, evidence suggests that the values, beliefs and preferences that underpinned their decision may in fact be unstable.

Capacity assessments are important events because a patient either retains or loses the right to make decisions for themselves and in accordance with their own values, beliefs and preferences. An aspect of respect for personal autonomy is that every effort should be made to assist even borderline patients to overcome their difficulties in making a contemporaneous medical treatment decision. Essentially if the person has or gains capacity to make a medical treatment decision they can refuse the relevant treatment at the material time or may exercise their right to change their decision and consent to the treatment in question.

In an appropriate case a finding that a patient retains decision-making capacity opens the door for them to review their prior choice, which may have been expressed at a time when they were in full health, in the light of their current situation. The issue of whether or not a person has capacity is treated as a question of fact to be determined by a doctor with responsibility for the patient. My concern is with the circumstances in which a patient may be found to retain decision-making capacity as it is difficult to eliminate the possibility of them feeling vulnerable as a result of their condition and afraid by what is entailed in their prior instructions and these are the very conditions which are known to engender a change of mind with a little persuasion.

Doctors are thereby reminded that legislation requires them to adopt a functional not outcome based test for capacity, i.e. a competent patient can decide for reasons that are rational, irrational, unknown or even non-existent. A two stage test is used to determine whether their patient has an impairment or disturbance that affects the way their mind or brain works and if they do they must then consider whether that means that they are unable to make the decision in question,[1] i.e. it is the capacity to understand treatment information[2] and retain it[3] so that it can be used or applied to ones values[4] to arrive at a choice that can be communicated[5] that is being appraised not whether what they decide is in their medical welfare interests.

However, it has been noted that doctors rarely question whether the patient is competent to consent when they are compliant with medical expert opinion but conversely are more likely to claim that a patient is not competent to consent if they raise objections or refuse a necessary and appropriate medical treatment or procedure. And in this respect the MCA determines that the relevant information that should be disclosed is that pertaining to the reasonably foreseeable consequences of a medical

[1] Mental Capacity Act 2005, s.2(1)
[2] Mental Capacity Act 2005, s.3(1)(a)
[3] Mental Capacity Act 2005, s.3(1)(b)
[4] Mental Capacity Act 2005, s.3(1)©
[5] Mental Capacity Act 2005, s.3(1)(d)

treatment[6] which places emphasis on what a reasonably prudent doctor,[7] not patient,[8] decides is material for them to weigh in the balance in order to come to a decision.

Yet, if autonomy is the primary principle of law and persons not values are sources of the normative claims we make on others, it is plain, in the context of medical treatment decision-making on behalf of formerly competent patients, that the value of autonomy may fall into decline or be subject to misuse absent an appropriate sustaining social practice to uphold its value at various critical points within the structure of the MCA and at various stages in the cycle of a medical treatment decision-making process.

My proposal is an attempt to plug these various gaps in the legislative scheme to create space for autonomy to triumph over beneficence. As an advance decision can be expression of values or of a value system the right to self-determination is being asserted through this particular construct. Although in this instance one is being used to protect and to give authority to the values or value system of a competent person on the basis that their values, beliefs and preferences underpin their decisions.

Even though a value system could not be interpreted as an actual advance decision one could be used in capacity assessments as well as to determine what should happen in the actual best interests of the patient, i.e. in which case a limited objective, not substituted judgment, standard would apply, the term ‘limited’ is used since it may still be possible to weigh values differently to the patient and to come to a decision that is not the one the patient would make. Nonetheless, when an appropriate welfare checklist, i.e. value system, is combined with an appropriate method for deciding, i.e. coherence theory, the problem is to an extent mitigated plus there is no actual advantage to doctors in stating that the patient is not competent merely because they refuse to consent to treatment as whatever is in their best interest must be rendered consistent with their prior disclosed values. Coherence theory thus makes an important contribution in the quest to change the emphasis away from contemporary towards precedent

[6] Mental Capacity Act 2005, s.3(4)

[7] The standard proposed in Sidaway v Board of the Bethlem Royal Hospital and the Maudsley Hospital and Others [1985] AC 871

[8] The standard proposed in Chester v Afshar 2004 WL 2289136

autonomy when third parties try to determine what should happen in another's best interests.

The possibility of affecting change under the MCA is apparent the question then is whether the principle, established in *Chester v Afshar*, that the patient's right to bodily inviolability determines that no gap should exist between beneficence and autonomy in relation to decisions concerning the life, health and welfare of patients, has become enshrined within the Act?

In this regard it appears that a fiduciary standard would make decisions-makers more acccountable for their decisions and actions. This is achieved in two ways. First, the standard removes the potential for conflict to arise in the interests of the relevant parties, i.e. between beneficence and autonomy. Second, a fiduciary standard changes the rules of accountability by upholding the value of transparency, honesty and integrity in decision-making processes which would tend to induce the necessary sense of loyalty to the aims and intention of patients that is needed to ensure that surrogate decision-makers carry out their duties to others appropriately and responsibly. The suggestion, in other words, is that a fiduciary standard encourages doctors to use their power beneficently in furthering the interests of the patient – i.e. it incorporates the moral principle do as you would be done by.

This is the only standard that acknowledges the special nature of the doctor of the doctor-patient relationship whilst also recognising the imbalance of knowledge and power that exists between the respective parties. Bearing in mind the interests that are at stake, i.e. human life has moral worth and dignity, and the facts of human nature there is every reason why this standard should be adopted in law.

Practical Application

The idea is given a foundation by Ronald Dworkin who argues that an individual right to autonomy makes self-creation possible which allows each of us to live our lives in accordance with our own unique personality or out of a sense of what is important to us. He proceeds to comment that people think it important not just that their life contain a variety of the right experiences, achievements, and connections, but that it have a structure that expresses a coherent choice among these and puts forward the view that a person's critical interests are what give their life a coherent narrative and in that sense differ from experiential interests which are more likely to fluctuate over time.

His analysis of autonomy demands that a person's critical and experiential interests should be the core features of a value system. Significantly the project requires persons to identify and set apart what is intrinsically valuable from the value of experience which is not deemed to be a source of intrinsic value. We are invited, in other words, to set out what we feel and act out of a sense of duty towards from those affairs that we show no settled commitment to, as well as from those things we do from pure inclination.

On this view autonomy allows people who have it to choose how far and in what form they will seek to realise that aim. Therefore, an integrity based view of autonomy, which the concept of precedent autonomy adopted by the MCA appears to support, is essential to considerations about what the personal consequences of this are for the person concerned.

However, if Rebecca Dresser is right, that establishing a coherent life theme is not the priority of most individuals, in that most often people respond to events as they arise, then this proposal is likely to have limited appeal and no real practical application under the MCA.

Suggestions for Further Research

As I have conducted a book based theoretical study one obvious suggestion to make is that empirical research may be needed to see whether, in fact, people can identify and organise their values in the manner intended, i.e. to separate them into critical and experiential interests. It would also be necessary to explore the issue of whether a third party decision-maker would be able to interpret and apply any resultant value system to achieve a result that is consistent with what the patient would decide, i.e. would they interpret and weigh values in the manner intended. This is important to ascertain because the intention is that a surrogate should use the patient's value system for capacity assessments as well as to determine whether a medical treatment should be administered, withheld or withdrawn. The issue is that a value system, based on critical and experiential interests, may be hard to apply. This is because the patient has determined what there good is but not how it should be pursued in every instance as a traditional advance decision would, i.e. it is non-specific and thus not a treatment decision. Critically, human judgment has not been eliminated from decision-making processes and therefore biases and prejudices may become manifest within the evaluative process leaving space for values to interpreted paternalistically.

BIBLIOGRAPHY

Books

Beauchamp, Tom L., Childress, James F., Principles of Biomedical Ethics, 2001, Fifth Edition, Oxford University Press

Bentham, Jeremy, An Introduction to the Principles of Morals and Legislation, 1823 (Re-Print), Clarendon Press

Berg, Jessica W., Appelbaum, Paul S., Lidz Charles W., Parker, Lisa S., Informed Consent, 2001, Second Edition, Oxford University Press

Brock, Dan W., Patient Competence and Surrogate Decision-Making, The Blackwell Guide to Medical Ethics, (2007, Blackwell Publishing)

Cassell, Eric, J., The Nature of Suffering and the Goals of Medicine, 2004, Second Edition, Oxford University Press

Dworkin, Ronald, Life's Dominion: An argument about Abortion and Euthanasia, Harper Collins

—. Justice in Robes, 2006, The Belknap Press of Harvard University Press

Gert, Bernard, Culver, Charles M., Clouser, K. Danner, Bioethics: A Systematic Approach, 2006, Second Edition, Oxford University Press

Gillon, Raanan, Philosophical Medical Ethics, 1986, John Wiley and Sons

Glover, Jonathan, Causing Death and Saving Lives, 1990, Penguin Books

Grubb, A., Principles of Medical Law, 2004, Second Edition, Oxford University Press

Harris, John, The Value of Life, 1985, Routledge Publishing, p.192

Herring, Jonathan, Medical Law and Ethics, 2008, Second Edition, Oxford University Press

Higgs, Roger, Truth Telling, in The Blackwell Guide to Medical Ethics, Edited by Rhodes, Rosamond, Francis, Leslie P., Silvers Anita, (2007, Blackwell Publishing)

Hill, Thomas E. Jr., Human Welfare and Moral Worth: Kantian Perspectives, 2002, Oxford University Press

—. Respect, Pluralism and Justice: Kantian Perspectives, 2003, Oxford University Press

Jackson, Emily, 'Informed Consent' to Medical Treatment and the Importance of Tort, In First Do No Harm, edited by Sheila McLean, (2006, Ashgate Publishing)

Jones, Richard, Mental Capacity Act Manual, 2008, Third Edition, Sweet and Maxwell

Kagan, Shelly, 1998, Normative Ethics, Westview Press

Kant, I, Groundwork of the Metaphysics of Morals, Edited by Mary Gregor, 2006, Cambridge University Press

Kennedy and Grubb, Medical Law, 2000, Third Edition, Butterworths

Koehler, Derek J., and Harvey, Nigel, Judgment and Decision-Making, 2007, Blackwell Publishing

Korsgaard, Christine M., The Dependence of Value on Humanity, in Raz, Joseph, The Practice of Value, (2003, Oxford University Press)

McGee, Glenn and Bjarnadottir, Dyrleif, Abuses of Science in Medical Ethics, In the Blackwell Guide to Medical Ethics, (2007, Blackwell Publishing)

Maclean, Alasdair, Briefcase on Medical Law, 2004, Second Edition, Cavendish Publishing

Mason J.K., McCall Smith, R.A., Laurie, G.T., Law and Medical Ethics, 2002, Sixth Edition, Butterworths

Mill, John Stuart, Utilitarianism, Second Edition, Edited by George Sher, Hackett Publishing Company

Moore, G.E., Principia Ethica, 1993, Revised Edition, Cambridge University Press

Newdick, Christopher, Who Should we Treat? 2005, Second Edition, Oxford University Press

Pippin, Robert, The Conditions of Value, in Raz, Joseph, The Practice of Value (2003, Oxford University Press)

Raz, Joseph, The Practice of Value, 2003, Oxford University Press

Rhodes, Rosamond, The Professional Responsibilities of Medicine, in The Blackwell Guide to Medical Ethics, Edited by Rhodes, Rosamond, Francis, Leslie P., Silvers Anita (2007, Blackwell Publishing)

Sandel, Michael J., Justice: What's the Right Thing To Do?, 2010, Penguin Books

Sidgwick Henry, The Methods of Ethics, 1981, Seventh Edition, Hackett Publishing Company

Smart, J.J.C. and Williams, Bernard, Utilitarianism For and Against, 2006, Cambridge University Press

Stauch, Marc, Wheat, Kay with Tingle, John, Sourcebook on Medical Law, 2002, Second Edition, Cavendish Publishing

The Blackwell Guide to Medical Ethics, 2007, Edited by Rhodes, Rosamond, Francis, Leslie P., Silvers, Anita, Blackwell Publishing

The Holy Bible, Cambridge University Press

Wallace, R. Jay, Introduction, in Raz, Joseph, The Practice of Value, (2003, Oxford University Press)

Wear, Stephen, Informed Consent: Patient Autonomy and Physician Beneficence within Clinical Medicine, 1993, Kluwer Academic Publishers

Reports

Dresser, Rebecca, Dworkin on Dementia: Elegant Theory, Questionable Policy, 1995, Hastings Center Report; Nov, 25, 6

Fagerlin, Angela, Schneider, Carl E., Enough! The Failure of the Living Will, 2004, Hastings Center Report, March-April

House of Lords, Report of the Select Committee on Medical Ethics, Volume 1, 1994, HMSO

Articles

Anderson, Emily E., What we Talk About when we Talk about Goals, American Medical Association, Journal of Ethics, Virtual Mentor, Jun 07, Volume 9, no.6, 407-409

Bartlett, Peter, Doctors as Fiduciaries: Equitable Regulation of the Doctor-Patient Relationship, 1997, Medical Law Review, No.5, pp.193-224

Bulger, Roger J., On Hippocrates, Thomas Jefferson and Max Weber: The Bureaucratic, Technologic Imperatives and the Future of the Healing Tradition in a Voluntary Society, The Tanner Lectures on Human Values, March 87

Dresser, Rebecca, Precommitment: A Misguided Strategy for Securing Death with Dignity, Texas Law Review, June 2003; 81 TXLR 1823

Epstein, Richard, A., The not so Minimum Content of Natural Law, 2005, Oxford Journal of Legal Studies, pp.219-55

Fellows, Lesley, K., Competency and Consent in Dementia, 1998, Journal of the American Geriatrics Society, Vol. 46; Part 7; 992-926

Gunn, M.J., Wong, J.G., Clare, I.C.H., and Holland, A.J., Decision-Making Capacity, 1999, Medical Law Review, 7(3) 269

Harris, John, The Right to Die Lives! There is no Personhood Paradox, 2005, Medical Law Review, 13, pp.386-392

Hui, E.C., Doctors as Fiduciaries: a legal construct of the patient-physician relationship; 2005, Hong Kong Medical Journal, Vol. 11, No.6, pp.527-29

Jacob R., Clare I.C.H., Holland A., Watson P.C., Maimaris C., Gunn M., Self-harm, capacity, and refusal of treatment: Implications for emergency medical practice, 2005, Emergency Medical Journal, 22: 799-802

Kagan, Shelly, Rethinking Intrinsic Value, The Journal of Ethics, 1998, 2, 277-297

Kuczewski, Mark G., Whose Will is it, Anyway? A Discussion of Advance Directives, Personal Identity, and Consensus in Medical Ethics, 1994, Bioethics, Volume 8, Number 1

Levinson, Jerrold, Intrinsic Value and the Notion of a Life, The Journal of Aesthetics and Art Criticism, 62:4, Fall 2004

McCullough, Laurence B., Medical Care for Elderly Patients with Diminished Competence: An Ethical Analysis, 1984, Journal of the American Geriatrics Society, vol.32 part 2 pp.150-153

Payton S., The Concept of the Person in the Parens Patriae Jurisdiction over Previously Competent Persons, Journal of Medicine and Philosophy, 1992, December, 17(6)

Pellegrino, Edmund D., and Thomasma, David C., The Conflict between Autonomy and Beneficence in Medical Ethics: Proposals for a Resolution, 1987, Journal of Contemporary Health Law and Policy, 3, 23-46

Rich, Ben A., The Values History: A New Standard of Care, 1991, Emory Law Journal, 40

Rodwin, Marc. A., Strains in the Fiduciary Metaphor: Divided Physician Loyalties and Obligations in a Changing Health Care System; American Journal of Law & Medicine, 1995, Vol. XXI Nos. 2&3, pp.241-257

Scanlon, Thomas M. Jr., The Status of Well-Being, 1996, The Tanner Lectures on Human Values

Tunzi, Marc, Can the Patient Decide? Evaluating Patient Capacity in Practice, 2001, American Family Physician, Vol.64 No.2

Veatch, Robert M., Doctor Does Not Know Best: Why in the New Century Physicians Must Stop Trying to Benefit Patients; 2000, Journal of Medicine and Philosophy, Vol 25, No. 6, pp.701-721

Wolpe, Paul R, Ethical and Social Challenges of Brain-Computer Interfaces, American Medical Association, Journal of Ethics, Virtual Mentor, Feb 07, Volume 9, no.2, 128-131